THE QUESTION OF PEACE
in Modern Political Thought

Laurier Studies in Political Philosophy Series

Global migration, MTV, transnational capital, and colonialism have given birth to a new and smaller world. To a greater degree than at any other time in remembered history, different cultures are brought together to live side by side. This close proximity has brought new mixtures and exciting possibilities—and also new struggles and conflicts. From many quarters comes an urgent call to build a sense of political belonging and unity in a diversity of voices. The call to unity is not, however, for uniformity or hegemony in one particular way of life. The unity to which we refer requires a rethinking and reconceptualization of existing philosophical paradigms that guide our relationships with others. In the spirit of intercultural dialogue, our Laurier Studies in Political Philosophy series is dedicated to exploring key challenges to our changing world and its needs. We are particularly interested in submissions that challenge dominant existing frameworks and approaches. We invite submissions in areas including Multicultural Theory, Aboriginal Studies and Philosophy, Post-colonialism, Globalization, Critical Race Theory, Feminism, and Human Rights Philosophy.

FOR MORE INFORMATION,
PLEASE CONTACT THE **SERIES EDITORS**

Ashwani K. Peetush	**Lisa Quinn**
Associate Professor of Philosophy	Acquisitions Editor
Wilfrid Laurier University	Wilfrid Laurier University Press
75 University Avenue West	75 University Avenue West
Waterloo, ON N2L 3C5	Waterloo, ON N2L 3C5
Phone: (519) 884-0710 ext. 3874	Phone: (519) 884-0710 ext. 2034
Fax: (519) 883-0991	Fax: (519) 725-1399
Email: apeetush@wlu.ca	*Email: quinn@press.wlu.ca*

THE QUESTION OF PEACE
in Modern Political Thought

Toivo Koivukoski and David Edward Tabachnick, editors

WILFRID LAURIER
UNIVERSITY PRESS

This book has been published with the help of a grant from the Canadian Federation for the Humanities and Social Sciences, through the Awards to Scholarly Publications Program, using funds provided by the Social Sciences and Humanities Research Council of Canada. Wilfrid Laurier University Press acknowledges the financial support of the Government of Canada through the Canada Book Fund for our publishing activities.

Library and Archives Canada Cataloguing in Publication

The question of peace in modern political thought /
Toivo Koivukoski and David Edward Tabachnick, editors.

(Laurier studies in political philosophy series)
Includes bibliographical references and index.
Issued in print and electronic formats.
ISBN 978-1-77112-121-7 (pbk.).—ISBN 978-1-77112-077-7 (pdf).—
ISBN 978-1-77112-078-4 (epub)

1. Peace (Philosophy). 2. Political science—Philosophy. I. Tabachnick, David, author, editor II. Koivukoski, Toivo, author, editor III. Series: Laurier studies in political philosophy series

| B105.P4D43 2015 | 172'.42 | C2014-905283-9 |
| | | C2014-905284-7 |

Cover design by David Drummond.
Text design by Janette Thompson (Jansom).

© 2015 Wilfrid Laurier University Press

Waterloo, Ontario, Canada

www.wlupress.wlu.ca

MIX
Paper from
responsible sources
FSC® C004071

This book is printed on FSC® certified recycled paper and is certified Ecologo. It is made from 100% post-consumer fibre, processed chlorine free, and manufactured using biogas energy.

Printed in Canada

CONTENTS

———

LATE-MODERN CRITIQUES OF THE SECURITY OF STATES AS APPROXIMATION OF PEACE

Foreword

John Gittings

If barbarism persists, then philosophy must protest.
If the sword is relentless, then civilization must denounce it.
– Victor Hugo, *Oration on Voltaire*, 1878

The voice of philosophy has a lot to say about peace, and in the present age we need to hear it more than ever. In a world that is globalized in its economy but still far from cosmopolitan in its outlook, the forces of prejudice, intolerance, and misunderstanding increase tension and generate conflict, both between and within nations. War, or the danger of war, exists at many levels—quite literally: on the ground, where ethnic and religious enmities spill over into violence, and in the upper atmosphere, where the cloud of nuclear war still hangs over us. Philosophers may not be the legislators of the world, but they can help us to clarify moral principles, understand reality, and distinguish true from false knowledge. That is what they are good at. The advice that past philosophers have offered on war and peace is still relevant today.

A group of these were the itinerant Chinese philosophers of the Hundred Schools of Thought, who would sit at the city gate of some small principality during the Era of Warring States (475–221 BC). Their role was to advise the ruler on strategy, such as whether or not to take advantage of a neighbouring state's weakness and invade. Most of the main Schools—the Confucians, the Mohists, and the Daoists (Taoists)—counselled against war, on both moral and practical grounds. Confucius's disciple Mengzi (Mencius) warned that wars to capture cities or territory always lead to disaster: they are a way of "teaching the earth how to eat human flesh."

Mohists would cite Mozi (Mo Tzu) himself, who held that states should cooperate for their universal advantage: "If rulers love the states of others as their own, no one will commit aggression." A Daoist might quote his Master Laozi (Lao Tzu): "The ideal relationship between states is one in which they are so close that they can hear their neighbour's chickens squawk and dogs bark, and yet they leave each other alone." All these philosophers would urge rulers not be seduced by the rival school of Strategists, who claimed to know the secret of victory.

Nearly two millennia later, in 1516, the great humanist Desiderius Erasmus—whose writings on peace were read by kings and popes, and who was invited to visit the royal courts of England and France—advised the young ruler of the Netherlands that his most important task was to "rule wisely in times of peace" so as to "preclude any future need for the science of war." An early advocate of what we would now call international arbitration, Erasmus argued from reason as well as morality. His most famous essay, *The Complaint of Peace* (1517), has been described as an effort "to induce men to see a crucial truth—that they were the victims of the tyranny of unsound ideas and corrupt men, and that practical alternatives did indeed exist."[1]

Two hundred years later, Bertrand Russell reflected in *The Ethics of War* (1916) on the real causes of the First World War—and how British public opinion was deceived by patriotism and hate. All the great powers of Europe, he pointed out, had precisely the same object: territory, trade, and prestige. The only difference was that the Germans had a lesser share, and wished to increase it; the British wanted to deny them. Both sides wanted total victory, no matter what the cost. "By concentrating attention upon the supposed advantages of the victory of our own side, we become more or less blind to the evils inseparable from war, and equally certain whichever side may ultimately prove victorious," Russell wrote fearlessly—and was promptly jailed for his views by an outraged British government. He was not the only philosopher to suffer for speaking his mind; but he is almost certainly the only one to be banned from approaching the seashore, for fear he might send signals to German submarines.

Perhaps, in these three examples, it may be said that the philosophers were not actually philosophizing. Mengzi was not reflecting on whether human nature is inherently good or bad; Erasmus was not weighing the balance between free will and predestination; and Russell was not applying himself to mathematical logic (a pursuit he abandoned during the war). They were, however, doing just what philosophers always do: applying their skills to the immediate problems of human existence, of life and death, of war and peace.

Yet there is a tendency for commentators to dismiss the thoughts of philosophers on the subject of peace, as though the thinkers have strayed into an alien area. Immanuel Kant's *Perpetual Peace* was long regarded as a marginal essay, a mere indulgence in utopianism, and the piece has only recently received proper attention. The pacific arguments of the Chinese Hundred Schools were long overshadowed by those of the Strategists, and by Sunzi's (Sun Tzu's) popular *Art of War*. Erasmus's writings on peace are substantial (amounting to more than 400 pages of modern printed text); yet while the works of his more war-minded contemporary Niccolò Machiavelli are available in any good bookshop, it is hard to find a single work by Erasmus—with the possible exception of his *In Praise of Folly*, the *jeu d'esprit* he wrote in 1510 to amuse his friend Sir Thomas More.

Similarly neglected are all the other humanitarian peace thinkers, from the Renaissance to the Enlightenment; these include Emeric Crucé, William Penn, the Abbé de Saint-Pierre, and Jean-Jacques Rousseau. Bertrand Russell's pro-peace arguments in the First World War, and his opposition in later life to the strategy of nuclear deterrence, are portrayed as political causes unrelated to his philosophy. Much the same happened to the peace speeches and poetry of Victor Hugo, and to the pacifist philosophy of Leo Tolstoy.

But one area of philosophical thought that does concern itself with peace (by way of its reverse) is the doctrine of Just War. We may hope that a proper understanding of the conditions that make going to war legitimate, and of the way it may most lawfully be waged, might help to deter the breaking of peace—or at least make the resulting war less inhumane. Still, we should bear in mind that the doctrine has served different purposes in its long history; that it has usually been honoured more in the breach; and that its continued relevance is questionable.

In the early Christian world, the issue of greatest concern was whether Christianity could be reconciled with serving in the Roman imperial army. Though St. Augustine is often described as the Father of Just War, his views changed over a period of forty years; and he himself increasingly urged peace as preferable to war. "It is a higher glory still to stay war itself with a word, than to slay men with the sword," he wrote, a year before his death. St. Aquinas rationalized the Augustinian doctrine of *jus in bello* when he and his fellow theologians of the early Middle Ages challenged the temporal rule of the Pope and his bishops. Their answer was the Crusades, when Just War became Holy War.

The theory took a different turn in 17th-century Europe, when secular nation-states competed with more sophisticated means of warfare (such as standing armies and field artillery). The contributions of the Netherlands jurist Hugo Grotius (1583–1645) paved the way for the Enlightenment philosophers, and laid the foundation for modern international law. In his major work *De juri belli ac pacis* (1625), Grotius looked to natural law to find a way to sanction and restrain war, based on rational and moral principles. Ideally, he saw the international community as governed less by Christian authority than by a framework of treaties and agreements between states. This argument would be carried further by the Swiss philosopher Emer de Vattel in his *The Law of Nations* (1758).

Since that time, the Just War doctrine changed little until quite recently: exposition continued to lean heavily on quotations from Vattel, Grotius, Aquinas, and even Augustine. Its actual effect on the conduct of war is debatable. Kant's judgment that the doctrine merely provided a fig leaf for aggression—he famously described Vattel's *Law of Nations* as a "sorry comforter"—often seems near the truth. Totalitarian regimes have been as likely as Liberal or democratic governments to claim its protection; and both sides in the Crimean, Boer, and First World wars insisted that theirs was a Just War. In the moralizing ideology of William Gladstone, the use of aggressive force (such as the occupation of Egypt in 1882) could be justified as "force armed with the highest sanction of law." We may also recall President William McKinley's justification of the war against Spain in 1898, and the virtual annexation of Cuba in the same year as being "in the name of human progress and civilization."

More positively, the Just War doctrine provided a basis for humanitarian measures such as the formation of the Red Cross, the development of the Geneva Conventions, and the creation of other international legislation seeking to limit the damage of war. The provisions restricting war in the Covenant of the League of Nations (and later in the Charter of the United Nations) are also based on its concept of justifiability. Just War thinking lay behind much of the argument in the late 1930s supporting collective security, and the fight against fascism and Nazism. Indeed, the Second World War is still viewed as the irrefutable example of a just war—despite the elementary violation (as historian Michael Walzer has observed) that the civilian death toll from "allied terrorism" in that war exceeded half a million men, women, and children.[2] In the post–Cold War period, there has been a rebirth of interest in the Just War, and a corresponding decline in the appeal of the "realist" approach that dominated Cold War thinking. From the Gulf War of 1990 onwards, the doctrine has provided an often-contentious yardstick against which wars of intervention or aggression are measured. The Just War concept was invoked by British prime minister Tony Blair to justify the armed intervention in Kosovo (1998–1999), and it was often cited by defenders of the US-UK invasion of Iraq (2003). In his Nobel Prize acceptance speech in 2009, US president Barack Obama sought to present his country's use of force as in the same tradition, the pursuit of a "just peace."

Whatever the usefulness of Just War theory, we should remind ourselves that philosophizing about war and about peace are two different exercises: one seeks to limit war, the other to prevent it. The peace argument is based not only on morality, but on an acute awareness of the long-term costs of war. Sadly, that awareness is not always shared. In the years leading up to 1914, the main critics of European war—peace advocates such as Jean de Bloch, Norman Angell, Bertha von Suttner, and Jane Addams—predicted, correctly, that such a war would be an economic and social disaster as well as a moral one. These thinkers recognized the fact that peace must be linked to a much broader agenda of justice and development. After the First World War, this philosophy began to be expressed through the economic and social agencies of the new League of Nations. As the opening words of the International Labour Organization's 1919 Constitution proclaim, "universal and lasting peace can be established only if it is based on social justice." These values informed the development of the economic and social organizations of the United Nations, and have since become integral to contemporary peace theory.

Part of the difficulty of talking about peace is that the word itself has often been misappropriated. After the Second World War, both superpowers claimed it: Soviet propaganda called Josef Stalin the greatest "fighter for peace," while the US Strategic Air Command claimed that "peace is our profession." To speak of peace was to run the risk of being accused of naïveté—or worse, of being a propagandist for the opposing superpower. It was safer to speak of "conflict resolution," a term chosen by peace-studies pioneer Kenneth Boulding and his colleagues at their research centre at the University of Michigan in 1956. Only a few lonely voices still used the word "peace," including the US peace philosopher John Somerville.[3]

In 1955, the Russell-Einstein Manifesto—Bertrand Russell's call for world leaders to ban nuclear weapons, signed by Albert Einstein—was supported by Albert Schweitzer. By the early 1960s, popular protest grew against the superpowers' policies on nuclear testing, deterrence, and mass destruction. Peace thinkers, including J. D. Bernal, C. Wright Mills, Seymour Melman, Erich Fromm, and Anatol Rapoport, began to reach a wider audience. Vehicles for international peace dialogue included the Pugwash movement, founded by Joseph Rotblat and Bertrand Russell (1957); the Stockholm Institute for Peace Research, founded by Gunnar Myrdal (1966); the *Journal of Peace Research*, established by Johan Galtung (1964); and the Conference on Peace Research in History, now the Peace History Society (also 1964). In a separate initiative, an international project involving nearly 200 thinkers from 40 countries led to a significant volume of essays on the philosophy of war, published in 1969.[4] By the 1970s the new discipline of peace studies, embracing the history and philosophy of peace, was well established, although it often encountered both academic and political hostility. British prime minister Margaret Thatcher, for instance, was enraged by the founding in 1974 of a Department of Peace Studies at Bradford University, and tried to have it closed.

In spite of these difficulties, the field has been considerably enriched in recent decades. The concept of "positive peace," first developed by Galtung in 1964, is now widely accepted: peace is not merely the absence of war, it must include freedom from hunger and oppression, and have as its goals economic development and social justice. In the age of economic globalization, peace should also be globalized. This is not a new concept. Seneca the Younger (c. 4 BC to AD 65) had a cosmopolitan vision of "a vast and truly common state, which embraces alike gods and men, in which we look neither to this corner of earth nor to that, but measure the bounds of our citizenship by the path of the sun."[5]

But although philosophy has more to say on the subject of peace than is generally supposed, in all honesty it must be concluded that this is not enough. Much analysis has concentrated on humanity "under the aspect of the eternal"—a position that regards war as being a given in the nature of things. For Aristotle and Plato, war seems to have been part of the fabric of human existence (as was slavery). Some comments attributed to Socrates that imply a critical attitude to war do not make up for this failure; and we must struggle to gain a coherent view of war and peace from any of their writing. This lack of classical thought on war and peace to inspire later thinkers, coupled with a frequent disregard of the thinkers from Erasmus onward who did explore the field, has resulted in a philosophical deficit with regard to peace.

This makes all the more important the efforts of the philosophers examined by the authors in this book: their goal is to reconstruct and rescue thinking about peace. Many of the thinkers (as the authors acknowledge) are not often regarded as having much to say on the subject. Yet one cannot think of a better cause for such an enquiry—particularly in the present decade, as we commemorate the centenary of the First World War. As Erasmus said so long ago: "Peace is the mother and nurse of all that is good for humanity."

Notes

1 Robert P. Adams, *The Better Part of Valor* (Seattle: University of Washington Press, 1962), 165.

2 Michael Walzer, *Just and Unjust Wars* (New York: Basic Books, 1972), 255.

3 John Somerville, *The Philosophy of Peace* (New York: Liberty Press, 1949).

4 Robert Ginsberg, *The Critique of War: Contemporary Philosophical Explorations* (Chicago: Henry Regnery, 1969).

5 Lucius Annaeus Seneca, *De otio* (*On Leisure*), trans. John Basore, *Seneca: Moral Essays* (London: Heinemann, 1932).

Introduction

Toivo Koivukoski and
David Edward Tabachnick

What is peace? This collection explores different conceptions of peace as they are articulated in works of modern political philosophy. From Luther to Spinoza, Hobbes to Locke, Kant to Habermas, these essays from contemporary political theorists consider the contributions that modern theory has made to our understanding of peace as a political concept.

Our starting point for the volume is the observation that how one thinks about peace depends very much on how one comes at the idea. So, in a practical sense, peace may mean something very different for an educator and a soldier, a civil servant and an activist. What matters—both in terms of formulating it as a concept, and in terms of political action—is what peace would look like in a particular situation. There are a whole range of potentially peaceful conditions: from a critically engaged classroom, to a secure border, to an open consultation with stakeholders, to a rallying cry of "No justice, no peace," with voluntary cooperation withheld.

The common element between these many contested perspectives has a kind of obviousness to it. We may agree that peace is not war, without defining just what peace is. Or we might find quietude in a coming to rest, rather like the peace of the graveyard that Immanuel Kant grimly jokes (in his 1795 essay *Perpetual Peace: A Philosophical Sketch*) will be humanity's lot if we do not take up peace as a cause of action. In instances when we already agree on what peace is, the concept itself is not particularly helpful: it either directs our attention to the opposite phenomenon—war—or else it eases us into a false sense of solace, in hopes that are beyond the promise of politics.

Held precariously in an impasse between fear for the other, and exasperation at the recurrence of war, our thinking about peace must clearly account for the tangle of working concepts that attach to that idea. These articulate the growing profusion of ways to bring form and substance to our inklings of a better world, formulated in terms of what is worth hoping for, what are our common goods, and how we may begin to work toward those ends. Like any political discussion, the starting point here is a field of opinions. Each is particular to a point of view, sometimes prone to change, sometimes equivocal, sometimes determined: if not a mass of diverse singularities, then at least a singularity that contains multitudes.

If we trace out that diversity, peace may appear as less of a monolithic, abstract imposition, a kind of *pax imperium*, and more as a political project helped along by philosophic clarification. Its theoretical dimensions are intended less to synthesize some unified idea than to define and analyze the differences between concepts—a multitude of potentials for action, circling like constellations attracted by the gravity of peace. In the apparent absence of an idea of peace that can be peacefully agreed upon, we are left with politicized concepts of peace: an idea as unfinished as the political itself, and one that throws back on the individual much of the work of peace realization. It is we who must ask ourselves what peace means to us, and what we can do to make our particular vision most real to us in our lives.

This provisional quality of the active question of peace implies a fundamental ethic of respect for differences, of a recognition of others that goes deeper than the mere reciprocity of shared fear. If peace does indeed share in the basic plurality of our political condition, and of cherished ideals of justice and voluntary association, then such differences are intrinsic values. We recognize this in every expression of peaceful agency.

What political philosophy can add to the praxis of ethical agency is the moderating consideration of the limits of action—a moderation that arises out of the pluralistic quality of the idea of peace. We see the same diversity in all the theories of peace outlined in this volume that we do in the works of actual peacemakers, be they educators or soldiers, civil servants or activists. These modern works of political philosophy also acknowledge the absence of a singular idea of peace, and lean toward a liberal recognition of difference rooted in respect for others. As a political concept, this is perhaps the one modest contribution that contemporary theory can make to peace studies—and, perhaps, to the actual realization of more just and peaceful relationships.

The fourteen essays in this volume are arranged in a roughly chronological order, covering an almost 500-year span in the history of European religious, philosophical, and political thought. They range from Luther's fiery 16th-century rhetoric—the radical ideas that kick-started the Reformation—to the 20th-century critical theorist Jürgen Habermas (of all the thinkers examined here, the only one still alive today). In between are a wide variety of keen minds: Benedictus Spinoza, Thomas Hobbes, John Locke, Emer de Vattel, Jean-Jacques Rousseau, Immanuel Kant, Georg Hegel, Henry David Thoreau (the only non-European), Martin Heidegger, Walter Benjamin, Hannah Arendt, and Jacques Derrida—together representing some of the most powerful thinkers in the Western tradition.

In Chapter 1, Jarrett A. Carty's reading of Luther describes an essential limit in the separation of powers between the earthly and heavenly realms. This theological distinction of faith and knowledge, each with its demands and duties, anticipates the modern separation of church and state. But the false conflation of divine and secular authorities can lead to two types of political excess and unjustified violence. On the one hand, this interpretation can encourage secular authorities to overreach their powers, claiming divine sanction for all-too-mundane acts of domination by force. On the other hand, it may stoke the fervour of revolutionaries who claim that God is on their side of history—thereby justifying violence by gnostic eschatology.

The rationales for both kinds of violence shift the discourse about war. From being a sometimes necessary, if often despised, means of action, it comes to represent a kind of redemption that promises more than force could ever offer—that is, either supreme political power, or total liberation from it. Beyond this basic confusion over what violence can accomplish, conflating secular and divine orders characteristically induces immoderate behaviour. A radicalized mentality of "the end justifies the means" often results not only in justifying any and all means; it actually demands their use.

The dangers that Luther saw in the peasant revolts that swept through Europe in the mid-16th century were apparent on both sides of the conflict: in the ruthless violence of an oligarchic class that claimed privileges by divine sanction, and in the radicals who claimed the right to revolt based on eschatological promise. This theological context for politics made the peaceful settling of contested claims extraordinarily difficult, short of totally cowing whole populations, or executing erstwhile nobility.

For Luther, the crucial significance of setting apart the two kinds of authority—one based on human laws and force, the other derived from divine laws—was a theological reasoning for what would become a defining feature of modern thought: separating church and state. This concept undercuts the justification of violence in the service of a higher cause, one that transcends all considerations of mere earthly means and ends. This early call for moderation is still sorely needed in our contemporary global politics, with its history of ideologically inspired violence—both by rulers and by those who would overthrow them.

The importance of a culture of peace as a basis for political security also informs Paul Bagley's essay on Spinoza in Chapter 2. By this reading of Spinoza, compelling myths and holy books are needed to mediate between the self-interest of the individual and the fervour of collective passions. Although reason may be able to subdue the passions and inform habits of virtue, such a philosophic balance is hard to develop and maintain. Something more is needed to build a peaceful society: a kind of template for understanding how individuals find their place in relation to the whole. A combination of received or imagined wisdom, coupled with the concord of religious ceremony, may be a more natural way to shape behaviours en masse.

This interpretation of the paradox of human nature, which is at once moved by desire and guided by reason, reveals the limits of a rational promotion of peace. Enlightened self-interest may not be enough to produce concord, either within states or between them. Myth and religion still hold sway over both policy-makers and political theorists. Bagley concludes that "so long as human beings are led more by the imaginative-affective life than by reason, Spinoza's teaching on peace, security and healthy life remains a cautionary tale."

In order to address political issues, the question of peace must be rooted in the motives and drives of human nature, in what would make peace desirable to both individuals and states. In Chapter 3, Laurie Johnson corrects a common misinterpretation of Hobbes—one that seems to make any form of cooperation between states impossible, and war the supposed norm for their relations. But for Hobbes, peaceful relations are manifestly possible. Granted, states are constrained neither by natural law (as are individuals, who feel the desire to seek and keep peace), nor by any supranational equivalent of sovereign law. Yet states are still limited by internal factors, such as the life-loving drives of their citizens—who, according to Hobbes's psychology of self-interestedness, have little reason to go to war for anything other than their own defence.

Still, although realistic thinking should incline states to prefer peace, as individuals do, sources of conflict are apparent in the psychology of even selfish individuals. (One of these is "diffidence," which according to Hobbes persists in individuals as in states.) To understand the persistence of challenges to peace, Johnson emphasizes the role of honour-seeking in Hobbes's political theory as a psychological source of conflict. Unlike the wild inclinations that characterize martyrs and the vainglorious, governments usually act in reasonable and peaceful ways—mainly out of self-interest, coupled with a healthy dose of fear. Even if readers of *Leviathan* are not inclined to internalize its logic of "fear death or die," they might accept the social psychology of: "If all people could fear death more than they love honour, they would be able to enjoy a lasting peace."

A necessary supplement to democratic peace theory is Jeff Sikkenga's reading of Locke in Chapter 4, in which he suggests that the presence of institutions like free markets and democratic governance is not enough to keep the peace. Beyond these frameworks for individual liberty there must be a liberal political culture—a set of practices sustained by people at once motivated by self-interest, yet capable of self-regulating behaviour. In the absence of such capacities, in a secular context, what is there to restrain naked striving for mastery, intolerance of others, or vengefulness? Sikkenga suggests that what is needed to cultivate a peaceful public sphere is the shaping of citizens who are inclined to peaceful coexistence. Such a spirit of unanimity is created by a liberal education that teaches the value of freedom, while at the same time addressing its limits. This thinking on the importance of fostering a liberal culture extends to contemporary experiments in exporting political and economic liberalism, via military occupations: democratic regimes do not appear inclined to peace unless their citizens are similarly inclined. "We do not need war and conflict," Sikkenga concludes. "But we will have them, unless liberal institutions are undergirded with liberal human beings."

The premise that peace is self-limiting implies a sense of moderation in the means to that end. In Chapter 5, Holland's examination of Vattel emphasizes peace as a necessarily messy business of compromise, of interests checked, and ideals clipped: in negotiations and settlements, solutions to differences are never entirely solved. Holland presents Vatell's "natural law" approach to international relations as one with justice as its goal, constrained from promoting war as the vehicle of a just cause. Instead, it is guided by the concept of peace—understood here as a contractual amnesty—as "morally non-discriminatory." As in war, the condition of peace must not to be judged by its ultimate justice. More important to Vattel is the efficacy and duration of the amnesty; a project made possible, Holland says, only by "burials in oblivion of claims against the other party."

This seems straightforward enough: securing an amnesty by contract means relinquishing claims against the other party, and being willing to resolve issues on conditions not entirely desirable to either antagonist. The strategy also works for peaceful settlements, in situations when war must be constrained: whenever one side is relegated to the status of absolute enemy, the hostilities become much more dangerous—and peace becomes increasingly unlikely. Holland points to the so-called War on Terror as typical of all incendiary notions of spurious "just causes" that are used to justify constabulary wars, along with the associated claims of a right to prosecute a war of global reach for an indefinite duration. If our ethical sensibilities draw us to a limited, contractual, and morally neutral form of peace, Vattel would caution us against this kind of combination of natural law and ideological violence.

René Paddags's Chapter 6 highlights the essential role played by Rousseau's definition of peace in the development of our traditional and modern conceptions of it. Rousseau felt that individuals could never truly enjoy a complete sense of peace—as they could in the original lost "state of nature"—because their safety is always vulnerable to potential harm by others; this limits their ability to love all people equally. Still, Rousseau argues that we can create "the political-institutional conditions of peace" domestically, through the rule of law and democratic legislatures—though this does nothing to mitigate the possibility of war with other states. For external peace to be established, the same conditions for domestic peace must be extended internationally: Rousseau suggested the creation of a European federation, based on common ties and customs. As the general will of a state trumps individual will, such an institution would subordinate state sovereignty to the federation's will.

But, Rousseau lamented, people are mostly driven by their passions rather than by reason, and so are unprepared to participate in this kind of institution. For one thing, monarchs would never be willing to subordinate their authority to a supranational body. The logic of a European federation seemed compelling but impracticable, and international peace remained out of reach. As Paddags explains, Rousseau's critique gives us some useful insight into the dysfunction of today's European Union.

Directly or indirectly, in agreement or disagreement, in anticipation or in response, every effort to define peace in modern political thought must come back to Kant. As Leah Bradshaw points out in Chapter 7, Kant's influential "realistic peace project"—founded on the notion of universal human rights—tried to explain how we might create practical peace in this world, rather than considering it in utopian terms. Although our individual rights are always contingent on the freedom of everyone else, Kant felt that this middle way could realize these rights through properly composed political institutions and the practice of public law, based on the willing consent of the governed. And rather than envisioning a world government overseeing a cosmopolitan citizenry, Kant recognized the practical need for republican states to protect the rights of their citizens.

But while the expression of these laws may differ, their basis in principles of universal right still renders international peace a practical possibility—even when violence, conflict, and war may seem to make the realization of a progressive peace project doubtful. As Bradshaw summarizes: "Perpetual peace is our ultimate goal, but one that has to be embraced and worked toward, in a realistic assessment of our present condition." Again, for Kant, rights are not natural or inalienable but political and practical. People without a state are people without rights. Informed by Arendt's reading of Kant, Bradshaw speculates whether this problem of rights affects not only the marginalized and stateless, but also those caught up in revolutions—when state protection is compromised, absent, or rejected. In the global dilemmas we face in the 21st century, is Kant's defence of "discrete sovereign republican states" still relevant? Should we move away from the framework of international treaties as a means for solving global injustices? If rights are practical and political (as both Kant and Arendt argue), then might "the transcendence of the state into the universal ether of cosmopolitan right" mean that this cosmopolitan order would have no institutions or laws to protect those rights?

It is of course possible to overstate the likenesses between states and individuals, however much states may draw on the natural dispensations of their citizens as motives for seeking peace. Mark Blitz makes a similar point in Chapter 8 when he asks whether it is universally desirable for states to seek peace; and he turns to Hegel for the distinction between a state's internal legitimacy and its international recognition. States are constrained by their constitutional relationships with their citizens—an identity experienced by the citizens themselves as a positive duty. The Hegelian synthesis of the part and the whole has no direct correlation in interstate relations. The sovereignty of states, via this bond of legitimizing duties and rights, means that they are not bound to other states in a similar manner. Such bonds may be reciprocal, but they are not mutually constitutive. As states, what they share in terms of global politics is more a matter of history than of identity. Here at the intersection of international relations and political theory, Blitz seeks to correct some predominating views of Hegel: as either a closet liberal, or a Marxist *avant la lettre*, or as a primary source of global capitalism, or as a prophet of worldwide socialist revolution. Blitz's goal is to put some distance between Hegel and Kant on the question of the desirability of perpetual peace as an end to history. In this reading of Hegel war is at times necessary, and thus remains a perennial possibility—one sustained by the duties claimed by states of their citizens. The question of the desirability of peace turns on the boundaries that delimit the sovereignty of states in their dealings with one another. The potentials of international action, and of a kind of world spirit, seem to remain circumspect, stopping short of (as Blitz put it) "self-conscious political crusades." In practical terms, he argues that a state's power to make war would be "limited or eschewed when foolish, and not prosecuted when agreements can be found whose effect would be to make a war unnecessary."

A blueprint for the kind of social order where justice reigns, peace is assured, and citizens are able to rise above mundane concerns such as merely provisioning their lives, and fearing violent death—such is the goal that makes peace the political project that it is. There is always an element of difference to political reality, whether it be a difference of perspective, of interests, or of identities set apart by history and geography. Toivo Koivukoski's reading of Thoreau in Chapter 9 outlines that division between human beings and nature, one that in many ways reflects our capacities for peaceful relations—which may be described as having as its goal both the ease of prosperity, and the state of harmonious communion with the natural world. In today's world, however, achieving such a state must involve dealing with issues such as ecological sustainability versus crisis, and economic resources versus inequality. The kind of systemic violence associated with those issues limits the potential for peace. Modern political thought is caught between these goals and these limits. Koivukoski's essay follows Thoreau in describing peace as an essentially political question, uplifted by ideals yet tangled in messy realities.

Drawing on an ontological critique of the cosmopolitan global order, David Edward Tabachnick takes on the challenge, in Chapter 10, of locating

Heidegger's definition of peace. As Tabachnick notes, "Heidegger seemed to think that a massive perpetration of external violence would in some way recapture a nearly lost 'inner harmony.'" For him, war and peace were linked not because there is peace at the end of war, but because "war is the father of all things," including peace. He sought an authentic peace that moved away from the naïveté he associated with contemporary culture and politics, including Kant's call for enlightened legislation and institutions designed to limit war. For Heidegger, the only way to arrive at this peace was through the necessary disruption of war—as in the ancient Greek *Polemos*, the mythological god or daemon of war. He believed that this paradoxical peace was the only way for human beings to arrive at a state of *Dasein*, authentic existence.

Today, such a spiritual journey is not only for individuals; Heidegger saw it also as a quest for the whole German *Volk*, in order to find its way out of the disorientation and deprivation of our modern technological society. Heidegger believed that violence, destruction, and conflict could wipe this away, and allow Germany to recapture a lost harmony with Being. As Tabachnick attempts to clarify, Heidegger's endorsement of the National Socialists, and of the destruction of the Second World War, can be interpreted as an extension of his definition of peace.

In Chapter 11, Hermínio Meireles Teixeira explains Benjamin's definition of peace as a direct challenge to the power of the sovereign state. In contrast to Kant, Arendt, and Habermas, Benjamin sees political institutions and laws less as facilitators of peace than as mere guises for authority. He points to the provisions for states of emergency, which allow the suspension of human rights in the name of security, to indicate that "legal violence" rather than legal peace is the true basis of the modern state. In fact, he views peace as "the historical struggle to sever this nexus between violence and law in political experience." As with Heidegger's view of disruption and war, Benjamin's idea of a peace that can only exist outside of the state takes the form of "divine violence." By destroying the state without any attempt at restoration, the source of legal violence is shattered—replaced by "a devastating indifference" to hierarchical order or government.

As Teixeira admits, what eventually replaces the fragmented sovereignty necessarily remains unclear. Citing Derrida, he acknowledges that Benjamin's vision bears rather too much resemblance to the Nazis' terrifying Final Solution. But the Nazi vision relied on restoring some form of the state, whereas divine violence "comes neither to restore or preserve the legal right of sovereign violence, but to depose it." So unlike Heidegger's version, Benjamin's peace does not depend on some great moment of destruction to recapture lost greatness or authenticity. Rather than the violent cycle of revolution and counter-revolution, he proposes a way to end the false security of the state, which is always backed up by the implicit threat of violence.

According to Diane Enns in Chapter 12, Arendt's contribution of "politicizing" peace can lead us away from our attraction to violence for political ends—whether committed by a state seeking security, or by citizens seeking revolution. Rather than embracing passivity or completely rejecting violence, such a peace would require real political engagement. Describing politics as "sheer human togetherness," Arendt emphasizes plurality, free speech and movement, and shared experience in the public space. Yet this plurality and interaction also offer opportunities for disagreement and conflict. As Enns writes, "Expressions of public discontent, dissent, disagreement, and moral outrage are as necessary as the negotiation and deliberation required for agreement—these are not destructive of politics, but constitutive of any human relations among individuals."

The problem is that most state systems, instead of maximizing political participation, are designed to create an us-versus-them mentality. For citizens, this often makes violence seem an easy choice; and this is why the totalitarian state is so profoundly isolated and anti-political, a place where peace is impossible. We have recently seen some revolutionary movements rise up against authoritarian regimes—a reminder that real power lies in the political plurality of the people, and not in the violence that props up dictators. Enns admits that such resistance sometimes ends with the regime becoming even more firmly entrenched; but the underlying concern is how revolution, successful or not, can be transformed into peaceful politics rather than spurring further violence. This highlights the fact that Arendt (unlike Gandhi) does not simply reject violence as a justifiable reaction to repression. The problem lies with the glorification of violence, which in many revolutions turns "dreams into nightmares." So even though she does not adhere to an "absolute principle of non-violence," Arendt sees politics as the most likely route to peace: for her it represents the finding and protecting of common spaces for agreement, disagreement, or engaging in peaceful relations.

To put the contested idea of peace in context, we must both adjust our expectations of what can reasonably be accomplished; and also reinvigorate the concept as a political project—one that needs action to fulfill its promise. As Pamela Huber suggests in her reading of Derrida in Chapter 13, politically peace works to moderate our behaviour: reality is often messy, and our categories for understanding it may often seem like caricatures. This notion of peace as a limiting factor may invite a poetic appropriation, challenging the margins of our knowledge and what we claim to know about the quality of peace. This view offers hope for limiting the domination of others, whether that domination arises out of ignorance, self-righteousness, or bully ethics that impose arbitrary absolutes. Such a political project would arise not out of some monolithic unity, but rather out of a condition of plurality.

In Huber's reading of Derrida, the experience of friendship offers a personal point of connection to peace—understood not in isolation, but as a relationship with "otherness." It is this otherness, this experience of real but imperfect relationships, that create the differences of perspective that make it possible to love others, and care about what is not our own. For Derrida, Huber proposes, this awareness of the limits of our knowledge is what moderates the self, and serves to pacify our relationships with others. This kind of peace contains a certain paradox: the differences between us— and indeed within ourselves as well—come to be treated as the source of what we have in common. Out of our differences and our divided beings, a kind of universality arises. As Huber concludes, "peace may ultimately mean being at war with ourselves."

Finally, Chapter 14 offers a critical encounter with perhaps the last remaining champion of high modernity. David Borman explores Jürgen Habermas's extraordinarily ambitious vision of "a positive conception of peace." Habermas tries not to impose Western liberal and democratic norms onto the global plurality, with all its cultural differences; and he also tries not to argue for a utopian vision. But the latter attempt involves a certain ambivalence. Borman notes that Habermas's effort to articulate a "realistic utopia" for the post–Cold War world muddles his genuine purpose. "Would the real Habermas stand up?" he quips.

In an effort to locate the "real" Habermas, Borman reminds us of his debt to Kant's "pacification through law" (discussed at length by Leah Bradshaw in Chapter 7). Rather than a Hobbesian negative peace, Habermas calls for "the transformation of political relations according to normatively legitimated rules and/or procedures." In Borman's view, this goes much further than Kant: peace is defined not simply as the elimination of war, but by the idea of non-violent intervention to relieve the tensions that lead to war. Critically, this notion recognizes the relationship between socio-economic conditions and political peace.

But does that make the project of global peace viable? Habermas argues that the rise of modern democratic states around the world—something that Kant could never have envisioned—offers a new potential for it. However, the mere fact that modern states no longer go to war with one another quite so often does not fully realize Habermas's vision of a just and equal society. The same problem persists in his consideration of the new possibilities for peace offered by economic globalization, and by the rise of the "global public sphere"—facilitated by advances in international communication such as the Internet. Again, these are things that Kant could not have anticipated.

In Borman's view, this area offers great potential for Habermas's positive vision. So do the developments in cosmopolitan legal order, backed by advances such as the Universal Declaration of Human Rights, and the establishment of an International Criminal Court. But there is a dilemma in embracing this global order: Habermas believed that the vision of peace required military interventions to respond to violations of human rights (in places such as Kuwait and Kosovo, for instance). Perhaps in the future such violence might be avoided if states voluntarily relinquish their power to regional or global bodies. Borman doubts, however, that even democratic states will choose to give up their sovereignty. He seems unconvinced that national legitimacy can be transferred to international organizations, especially if the latter are not democratic. For Habermas's peaceful project to be viable, it must in fact embrace a negative peace rather than a positive one. Surprisingly, the "real Habermas" may stand closer to the realists than to the idealists.

As we can see, the history of political thought contains a rich diversity of modern definitions of peace: idealist and realist, secular and religious, state-centric and individual-centric, political concept or philosophical idea. The act of asking what peace means, in any particular situation, is designed not so much to settle the question of what peace is, but rather to cast into relief its contested dimensions. Intimately associated with this question is another: what constitutes a just society? The association of peace and justice may lead to the paradox that peace becomes an end worth fighting for. But it is insufficient for us to define peace simply in terms of what it is not, or else peace studies may morph into the study of war. So the search for a definition of peace has a dangerous quality—but also a potential saving grace, if we recognize that our very being is at stake in this matter.

PART I

TRANSITION TO MODERNITY:
THE PLACE OF GOD AND MYTH

CHAPTER 1

By the Grace of God: Peace and Martin Luther's Two Kingdoms

Jarrett A. Carty

Introduction: Luther's Beliefs

The Reformation began in Germany with Martin Luther's protest against the sale of indulgences in 1517, and shortly expanded into a general schism within the Western church. Reform, Luther soon discovered, needed the cooperation of government, in which the civil authorities had a crucial role. Luther also needed theoretical justification for his Reformation, and guidance on its proper jurisdiction and limits. He looked for this guidance to the Bible and to the time of the apostles, believing that temporal government had once been independent of spiritual authority—and that the political tumult of his age was the result of spiritual authority having usurped government. True and lasting peace, he felt, could only come about through a proper respect for both of the distinct yet complementary "two kingdoms." The spiritual realm was ruled by Jesus Christ, through his Word; the secular realm was ruled by kings and civil authorities, through law and coercion. Its responsibilities were maintaining law and order, ensuring the protection of life and property, and promoting peace.

Luther held that wherever peace did not reign, and rebellion, war, or chaos, prevailed, the fault lay with the confusion of the two kingdoms—and the corruption of the spiritual by the temporal. The peace he sought, though, would prove to be tragically elusive. During his career, two major political controversies erupted: the Peasants' War of 1525, and the Protestant resistance against the Holy Roman Empire that began in 1530. And after his death in 1546, his views were challenged by the hardening of confessional church doctrines, and by the civil control of the churches in the wake of the Peace of Augsburg (1555).

Luther, Grace, and Reform

Around 1516, early in his teaching career at the University of Wittenberg, while lecturing on the Psalms and Paul's Epistle to the Romans, Luther devised his theological doctrine of justification: God's act of declaring a sinner righteous by faith alone.[1] Luther had once understood justification in terms of God righteously punishing sinners: if sinners met the requirement, they would be justified; if not, they remained unrighteous, and suffered the wrath of a harshly judging God. Luther struggled with this concept as a barrier to mankind's salvation, for it seemed to him beyond the capacity of human beings to achieve. He began to view sinners as initiators of their own salvation, and justification as the freely given (if unmerited) gift of God. Sinners did not have to meet any preconditions; they were already justified, by their faith in Christ's death and resurrection.[2]

But Luther's new doctrine of "by faith alone"—*sola fide*—directly challenged aspects of the medieval church's penitential system, which he felt was based on erroneous theology. The misuse of indulgences was a conspicuous example. Ordinarily, these were sanctioned reductions, remissions, or commutations of penances and punishments imposed on the contrite, in the form of almsgiving or pilgrimages—*after* they had duly confessed their sins and been absolved by a priest. Hitherto, indulgences had been generally uncontroversial. But the Archbishop of Mainz, in order to raise money to pay the massive debt he had incurred in buying his bishopric, allowed a special sale of indulgences in his territory (with the approval of Pope Leo X), in exchange for a cut of the proceeds. Luther heard from his parishioners that the priests in charge of this sale were allowing the public to buy indulgences, as though the instrument was itself confession and absolution. This practice, Luther held, turned penance into a mere financial transaction rather than genuine contrition; in effect, it put God's divine forgiveness up for sale. Luther was compelled to denounce what he believed was a serious theological error.

When Luther published his seminal work, *Disputation on the Power and Efficacy of Indulgences*[3] (commonly known as the *Ninety-Five Theses*) on October 31, 1517, he could not foresee the explosive controversy that his criticisms would evoke.[4] In the debate that followed, Luther increasingly found himself at odds with ecclesiastical authority, and with the politics of the Holy Roman Empire. Although Luther had intended his theses to be merely a scholarly exploration, several prominent theologians quickly took issue with them. They viewed the document as an attack on papal supremacy, and Luther as a radical conciliarist (that is, one who believed that authority rested with a church council rather than the pope).[5]

Over the next two years, several debates, disputations, and hearings would convince Luther's opponents that he was in fact attacking the papacy; and convinced Luther himself of the serious crisis within the church.[6] One such debate, at Leipzig in July 1519, was a turning point for Luther's theology and political thought. Debating against Johann Eck (1486–1543), he publicly stated his conception of the church and the Bible as the final authorities in all matters of doctrine and faith.[7] Luther also argued that both popes and councils had erred, and that only wholesale reform would correct the insidious errors that had enveloped the church, and thus imperilled all Christendom. This position, of course, virtually guaranteed his excommunication.

Any doubt about Luther's commitments to reform was erased by his activity in 1520: in that year he published several of his most famous works. These included a bold indictment of the church's practices, *The Babylonian Captivity of the Church*,[8] and a defence of his doctrine of justification and its ethical implications, *Christian Liberty*.[9] But the document that laid out the political implications of reform was his *An Open Letter to the Christian Nobility of the German Nation Concerning the Reform of the Christian Estate*[10]—a statement of his unabashed plans for programmatic reform.

To the Christian Nobility proposed a whole litany of reforms: the amalgamation of existing mendicant orders (and a end to creating new ones); the abolition of mandatory celibacy for the clergy; and a drastic reduction in masses said for the dead (a major source of church revenue at the time). Luther also advocated more discipline in popular religion, through the reduction in the number of festivals, and the abolition of certain shrines and chapels; he called for an end to the practice of begging, recommending instead that cities care for their poor through community charity for the poor; and he even called for a change to the degrees of consanguinity within which marriage was forbidden.

Most of all, however, the publication attacked what Luther called the "three walls" of the papacy: the pope's claim to superiority over all temporal powers, and the exclusive authority to interpret Scripture and summon a church council. He emphatically denied the temporal authority of both church and papacy, and recommended that those in positions of civil power should have a major role in overseeing reform. In the early years of the German Reformation, Luther had to defend what he saw as the God-given responsibility of temporal authority to maintain its distinction from the church.

The Two Kingdoms

Luther's first major political treatise was his famous *Temporal Authority: To What Extent it Should be Obeyed*, published in 1523. The work became the foundation of his treatment of the nature of civil government. He considered it one of his most important works: years later, after citing it in his treatise *Whether Soldiers too Can be Saved*, Luther wrote that "not since the time of the apostles have the temporal sword and temporal government been so clearly described or so highly praised by me."[11] *Temporal Authority* was divided into three parts. The first and second addressed the basis of temporal authority, and particularly its extent and limits. The third dealt with his vision for internal and external peace.

In the first part of *Temporal Authority*, Luther pointed out that the Bible clearly indicated the divine basis of government, to which Christians were commanded to submit.[12] Government, along with its power to coerce, was nearly as old as humanity itself; even the antediluvian stories of Genesis attested to its existence. But what of the apparent contradiction of Jesus' teachings—particularly his command to the faithful (in the Sermon on the Mount) to "turn the other cheek" and love their enemies?[13] Could both secular authority and Christ's commands be justly obeyed? Luther argued that they could: both must be accepted as true. He reconciled them in his Two Kingdoms doctrine: the world was divided into the spiritual kingdom, ruled by the Word of Jesus Christ as expressed by the church, and the temporal kingdom, governed by worldly powers through the law and the sword.[14]

This doctrine is rightly considered the centrepiece of Luther's political thought; but it should not be overlooked that he considered it based wholly on biblical revelation. He never explicitly acknowledged any significant influence by St. Augustine's concept of the two cities, or the medieval doctrine of the two swords.[15] Besides, his were very different from the other teachings. Unlike Augustine's cities, Luther's two realms were complementary, showcasing God's love and order for humanity; and unlike the swords, his spiritual kingdom had no jurisdiction over temporal matters. In contrast to his silence on medieval sources, Luther abundantly acknowledged the Bible as his source. His concept was the answer to the apparent biblical conflict between "turning the other cheek," and Paul and Peter's command to honour and obey political authorities.[16] He sought to explain the paradox of being fully justified by God, yet remaining in this life.

But although Luther believed that true Christians had no need of temporal government to live in peace with God and one another, he also believed that no one is righteous or justified by their own merit. Therefore secular government was divinely instituted by God to keep the peace, by curbing human tendencies to sin and lawlessness. Both kingdoms were divine gifts to humanity; the spiritual nourished the teaching of Jesus' justification for all believers, and the worldly tried to create peace through good laws and the just punishment of wrongdoing. Hence the first part of Luther's treatise could comfort any Christian prince troubled by the apparent conflict between the commands to love enemies and to punish the lawless: by fulfilling the divine call to keep the peace and punish violence, he was also fulfilling Jesus' command to love his neighbour.

In the second part of his treatise, which he felt was the main part, Luther sketched the extension and limits of temporal authority. The importance of this section for Luther's understanding of peace was paramount: so long as government knew its proper scope, and kept within it, peace would flourish. He argued that its proper jurisdiction was over external things like life and property, while spiritual jurisdiction was over the inner realm of the soul. For Luther, secular government had no authority over any matters of faith such as belief, justification, and salvation. Government could not justly legislate faith or coerce belief; in fact, if it ever attempted to do so, upheaval was sure to follow. This, Luther believed, was precisely what was happening in Germany. When princes banned his translation of the New Testament, thereby assaulting the preaching of the Word, they were crossing the boundary of government's rightful authority and trespassing on spiritual matters.

For Luther, the main result of harmony between the two kingdoms would be a substantial peace. If a ruler secured the temporal world by ruling with justice and keeping general order, this would provide fertile conditions for spiritual leaders to preach the Word. A healthy spiritual realm—one characterized by the doctrine of *sola fide*, biblical teachings, and the holy sacraments of communion and baptism—would in turn nurture virtuous subjects. According to divine purpose, mutual benefit was the result of working in tandem. The harmony of the two kingdoms brought body and soul under two means of divine governance that were distinct from one another, each fit for its own purpose but not the other's, unified under the rule of God that brought order to bodies and grace to souls.

Luther intended this harmony to be eminently practical for rulers, and so the next section of *Temporal Authority* was essentially a pastoral address to princes with troubled consciences. (The writing of the treatise was originally prompted by the actual concerns of Luther's own prince, Frederick the Wise of Saxony.) Princes and magistrates could rule within the bounds of their offices and duties, and still be justified by faith rather than by their own merits. The true Christian prince, Luther instructed, ought to fulfill his godly duty by devoting himself to the public good, and resisting all the temptations of political power—especially the corruptions of luxury and licentiousness that accompany courtly life. He must be on his guard against the mighty, punish all evildoing, and obey the secular powers over him (which, in the complex political realities of the Holy Roman Empire, was no easy task). He must rule wisely and enact reasonable laws (which Luther provided in the appendix).

In the third part of the treatise, Luther outlined his vision for internal peace that would accompany an enduring peace in the external world. His goal was to soothe the heart of a conflicted Christian (such as a troubled prince or magistrate) by assuring him that there was no conflict between the necessities of governing, and the prospect of being saved by grace. The need to execute a murderer could in fact be reconciled with "turning the other cheek": since God had ordained the justly undertaken actions of temporal authority, then all its offices—from prince and magistrate to soldier and hangman—were also divinely instituted, and crucial parts of God's reign on earth.

Temporal Authority did not exhaust Luther's views on the Two Kingdoms doctrine, particularly as it applied to secular government. He continued to have a great deal to say on the subject, in the form of treatises, biblical commentaries, letters, and polemics, throughout his whole life.[17] He would also considerably develop his ideas on many more issues, such how far secular authority could be exercised over questions such as liturgical practices, preaching, and the adoption of Reformation ideas—especially as the Reformation hardened into divided confessional churches. (In this context, "confessional" refers to the emerging separate church denominations such as Reformed, Lutheran, Roman Catholic, etc., rather than to the actual ritual of confession.) But shortly after Luther published *Temporal Authority*, two violent controversies arose that seemed to demonstrate the corruption of the two kingdoms, and to shatter the promise of peace. These were the Peasants' War in 1525, and the crisis of resistance to the Holy Roman Empire in 1530.

The Peasants' War

As the Reformation spread, certain radical agendas for reform began surfacing, supposedly based on rediscovered biblical teachings.[18] These caused a wave of dissent in Germany, and even threatened revolution. Several reformers denied the need for government altogether, advocating complete withdrawal from society, or else simply ignoring political authority. Others attempted wholesale political reforms, proposing to abolish old political forms and offices and establish new ones that conformed to their doctrines. Luther himself vociferously opposed the radical tendency to spiritualize politics, which confused the spiritual and secular realms. Defending the separation of his two kingdoms, he wrote a number of treatises and polemics against the radicals themselves, and against the cities and territories that adopted their faith and politics.[19]

Luther's objections may appear to be primarily for the sake of the purity of evangelical reform and church purification. The reformers drew no distinctions between the spiritual and the temporal: both would be governed by what they considered to be the commands of God, revealed either directly, or through gospel or Scripture. But for Luther, the survival of both kingdoms was at stake. To be sure, the radicals' mingling of spiritual and worldly authority would imperil souls—but it would also unleash violence in the temporal world.

The Peasants' War of 1525 was the first and most acutely felt upheaval of the radical Reformation.[20] Though the causes of the uprising were complex, with deep roots in the 15th century, the primary cause was the annulment of peasant rights by nobles and landlords in the early 16th century. Smouldering widespread resentment, sparked by the winds of church reform, culminated in a violent revolt that spread throughout several regions in Germany and central Europe. In early 1525, a group of peasants from Upper Swabia published a pamphlet titled *The Fundamental and Proper Chief Articles of all the Peasantry and Those Who are Oppressed by Spiritual and Temporal Authority*, commonly known as the Twelve Articles. Though the document rejected outright revolution, it based its grievances on the Bible; and it called on theologians like Luther to weigh in on the conflict.[21]

Luther vehemently rejected their cause. He wrote three works in response,[22] all heated, even violent, in their language and tone: he argued consistently for maintaining the two separate realms. His first response, *Admonition to Peace, A Reply to the Twelve Articles of Swabia*,[23] sharply criticized the supposed biblical support for the peasants' grievances. Luther readily acknowledged that they were indeed suffering great injustices, and even that the present tumult was a just punishment for the recalcitrance of the nobility. But he unequivocally denied that the peasants had any biblical justification for rebelling against temporal authority. His objection to the Twelve Articles was twofold: by attacking the divinely ordained separation of the two kingdoms, the manifesto threatened both the preaching of the gospel, and the peace of a well-ordered government. He held the appropriation of biblical principles for the sake of political and social revolution to be deeply flawed, even blasphemous. In his view, the Twelve Articles promised only further violence, rather than the new order of peace the peasants hoped to bring about.

Luther's second response, *Against the Robbing and Murdering Hordes of Peasants*,[24] was notoriously severe. By the time he wrote his polemic, Luther had learned that the peasant revolt had become openly violent and destructive. Yet he remained consistent in his vehement defence of secular authority, and his opposition to those who challenged it. His fiery rhetoric was fuelled by what he saw as a threat to both worldly government, and the gospel, since the former functioned as a safe haven for the latter. The peasants had violated their duty to submit to law and government by rebelling; most perversely of all, by claiming to act in the name of God, they were corrupting the gospel. For this reason, Luther endorsed a merciless crushing of the revolt: rulers could in good conscience take up the sword if their subjects were unwilling to obey. Infamously, he wrote: "Let whoever can stab, smite, slay. If you die in doing it, good for you! A more blessed death can never be yours, for you die while obeying the divine word and commandment ... and in loving service of your neighbour, whom you are rescuing from the bonds of hell and of the devil."[25]

Luther's polemic was so harsh that enemies and friends alike excoriated him; even fellow reformers like Philipp Melanchthon thought it extreme. Rather than furthering the cause of peace, Luther seemed to endorse more bloodshed, and the indiscriminate quashing of subjects by bloodthirsty nobles. Luther responded to these criticisms with a third work, *An Open Letter on the Harsh Book Against the Peasants.*[26] But far from retreating from his position in the previous two publications, Luther defended it—repeating his belief that the peasants had no justified biblical grounds for revolt, and were thus undermining both the two kingdoms. To be sure, the bloodlust of the princes and nobles in suppressing the revolt was also an affront to the worldly kingdom; cruelties were not justified, and undermined constituted authority. On the one hand, Luther felt that the secular powers deserved the upheaval; but on the other hand, the peasants too deserved the harsh suppression of their rebellion for disrupting the peace. He also considered their pleas for clemency after their defeat the height of hypocrisy, for asking mercy from the very authorities they had sought mercilessly to destroy.[27] When radical reformers aimed to enforce the gospel by the sword, he believed, their uprising could only wreak destruction on both governments and souls.

Resistance to Empire

After the Peasants' War, the second major challenge to Luther's vision of peace came with a crisis of empire. The Diet of Augsburg, in June 1530, was an attempt by church authorities to calm rising tensions over Protestantism, especially due to fears of the rising Ottoman threat. In its aftermath, the German territories supporting church reform were threatened with prosecution if they did not return to the ecclesiastical fold of the Roman church. At Augsburg, the Protestants—as they now were being called, for their protest against some of the church's beliefs and practices—were given the chance to defend reform and clarify their beliefs, in what famously became known as the Augsburg Confession. The Catholic Confutation then attacked the doctrine of reform; and this was accepted by the Holy Roman Emperor Charles V as the final word on the matter.

Protesting Germans were given a grace period of six months (known as the Augsburg Recess) to accept the Confutation. But Luther's own prince, John the Constant of Saxony (Frederick the Wise had died in 1525), instead of capitulating, responded by proposing a defensive Protestant league. He summoned lawyers, courtiers, and theologians (including Luther) to meet in Torgau in October 1530. The result of that meeting was the Torgau Declaration, which approved the principle of armed defence against the empire. Luther endorsed the Declaration, and began composing his treatise titled *Martin Luther's Warning to His Dear German People*.[28] It was published in March 1531.

In *Temporal Authority* and elsewhere, Luther had always maintained that no subjects should ever rise up against their superior (though there were grounds for limited disobedience). Christians could not revolt against temporal authority without destroying both the government and their souls. But despite his long-standing ban on rebellion, in *Warning to His Dear German People* he developed a clear doctrine and justification of political resistance—including armed resistance—against the Holy Roman Empire. How could such a stance be reconciled with his doctrines of peace and the Two Kingdoms?

Luther argued that he was being entirely consistent. He would never counsel war, but he would also not decry self-defence—and though the resistance in 1530 had the appearance of rebellion, it was in fact an act of defence of the temporal kingdom.[29] Responding to accusations that he had reneged on his earlier positions regarding obedience, Luther turned the issue around: the empire itself was essentially waging war on the integrity of secular authority, he argued, which was contrary to divine, natural, and even imperial law. Peace could not be gained by allowing the Catholic political and ecclesiastical authorities to prosecute a war against Protestants, without any due legal process, or recourse for the defendants. Luther's stance at Torgau, and in his *Warning to His Dear German People*, was therefore—from his perspective—one taken for the sake of peace. Resistance against the empire was for the sake of honouring the temporal kingdom.

Conclusion: An Elusive Peace

Luther's doctrine of the Two Kingdoms envisioned peace as a result of the separate and harmonious cooperation of secular power and spiritual authority. Whenever chaos reigned—as it did during the Peasants' War or the crisis of empire—the reason, he believed, was the confusion of the kingdoms. Luther saw evidence of corruption all around him in the ecclesiastical and temporal authorities. Still, there were major complications to his position. For one thing, Luther's advocacy for peace was deeply paradoxical: he pushed for church reform and argued for proper bounds for government, yet at the same time he believed that the apocalypse was nigh.[30] The true separation of the two kingdoms was ultimately beyond human agency, Luther believed; only God could fully restore it—and that full restoration would likely come about only with the remaking of the world.

As well, matters closer to home (and within human power) challenged his doctrine, and his vision of earthly peace. For instance, could secular authority be expanded to include, in case of emergency, special powers over the local church? Luther determined that exceptions could be made, particularly when caused by the recalcitrance of the Roman church. In such circumstances a secular magistrate—as a result of his leadership status in the community of believers—could also wield authority in the spiritual kingdom as an "emergency bishop" (*Notbischof*). This issue would prove to be the beginning of a long and hotly disputed topic during the Reformation. Many of Luther's own followers believed in some version of the Two Kingdoms, yet affirmed that worldly governments had a duty to see that true religion flourished in their territories: they must institute discipline, good morals, sound preaching, and generally oversee the clergy.[31] Philipp Melanchthon and Johannes Brenz, for example, both held that civil authorities had an obligation to maintain a Christian society in all its public observances.

This debate over the role of political authorities in overseeing the clergy and religious observance showed that Luther's vision of two strictly separated kingdoms may not have been as practical as he believed. As the Reformation gained momentum and positions hardened, one result was the emergence of confessional churches as the ultimate goal, rather than a worldwide church reform. The boundaries of Luther's spiritual and temporal kingdoms became blurred; and what had hitherto seemed like harmony between them became more like a theoretical separation, with increasingly greater oversight of church affairs by secular powers, both Catholic and Protestant. These grew in power and authority over many aspects of life and society, and also appropriated more and more control over churches. The Peace of Augsburg (1555), and the agreements between Catholic and Lutheran territories in the decades after, gave German princes the right to determine the religion of their subjects.

But the harmony Luther envisioned, when each kingdom reigned in its proper sphere, was never permanently realized. In the short term, for the next half-century or so, the system produced a tenuous peace. But in the long term, tragically, it led to one of Europe's most devastating cataclysms: the Thirty Years War (1618–1648). Fuelled by Reformation divisions and the power-politics of expanding and clashing monarchies, the war obliterated a third of Germany's population. This exceeded the death toll of all previous wars or plagues, including the Black Plague of the 14th century, and remained unsurpassed until the World Wars of the 20th century.

One remarkable contrast between 16th- and 17th-century views was that in the former, most thinkers—like Luther, and largely like his century— believed that territories divided by different Reformation churches could not be governed; and that only the dominant religion of the territory promoted peace and order. But the 17th century began to challenge the political necessity of doctrinal uniformity. In this regard, Thomas Hobbes (1588–1679) and Baruch Spinoza (1632–1677) were perhaps the most radical thinkers. For Hobbes, the greatest challenge to peace was controlling those in the regime who desired honour and glory. (See Laurie M. Johnson's essay on Hobbes in this volume.) Otherwise, Hobbes believed, all government and church authority ought to be subsumed under sovereign authority, for the sake of peace and good order. Security would be brought about only by such a contract, rather than by confessional uniformity; and doctrinal disputes were mere vain talk. And in Spinoza's controversial *Theological Political Treatise*, he argued that only a general religiosity could benefit public order by controlling the passions of the masses. Otherwise, political rule should avoid religious doctrine altogether, and give as much freedom of thought and speech as possible. (See Paul Bagley's essay on Spinoza in this volume.)

But in the time of the Reformation, the idea that doctrinal uniformity brought peace was still commonplace, and allowed the political authorities to effect their consolidation over their territorial churches. When this commonly accepted notion began to lose ground, in the aftermath of the Thirty Years War, the change came just as the notion of the nation-state began to arise. Even if Luther's doctrine of Two Kingdoms did not prevail, and his vision of peace was tragically frustrated, his political thought was still an important part of this crucial period of European political history. It reveals the profoundly theological roots of the modern secular state[32]—a system often assumed to have come about as a secular alternative to failed reform, in the aftermath of the Reformation and the religious wars.

In fact, the hallmarks of the modern state—like the consolidation of the rule of law, and a monopoly over public order—derived largely from the political context of church reform in the 16th century. Without the Reformation, one could argue, there might not have emerged the coherent, territorially based bodies of law that we now take for granted.[33] Luther's ideas, while not in themselves responsible for this development, nevertheless point the way to the principles on which modern political life was originally built: on the religious, social and political problems of church reform, and the search for peace amidst a deep political and spiritual crisis.

Notes

1   Alister McGrath, *Luther's Theology of the Cross: Martin Luther's Theological Breakthrough* (New York: Blackwell, 1985), 141–47.

2   For a detailed historical account of Luther's theological development, see Bernhard Lohse, *Martin Luther's Theology: Its Historical and Theological Development*, trans. Roy A. Harrisville (Minneapolis: Fortress Press, 1999), 43–95.

3   The text of *Disputation on the Power and Efficacy of Indulgences*, and all other English versions of Martin Luther's writing, is taken from *Luther's Works* (hereafter referred to as *LW*). Jaroslav Pelikan and Helmut Lehmann, ed., *Luther's Works* (St. Louis: Concordia Publishing House and Philadelphia: Fortress Press, 1955–1986). German and Latin references to Luther's texts are from D. Martin, *Luther's Werke: Kritische Gesamtausgabe* (Weimar: Herman Böhlau, 1883), hereafter referred to as *WA*. *LW* 31: 9–16; *WA* 1: 233–38.

4   Lohse, 96–109.

5   For an introduction to the conflict between conciliarism and papalism, including primary sources, see J. H. Burns and Thomas M. Izbicki, *Conciliarism and Papalism* (Cambridge: Cambridge University Press, 1997).

6   This escalation took place in discernible stages. See Scott H. Hendrix, *Luther and the Papacy: Stages in a Reformation Conflict* (Philadelphia: Fortress Press, 1981).

7   Lohse, 118–26.

8   *LW* 36: 3–126; *WA* 6: 497–573.

9   *LW* 31: 333–77; *WA* 7: 1–38.

10   *LW* 44: 115–217; *WA* 6: 404–69.

11   *LW* 46: 95; *WA* 19: 624. For a more extensive survey of Luther's political thought, see these writers:

> W. D. J. Cargill Thompson, *The Political Thought of Martin Luther* (Sussex: Harvester Press, 1984).
> Quentin Skinner, *The Foundations of Modern Political Thought, Vol. 2, The Age of Reformation* (Cambridge: Cambridge University Press, 1978).
> David M. Whitford, "Luther's Political Encounters," *The Cambridge Companion to Martin Luther*, ed. Donald McKim (Cambridge: Cambridge University Press, 2003).

12   Luther's "go to" text for this subject was Paul's Epistle to the Romans, 13:1–2.

13   Matthew 5:38–48; compare Luke 6:27–36.

14   For excellent theological and historical studies of Luther's Two Kingdoms, see these writers: Heinrich Bornkamm, *Luther's Doctrine of the Two Kingdoms*, trans. Karl H. Hertz (Philadelphia: Fortress Press, 1966); David C. Steinmetz, "Luther and the Two Kingdoms," *Luther in Context* (Bloomington, IN: Indiana University Press, 1986); and William J. Wright, *Martin Luther's Understanding of God's Two Kingdoms* (Grand Rapids, MI: Baker Academic, 2010).

15   Those doctrines were also considered to be biblically supported.

16   Luther's letter to Philip Melanchthon (July 13, 1521), while he was forming his Two Kingdoms doctrine, shows his struggle with the divine gift of governmental authority and its relationship to the gospel. "I cannot allow you to reject the statements of the Apostles Paul in Romans 13 [:1–2] and Peter in I Peter 2 [:13–14] as if they were not applicable here, or as if they were only instructing the citizens," he wrote. "You will not accomplish this, my Philip! These are words of God—of great importance—when Paul says: [temporal] authority is from God, and whosoever resists [temporal] authority resists God's ordinance, and [temporal authority] is the servant of God." *LW* 48: 260; *WA Br* 2: 357.

17   See, for example, the extensive collection of Luther's writing in Jarrett A. Carty, *Divine Kingdom, Holy Order: The Political Writings of Martin Luther* (St. Louis: Concordia Publishing House, 2012).

18   For the authoritative overview of radicalism in the Reformation, see George H. Williams, *The Radical Reformation* (Philadelphia: Westminster Press, 1962). For a fine introductory essay and a collection of important radical writings, see Michael G. Baylor, ed., *The Radical Reformation* (Cambridge: Cambridge University Press, 1991).

19   Luther's attack on radical reform politics began early, after he witnessed first-hand (though in disguise, as he remained hidden by Prince Frederick of Saxony at the Wartburg after the Diet of Worms) the public disorder in Wittenberg following the radical turn of several colleagues. See his 1522 treatise, *A Sincere Admonition By Martin Luther To All Christians To Guard Against Insurrection and Rebellion*, *LW* 45: 51–74; *WA* 7: 676–87.

20   For more on the Peasants' War, see these two writers: Peter Blickle, *The Revolution of 1525: The German Peasants' War from a New Perspective*, trans. Thomas A. Brady, Jr. and H. C. Midelfort (Baltimore: Johns Hopkins University Press, 1985); and Tom Scot and Robert W. Scribner, ed., *The German Peasants' War: A History in Documents* (Atlantic Highlands, NJ: Humanities Press, 1990).

21   An English translation of the Twelve Articles is contained in *LW* 46: 8–16.

22   For an overview of Luther's involvement, see Martin Brecht's three-volume biography of Luther—the most authoritative and richly detailed biography written to date. Martin Brecht, *Martin Luther: Shaping and Defining the*

Reformation, 1521–1532, trans. James A. Schaaf (Minneapolis: Fortress Press, 1990), 172–94.

23 *LW* 46: 3–43; *WA* 18: 291–334.

24 *LW* 46: 45–55; *WA* 18: 57–361.

25 *LW* 46: 54–55; *WA* 18: 361.

26 *LW* 46: 57–85; *WA* 18: 384–401.

27 *LW* 46: 70; *WA* 18: 391.

28 *LW* 47: 3–55; *WA* 30III: 276–320.

29 Luther's counselling resistance against the Holy Roman Empire remains a controversial topic in Luther and Reformation scholarship. For more information, see these writers:

> W. D. J. Cargill Thompson, "Luther and the Right of Resistance to the Emperor," *Church History* 12 (1975): 159–202.
> Cynthia Grant Schoenberger, "Luther and the Justifiability of Resistance to Legitimate Authority," *Journal of the History of Ideas* 40 (1979): 3–20.
> David M. Whitford, *Tyranny and Resistance: The Magdeburg Confession and the Lutheran Tradition* (St. Louis: Concordia Publishing House, 2001).

30 Luther's apocalyptic battle with the Devil forms the interpretive foundation of Heiko Oberman's provocative biography *Martin Luther: Man Between God and the Devil* (New York: Doubleday, 1992).

31 For more on this subject, see these writers:

> E. J. Brill and Timothy J. Wengert, *Philip Melanchthon, Speaker of the Reformation: Wittenberg's Other Reformer* (Surrey: Ashgate Publishing, 2010).
> James M. Estes, *Peace, Order, and the Glory of God: Secular Authority and the Church in the Thought of Luther and Melanchthon* (Leiden, Netherlands: Brill, 2005).
> James M. Estes, *Christian Magistrate and Territorial Church: Johannes Brenz and the German Reformation* (Toronto: Centre for Reformation and Renaissance Studies, 2007).

32 See Michael Allen Gillespie, *The Theological Origins of Modernity* (Chicago: University of Chicago Press, 2008).

33 See Harold J. Berman, *Law and Revolution II: The Impact of the Protestant Reformations on the Western Legal Tradition* (Cambridge, MA: Harvard University Press, 2003); and also John Witte Jr., *Law and Protestantism: The Legal Teachings of the Lutheran Reformation* (Cambridge: Cambridge University Press, 2002).

CHAPTER 2

A Secure and Healthy Life: Spinoza on the Prospects for Peace

Paul Bagley

In his *Tractatus politicus*, Benedictus Spinoza asserts that the optimal condition and goal of a civil state "is nothing other than peace and security of life."[1] That condition, he says, is best achieved when individuals "transact their lives in harmony, and laws are preserved inviolate." In civic life, enmity and contempt, or breach of the law, are not to be imputed to the malice of the subjects; instead they result from the depravity of the state. People, Spinoza declares, "are not born citizens but must be made so." It is incumbent on the governing authority to foster an environment in which concord, safety, and obedience to law are advocated and enforced. Just as a state deserves rebuke when it fails to cultivate such dispositions among its citizens, so too the citizens' virtue and "constant observance of the law, for the most part, are to be assigned completely to the virtue and authority" of the state.[2] Spinoza concludes that "peace is not being free from war but a virtue that arises from strength of mind; for in fact, obedience [is] the constant will of following what ought to be done, according to the common decree of the governing authority."[3]

In Spinoza's view, the prospects for peace among citizens demand obedience to law, arising from a strength of mind that he characterizes as a virtue. Attaining that condition, however, is difficult, since the natural inclination of individuals to seek preservation, security, health, and peace derives from the same natural inclination by which they act selfishly, passionately, impulsively, and destructively. The problem of human nature must be understood and resolved before peace through the civil state can be made practicable.[4] The *Tractatus* offers a brief description of human nature, and the adversities that individuals suffer because of the tensions between reason and passion—both within themselves, or in relation to others.[5] But in another work, the *Tractatus theologico-politicus*, Spinoza elaborates more fully on the natural problem.[6] The solution he proposes is for individuals to surmount their basic selfish interests by adopting a plan of living that makes peace possible.

The Natural Problem

In the *Tractatus theologico-politicus*, Spinoza says that all we properly desire may be referred to three chief things: comprehending things through their primary causes; acquiring the habit of virtue and subduing the passions; and living securely with a healthy body.[7] He asserts that the first and second objects may be attained by powers that are contained in human nature itself, since they depend entirely on the laws of our nature, and may be acquired through our power alone. But the satisfaction of the third object of desire lies mainly in external things such as gifts of fortune—"whatsoever nature affords man without his help." Spinoza therefore concedes that the ignorant and foolish may be as happy or unhappy in life as the prudent and vigilant.[8] Acquiring knowledge and virtue is not sufficient to attain a secure and healthy life; the peace sought by both knowledgeable and ignorant individuals requires something more. External things such as natural resources are indispensable but inadequate.

Satisfying the third objective—security and health—entails the formation of societies with certain laws. Political association is another necessary thing, one that can be aided greatly by direction and vigilance.[9] Rather than surrender the formation of societies to chance, it is more advantageous that they be organized and established by sensible and perceptive persons. In other words, although satisfaction of the first and second objects of desire is not sufficient to assure secure and healthy life, knowledge and virtue can be very useful in bringing about those things that can make the third objective feasible. Few people are capable of subduing their passions and acquiring the habit of virtue through the exercise of reason alone. Most hope to obtain knowledge, acquire virtue, or live in security and health based on the opinions they construct from their vague experiences of things.[10] Furthermore, individuals tend to look to novelties, rarities, or exceptions to inform their basic regard for things. Opinion is their element.

In his treatise, Spinoza discusses the appeal of society and the reasons for its formation.[11] In his view "those who live rudely without [society] make a miserable and almost brutish life." Discussing the reasons for founding a republic, he repeats that verdict: people fail to afford one another mutual assistance, and they lack cultivation of reason in circumstances devoid of civil society.[12] He maintains that the universal foundations of society can be deduced from human nature: individuals' impetus toward self-preservation compels them to recognize the utility and necessity of participation in civil society. Its appeal resides in the fact that it promotes security from enemies, and "easily abbreviates many things," such as labour. Indeed, without such cooperation, individuals would lack the time and development of skills to sustain themselves; for "not all are equally apt for all things," and people living alone would not be able to provide for themselves.[13] Society affords conveniences and comforts, as well as fostering the development of the arts and the sciences—which Spinoza asserts are indispensable to the "perfection of human nature and its blessedness."[14]

But despite the incentives to participate in society, the elemental characteristics of human nature can threaten it or prevent it from achieving its goals.[15] Since without society human lives are miserable and brutish, it must be inferred that their primordial condition is asocial. Indeed, if human beings are considered only under the "*ius et institutum naturae*"—the right and order of nature—then their natural right, or fundamental condition, "is determined not by sound reason but by desire and power."[16] Moreover, by nature, all pursue what they esteem to be in their own interest to the exclusion of others.

For this reason, all social or political arrangements involve an inherent paradox.[17] Individuals seek only their own interest; and they have "the highest right of nature," in Spinoza's view, to pursue that interest to the neglect, or even the injury, of others.[18] As a result, societies require a remedy to counter such detrimental human interests and behaviours. If individuals were constituted by nature to seek nothing except what true reason indicates, society would have no need for laws; it would be enough to teach true moral lessons, and people would respond to them by doing only what was truly useful. But because people are driven more by power and desire than by reason, this is not enough. Instead, Spinoza concludes, "no society can subsist without a governing authority, force, and consequently laws that moderate and restrain human lust and unbridled impetuses."[19] By this means "men are made citizens," and develop the virtue and strength of mind that result in peace. This fact makes the state the most significant external thing needed to satisfy the third object of desire.

Solutions to the Natural Problem

Most individuals can be swayed to obey laws because the polity either promises them what they love most, or threatens them with what they fear most. Political leaders understand what moves their citizens most effectively, and know that passionate and unreasonable individuals are not moved to citizenship by rational arguments or mathematical demonstrations. Instead, they are moved by the telling of stories—stories that attract the imagination; that reflect common opinions, sentiments, biases, and habits; and that carry the authority to influence the desires, hopes, and fears of the multitude.[20]

The most efficient stories to move people to engage in political life, and to moderate their conduct, are contained in the Scriptures. Their great advantage, Spinoza writes, is that the Scriptures were "revealed first for the use of an entire nation, and in the end revealed to the whole human race." As a result, their lessons have been "accommodated greatly to the grasp of the plebs [and] confirmed by experience alone."[21] Scripture can induce people to adopt a sensible plan of living that contributes to their security and health; and Spinoza identifies their lessons with the dogmas of revelation, theology, faith, or piety. They demand that people obey the law, cultivate strength of mind or virtue, and love their neighbours; and they also promise *salus*, in either its theological or political sense.[22]

Theology proposes that its guidance is sufficient for the proper conduct of human life: because most people are led more by passion than by reason, they will be disposed to the kind of instruction that is communicated though dramatic narratives. Such stories appeal to the opinions, sentiments, biases, and beliefs about their experiences of the world that are common to the imaginative-affective life. Furthermore, Spinoza believes, people are naturally prone to credulity and superstition whenever they cannot govern their affairs with some kind of dependable counsel, or whenever they feel that fortune has failed them.[23] As an alternative, the suprarational dogmas of religion promise individuals the satisfaction of their hopes and desires, and the alleviation of their miseries or fears, if they follow Scripture's prescribed plan of living. To solve the problem of human nature, Spinoza is willing to invoke theology to move people to obedience—since reason or philosophy cannot do so.[24]

The motive for this recourse to religion is Spinoza's belief that the *ius et institutum naturae* determines beings to act in a certain way: fish swim, and big fish eat little fish, because it is their nature to do so. Whatever any being does by its own nature, it has the highest right to do because "the right of the individual is coextensive with its determinate power."[25] The identification of natural right with natural power extends to every being in nature, and hence to all aspects of human nature. Consequently, people who are not yet acquainted with reason, or have not yet "acquired a virtuous disposition," live under the control of appetite alone—but with as much right as people who conduct their lives under the rule of reason. The reasonable and sensible human being has the right to do all that reason dictates; but so too has one who is ignorant and wanton, who may "do all that is urged on him by his appetites."[26] Furthermore, Spinoza says, since in nature every being endeavours to persist in its state as much as it can, taking no account of anything but itself, so too every individual has a right to exist and function in its natural state." Spinoza makes no distinction, in their exercise of rights or powers, between people who have discovered the advantages of using reason and fools and madmen "to whom true reason is unknown."[27]

The concept of nature, in Spinoza's account, exposes the root of the natural or philosophic problem. "The natural right of every human being is determined not by sound reason, but by desire and power," he says. Whatever people believe to be to their advantage—whether they are under the guidance of reason or the sway of passion—they may get for themselves by any means, be it force or deceit or entreaty. A man "may regard as an enemy anyone who tries to hinder him from obtaining what he wants," Spinoza concludes.

Most striking is his deduction that under the *ius et institutum naturae*, the life of passion is just as legitimate as the life of reason. Solving the natural problem demands that rational individuals be able to live peacefully and securely among individuals guided chiefly by their passions, who regard as enemies anyone they perceive as impeding them from satisfying their desires, impulses, or lusts. The highest natural right allows all individuals to employ any means at their disposal to obtain what they seek; and "only that which no one desires, or that no one can do, is excluded from anyone's right or power." [28]

Nobody is prevented by nature from wresting from others by force whatever advantage they perceive; and even those who ignore reason for the sake of passion are as much at risk from others who live the same way as those who live by the dictates of reason.[29] To avoid the dangers inherent to the natural condition, laws must be instituted; citizens must be brought to comply with them; the polity must threaten punishment for those who violate them; and it must also offer rewards for those who abide by them. Thus the obvious practical solution to the natural problem would seem to be a political one. Ironically, though, the right and order of nature has the effect of making human life precarious. Because natural right is determined more by appetite than by reason, there is no good reason to believe that the law of self-preservation actually tends to preserve or protect individuals.

Still, Spinoza insists that it is far more salutary to live in accordance with laws and reason that serve the true advantage of individuals.[30] All people seek to conduct their lives and affairs free from anxiety, struggles, hatred, and anger; but such a situation cannot be realized as long as all people may do as they please, and "reason can claim no more right than hatred or anger." To forestall those negative influences, individuals must be moved to unite into one body, agreeing that unrestricted natural right be converted to common right and pledge to be guided in all matters only by the dictates of reason. They must keep those appetites in check that tend to others' hurt, do nothing they would not want done to themselves, and uphold others' rights as they would their own.[31]

Fortunately, nature itself gives individuals the means to foreswear the unrestricted exercise of natural right. The same elements that permit them to use any measure to satisfy their desires, also permit them to enter political life and submit to laws that constrain harmful behaviour. The universal law of self-preservation means that people do not reject what they judge to be good, "except through the hope of a greater good or the fear of a greater evil." Conversely, no one endures any evil except to avoid a greater evil, or to gain a greater good.[32] Because self-preservation is the *lex summa naturae*, and polities are designed to improve the lives, security and health of citizens, even individuals ruled more by passion than reason could be persuaded to enter political life. For them, abdicating their entitlement to some rights or powers would be perceived as a lesser evil that could be endured for the sake of attaining a greater good. Indeed, safety from harm is the professed aim of that plan of living designed to protect life and the republic.[33] However, a person's manner of discriminating between or among goods and evils is entirely idiosyncratic. According to Spinoza, it is a principle of human nature—a law so firmly inscribed that it should be placed among the eternal truths—that everyone will choose of two goods that which each judges to be the greater, and of two evils that which seems the lesser.[34] But he expressly points out that this is purely a matter of belief, and that actual facts may not correspond with a person's judgment.

Still, an individual's perception of advantage is neither constant nor consistent. Even the advantages of participation in political life may not be strong enough to induce some people to comply with the law. Spinoza concludes that "an agreement has no force except because of its utility, without which the agreement is annulled and held void."[35] The stability of any polity depends on the estimation of that utility by its citizens. If they cease to regard it as useful, then they are no longer bound by the terms of their allegiance to it. In that crucial respect, however, the assumptions that can lead citizens to participate in a polity—choosing it as the greater good based on its utility—are the same that can undermine a polity: regarding participation in it as a greater evil because of its lack of utility. An exclusively political solution to the natural problem, designed to secure a peaceful life for both rational and passionate individuals, is inherently inadequate.

From that eternal truth, it necessarily follows that no one will "promise in all good faith to give up his unrestricted right, [or] keep any promises whatsoever, except through fear of a greater evil or hope of a greater good."[36] Since natural right is determined by power alone, one may act deceitfully in dealing with an assailant, for example, and promise whatever is demanded— even though the victim has no intention of honouring the promise. The law of self-preservation allows deceit as a perfectly legitimate exercise of right whenever an individual perceives the necessity for it. Human nature dictates that agreements are made and considered valid only because of their perceived utility to the assenting parties; and that fact, Spinoza says, deserves special attention when constituting a polity. If all people could be induced to follow reason and to recognize "the supreme utility and the necessity of the Republic's existence," they would foreswear deceit entirely. Furthermore, from their desire to secure the highest good—that is, the preservation of the Republic—they also would observe their agreements with others in complete good faith; and they would regard keeping their word their most important civic function, since honesty is "the strongest shield of the Republic."

The problem is that most individuals are not readily guided by reason. Rather, as Spinoza points out, "each of them is drawn by his own pleasure, and the mind frequently is so occupied by avarice, glory, envy, hatred, etc., that no place remains for reason." So although people may make promises and pledges, their faith is not assured unless the promise is strengthened by something else that has the power to prevent deceit.[37] Spinoza's view of keeping faith displays an important tension between the interests of citizens and the governing authority, which is compounded by another fact of human nature: obedience cannot be known from nature, and therefore cannot be taught by philosophy or reason.[38] Spinoza resorts to theology and its stories in order to justify the political practice of obedience.

Making Citizens Obedient for the Sake of Peace

Describing the formation of civil societies, Spinoza defines social aspects such as justice and injustice, civil right and wrong, alliances and enemies.[39] These definitions frame the rights of the polity against the rights of citizens. In his consideration of crimes, where natural right conflicts with civic right, Spinoza poses this question: Does someone who lives entirely by appetite, even with *summum ius*, contradict God's divine command for everyone to love their neighbour and avoid doing injury to others?[40] How does the right and power of nature relate to the right and power of divine law? In fact, Spinoza resolves the question without difficulty. In his view the natural state predates religion, and so no one knows by nature that any obedience is owed to God. Indeed, such knowledge cannot be attained by any process of reasoning. Before the revelation of divine law, and its requirement of obedience to God, the people are not bound by a divine right of which they were ignorant.[41]

Spinoza's account of crime in civil society is conventional: the sovereignty of the governing authority surpasses the rights of the individual. But he also raises another question. In the natural state, and absent a lawful polity, are not individuals still bound to constrain their injurious behaviours—in accordance with divine law, which obliges everyone equally to love their neighbour? Spinoza replies that people are not bound by any such obligation if they live only according to their natural condition; for the state of nature predates religion, just as it predates political life. Indeed, Spinoza maintains that the origin of religion is identical with the origin of a civil state: both require individuals to transfer natural rights to a governing authority, whether civil society or God.[42] Only through such a transfer, together with an agreement to live in a certain way, does obedience come into existence.

For just as no one knows by nature that any obedience is owed to God, individuals also do not know that they owe any obedience to their fellows or equals—at least before their pledge of faith to the governing authorities.[43] Obedience, either to God or to other people, derives not from nature but from a contractual construct.

Reasonable individuals who understand what serves their true good will always conduct their lives either by the dictates of reason, or by some dependable counsel in both the natural and political conditions. Their rational and self-determined actions do not involve acting at the bidding of others, and hence do not involve any kind of obedience. Spinoza's conclusion regarding reason and action explains his idea that no one knows by nature about obedience to God. Knowledge of nature is the province of reason or philosophy; and so knowledge of obedience cannot be attained by any process of reasoning, because it cannot be known from nature—which contains no claim of obedience. Instead, obedience must be introduced through the suprarational means of "revelation confirmed by signs."[44] Spinoza invokes the stories from the Scriptures to convince passionate individuals of the need for obedience. He presses theology into the service of politics in order to make people into citizens—justifying the virtue that entails a constant will to obey the law and keep faith with others.

Passionate individuals, who spurn reason and live by desires or impulses, can reject or ignore the dictates of reason as well as the reasonable decrees of the state; and they will comply with the latter only if forced to do so. Neither nature nor reason can teach them obedience, and attempts to instill it by appealing to its utility will be accepted or rejected on the basis of idiosyncratic perceptions of whether it is to their advantage or disadvantage. Naturally prone to superstition, such people refuse to address problems of sociability through the exercise of reason. They consider "reason to be blind and they take human sensibility as vain," and thus prefer to turn to fortune or chance to favour them.[45] However, the superstitious inclinations of passionate individuals can be exploited by the more reasonable, since the passionate will yield to lessons and dictates that promise them advantages— especially when those dictates emanate from sources that are above reason. Accordingly, Spinoza believes the utility of Scripture to be very great, and without it "we would have to doubt of the *salus* of nearly all."[46] Furthermore, though very few of mankind are capable of acquiring the habit of virtue by reason alone, all are able to obey.[47]

Spinoza contends that the problem of human nature cannot be solved naturally or philosophically because the life of passion is as legitimate as the life of reason; and neither philosophy nor reason can demonstrate that a life of obedience is superior to a life of appetite. Nor can the natural problem be solved by political means. For the political solution still requires obedience to laws predicated on an individual's promises to live within certain agreements or constraints. However, Spinoza's interpretation of theology focuses on its instruction to obedience, in the command to love God above all and your neighbour as yourself.[48] His interpretation of its fundamental doctrine is expressed in the same terms as his description of the constitutional foundations of a liberal democratic polity. That is, all citizens are bound to keep their appetites in check "insofar as it would tend to another's hurt"; must do to no one what they would not want done to themselves; and must uphold others' rights as they would their own.[49]

Affiliating the terms of obedience to God with the terms of obedience to civil society has a significant consequence. Whereas violations of human law carry the threat of punishment by other humans, violations of divine law have far more severe repercussions: "God bids that the faith pledged be altogether kept"—that is, one must abide by promises of obedience to the polity or risk divine sanctions.[50] Life *in optima Republica* (one founded on freedoms of thought and speech, especially the freedom to philosophize) fosters the strength of mind that leads to compliance with law, and the realization of peace, security and health.[51]

Spinoza's solution to the natural problem is a theologico-political one, though not a theocratic one. He rejects "the system of the Turks"—that is, the Islamic character of the Ottoman Empire—because it does not permit individuals to reason or doubt.[52] He also asserts that the Hebrew *imperium* should not be repeated, although he admits that some of its features may be worthy of imitation.[53] The most imitable, he says, was its identification of piety with patriotism—such that pledging faith to the polity and the people was no less than pledging faith to God.[54] Such a bond enhanced the "constant will of following what ought to be done according to the common decree of the governing authority." Living in that condition, says Spinoza, is peace.

Spinoza and Peace beyond 1670

In his theologico-political treatise, Spinoza's solution to the natural problem—and his answer to the question of how to achieve peace—involves a liberal and democratic interpretation of Scripture, theology, and religion. Individuals are accorded the right to interpret and accept whichever doctrines enhance their piety, which is demonstrated in their obedience to God.[55] Furthermore, piety was determined only by actions and good works rather than by professions, since "faith without works is dead."[56] The predominance of Christianity throughout Europe in the 17th century, and the emergence of republicanism, meant that Spinoza's interpretation of religion in relation to political life appealed to many of his readers. Even if they disagreed on their preference of political regime, all Christian sects could approve the fundamental relevance of the divine law to love God above all, and to love one's neighbour as oneself.

Perhaps it is difficult to conceive how Spinoza's lessons on peace could be applied today. It seems inadvisable to prefer one religion over another for the sake of making individuals obedient; and not many would wish to resort to his solution to the question of sociability and peace—although (as he says of the Hebrew kingdom) perhaps it has imitable aspects. His reinterpretation of Christianity liberalizes and democratizes it. He retains the skeletal elements of dogma, but leaves individuals to judge its meaning as they wish—as long as their interpretations demonstrate piety and obedience to God since obedience better exhibits piety than any professions of faith. Indeed, Spinoza goes so far as to subordinate religious life, and the practice of justice and charity, to civic authorities. He even holds that divine justice is represented by the rule of just individuals on earth.[57]

The *Tractatus theologico-politicus* frames a theological doctrine that can be pressed into the service of politics. Polities cannot rely on their own devices to correct the problem of human nature, since they tend to compel obedience rather than inviting it, as religion does.[58] States often also operate on the basis of coercion, repression, or trepidation, which are repugnant to human nature. On that point, Spinoza cites Seneca's observation that human nature is reluctant to submit to compulsion : "no one continues in a violent regime for long, moderate ones endure."[59]

History is full of the many wars, liberations, and revolutions that have resulted from the complete or partial fusion of theological and political ideas. Anxiety, struggle, hatred, and anger have long been part of human life, even though everyone would prefer to live free of those conditions; and Spinoza's own theologico-political solution was devised to alleviate them. But it also must be conceded that invasions, genocides, displacements, and persecutions also often have resulted from theologico-political doctrines. In other words, benefit as well as harm can result from them.

It may be said that Spinoza's answer to the question of peace is to promote liberty and tolerance through obedience to law. His ideas focus on the detrimental effect that lives guided solely by the passions have on peace, security, and health, and of the usefulness of religious doctrines in constraining those passions. What every religion communicates is devotion to a Supreme Being, best realized through a certain conduct of life that demonstrates care for others. If all individuals are led by reason, there is no need of law and thus no need for obedience. Societies would form naturally; citizens would adhere to the dictates of sound reason; and people would achieve their true good.[60] Much of political (and diplomatic) life currently is conducted on the basis of modern rationalism and enlightened self-interest.[61] Yet, so long as people are led more by imaginative-affective impulses than by reason, Spinoza's plan for achieving peace, security, and healthy life may remain a cautious reminder. A sensible religious piety could inform civic virtue.

Notes

1   *Tractatus politicus, BDS Opera posthuma* (Amstelodami, 1677), p. 289. The posthumous works of Benedictus de Spinoza were collected and published anonymously by the author's friends after his death in 1677. The volume contained his *Ethica ordine geometrico demonstrata*; the *Epistolae* (selected letters); his work on Hebrew grammar, the *Compendium grammatices linguae Hebraeae*; together with two unfinished treatises, the *Tractatus intellectus emendatione* and the *Tractatus politicus*. The latter work is divided into chapters and sections. Hereafter, citations from the *Tractatus politicus* will use an abbreviated form of the title, viz., *TP*, followed by the chapter number and section number(s): for example, the quotation in the text is from *TP* 5§2. Translations from the Latin are made by the author.

    A more precise indication of what is at issue in achieving *securitas* may be found in the *Ethica*, particularly *Affectuum Definitiones* 14. Spinoza provides this definition: "Security is Joy (*laetitia*) arising from the idea of a thing future or past about which any cause for doubting has been removed" (*Ethica* 3, P18, Scholium 2). Spinoza also asserts that *fluctuatio* and *dubitatio* are the same thing, or "there is no difference between them" (*Ethica* 3, P17, Scholium). The condition of fluctuation is one of inconstancy or irresolution about a matter which subjects an individual to vacillations "between hope and fear" (*Ethica* 3, Aff. Defs. 12, 13). Security, for Spinoza, means the elimination of the causes for doubt about things which concern us, such as health, livelihood, threat of war, etc., such that we have no occasion to vacillate between a state of hope and a state of fear in regard to them.

2   *TP* 5§3.

3   *TP* 5§4. Spinoza refers readers to *TP* 2§19, where he expresses the same idea
     that obedience implies willingness to comply with the governing authority's
     decrees on what is good for the community. Spinoza's conclusion about
     peace and war contrasts with the doctrine advanced by Thomas Hobbes, who
     contends that "the state of nature is a state of war," and that entrance into
     political society is sufficient to occasion peace. Thomas Hobbes, *Leviathan*
     (London: Andrew Crooke, 1651), 62–63. For a more insightful account of
     Hobbes's ideas, see Laurie M. Johnson's Chapter 3 in this volume, especially the
     section entitled "The Third Cause of Quarrel."

4   In Chapters 13 and 14 of *Leviathan*, Hobbes recognizes the same problem and
     the need to curtail it through the abdication of rights and the institution of
     coercive laws for the sake of sociability. But Immanuel Kant, in "Idee zu einer
     allgemeinen Geschichte in weltbürgerliche Absicht," *Berlinische Monatsschrift*
     4 (11 November 1784), recognizes that the same difficulty in human nature
     also is the catalyst for beneficent social organization and human development.
     Kant states in the Fourth Thesis of the essay that the natural human propensity
     to "unsocial sociability" (*ungesellige Geselligkeit*) is what spurs competition,
     prevents laziness, and encourages the improvement of the human condition
     toward its full capacity. This state is to be realized in "the constitution of a
     universal [rational] civic society that administers laws among men" (Fifth
     Thesis). See G. Hartenstein, ed., *Immanuel Kant's sämmtliche Werke*, 8 bände
     (Leipzig: Leopold Voss, 1868), 4: 146; 148.

5   *TP* 1§5; compare 2§§3–5 & 11–14.

6   Benedictus Spinoza, *Opera* (4 vols.), ed. Carl Gebhardt (Heidelberg:
     Universitæsbuchhandlung, 1925), 3: 179. Hereafter citations of this work will
     appear with the abbreviated form of the title, *TTP*, followed by the volume
     number and page number in the Gebhardt edition (*TTP* 3: 179). The original
     title page of the *TTP* in 1670 bore the name of Henricum Künrath as the
     publisher, and Hamburg as the place of publication. However that information
     was false, and was decried as such by Johannes Musaeus, a German Protestant
     theologian, in his *Tractatus theologico-politicus ad veritatis lumen examinatus*
     (Jena, 1674).

7   *TTP* 3: 46–47.

8   *TTP* 3: 47.

9   *TTP* 3: 73; compare 47.

10   *Ethica* 2, P40, Scholium 2. Spinoza describes "knowledge of the first kind" as
     being derived *ab experientia vaga*. The first kind of knowledge is connected
     with objects of the imagination together with those things which we come to
     think "*ex auditis aut lectis.*" The phrase, "vague or wandering experience," is
     Baconian in origin (*Novum organum*, I Aphorism 100): "for experience, when it
     wanders in its own track, is, as I already have remarked, a mere groping in the

dark, and confounds them rather than instructs them."

11   *TTP* 3: 73–75.

12   *TTP* 3: 191.

13   *TTP* 3: 73.The basic or natural inclination toward sociability, as explained by Spinoza, has an ancient pedigree. Both Plato (*Republic* 369a-d) and Aristotle (*Politics* 1252a24–1253a18) acknowledge that awareness of basic human insufficiency—that is, the fact of need—is what initially impels human beings to enter into social or political arrangements with one another.

14   *TTP* 3: 73.

15   *TTP* 3: 189; compare 46–47 and *TP* 2§§1–5.

16   *TTP* 3: 190; compare *TP* 2§§1 & 3–5.

17   *TTP* 3: 190-93; compare *TP* 1§§6–7. For a different perspective on the natural problem and possible solutions to it, see Benjamin Holland's "Vattel on Morally Non-Discriminatory Peace" in Chapter 5 of this volume, especially the section entitled "Vattel's Philosophic Precursors: Leibniz and Wolff." Holland's treatment of Wolff's ideas, which may be understood as a counterpoint to Spinoza's doctrine and its influence on Vattel, is particularly noteworthy.

18   *TTP* 3: 189.

19   *TTP* 3: 73–74.

20   *TTP* 3: 76–77.

21   *TTP* 3: 118. Recourse to stories or tales, in the service of the foundation and formation of a political society, is also acknowledged by Plato, who advocated the utility, necessity, and benefit of employing a "*gennaion pseudos*," *Republic* 414 b–c (compare 389b).

22   *TTP* 3: 69–71. For Spinoza, the Latin word *salus* possesses a useful ambiguity. In its early significance the word conveys good health, safety, prosperity, welfare, or preservation. But in later uses of the word, its early connotation is extended to mean "salvation" in a religious sense. I believe that Spinoza's choice of *salus* to signify health and well-being, as well as salvation, is determined by two facts. First, the one word applies equivocally to both political and theological situations; and second, Spinoza needs to rely on theology regarding obedience in order to bring about peace by satisfying the third proper object of desire.

23   *TTP* 3: 5.

24   *TTP* 3: 193; compare 165.

25   *TTP* 3: 189; compare TP 2§4. Compare Hobbes, *Leviathan*, Chapter 13.

26   *TTP* 3: 189–90.

27   *TTP* 3: 190.

28   *TTP* 3: 189.

29   In accordance with the philosophic teaching of the treatise, which is to say the teaching of nature, the life of passion and the life of reason are equally natural and equally legitimate. Still, the conclusion that the life of reason is

superior to the life of passion is supported by Spinoza's identification of living in accordance with "the dictates of sound reason" and living in accordance with one's "true advantage" (*TTP* 3: 73–74). Moreover, if "a human being's true happiness" demands "knowledge of the truth" (3: 44) and only philosophy or reason is devoted to truth (3: 179) then the life of reason must be superior to the life of passion and the various ways that the passionate life can express itself, including the acceptance of various forms of religious prejudice or superstition. Common to both the passionate life and the superstitious life are the emotions of "anger, hatred, and deceit" (3: 6; compare 190); and Spinoza plainly affirms that superstition itself originates from the "most powerful kinds of affect" and not from reason (3: 6). In a recent study, Susan James traced the development of early modern philosophic conceptions of the relationship between passion and reason (Susan James, *Passion and Action: The Emotions in the Seventeenth Century* (Oxford: Clarendon Press, 1997). See especially 136–56 for her treatment of the affects or emotions in Spinoza. As Marlene Rozemond has observed, James encourages a reconsideration of the supposed divide between reason and passion in early modern philosophy, wherein reason is good and passion is bad. See Marlene Rozemond, "Review of Passion and Action," *Philosophy and Phenomenological Research* 61.3 (2000): 723–26.

30 *TTP* 3: 191; compare 73–75.

31 *TTP* 3: 191; compare TP 2§§13–17.

32 *TTP* 3: 191–92.

33 *TTP* 3: 59; compare TP 5§1.

34 *TTP* 3: 192. The word "firmly" (*firmiter*) was italicized in the original 1670 edition.

35 *TTP* 3: 192.

36 *TTP* 3: 192; compare 58–59 & TP 2§12.

37 *TTP* 3: 192–93; TP 2§§21–22.

38 *TTP* 3: 189; compare 98–99. Spinoza's identification of the teaching of philosophy or reason with the teaching of nature is established in Chapter 14 of the *TTP*. "The object of Philosophy is nothing other than truth.... The bases of Philosophy are common notions and one is bound to endeavour to obtain them only from nature itself" (*TTP* 3: 179; compare 180, 183, 186).

39 *TTP* 3: 195–99.

40 *TTP* 3: 197.

41 *TTP* 3: 198.

42 *TTP* 3: 198–99.

43 *TTP* 3: 199.

44 *TTP* 3: 198. By "signs" Spinoza means "miracles" (compare 3: 35–36 with 3:92). However, Chapter 6 of the *TTP* argues that miracles are impossible. Spinoza's appeal to religion or theology in order to introduce obedience is determined

more by its utility than its truth.

45   *TTP* 3: 3–5.

46   *TTP* 3: 188; compare 179. Spinoza expressly denotes the usefulness of the teaching of theology for achieving political stability.

47   *TTP* 3: 188.

48   *TTP* 3: 179–85.

49   *TTP* 3: 191; compare 3: 70–71; 84–85; and 177–80. These passages indicate the specific practical implications or consequences of the divine law for human behaviour and action in ordinary daily affairs.

50   *TTP* 3: 199–200.

51   *TTP* 3: 194–95.

52   *TTP* 3: 6–7.

53   *TTP* 3: 206.

54   *TTP* 3: 210–12.

55   *TTP* 3: 102; 104; 116–17; 165; 178–80; 184–85; 188.

56   *TTP* 3: 172.

57   *TTP* 3: 228–29; 31. According to Spinoza, it is a responsibility of a "good republic" to set conditions so that it cannot be "expedient for evil human beings to be evil" (3: 104); compare *TP* 2§22. Whether to integrate faith and politics or to separate them is a persistently vexing question. Indeed, from the inception of the Reformation, Martin Luther was acutely aware of the need to balance carefully the claims of religious commitment against the claims of civic commitment. For a thoughtful consideration of the matter, see Jarrett A. Carty's "By the Grace of God: Martin Luther's Two Kingdoms and Peace" in Chapter 1 of this volume, especially the section titled "The Two Kingdoms."

58   *TTP* 3: 151–56.

59   *TTP* 3: 74.

60   *TTP* 3: 73–74; *TP* 3§§6–7.

61   Recognition of the rational utility and necessity of political life, for the sake of achieving peace, are commonplaces of modern political thinking. But perhaps nowhere has the subject received a more systematic, comprehensive, and developed treatment than in the teaching of Hegel. For a lucid account of the rationality of political life in peace, see Mark Blitz's "Hegel on Peace," Chapter 8 of this volume.

PART II

MODERN DEFINITIONS OF PEACE:
STATE AND LAW AS MEANS TO PEACE

CHAPTER 3

Thomas Hobbes on the Path to Peace: Love of Glory versus Realist Foreign Policy

Laurie M. Johnson

Realist and neo-realist scholars have often looked to Thomas Hobbes as an intellectual father. As Michael Williams put it: "To invoke Hobbes is to call forth the image of a world of conflict and perpetual danger, a [vision] of international politics as a 'state of nature' defined by continual insecurity, competition, and potential or actual conflict."[1] While the realist adoption of Hobbes is not entirely wrong, this chapter will hopefully show that Hobbes thought about the way to peace in a more focused way than merely coping with a continual state of war, even in his treatment of international relations.

First, I will show that Hobbes himself does not equate individuals in the state of nature with nations in anarchy, that he does not apply the social contract to international relations, and that he does not argue for a world government. Second, I will show that in Hobbes's view the fear of violence and death is not the sole, or even the chief, cause of conflict; and I will explore how Hobbes does view individuals' desire for honour and glory as the main cause of conflict, especially in civil society.[2] Third, I will discuss how Hobbes treats the desire for honour and glory in individuals in different contexts: in the state of nature, in civil war, and in the English Civil War. This shows us that in his view, the problem was fearlessness caused by ambition and love of glory, not the fearfulness required for survival. Fourth,

I will discuss how Hobbes's views on military honour evolved, to the point of viewing the idea mainly as a cause of irrational violence rather than as a cause of noble restraint and heroism. Fifth, I will briefly look at Hobbes's historical works that analyze England's international wars of his day, and demonstrate his view of individuals who stir up trouble.

Lastly, I will try to sum up Hobbes's "prescriptive realism," in which he strongly links national unity and order, international defence, and the ability to conduct trade and diplomacy. In his view, fear should be the guide in both domestic government and international relations, though it most often is not. For Hobbes, peace among nations is simply the absence of hostilities. Since nations cannot escape from anarchy, they cannot abandon the posture of war (that is, the readiness and willingness to use force if necessary). However, Hobbes thinks that a strong state can more successfully pursue alliances and treaties, and can more reasonably take the laws of nations into account—making peace among nations much more likely than peace among individuals in the state of nature.

Nations Are Different

The interpretation of Hobbes's views on international relations most accepted today seems to show him as a realist of some sort. There are good reasons for this view. Hobbes understands the influence of situations on people's decisions, an understanding he demonstrates in his theory of the state of nature. He confirms the influence of external structure in decision-making when he acknowledges that not all individuals have the same desire for power; but given the situation of anarchy, all of them must act as if they do to survive. Given the strong human instinct for self-preservation, and the uncertainty of the state of nature (not being able to know others' intentions, and knowing that at least some people pose serious threats), a war of "all against all" is the predictable result. Each person must assume that every other person is a threat to his life, and act accordingly—that is, take pre-emptive action. This creates the situation of mistrust and escalating tensions that scholars of international relations have termed a "security dilemma."[3]

Hobbes does compare the state of nature to civil war, and also to the relationships among sovereigns.[4] Like individuals in Hobbes's "natural condition," states exist in an environment in which there is no higher power to stop them from fighting. Further demonstrating the similarity of the state of nature and international relations, Hobbes also applies his ideas about the laws of nature to the international realm. "As for the law of nations, it is the same with the law of nature," he writes. "For that which is the law of nature between man and man, before the constitution of the commonwealth, is the law of nations between sovereign and sovereign after."[5] In *Citizen* (*De Cive*), he further elaborates:

> The precepts of both are alike. But because cities once instituted do put on the personal properties of a man, that *law*, which speaking of the duty of single men we call *natural*, being applied to whole cities and nations, is called the *right of nations*. And the same elements of *natural law and right*, which have hitherto been spoken of, being transferred to *whole cities and nations*, may be taken for the elements of the *laws* and *right of nations*.[6]

It would seem that all the imagery and ideas that emerge from Hobbes's "state of nature" individuals also apply to his understanding of international relations. However, he does note a major difference: states could never feel as insecure as individuals in a state of war. Kings could lose battles and even wars, and still hope that their states would survive in some capacity. They would never feel the same fear as individuals whose lives could be instantly annihilated. As A. Nuri Yurdesev puts it, "While the interpersonal state of nature is unbearable, the international state of nature is bearable."[7] Unlike Rousseau—who, as René Paddags points out in Chapter 6 of this volume, proposes a social contract or federation among nations as the only sure way to peace—Hobbes concludes that sovereign nations (unlike individuals in a state of nature) do not feel enough need to form a world government for a solution.[8] Government over individuals makes sense, but an international social contract does not.[9] Paddags points out that even Rousseau admitted his plan would not work unless individuals developed sufficient reason and courage to follow through. But Hobbes does not want to rely on that much of a change in human nature to obtain peace.

Likewise, Hobbes does not merely equate the law of nature with the law of nations. For individuals in a state of nature, the right of nature—which dictates survival—takes priority over the laws of nature. This means that individuals must often disregard the laws of nature to survive, since those laws are only real if they are enforced by a real power. For this reason, most of Hobbes's laws of nature read less like actual enforceable laws for behaviour in nature, and more like prescriptions to guide government once the social contract has been made. To avoid a breakdown of civil order, citizens should be forgiving and accommodating to each other, and government should be equitable and predictable. Hobbes believes that the sovereign in a commonwealth should be the source of all law; so even in civil society, the laws of nature are not strictly laws, but rather norms that the sovereign would be wise to consider when legislating. But the law of nations can never be made into social norms, let alone civil law, in the same way.

As we know, the right of nature allows any action necessary for self-preservation, while the laws of nature are rules of reason that are conducive to peace. Sovereigns, who have no chance of creating a world government with other sovereigns, can listen to the laws of nature in their conscience, but they must also continually assert their right to defence.[10] In the international state of nature, "there is no faith kept in promises,"[11] and sovereigns retain the right to do whatever is necessary to preserve the state, including hurting enemies in war.[12] Hobbes thinks there is no way out of the natural condition for states; except perhaps for a time, and imperfectly, by imperial conquest.[13] States must find ways to seek peace with each other as frequently as possible—Hobbes's top priority is peace at all levels. But unlike individuals, who can form a social contract, states must continue to resort to war.

So one big difference between the situation of individuals and nations is that individuals can get out of the state of nature, and (if they have a good sovereign) be governed by the laws of nature via the social contract. But nations cannot escape the state of nature, and there can be no government over them. This fact leads to another notable difference between individuals and nations. Sovereigns are able to act in concert and consult the laws of nations (if they so desire) more frequently than individuals, for the very reason that they will never enter into a social contract: their relative security. Agreements and treaties among them, though unenforceable, may still emerge from time to time and remain relatively stable, as long as they are in the best interests of the sovereigns—that is, until one or more of the parties no longer find them convenient. As Noel Malcolm points out, Hobbes's work contains much discussion of alliances of various sorts, including (most prominently) those for security and trade.[14] As Hobbes writes in *Behemoth*, his history of the English Civil War: "It is indeed commonly seen that neighbour nations envy one another's honour, and that the less potent bears the greater malice; but that hinders them not from agreeing in those things which their common ambition leads them to."[15]

In sum, Hobbes believes that sovereign nations actually have more of a chance of maintaining peace—though admittedly an imperfect and temporary peace—than individuals do. But what causes them to abandon treaties, treacherously shift alliances, and disregard the laws of nations in favour of war? Hobbes's words quoted above seem to suggest that love of honour and glory has a great deal to do with those decisions. Does he really believe, as realists do, that fear induced by the anarchical structure of international relations is the sole, or even the main, cause of war among nations?

The Third Cause of Quarrel

A great deal of the literature on Hobbes focuses on his concept of anarchy within the state of nature, and how the fear of death, or the imperative for survival, necessitates the pursuit of power.[16] Instead, we know that Hobbes learned from Thucydides that men have three compelling motivators for going to war: honour, fear, and profit. The Athenians attributed their pursuit of empire to all three.[17] Hobbes repeats these causes of quarrel often in his works—most memorably in *Leviathan*, where he writes:

> In the nature of man, we find three principal causes of quarrel. First, competition; secondly, diffidence; thirdly, glory. The first, maketh men invade for gain; the second, for safety; and the third, for reputation. The first use violence, to make themselves masters of other men's persons, wives, children, and cattle; the second, to defend them; the third, for trifles, as a word, a smile, a different opinion, and any other sign of undervalue, either direct in their persons, or by reflection in their kindred, their friends, their nation, their profession, or their name.[18]

Although Hobbes writes of all three causes, his ideas on the third— on outrage caused by "trifles" or "signs of undervalue"—and on the task of applying these ideas to international conflict, have garnered much less attention than they should. Some authors have provided some insights into Hobbes's ideas on the importance of honour as a cause of war. For instance, George Kateb argues that the love of honour influences civil and international conflict through individual leaders, who inflame the people's ambitions, and "ignite turbulence, sedition, and civil war."[19] As well, David Boucher notes that honour may play a role in the length of hostilities when military leaders encourage a sovereign to continue a conflict. Such men, Kateb observes, are often inclined to prolong war, "because honour in their profession can only be attained by war."[20]

Jean Hampton and William Sacksteder also deal with this topic in their discussion of the related concept of glory as a cause of war.[21] Hampton seeks to apply Hobbes's general ideas on the desire for glory, as a cause of conflict among individuals, to the idea that nations seek glory. But she notes that "Hobbes does not consider the way in which a nation's longing for glory can provoke war with other nations."[22] Sacksteder argues that "glory, although the more evanescent origin of conflict, is also the more insidious and destructive cause of quarrel among nations."[23] However, his method consists of an "inquiry into likenesses between international affairs and mankind under supposed natural conditions."[24] Arthur Ripstein argues along the same lines, with a caveat: "Any attempt to develop a Hobbesian account of international relations carries with it an inherent danger. There are perils involved in taking the metaphor of nations as persons writ large too seriously."[25]

While it is true that one can compare Hobbesian individuals and nations by way of metaphor, one does not have to rely solely on such comparisons. Hobbes often shows how individuals—both leaders, and those who want to be leaders—can move nations' foreign policy for their own personal ambitions, and persuade others to adopt their own motivations. Hobbes's views on the roles of honour, glory, vain-glory, and pride in war and international relations are fairly plentiful, and I will focus on his ideas here. Though scholars often like to distinguish those terms (honour, glory, vain-glory, pride), Hobbes treats them as similar in one important respect: all those emotions stop people from being motivated enough by fear, or even rational self-interest.

As Martin Bertman points out, the lessons Hobbes learned from Thucydides (whose work Hobbes translated at the beginning of his career) and Homer (whose work he translated at its end) taught him to reject the "Homeric warrior culture" in favour of taking the dangers of war much more seriously.[26] Hobbes was a critic of his own culture, which in his view also too often elevated honour, glory, and pride above survival. In fact, he did not so much confirm realism in politics as promote it as a substitute for irrational love of glory.

Honour in Action

After we examine how the struggle for honour influences the state of nature among individuals, we might guess how Hobbes's ideas on individuals might be applied to international relations. Then we will turn to what he says specifically about civil war and international war.

For individuals, it might be assumed that fear is the strongest motivator for both violence and peacemaking. But a closer look at Hobbes's ideas casts doubt on this conclusion. Granted, he depicts the state of nature in the direst terms, as producing great anxiety, misery, and fear of violent death. However, if we consider his reasons for employing the theory in the first place, the situation becomes less clear. The desire for honour, and the enjoyment of glory, produces much of mankind's most aggressive actions;[27] and Hobbes argues that it is inherent in human nature that every man "looketh that his companion should value him, at the same rate he sets on himself."[28] This is one of the main reasons for war, yet he repeatedly suggests that it is the least legitimate reason.[29] Such desires cause people to be fearless, to risk their lives for others' esteem. Far from thinking that individuals are by nature fearful, he feels they are not fearful enough.

Hobbes's political works, chief among them *Citizen* and *Leviathan*, had as their primary aim the avoidance of civil war. If people were consistently as afraid of violent death as Hobbes wished, conflict would never occur. He blames civil war squarely on the natural human desire for honour, which overwhelms people's fear of physical harm as well as their true self-interest. In his account of how humanity compares to animals (an answer to Aristotle's assessment of human nature), Hobbes makes it abundantly clear that the desire for honour is our most uniquely human, and most unattractive, characteristic.[30] Most of the differences between us and animals, such as the desire for eminence or for showing off, relate to the goal of what Hobbes terms "preferment." Also in *Citizen*, he states that it is the powerful elites (who, of course, make most of the decisions about war) who want honour the most. All people want honour, he writes, "but chiefly they, who are the least troubled with caring for necessary things."[31]

Behemoth nicely illustrates the point that real people are as often motivated by pride as by fear or self-interest. As Robert Kraynak points out, "Hobbes's history shows that the civil war was caused by opinions and doctrines of right, which were created and exploited by ambitious intellectuals solely for the purpose of displaying their wisdom and learning."[32] Hobbes himself attributes the rebellious behaviour of dissenting ministers during the civil war less to feelings of insecurity than to outright arrogance. He pointed out that the ministers wanted a popular form of government so that religion would dominate politics, and so that "they might govern, and thereby satisfy not only their covetous humour with riches, but also their malice with power to undo all men that admired not their wisdom."[33]

The gentry and nobility who supported the rebellion also did so because of their desire for honour, according to Hobbes: "Certainly the chief leaders were ambitious ministers and ambitious gentlemen; the ministers envying the privy-council and principal courtiers, whom they thought less wise than themselves."[34]

As Stephen Holmes explains, one of Hobbes's most strident arguments in *Behemoth* is that the competition for status or recognition at this time flew in the face of any rational fear. "In most cases, the irrationality of behaviour has its origins in the irrationality of an individual's motives—notably, in an unreasonable skittishness about insult and public humiliation," he points out.[35] Peter Hayes also notices this theme in Hobbes's treatment of civil conflict.[36] We can conclude that in analyzing the causes of civil war in the hypothetical state of nature, among individuals or among groups, people too often forget about fear and rational self-interest and let the desire for honour and glory produce irrational conflict.[37] This human tendency is the reason why Hobbes devises his theories on the state of nature and the social contract—to try to impress on his readers the idea that such desires will get them killed, and that they should listen to their fears instead. Hobbes's realism is a recommendation for people on how to think and act when in danger, rather than an analysis of how they actually do think and act.

In contrast to John Locke (who, as Jeffrey Sikkenga points out in Chapter 4 of this volume, believes that peace requires educating individuals to be tolerant and liberal), Hobbes does not require any remaking of human nature. While Hobbes would agree with Locke about the dangers of dominating pride, his solution is not to transform people into truly tolerant and liberty-loving creatures. As Sikkenga points out, this is difficult to do because so much depends on the existing culture of the country. Instead, the solution is to persuade people to see the primacy of self-preservation— meaning that the Hobbesian road to peace is not democratic but autocratic: he hopes to turn unrealistic people into realists.

Honour-Seeking in International Warfare

If individuals are motivated to brush aside their fear and desire for self-preservation, and risk their lives in civil conflicts, does that mean honour is the chief cause of international wars as well? Hobbes often blurs the distinction between the two, using the term "war" for both. To get a clearer idea of his thoughts we can examine one of his early works, *The Elements of*

Law, Natural and Politic. This book indicates that he thoroughly rejects the honour-seeking character, precisely because this type of person is a major cause of both civil and international war.

Hobbes seemed to admire military honour when he wrote *The Elements of Law* in 1640, but at that time he viewed the quality less as irrational and reckless behaviour than as a sort of noble self-restraint. A man's safety comes first in war, he argued, and fear for one's own life is the only legitimate motivation for taking someone else's life. (He defined cruelty as violence that goes beyond fear, and involves enjoyment of destruction and killing.)[38] So while Hobbes acknowledged that there was no "law of war" in the strictest sense, he encouraged those engaged in it to do only what was necessary for self-preservation.

The Elements of Law mentioned people of a "timorous" nature in a negative way, placing them in the same category as "superstitious" individuals whose imagination can deceive them.[39] In contrast, Hobbes described courage as "the absence of fear in the presence of any evil whatsoever; but in a stricter and more common meaning, it is contempt of wounds and death, when they oppose a man in the way to his end."[40] He expressed a favourable view of courage in battle when he wrote: "Courage may be virtue, when the daring is extreme, if the cause be good." (He also conceded the opposite virtue, opining that "extreme fear [is] no vice when the danger is extreme.")[41] The tone of the first comment indicated that in this early iteration of his political views, Hobbes admired the fearlessness in warfare that was associated with old aristocratic notions of honour; he did not yet completely associate it with egoism and a reckless disregard for life. But he would soon come to criticize that view.

In *Citizen*, Hobbes argues forthrightly for the sovereign's duty to defend the commonwealth—holding it "unlawful" (presumably against the law of nature) for a sovereign to fail to maintain and supply a military force for national defence. In his view, lack of money is the prime obstacle: sovereigns often find it difficult to "wring suddenly out of close-fisted men so vast a proportion of monies" as are necessary to raise a standing army, one that is always prepared to fight.[42] But in the same work, Hobbes also moves toward condemning the desire for martial honour and glory. Discussing how sedition spreads in the military, he notes that soldiers who take honour seriously ("what seems right and good in their own eyes") often follow a commander out of a desire to share in his glory;[43] and such people are most likely to follow an insubordinate commander. The man whose courage is good, if he follows a good cause, may still exist; but Hobbes drops any mention of him. Instead he emphasizes the arrogance of military honour-seekers, who respect their commander because of some perceived quality such as heroic virtue or military prowess. They judge him worthy of respect, and are ready to follow him in his actions, on the basis of their personal opinions and preferences about honour—instead of being loyal to the sovereign power. Cast in this light, pride and the courage to obtain honour seem wholly bad and destructive.

In Hobbes's mature thought, individuals motivated by honour and glory are destructive to civil order. Pretensions to heroism and valour are most often born of arrogance and ambition; they are the fruit of self-love, not the desire for self-preservation or the preservation of society, and most often simply get people killed. "Competition of riches, honour, command, or other power, inclineth to contention, enmity, and war: because the way of one competitor, to the attaining of his desire, is to kill, subdue, supplant, or repel the other,"[44] he writes. Timorousness now appears much more acceptable than the destruction that can be caused by the honour-seeking man—who by the time Hobbes wrote *Leviathan* is most often identified as the "vain-glorious" man.[45] Such a character is treated as prideful, one whose passions are mostly self-centred, despite their principled rhetoric. Courage and "virtue military" Hobbes views as the destructive values of the "great and ancient gentry."[46] In Chapter 11 of *Leviathan*, he clearly abandons the aristocratic notion of honour for a very different set of values:

> Desire of ease, and sensual delight, disposeth men to obey a common power: because by such desires, a man doth abandon the protection that might be hoped for from his own industry, and labour. Fear of death, and wounds, disposeth to the same; and for the same reason. On the contrary, needy men, and hardy, not contented with their present condition; as also, all men that are ambitious of military command, are inclined to continue the causes of war; and to stir up trouble and sedition: for there is no honour military but by war; nor any such hope to mend an ill game, as by causing a new shuffle.[47]

Hobbes now seems inclined to prefer the timorous man, who fears pain and death, and cares about his daily comforts, over those hardy or needy men who are ambitious for military honour. In creating the circumstances for them to display their superiority, take revenge against those who slight them, and compete for command, they cause unnecessary war. These individuals are treated as objectively less admirable than those who run from danger, and seek their own safety and comfort. Hobbes accuses such warlike men of being rhetoricians, combining eloquence and flattery with "military reputation" to gain followers.[48] Their courage springs from unrealistic self-love, not true adherence to principle. For this reason Hobbes says that "amongst the passions, *courage*, (by which I mean the contempt of wounds, and violent death) inclineth men to private revenges, and sometimes to endeavour the unsettling of the public peace."[49]

While the culture of courage is conducive to a strong military force, Hobbes clearly views it a lesser good than its opposite. Timorousness, he says in the same sentence, "many times disposeth to the desertion of the public defence"; yet we know that Hobbes does not condemn this attitude, indeed prefers it—problematic though it is for national defence. His preference for timidity, and his refusal to promote courage, represent a complete rejection of a prideful love of honour in favour of a new idea, one more useful to more of the people, more of the time: the "fearful bourgeois civic spirit"[50] that makes individuals peaceful, productive, and reconciled to submission.

England's Wars

An overriding theme in *Leviathan* is that if everyone feared death more than they loved honour, they would be able to enjoy peace. Applying this observation to sovereigns and their decisions to engage in warfare, Hobbes writes that "Kings, whose power is greatest, turn their endeavours to the assuring it at home by laws, or abroad by wars: and when that is done, there succeedeth a new desire; in some, of fame from new conquest; in others, of ease and sensual pleasure; in others, of admiration, or being flattered for excellence in some art, or other ability of the mind."[51] The events of Hobbes's day confirms his view of these motivations.

In theoretical or philosophical terms, Hobbes believes that some leaders view war more as an opportunity to display their valour, or to enjoy their power over others, than for the sake of security or rational self-interest.[52] In practical terms, his treatment of actual wars fought between England and its enemies yield an even better view of what he thinks of war, and hence of what might bring peace. He seems quite clear that many wars are started not out of fear, but from a desire for honour. As he says in *A Dialogue between a Philosopher and a Student of the Common Laws in*

England, there are Kings who "for the glory of conquest, might spend one part of their subjects' lives and estates in molesting other nations, and leave the rest to destroy themselves at home by factions."[53] He outlines this view in his treatment of the international wars England engaged in during the same period as the Civil War (1642–1651).

The most memorable example Hobbes gives, in *Behemoth*, discusses in depth the war between England and Scotland—a conflict that was integral to the development of his own country's civil war.[54] In the mid–17th century, although Charles I was King of Scotland and Ireland as well as England, the nations often behaved as if they were separate and independent. (In *Behemoth* Hobbes points out that many English viewed the Scots as "foreigners.")[55] The trouble began when Charles I tried—"by the advice, as it was thought, of the Archbishop of Canterbury"—to impose the English Book of Common Prayer on the Scots, who were largely Presbyterian.[56] In Hobbes's view, the ministers of the Church of England were ambitious rather than principled, and wanted to expand their own influence and power at the expense of the King.[57]

Unsurprisingly, the Scottish nobles took great offence at this imposition on their worship, and rose up against Charles. They took courage from the fact that there were a great many Presbyterians in the English Parliament, and the King needed the help of Parliament in order to raise an army to put them down. Charles, however, raised a private army, marched into Scotland—and then, out of a desire to end the conflict, agreed not to impose Church of England practices on the Scots after all. But this manoeuvre provided little security for the realm. As Hobbes writes, the "democraticals," although "formerly opposers of the King's interest, ceased not to endeavour still to put the two nations into a war; to the end the King might buy the Parliament's help at no less a price than sovereignty itself."[58] As the Scottish army threatened to invade, Charles was forced to convene Parliament; which caused the very situation his enemies hoped for—the opportunity for open rebellion and civil war.

Hobbes describes the nobility of Scotland as motivated not by fear of attack from England, or even by religious conscience, but by pride. They did not want "poor scholars" (as they termed the Church of England) to tell them how to worship. Also, they wanted to stir up trouble in England, hoping for a reward from the English Parliament for their help during the rebellion. As Hobbes writes, "from the emulation of glory between the nations, they might be willing to see this nation afflicted by civil war, and might hope, by aiding the rebels here to acquire some power over the English, at least so far as to establish here the Presbyterian discipline; which was also one of the points they afterwards openly demanded."[59]

At roughly the same time, the Catholics in Ireland saw the turmoil in England as an opportunity to rebel against their Protestant oppressors. Parliament, busy struggling with Charles, invited men to "bring in money by way of adventure." The proposition, Hobbes tells us, was that the "adventurers," if successful, would be assigned "two millions and five hundred thousand acres of land in Ireland."[60] He blames those individuals who had spread pernicious beliefs, to feed their own desire for supremacy, for the Irish conflict. Later, when Oliver Cromwell subdued both Scotland and Ireland, Hobbes characterizes his motivation as entirely one of personal ambition, seeking power and glory, rather than any care for the safety of England.[61]

During the rule of the Rump Parliament in 1648, war also broke out between England and the Netherlands. The conflict between the two nations was over fishing rights, trade, and the English demand that the Dutch make amends for previous wrongdoings.[62] Like his favourite historian, Thucydides, Hobbes analyses the underlying causes of the war as a combination of pique and profit. "The true quarrel, on the English part, was that their proffered friendship was scorned, and their ambassadors affronted; on the Dutch part, was their greediness to engross all traffic, and a false estimate of our and their own strength."[63]

The war officially began in 1652 with a skirmish between Dutch and English ships. The Dutch refused to lower their flags to acknowledge that they were in English waters, the English fired on them, and the Dutch backed down. But it was too late to stop the conflict from escalating, as the two sides continued to threaten each other.[64] Hobbes unequivocally states that the Dutch started the war by refusing to lower their flag; he attributes this to their desire for honour, "knowing the dominion of the narrow seas to be a gallant title, and envied by all the nations that reach the shore."[65] Hobbes illustrates the honour mentality by pointing out the Dutch commander's provocative behaviour: "with a childish vanity [he] hung out a broom from the main-top-mast, signifying he meant to sweep the seas of all English shipping."[66] Still, he depicts both sides as desiring conflict and avoiding opportunities to back down. The advantage went back and forth for some time; but in the end the Dutch lost, and had to pay the expenses of the war and acknowledge English dominion of the narrow seas.

When Hobbes analyzes the war between the English and the Scots, the English invasion of Ireland, and the Dutch and English war, he finds no hint that the belligerence on any part was caused by fear, or the need for pre-emptive action or deterrence. Instead, he claims that the wars were caused by individuals—such as the Archbishop of Canterbury, the nobles and gentry of Scotland, the Catholic leaders in Ireland, the Presbyterians in the English Parliament, and the glory-seeking military and naval commanders—who acted on their outsized desires for honour, supremacy over other nations, and personal profit. The competition for such benefits made them set aside any fear they might have had for their personal safety, or even their nations' welfare. Issues of fear and security had no part of the calculations that led to these conflicts, in Hobbes's view.

Prescriptive Realism

Hobbes does not believe there will ever be permanent peace among nations, because they have no compelling reason to make a social contract with each other. Instead, he focuses on creating domestic peace through such a contract. His treatment of the subject shows a faith reminiscent of the later Enlightenment, in the power of reason to overcome the foibles of honour-seeking and arrogance.[67] It is not surprising that he links the issues of international and domestic peace, as in this statement from A Dialogue:

> You are not to expect such a peace between two nations; because there is no common power in this world to punish their injustice. Mutual fear may keep them quiet for a time; but on every visible advantage they will invade one another; and the most visible advantage is then, when the one nation is obedient to their King, and the other not. But peace at home may then be expected durable, when the common people shall be made to see the benefit they shall receive by their obedience and adhesion to their own sovereign, and the harm they must suffer by taking part with them, who by promises of reformation, or change of government, deceive them.[68]

Hobbes argues that a nation is stronger and more formidable when it can present a united front, with all its domestic issues resolved (and ambitious would-be politicians and commanders suppressed).[69] Donald W. Hanson explains that the civil strife Hobbes wants to suppress invites international peril: "Domestic ambitions are apt to be expressed in imperialistic ventures, or a weakened polity may find itself exposed to foreign intervention."[70] Most often, the state is much more fractured than a "fictitious artificial person," embodied by its sovereign.[71] If people could see the benefit of unity and obedience, the state could act as one, increasing its prospects for domestic and international peace. National security is one of the main reasons for entering into the social contract to begin with, as Hobbes points out: "That if there needs must be war, it may not yet be against all men, nor without some helps."[72] He makes the point again in *Citizen*:

> In vain do they worship peace at home, who cannot defend themselves against foreigners; neither is it possible for them to protect themselves against foreigners, whose forces are not united. And therefore it is necessary for the preservation of particulars, that there by some one council or one man, who hath the right to arm, to gather together, to unite so many citizens, in all dangers and on all occasions, as shall be needful for the common defence.[73]

Under the social contract sovereigns must have absolute power in their own country, along with authority to make war and peace; they must have at their full disposal both the domestic sword of justice, and the military sword of war. When subjects are obedient, sovereigns can more credibly threaten foreign powers, and have those threats heeded. As Hobbes writes, "no King can be rich, nor glorious, nor secure; whose subjects are either poor, or contemptible, or too weak through want, or dissention, to maintain a war against their enemies."[74] In order to achieve this situation, sovereigns must eschew the pursuit of honour and glory, and act rationally at home and abroad. They must (perhaps by consulting Hobbes's writing) be knowledgeable about many subjects: human nature, domestic law, economics, diplomacy, foreign policy, and the "designs of all nations."[75] Such a sovereign, secure in power, can rule in a way that brings unity and prosperity to the nation, which will in turn support the sovereign by raising and maintaining the army necessary to secure peace. A nation forearmed and well garrisoned is able to pre-empt the hostility of other nations, instead of having to wait until too late to properly prepare.[76] But if—as was the case with Charles I—the sovereign cannot even control his own military because of dissension within the government, he will be unprepared for war, and will probably lose.[77]

If nations would unite, not only would they be more secure against enemies, but their very security might lead them to cooperate more with one another in beneficial ways. Hobbes believes that the laws of nature can be better observed among nations than among individuals. Indeed, unity and strength make it quite possible for states to form effective alliances, treaties, and other forms of cooperation designed to avoid war and encourage trade. István Hont points out that although Hobbes saw much of the European quest for trade as "the aggressive pursuit of *grandezza*, and therefore dangerously vainglorious," he nevertheless approved of trade "in the traditional sense of exchanging qualitatively different products among different regions and climes."[78] This could only take place in a relatively stable and peaceful international environment. As Glen Newey puts it, "Civil peace allows cooperation within civil societies and between them.... [Hobbes] thus allows for at least a rudimentary form of international civil society."[79]

In his own time, although Hobbes was not primarily an international theorist, he offered his political philosophy as a means of producing international peace through a realist, non-bellicose foreign policy. The philosophy of prescriptive realism teaches sovereigns to pursue domestic peace and prosperity, combined with military preparedness, instead of engaging in wild adventures for the sake of glory.[80] Hobbes's social contract affirms that the true purpose of government is to protect the people's lives; and he argues against the honour-seeking characters who meddle in national and international affairs purely for their own elevation—in the process disrupting domestic peace and commerce, and potentially causing wars. If fear really was the major motivator in international relations, there would be little intrigue, sabre-rattling, or war. Hobbes certainly knew that this is not the case, but evidently hoped his teachings could make it so.

Notes

1   Michael C. Williams, "The Hobbesian Theory of International Relations: Three Traditions," *Classical Theory in International Relations*, ed. Beate Jahn (Cambridge: Cambridge University Press, 2006), 253.

2   Hobbes distinguishes between honour and glory. Honour is something that is bestowed on someone by others, and Hobbes sees it as a source of conflict if it is not tightly regulated by a knowledgeable sovereign. It should not be defined by independent individuals and groups. Glory is a feeling that people have when they feel a sense of superiority over others, and the quest for this feeling is seen by Hobbes as an illegitimate motivation for conflict. He often uses the term "vainglory" to emphasize the self-regarding and ultimately destructive nature of this motivation; but he also treats it as a natural and permanent human motivation that needs to be rigorously controlled (and hopefully eliminated) by a knowledgeable sovereign. Both terms are used in this essay in close proximity,

since both qualities come from the same basic source: the human desire to distinguish oneself above others. Hobbes sees both as related sources of conflict that must be overcome for individuals to have peace.

3   John Herz, *Political Realism and Political Idealism* (Chicago: University of Chicago Press, 1951).

4   Thomas Hobbes, *Leviathan*, ed. Michael Oakeshott (New York: Macmillan, 1962), 101.

5   Thomas Hobbes, *The Elements of Law, Natural and Politic*, ed. Ferdinand Tönnies, 2nd ed. (London: Frank Cass, 1969), 190.

6   Thomas Hobbes, *Man and Citizen*, ed. Bernard Gert (Indianapolis: Hackett, 1991), 275.

7   A. Nuri Yurdesev, "Thomas Hobbes and International Relations: From Realism to Rationalism," *Australian Journal of International Relations* 60.2 (2006): 315.

8   *Leviathan*, 101. Some authors insist on either arguing with Hobbes about this logic, or else arguing that Hobbes would, after all, somehow approve of world government. Most of the time, these authors do not employ textual analysis but extrapolate from a few basic ideas from Hobbes. For an example of this approach, see Peter Caws, *The Causes of Quarrel: Essays on Peace, War, and Thomas Hobbes* (Boston: Beacon Press, 1989).

9   Yurdusev, "From Realism to Rationalism," 316.

10   Hobbes, *Leviathan*, 260.

11   Hobbes, *Man and Citizen*, 301.

12   Hobbes, *Leviathan*, 234.

13   Hobbes was a student of Roman history, and often referred to the Empire in his writings; but he does not generally treat their conquests as instruments of peace, or as improvements in the lives of the people they subjected. (See, for instance, his letter of dedication to William, Earl of Devonshire; *Man and Citizen*, 89–90.) However, he does approve of the Roman strategy of forcing Roman citizenship and service on subject nations. See *Leviathan*, 150.

14   Noel Malcolm, *Aspects of Hobbes* (Oxford: Clarendon Press, 2002), 452.

15   Thomas Hobbes, *Behemoth, or The Long Parliament*, ed. Ferdinand Tönnies (Chicago: University of Chicago Press, 1990), 32.

16   Malcolm, *Aspects of Hobbes*, 435.

17   William Schlatter, ed., *Hobbes's Thucydides* (New Brunswick, NJ: Rutgers University Press, 1975), 70.

18   *Leviathan*, 99–100.

19   George Kateb, "Hobbes and the Irrationality of Politics," *Political Theory* 17.3 (1989): 363.

20   Kateb, "Irrationality of Politics," 228.

21   See two essays in Caws's *The Causes of Quarrel*: Jean Hampton, "Hobbesian Reflections on Glory as a Cause of Conflict," 78–96; and William Sacksteder, "Mutually Acceptable Glory: Rating among Nations in Hobbes," 97–113.

22   Hampton, "Hobbesian Reflections," 95.

23   Sacksteder, "Mutually Acceptable Glory," 97.

24   Sacksteder, "Mutually Acceptable Glory," 104.

25   Arthur Ripstein, "Hobbes on World Government and the World Cup," *Hobbes: War Among Nations*, ed. Timo Airaksinen and Martin A. Bertman (Brookfield: Avery, 1989), 121.

26   Martin A. Bertman, "What Is Alive in Hobbes?" in *Hobbes: War Among Nations*, 11.

27   Hobbes does distinguish between glory and honour, as Gabriella Slomp points out. Glory is an entirely subjective thing—an internal quality or feeling. Honour is something that others give you. For purposes of this article, however, the two can be referred to as the same type of motivator. A thorough discussion of both terms, as Hobbes uses them, can be found in Slomp's article, "Hobbes on Glory and Civil Strife," in *The Cambridge Companion to Hobbes's Leviathan*, ed. Patricia Springborg (Cambridge: Cambridge University Press, 2007); and also in her own book: Gabriella Slomp, *Hobbes and the Political Philosophy of Glory* (New York: St. Martin's Press, 2000), 181–98.

28   Hobbes, *Leviathan*, 99.

29   Hobbes, *Leviathan*, 99–100.

30   Hobbes, *Man and Citizen*, 168.

31   Hobbes, *Man and Citizen*, 252.

32   Robert P. Kraynak, "Hobbes's *Behemoth* and the Argument for Absolutism," *American Political Science Review* 76.4 (1982): 838.

33   Hobbes, *Behemoth*, 159.

34   Hobbes, *Behemoth*, 23.

35   Stephen Holmes, "Political Psychology in Hobbes's *Behemoth*," *Thomas Hobbes and Political Theory*, ed. Mary G. Dietz (Lawrence: University of Kansas Press, 1990), 123.

36   Peter Hayes, "Hobbes's Bourgeois Moderation," *Polity* 31.1 (1998): 70. Hayes writes: "In distinguishing men of moderate, limited ambition from those who are immoderate, Hobbes describes how limitless power-seeking is indeed driven by pride, and that those who would lead a commonwealth into civil war are little motivated by fear."

37   Emblematic of this view are the comments of medieval author of chivalry, Geoffroi de Charny: "And while the cowards have a great desire to live and a great fear of dying, it is quite the contrary for the men of worth who do not mind whether they live or die, provided that their life be good enough for them to die with honour." Richard W. Kaeuper and Elspeth Kennedy, ed., *The Book of Chivalry* (Philadelphia: University of Pennsylvania Press, 1996), 189. There can be no greater contrast between Hobbes and earlier authors than on the worth of dying in the pursuit of honour.

38   Hobbes, *Elements*, 101.

39   Hobbes, *Elements*, 10.

40   Hobbes, *Elements*, 38. Later, Hobbes also defines courage as "to resolve to break through a stop unforeseen" (48).

41   Hobbes, *Elements*, 94.

42   Hobbes, *Man and Citizen*, 262.

43   Hobbes, *Man and Citizen*, 253.

44   Hobbes, *Leviathan*, 81.

45   Hobbes, *Leviathan*, 220–21.

46   Hobbes, *Leviathan*, 78.

47   Hobbes, *Leviathan*, 81.

48   Hobbes, *Leviathan*, 83.

49   Hobbes, *Leviathan*, 503.

50   Peter Hayes, "Hobbes's Bourgeois Moderation," *Polity* 31.1 (1998): 69.

51   Hobbes, *Leviathan*, 80.

52   It has frequently been noted that Hobbes's thoughts on some issues evolved over time, such as on the value of things like honour-seeking, courage, and valour in warfare. Leo Strauss points out that Hobbes had rejected honour as a positive force in war by the time he wrote his mature works: "While Hobbes could still say in the *Elements* 'the only law of actions in war is honour,' in *Leviathan* he says: 'Force and Fraud, are in warre the two Cardinall virtues.' When Hobbes replaces 'honour' by 'force and fraud,' he gives us to understand that what he formerly esteemed as 'honour' he has now detected as fundamentally unjust and a pretext for injustice." Leo Strauss, *The Political Philosophy of Thomas Hobbes, Its Basis and Genesis* (Chicago: University of Chicago Press, 1984 [Midway reprint]), 114.

53   Thomas Hobbes, "A Dialogue between a Philosopher and a Student of the Common Laws in England," *The English Works of Thomas Hobbes*, Vol. 6, ed. Sir William Molesworth (London: J. Bohn, 1839), 17.

54   Malcolm, *Aspects of Hobbes*, 453. He mentions this episode briefly in his chapter on international relations.

55   Hobbes, *Behemoth*, 33.

56   Hobbes, *Behemoth*, 28.

57   Hobbes, *Behemoth*, 47.

58   Hobbes, *Behemoth*, 29.

59   Hobbes, *Behemoth*, 30.

60   Hobbes, *Behemoth*, 99–100.

61   Hobbes, *Behemoth*, 166.

62   Hobbes, *Behemoth*, 174.

63   Hobbes, *Behemoth*, 174.

64   Hobbes, *Behemoth*, 175.

65   Hobbes, *Behemoth*, 176.

66   Hobbes, *Behemoth*, 178. Hobbes's version of events may not be historically accurate: some interpreters believe this story is apocryphal. However, what holds our attention here is what Hobbes makes of his version of events.

67   For instance, Hobbes wrote in his letter of dedication in *Man and Citizen*: "For were the nature of human actions as distinctly known as the nature of quantity in geometrical figures, the strength of avarice and ambition, which is sustained by the erroneous opinions of the vulgar as touching the nature of right and wrong, would presently faint and languish; and mankind should enjoy such an immortal peace, that (unless it were for habitation, on supposition that the earth should grow too narrow for her inhabitants) there would hardly be left any pretence for war." Hobbes, *Man and Citizen*, 91.

68   Hobbes, *A Dialogue*, 7.

69   Hobbes hoped that his doctrine would be taught, not just in England, but around the world. He gave much advice (all outside the scope of this paper), concerning what strong sovereigns should teach their citizens, especially in the area of the Christian religion, so that they would be prone to unity instead of dissension. It is particularly telling, though, for the subject of this argument, that Hobbes's Christianity stressed the theme of pride as a sin. He sought a Christianity that was compatible with peace instead of one that provided men with an excuse to go to war. In his view, pastors should emphasize Christ-like meekness. Hobbes wrote of the inherent dangers he saw in a religion based on a book that all could read and interpret. Sensing the implications of Hobbes's Christian teaching of meekness and obedience on traditional manly ideals like honour and glory, Stephen Holmes comments: "So valuable is this un-manning or dis-couragement to the state that the appalling risks of a book-based religion must be run" (Holmes, 142). One of Hobbes's goals was to teach average citizens that their Christian faith could be misused by leaders, and that it did not require them to sacrifice their lives for any political or even religious cause. He comments with an obvious smile in *Leviathan* that, "To die for every tenet that serveth the ambition, or profit of the clergy, is not required" (365–66). He writes a very similar sentiment on the last page of *Man and Citizen*, implying that most cases of martyrdom are the result of misguided followers of some ambitious individual or institution (386).

70   Donald W. Hanson, "Thomas Hobbes's 'Highway to Peace,'" *International Organization* 38.2 (1984): 338.

71   In making this statement, the writers clearly do not quite make the distinction between what Hobbes wants, and what he thinks actually exists. Camilla Bolsen and David Boucher, "Hobbes, Law and Morality," *International Political Theory after Hobbes: Analysis, Interpretation and Orientation*, ed. Raia Prokhovnik and Gabriella Slomp (New York: Palgrave Macmillan, 2011), 95.

72 Hobbes, *Man and Citizen*, 118.

73 Hobbes, *Man and Citizen*, 177.

74 Hobbes, *Leviathan*, 144.

75 Hobbes, *Leviathan*, 195.

76 Hobbes, *Man and Citizen*, 262.

77 As Hobbes writes in *Leviathan*:

> … annexed to the sovereignty [is] the right of making war and peace with other nations, and commonwealths; that is to say, of judging when it is for the public good, and how great forces are to be assembled, armed, and paid for that end; and to levy money upon the subjects, to defray the expenses thereof. For the power by which the people are to be defended, consisteth in their armies; and the strength of an army, in the union of their strength under one command; which command the sovereign instituted, therefore hath; because the command of the militia, without other institution, maketh him that hath it sovereign. (138)

78 István Hont, Jealousy of Trade: International Competition and the Nation-State in Historical Perspective (Cambridge, MA: Harvard University Press, 2005), 18–19.

79 Glen Newey, "*Leviathan* and Liberal Moralism in International Theory," Prokhovnik and Slomp, 78.

80 Hanson, "Thomas Hobbes's 'Highway to Peace,'" 349.

CHAPTER 4

John Locke's Liberal Path to Peace

Jeffrey Sikkenga

How do we spread peace in the world? Democratic peace theory argues for fostering commerce and democracy—which certainly help.[1] But commerce does not always eliminate or overcome conflict even between trading partners; and as we have seen in the recent toppling of dictatorships, "democracy" can give vent to (or permit cultivation of) political passions that can heighten the risk of conflict and even war.[2] Something else must be present.

According to John Locke, that something else is liberalism—a politics based on attachment to individual liberties, government by consent, the rule of law, private property, and a significant role for reason in politics.[3] But liberal institutions alone do not make a society peaceful. Liberalism—liberal habits, customs, and ideas—must be the reigning ethos.[4] This is not to say that only liberal democratic societies avoid war; according to Locke, however, liberal societies are essentially peaceful—their fundamental principles promote "good will, mutual assistance, and preservation" within and between political societies.[5] Liberal societies inherently resist entering into the state of war, which Locke defines (in the second of his *Two Treatises of Government*) as "a state of enmity and destruction" marked not by passionate and hasty disputes but by settled designs on other men's lives.[6] This is because only a liberal society, like a liberal individual, rejects all "attempts to get another man into his absolute power," which "does thereby put himself into a state of war with him."[7] If non-liberal societies do not try to dominate others, it is more by accident than principle: they are too weak to fight; their neighbours are too strong; they are internally divided, their ruler is cautious, they lack the resources, or they are concentrating on other things. Unlike liberal societies, they have not conquered the desire to dominate others: they either do not have the capacity to act on the desire, or they have directed it inward (as in when one class or group dominates another). Liberal societies, in contrast, do not try to dominate the lives, liberties, or properties of people in their own or in other societies, because that goes against liberal principles of justice. Liberals take pride in ruling themselves, not others.

But liberalism can reign only where the people of a civil society are liberals. As Locke knows, it is difficult to create real liberals—people who are reasonable and peaceful, yet spirited in the defence of their freedom and that of others. As Laurie M. Johnson points out in Chapter 3 of this volume, Locke's predecessor Hobbes seemed to think that such a combination is impossible. She notes that Hobbes's "preference for timidity, and his refusal to promote courage, represent a complete rejection of a prideful love of honour in favour of a new idea, one more useful to more of the people, more of the time: the 'fearful bourgeois civic spirit' that makes individuals peaceful, productive, and reconciled to submission."[8] But that bourgeois spirit is unacceptable to Locke, who believes that peaceful people can be afraid or incapable of defending their freedom against threats—either from external enemies, or from their own government.

Locke knows, of course, that spirited people can be too proud and therefore too inclined to fight—a spirit to which he attributes "the greatest part of those Mischiefs which have ruin'd Cities, depopulated Countries, and disordered the Peace of the World."[9] But unlike Hobbes, he believes that education can transform the love of dominion over others into a politically salutary "love of liberty" that satisfies individuals without fuelling national or religious conflicts. So Locke would not accept Rousseau's view that peace can extend within a society but probably not between societies. (Except, as René Paddags points out in Chapter 6 of this volume, "through the actions of a founder-statesman" who creates a federation of nations "through force and fraud.")[10] That is because, according to Locke, peace is not based on extending "the love of one's own existence" to one's fellows "through *amour de patrie*," an action that is inherently limited to a small-scale political community.[11] Rather, Locke believes that pride (Rousseau's *amour propre*) can be used to extend peacefulness between societies. The key is to make liberal people proud of ruling themselves, not others. In Locke's view, a nation of such individuals would defend its liberties assertively when necessary, but would otherwise direct itself to peaceful enterprises that promote prosperity and goodwill. If Locke is right, democratic peace theory needs an important supplement. We must remember that without liberalism, commerce and democracy are not enough to produce peace; and also that the success of liberalism itself depends on the right education.[12] The goal of all education should be to instill liberalism.

From Love of Dominion to Love of Liberty

For Locke, proper education is not about training warriors, initiating tribe members, or inculcating religious believers.[13] Its goal is to create the kind of people he calls "Industrious and Rational"—those who labour diligently, have a spirited attachment to "life, liberty, and estate," and guide their actions by reason (or at least opinions formed from reason).[14] People, in short, who are freely able to "order their Actions, and dispose of their Possessions, and Persons as they think fit, within the bounds of the Law of Nature, without asking leave, or depending upon the will of any other Man."[15]

The problem is that people do not come into the world as industrious and rational lovers of freedom. We are all born with the same original innate impulses to preserve our lives and be happy—that is, to have pleasure with no admixture of pain.[16] Very early, however, we also develop the desire for power—of wanting to get and keep objects that remove pain and give pleasure. Acquiring power gives rise to pride, the feeling of pleasure produced by having the opinion of power over external objects.[17] Pride is a delightful sense of self-power—the stronger the feeling of one's power, the stronger the pride (and pleasure). Since even infants quickly learn that they have some small power to attain the objects of their desire, pride is natural in human beings "even from our cradles."[18]

Such pride and desire for power can very easily take two dangerous forms. The first is a wilful desire for liberty from any constraint on our immediate gratification—what Locke calls "license" in *Some Thoughts Concerning Education*.[19] The second is a desire for dominion—of having "Absolute, Arbitrary, Despotical Power" to use something as one chooses.[20] The love of dominion begins when individuals perceive (starting in infancy) that they can satisfy their desire for external objects by having power over others, especially those who might give (or take away) these objects. At the moment of that perception, the desire for power is changed; it changes from a desire to control objects to a desire to control other people. Children, for example, begin to test their parents to see if they can assert their will over them.[21] The experience of dominion over something is a deep pleasure, Locke says: "I told you before that children love *liberty.... I* now tell you that they love something more: and that is *dominion*."[22]

Such love becomes especially dangerous when it mixes with another fact of human nature: self-love. Self-love is the feeling of strong attachment to the faculties, labour, and products of one's mind and body.[23] "Our first actions," Locke argues, are guided "more by self-love than reason or reflection."[24] On its own, self-love is not evil: it promotes self-preservation and happiness. But by inclining people to regard only themselves, it can inflate the original love of dominion into the sole filter through which people see themselves or others. Once roused by a perceived harm, for example, "Self-love will make Men partial to themselves and their Friends," and may give rise to "Ill Nature, Passion, and Revenge."[25] In this way, self-love makes every situation into a competition of "whose wills shall carry it over the rest" rather than a matter of preservation or comfort.[26] The inflated love of dominion, Locke says, "is the first origin of most vicious habits that are ordinary and natural."[27]

The love of dominion can also become a source of unnatural vices that go beyond "insolent domineering."[28] People possess both imagination, which "is always restless and suggests variety of thoughts," and will, which "reason being laid aside, is ready for every extravagant project."[29] When combined with a strong love of dominating others, imagination can create the desire for conquest that leads people to aggressively pursue enterprises that promise glory, such as war. But according to Locke, such desire is not original to individuals, nor is it any original part of the desire for happiness. It is more a "fantastical itch," as he writes in *An Essay Concerning Human Understanding*, settled in us by "Fashion, Example, and Education."[30] (Cruelty to others is also not part of our original humanity, and where it exists it has also been planted in people "by fashion and opinion.")[31]

How can the natural desire for power be prevented from becoming a proud desire to dominate and conquer others?[32] The only natural passion strong enough to countervail excessive self-love is the desire for self-preservation, which generally disposes people to listen to reason and avoid any confrontation or danger.[33] Unfortunately, in many cases people's pride (or vengeful anger) can overcome their rational fear, and hurry "them on headlong, without sense, and without consideration" into danger.[34] In such cases, people must cultivate the habits and ideas that subdue the striving for mastery, but without their spirits being "abased and broken." If that happened they could "lose all their vigour and industry," which would put them in a worse state than "extravagant young fellows that have liveliness and spirit"—who can sometimes be set right and made into "able and great men."[35]

The combination of spiritedness and peacefulness is difficult to attain, and possible only when dominion over others is sought not for its own sake, but for the sake of power over objects that give us security and pleasure. If individuals believe that they can acquire and securely possess their desired goods without the need for mastery, they will not want to dominate others.[36] People taught to abhor fighting and killing will not want become conquerors (who, Locke says, "for the most part are but butchers of mankind").[37] While the desire for power cannot and should not be quite eradicated, the unreasonable love of dominion and conquest can be weeded out: proper education forms rational, free individuals who do not want to either dominate others, or be dominated by them.[38] Their "outward actions come from themselves."[39]

Education: Acquiring Liberal Habits and Ideas

The Right Habits: Self-Denial

According to Locke, the process of education must begin at birth, when children are like paper that can receive any characters impressed on them.[40] He argues that virtue is "the first and most necessary of those endowments that belong to a man or a gentleman, as absolutely requisite to make him valued and beloved by others, acceptable or tolerable to himself."[41] Virtue is founded on two things: the habit of self-control, and the idea of God. Self-control and self-denial refer to the capacity "to resist the importunity of present pleasure or pain for the sake of what reason tells him is fit to be done."[42] This capacity is not innate; indeed, it runs "contrary to … our natural propensity to indulge corporal and present pleasure, and to avoid pain."[43] So the habit must be developed in children "by all the care and ways imaginable" by those responsible for young people's education.[44]

For children to acquire the unnatural habit of self-denial, they must first learn to master their own desires by submitting their emotions to their parents' command.[45] This submission helps to make "their minds supple and pliant to what their parents' reason advises them," and will later allow them to submit to their own reason.[46] Such training must begin at a very young age, when babies first begin to cry. According to Locke, parents must learn that their "crying is of two sorts: either stubborn and domineering, or querulous and whining."[47] He admits that "sometimes their crying is the effect of pain or true sorrow, and a bemoaning themselves under it."[48] Nevertheless, no crying "must be suffered, much less encouraged."[49] When children have a good reason to cry, parents should help them and ease them as best they can by removing the cause of their pain, but "by no means bemoan them" or let them continue crying.[50] Such indulgence, he claims, leads to querulous and whining crying; and encourages them to cry at the "first approach" of pain. This in turn "softens their minds and makes them yield to the little harms that happen to them, whereby they sink deeper into that part which alone feels and make larger wounds there than otherwise they would."[51] Locke believes that children must acquire the "brawniness and insensibility of mind" that "is the best armour we can have against the common evils and accidents of life."[52] Without such toughness, children's minds will be too overpowered by pain and anger to allow them to think and act reasonably.

The other kind of crying, stubborn and domineering, is "an open declaration of their insolence or obstinacy when they have not the power to obtain their desire," Locke declares. Parents must suppress it by any means necessary, including physical force.[53] Still, he is no friend of beatings or corporal punishments, which he generally rejects as both unnecessary and unproductive: they operate on the principles of physical pain and pleasure, the very impulses from which children must be drawn away. Except in cases of extremity when nothing else can subdue children's minds and make them obey their parents, such punishment is to be avoided. It either produces a child of "slavish temper" who "submits and dissembles obedience whilst the fear of the rod hangs over him," but acts wildly when not confronted by force; or it is so brutally effective that it breaks children's minds, making them apathetic and inactive. Such a child's life is then "a useless thing to himself and others."[54] In neither case is rational self-denial inculcated.

Instead of the rod, Locke prefers two opposing methods for child-rearing: praise and shame. Used both together, he says, they "keep a child's spirit easy, active, and free, and yet at the same time restrain him."[55] Children are susceptible to both because they feel deeply about how others view them, particularly their parents. This concern is rooted in their desire to possess and control the objects they believe can preserve their comfort or give them pleasure[56]—a desire that is not entirely innate, but is acquired at a very early age—almost from birth, when babies first begin to feel the pain of unsatisfied needs.[57] From this experience, even small children gain the desire to control the things that satisfy their wants.[58] They also quickly realize that the world contains other people—most obviously their parents—who have the power to give or take away what the infants want; and so they begin to acquire some sensitivity about how others perceive them. [59] In particular, they "find a pleasure in being esteemed and valued, especially by their parents and those whom they depend upon."[60]

According to Locke, parents must use children's love of being esteemed to begin their moral education. To use praise and shame effectively, parents must first instill in their children awe and respect for themselves, as well as love and esteem, at a very young age—even "before children have memories."[61] Love is created both by parents allowing children to be children—indulging "their innocent folly"—and also by their tender care: removing any pain or discomfort that is too much for them. This care establishes in young minds, through experience, the concept that their parents are the benevolent source of all good things; which in turn creates the feelings of gratitude, and hope for more benefit, that constitute love in children.[62] Also important, Locke notes, is the idea of delight for children, which may be produced by "any present or absent thing."[63] The child esteems the parents because it knows they have the power to bestow pleasure and remove pain.[64]

The opposites of praise and care are shame and fear, which parents must also instill. Children must learn from experience that if they make wilful demands or disobey, their parents will take away or refuse to give desired things.[65] Locke counsels that these objects should not be used explicitly to reward or punish, since then children will not value the behaviour itself but merely the reward—and will have no incentive to behave well if there is no reward. Rather, any benefit or harm should seem to naturally accompany a state of good or bad parental grace.[66] If parents remove or withhold pleasant objects when children are disobedient, this causes some distress—"the only thing we naturally are afraid of."[67] By turning a cold shoulder, parents create in children the healthy fear that if they incur their parents' disapproval, they will fall into a state of "neglect and contempt," left without "whatever might satisfy or delight."[68]

Once parents have established the love of credit and the fear of shame, children will want to act as they know their parents wish.[69] According to Locke, this is the great secret of education: "by insensible degrees" to take children's natural impulse to feel pleasure and avoid pain, and use it to make them "in love with the pleasure of being well thought on."[70] This lively love of credit, combined with a sense of shame at displeasing, will serve children well throughout their lives, since through this education they acquire the disposition to check their own passions—at first out of love and fear of their parents; later out of habit; and finally, "when they grow able to judge for themselves" because they have learned to follow what their own reason advises.[71]

The Right Habits: Civility

Another critical habit of peacefulness, in Locke's view, is good breeding. By this he does not mean aristocratic haughtiness or meek humility, but the "due and free composure of language, looks, motion, posture, place, etc."[72] Such quiet self-assurance, he opines, is produced by never thinking meanly of ourselves, or of others.[73] Two things are necessary to abide by this principle: "a disposition of the mind not to offend others" and "the most agreeable way of expressing that disposition."[74] The polite disposition of mind is called civility, and the agreeable expression of civility is manners.[75] Civility is the principal "of all the social virtues," according to Locke, because it teaches people the habit of accommodating themselves to others, and living in harmony with them. This is important for preventing conflict in a liberal commonwealth that may be made up of citizens from many different races, religions, colours, and ethnic groups. Because of its central role in promoting peace, Locke concludes that civility is the first lesson that children and young people should be taught, with great care, until it "be made habitual."[76] Civility and manners allow people to communicate the "general good will and regard for all people" that is the core of good breeding.[77]

This rational and civil spirit procures children general respect, love, and esteem, and "they lose no superiority by it." Conversely, if the parents fail to cultivate these polite traits, children might learn by experience that there is no advantage in being civil when it is not to their immediate advantage.[78] Locke illustrates this lesson by examining the quality of liberality. Sharing possessions liberally is contrary to people's natural desire to control their objects. However, if parents teach children "to part with what they have easily and freely to their friends; and let them find by experience, that the most liberal has always the most plenty, with esteem and commendation to boot," then children will learn to believe that they need not dominate others in order to have all the control they need, (In fact, they will learn that they will actually lose power, and be punished, if they try to dominate others).[79] Under these (admittedly artificial) conditions, good nature may be settled into a habit, and "they may take pleasure ... in being kind, liberal, and civil to others."[80] Indeed, Locke says, well-raised children take more pleasure in being civil than in being insolent.[81]

To cement such a civil disposition, he recommends, "children from the beginning should be bred up in an abhorrence of killing or tormenting any living creature" and must "be taught not to spoil or destroy anything, unless it be for the preservation or advantage of some other that is nobler."[82] With such habits established early, youngsters will quickly learn to practice civility; and will become adults of liberal sentiments who go about their business with consideration and respect for their fellow citizens.[83]

The Right Habits: Mathematics

Another disposition necessary for peaceful individuals, in Locke's view, is the habit of reasonable thought learned through basic studies. In addition to learning to read and write, children must also be taught arithmetic—"not so much to make them mathematicians, as to make them reasonable creatures," able to observe "the connection of ideas."[84] Indeed, Locke argues in *On the Conduct of the Understanding*, "nothing does this better than mathematics."[85] The mathematical habit of reasoning gives students useful skills that they can transfer to other aspects of knowledge. In many fields, he points out, logical arguments "should be managed as a mathematical demonstration, the connection and dependence of ideas should be followed, until the mind is brought to the source [and] observes the coherence all along."[86] By acquiring the mathematical habit early on, children can become accustomed to thinking clearly and deductively on all issues; which not only improves their capacity for further study, but also teaches them to think through their moral opinions and actions for rational consistency.

The Right Ideas: God

In addition to the right habits, people must acquire certain fundamental ideas and intellectual content in order to be liberal: education must direct the imagination toward what reason authorizes. According to Locke, perhaps the most important is the idea of God. Like all ideas, this is not innate, and so it should be imprinted very early on children's minds.[87] But as Locke wrote in *A Letter Concerning Toleration*, teaching the proper notion of God is critical because religious zeal can be used by "Men striving for Power and Empire over one another" to justify persecution and war.[88] At an early age, children should learn about the true notion of God, "the independent Supreme Being, Author and Maker of all things, from whom we receive all our good, who loves us and gives us all things."[89] They must be taught to love and reverence the Supreme Being who "does all manner of good to those that love and obey him."[90]

This God requires "Charity, Meekness, and Good-will in general towards all Mankind," and opposes "those that persecute, torment, destroy, and kill other men upon pretence of Religion."[91] Such a liberal, benevolent concept of deity is crucial to the practice of virtue, because it reassures people that they will (eventually) be rewarded for their good behaviour. Even if justice is not done in the immediate here and now, virtue will triumph and "Quarrelsom and Contentious" individuals will be punished.[92] People with such an idea will embrace religious toleration and accept reason as humanity's "only Star and Compass" in all matters, including "religion, politicks, and morality."[93]

Locke argues that without a religious inducement, virtue loses its appeal for most people because it is too hard. He criticizes "the old Heathen Philosophers" for teaching that immorality must be avoided because it is "dishonest, below the Dignity of a Man, and opposite to Vertue, the highest Perfection of human Nature."[94] While the ancients' teachings "drew men's eyes and approbation" to the beauty of virtue, they did not instill in people any hope of future reward, or fear of punishment.[95] As a result, very few were willing to espouse virtue—not surprising, since reward and punishment "are the only motives to a rational creature."[96] In contrast, Locke's basic theology builds on reward and punishment, especially the idea that God has "the Power of eternal Life" and can reward the virtuous with "the endless, unspeakable joys of another life." This can open people's eyes to the goodness of virtue, and give them "something solid and powerful to move them."[97]

The Right Ideas: Science

Grounded in the right idea of God as a benevolent and lawful "Supreme Being," children can proceed to more advanced studies, including the sciences. These should not include logic or the metaphysical sciences, because in Locke's view too early a study of such subjects is "fitter to amuse than inform the understanding in its first setting out toward knowledge."[98]

As he knew from personal experience, abstract speculations are so difficult that young people "are tempted to quit their studies and throw away their books as containing nothing but hard words and empty sounds; or else to conclude that if there be any real knowledge in them, they themselves have not the understandings capable of it."[99] To avoid setting children against complex subjects, he recommends acquainting them first with subjects based on images or events, such as geography, astronomy, and chronology.[100] These provide a jumping-off point for the more formal and abstract study of geometry, which Locke praises for its logical process of building simple ideas on others.[101] More advanced scientific study should include also the studies of nature and physics" (particularly the work of "the incomparable Mr. Newton").[102] The goal should not to make students into scientists or physicists, but to habituate them to the scientific method, and to teach them to "understand the terms and ways of talking of the several sects" of scientists.[103] The crowning achievement of scientific study should be to make students view the "incomprehensible universe" not as a mystical organism, or a constant miraculous intervention of mysterious higher powers; but as a "stupendous machine" whose workings can (in principle) be known by diligent empirical observation and rational deduction.[104] Such a world view opens people's minds, and makes them more inclined to be open to the claims of reasonable argument—even to insist on reason as their "only Star and Compass" on the most important questions in life.[105]

The Right Ideas: Natural Rights

Locke also discusses history as perhaps the most important branch of advanced learning. Young people must study history in the right spirit: not just out of curiosity, or a scientific desire to reconstruct the past, but as part of a general study of "morality."[106] History, Locke, believes, is particularly able to spur people to acquire "knowledge of virtue," because its vivid stories of human excellence help students to remember general moral rules through specific examples, which are easier to remember.[107] Locke concludes that "nothing delights more than history."[108]

The study of history must include "the affairs and intercourse · of civilized nations in general, grounded upon principles of reason."[109] For this task Locke recommends the works of Grotius, and two books by the 17th-century German writer Samuel Pufendorf: *De officio hominis & civilis* and *De jure naturali & gentium*.[110] These last two books are especially important because they can help to instruct students on "the natural rights of men, and the origin and foundations of society, and the duties resulting from thence."[111] General knowledge of civil law and history is a field that young people "should not barely touch at, but constantly dwell upon and never have done with."[112] As the culmination of studying the "natural rights of men," Locke recommends his own *Two Treatises of Government.*

Locke believes that knowledge of natural rights is absolutely necessary for the success of a liberal commonwealth, and should be second nature for all students and citizens. Ignorance of this subject, unlike other areas of learning, not only harms material progress but also threatens civil society. Citizens do not inherently understand the concepts of political power unless they are taught about its foundation in the natural equality and liberty of all mankind. Without such knowledge, they cannot become enlightened—that is, learn to respect each other's rights; keep government limited to its true purpose of protecting life, liberty, and estate; and keep a watchful eye on any leaders who might try to lead the nation to war for their own ambition or imaginary visions of national glory.[113] Indeed, Locke goes so far as to say that if individuals do not have the right opinions about these political principles, peace will be impossible. People must "live together by no other Rules but that of Beasts, where the strongest carries it, and so lay a Foundation for perpetual Disorder and Mischief, Tumult, Sedition and Rebellion."[114]

The Right Ideas: Peaceful Extracurriculars

Locke's concern for education extends to extracurricular activities. He strongly recommends teaching young people—even upper-class children—"a manual trade, nay two or three," particularly "merchant's accounts."[115] Such training not only gives young people worthwhile skills, and provides them with healthy recreation for when they are not "employed in study, reading, and conversation."[116] Most importantly, perhaps, learning manual trades deflates "the vanity and pride of greatness" that might arise in intelligent or ambitious students, and prevent any urge in them to dominate others.[117]

The principle of educating against pride extends to areas such as dancing, music, fencing, and horsemanship. For example, Locke supports learning to dance as a means of cultivating a "graceful carriage," but claims that boys should not take up fencing: "a man that cannot fence will be more careful to keep out of bullies' and gamesters' company."[118] Although riding was viewed in 17th-century England as so necessary to good breeding that it would be a serious omission to neglect it in a boy's education, Locke leaves the matter to the discretion of parents and tutors—noting only that such activity has "very little to do with civil life" or promoting virtue and wisdom.[119] Even in matters of recreation, Locke's fundamental goal is always to make young people into rational creatures who are in the habit of reasoning, who have "right notions and a right judgment of things," and who can be always convinced by "plain reason and the conviction of clear arguments."[120]

The Right Ideas: Education and Tolerance

In a liberal commonwealth, this passion for inquiry and free-thinking—especially for philosophers who investigate explosive subjects like theology—is particularly important because many citizens may hold significantly different views on political, philosophical and religious matters.[121] Such a society needs proper education, to produce tolerant dispositions combined with the firm belief that others are also entitled to their opinions (and may even be right). Locke believes that if citizens have this liberal attitude, differences of religious opinion are much less likely to become occasions of "strife, faction, malignity, and narrow impositions."[122] Absent universal enlightened education, though, such reasonable and peaceful attitudes will be confined to only the best-educated and best-natured citizens.[123]

However, Locke is confident that once citizens are set right by their education, "they will quickly bring the rest into order" and diffuse a more liberal spirit throughout the commonwealth.[124] Granted, most ordinary citizens will have neither the time nor the desire to further investigate complex matters of religious or philosophical doctrine, which have little connection to their lives and businesses. But that is for the best, Locke claims: they will have little opportunity to be inflamed by abstract disputes that are beyond their "weak Capacities" to understand.[125] By directing people's minds away from such disputes, proper education will establish religious toleration, and ensure that theological and political differences do not spark deadly conflict.

The Liberal Path to Peace

Locke is clearly more optimistic than previous thinkers—ancient, medieval, or modern—about the possibility of transforming the desire for power into a passion for peace and liberty. While he acknowledges that many individuals too readily incline to being either "Quarrelsom and Contentious" or abject and slavish, he firmly believes that proper education can weed out bad desires and transform people into "Industrious and Rational" citizens. Admittedly, Locke never claims that such people will be rational enough to logically argue the truth of their opinions; only that they will be "reasonable" in the sense of being able to think calmly and logically about moral, political, and religious questions.[126]

In his view, citizens must have the right habits and ideas—ideas that make them liberal, practical, civil, committed to natural rights, open to rational discussion and argument, and sympathetic to others who pursue truth in different directions. They must be proud of their freedom, and have a vigorous love of liberty that prevents any tendency to become unable or unwilling to defend themselves and their society. Such a reasonable pride makes them fundamentally sober, moderate, and peaceful. According to Locke, this unique combination of "peaceful but spirited" sets the new liberal citizens apart from those produced by the old custom of moral education.[127]

Despite this optimism, though, we may wonder: what about nations that lack a culture of industrious rationality? If custom is so powerful, in Locke's view, how do people with "quarrelsom and contentious" habits and ideas ever begin to acquire the right ones? If they cannot do so, will they not be in a continual state of conflict and hostility with the industrious and rational nations? How can they become liberal?

Locke suggests three possible solutions: conquest, colonization, and example. The first option is limited by Locke's own fairly strict argument (in the *Second Treatise*) against going to war. Countries are authorized by reason only when threatened or attacked; and they cannot permanently take over another territory, enslave non-combatants, or use force against the local religion.[128] In his Article 97 of the Fundamental Constitutions of Carolina, for example, Locke writes that the native inhabitants' "idolatry, ignorance, or mistake gives us no right to expel or use them ill." These limitations seem to rule out conquest, even if its goal is merely to liberalize other countries. It might, however, be justifiable against a country that starts an unjust war, as Nazi Germany and Imperial Japan did. Even then, an occupation could only morally last long enough to punish those who "actually aided and concurred in the war,"[129] and to rehabilitate the population. Such rehabilitation could certainly include liberal reforms; but they would only become permanent if the next generation consented to them. As Locke points out, "a father hath not, in himself, a power over the life or liberty of his child." The children of the conquered, whatever happened to their fathers, are free men; "and the absolute power of the conqueror reaches no farther than the persons of the men that were subdued by him, and dies with them."[130]

The other two ways to liberalize countries use only moral force. Establishing colonies could spread liberal ideas and habits to populations that come in contact with them, so that—as Locke says with respect to Christianity in the New World—the native inhabitants may have the opportunity to acquaint themselves with "the peaceableness and inoffensiveness" of religious or social truth. By "good usage and persuasion" and "convincing methods," illiberal nations might also "be won ever to embrace and unfeignedly receive the truth."[131]

Alternatively, industrious and rational people can simply act as an example of the success of their liberal ideas and habits. This will not immediately lead other nations to embrace those same ideas and habits; their own customs—especially when believed to be of divine origin—may still make them believe and act in illiberal and unreasonable ways.[132] But over time, even unenlightened peoples will be unable to deny the advantages enjoyed by liberal societies. While "Fashion, Example, and Education" may have convinced them that concepts such as tribal identity, racial honour, and religious purity are more important than the goods of liberalism such as security, prosperity, and freedom, Locke believes that the attraction of liberal goods is rooted in the basic principles of human nature; and that once people experience security, prosperity, and freedom, desire for them may be denied or suppressed, but not eliminated.[133] Their benefits undermine the perceived value of the other, less liberal, concepts.

In Locke's mind, the benefits of liberal societies speak to the irresistible impulses of all peoples to preserve themselves comfortably, and to pursue their happiness free from every kind of slavery, whether of body or mind.[134] So while the mere example of successful free societies may not give the right habits or ideas to societies that lack them, it can make them want the goods and comforts that only such habits and ideas can produce; and may gradually open their minds, and lead them to start acquiring them. The process would likely be long and difficult, with many fits and starts and no guarantee of success. It is possible, though, if the right education can take hold.

If Locke is right, democratic peace theory needs an important supplement. We must remember that neither commerce nor democracy can produce peace without liberalism, and also that the success of liberalism depends on the right education. The contemporary failure of liberalism to take root in many modern countries would therefore not surprise Locke. From his point of view, physical resources, democratic elections, and written constitutions are not enough: rulers and citizens must also have moral and intellectual characters capable of supporting a liberal regime. Whatever praiseworthy characteristics people in non-liberal countries may possess, no amount of democracy or commerce can replace education. Love of dominion inevitably produces lawlessness, corruption, and conflict. They must instead become Lockean individuals: reasonable, self-controlled, civil, industrious, and proud of their rights.

In Locke's view, this sensible pride—this love of oneself as a rational, self-governing individual—is enough to satisfy people. We do not need war and conflict. But we will always have it, unfortunately, unless liberal institutions are made up of liberal individuals. As Locke's intellectual heirs, we should ponder this insight if we want to follow his path to peace.

Notes

1   See, for example, Bruce Russett, *Grasping the Democratic Peace: Principles for a Post-Cold War World* (Princeton: Princeton University Press, 1994).

2   István Hont shows that thinkers such as Samuel Pufendorf, Adam Smith, and David Hume promoted the idea that commerce can foster sociability (or at least non-violent competition) between nations without the "jealousy of trade" that causes political or military conflict. Locke believes that industrious and rational people can take pride in their commercial or trading success, without such pride becoming the "grandeur" that stokes war. In this respect, Hont is a kind of successor to Pufendorf (whom Locke recommends for understanding the rights of nations), and a predecessor of Hume and Smith. István Hont, *Jealousy of Trade: International Competition and the Nation-State in Historical Perspective* (Cambridge, MA: Harvard University Press, 2005), 10.

3   C.B. Macpherson argues that Locke's work "stood nearly at the beginning of the liberal tradition" and "seems to have almost everything that could be desired by the modern liberal democrat." Locke has been held responsible for the birth or development of many of today's dominant political notions, such as "government by consent, majority rule, moral supremacy of the individual, and the sanctity of private property." C.B. Macpherson, *The Political Theory of Possessive Individualism: Hobbes to Locke* (New York: Oxford University Press, 1962), 194.

4   John M. Owen IV, *Liberal Peace, Liberal War: American Politics and International Security* (Ithaca, NY: Cornell University Press), 15–21.

5   *Second Treatise of Government*, sec. 19. From John Locke, *Two Treatises of Government*, ed. Peter Laslett (New York: Cambridge University Press, 1988). All citations from *First Treatise* and *Second Treatise* come from the Laslett edition.

6   Locke, *Second Treatise*, sec. 16

7   Locke, *Second Treatise*, sec. 17

8   Laurie M. Johnson, "Thomas Hobbes on the Path to Peace: Love of Glory versus Realist Foreign Policy," Chapter 3 of this volume,

9   Locke, *First Treatise*, sec. 106.

10 René Paddags, "In Search for Laws above Nations: Jean-Jacques Rousseau on Perpetual Peace," Chapter 6 of this volume,

11 Paddags, "In Search for Laws above Nations."

12   In laying out Locke's account of the moral basis of international relations, Lee Ward helpfully suggests the importance of education in Locke's hope for peace. Ward concludes that "Locke's account … may speak more to his cautious hope for general moral and intellectual progress, than to a radical transformation in the international state of nature. The natural, if more distant, corollary to the creation of citizens who develop the proper rational habits and conduct befitting rights bearing individuals in liberal society may be the global citizen who respects and secures rights at home and in international society. Perhaps the prescriptive thrust of Locke's theory of international society aimed toward the inculcation of liberal principles in areas and aspects hitherto scarcely observed." Lee Ward, "Locke on the Moral Basis of International Relations," *American Journal of Political Science*, 50.3, July 2006, 704.

13   This discussion of Locke's education is indebted to the seminal work of Nathan Tarcov, *Locke's Education for Liberty* (Chicago: University of Chicago Press, 1984).

14   Locke, *Second Treatise*, ss. 34, 124.

15   Locke, *Second Treatise*, ss. 6, 4.

16   John Locke, *An Essay Concerning Human Understanding*, Book II, Chapter XX, ed. Peter H. Nidditch (New York: Oxford University Press, [1690] 1975). All citations from *Essay* are taken from this edition, which is hereafter cited as *ECHU*.

17   John Locke, *Some Thoughts Concerning Education*, ed. Ruth Grant and Nathan Tarcov (Indianapolis, IN: Hackett, [1693] 1996), sec. 81. All citations from *Some Thoughts* are taken from this edition, which is hereafter cited as *STCE*.

18   Locke, *STCE*, sec. 117.

19   Locke, *STCE*, sec. 103; *Second Treatise*, sec. 6.

20   Locke, *Second Treatise*, sec. 24.

21   Locke, *STCE*, sec. 105.

22   Locke, *STCE*, sec. 103.

23   Locke, *STCE*, sec. 115; *ECHU*, II, XXVII, sec. 17.

24   Locke, *STCE*, sec. 115.

25   Locke, *Second Treatise*, sec. 13.

26   Locke, *STCE*, sec. 109.

27   Locke, *STCE*, sec. 103.

28   Locke, *STCE*, sec. 109.

29   Locke, *First Treatise,* sec. 58

30   Locke, *ECHU*, II, XXI, sec. 45.

31   Locke, *STCE*, sec. 116.

32   This same problem confronts Locke on a theoretical level in his discussion of the state of nature and the state of war. While he argues that the state of nature is "not identical" to the state of war, he admits that the former quickly

degenerates into the latter, or at least that war constantly breaks out in it. Robert Goldwin, "Locke," *History of Political Philosophy*, ed. Leo Strauss and Joseph Cropsey (Chicago: University of Chicago Press, 1987), 479.

See also Richard Cox, *Locke on War and Peace* (Oxford: Clarendon Press, 1960), who claims that self-love pulls people away from what reason dictates—either by making them too timid in enforcing the law of nature, or by propelling the love of power beyond the bounds of reason. This makes most of mankind, as Locke observes, "no strict Observers of Equity and Justice." As a result, "the enjoyment of the property he has in this state is very unsafe, very unsecure. This makes him willing to quit a Condition, which however free, is full of fears and continual dangers." *Second Treatise*, ss. 3, 123.

33 Locke, *STCE*, sec. 115.
34 Locke, *STCE*, sec. 115; *ECHU*, II, XXI, ss. 12, 14.
35 Locke, *STCE*, ss. 111, 46.
36 Locke, *STCE*, sec. 111.
37 Locke, *STCE*, sec. 116.
38 Locke, *STCE*, ss. 109–10.
39 Locke, *STCE*, sec. 73.
40 Locke, *ECHU*, I, III, sec. 22.
41 Locke, *STCE*, sec. 135.
42 Locke, *STCE*, sec. 45.
43 Locke, *STCE*, sec. 135.
44 Locke, *STCE*, sec. 45.
45 Locke, *STCE*, sec. 112.
46 Locke, *STCE*, sec. 112.
47 Locke, *STCE*, sec. 111.
48 Locke, *STCE*, sec. 112.
49 Locke, *STCE*, sec. 112.
50 Locke, *STCE*, sec. 113.
51 Locke, *STCE*, sec. 113.
52 Locke, *STCE*, sec. 113.
53 Locke, *STCE*, ss. 111–12.
54 Locke, *STCE*, ss. 50–51.
55 Locke, *STCE*, sec. 200.
56 Locke, *STCE*, ss. 35, 105.
57 Locke, *ECHU*, II, XX, sec. 36.
58 Locke, *Second Treatise*, sec. 35.
59 Locke, *STCE*, ss. 40, 57, 110.
60 Locke, *STCE*, sec. 57.
61 Locke, *STCE*, sec. 44.
62 Locke, *STCE*, ss. 57, 63, 167.

63   Locke, *ECHU*, II, XX, sec. 14.

64   Locke, *STCE*, sec. 76.

65   Locke, *STCE*, ss. 57, 167.

66   Locke, *STCE*, sec. 55.

67   Locke, *STCE*, sec. 115.

68   Locke, *STCE*, sec. 59.

69   Locke, *STCE*, sec. 56.

70   Locke, *STCE*, sec. 56.

71   Locke, *STCE*, ss. 56, 58, 61.

72   Locke, *STCE*, sec. 141; *STCE*, sec. 93.

73   Locke, *STCE*, sec. 141.

74   Locke, *STCE*, sec. 143.

75   Locke, *STCE*, sec. 143.

76   Locke, *STCE*, sec. 143.

77   *STCE*, sec. 143.

78   *STCE*, sec. 109.

79   *STCE*, sec. 110.

80   *STCE*, sec. 109.

81   *STCE*, sec. 110.

82   *STCE*, sec. 116; also compare *Second Treatise,* sec. 6.

83   *STCE*, sec. 116.

84   John Locke, *On the Conduct of the Understanding*, ed. Ruth Grant and Nathan Tarcov (Indianapolis, IN: Hackett, [1704] 1996), sec. 6. All citations from *Conduct* are taken from this edition, hereafter cited as *TCU*.

85   *TCU*, sec. 6.

86   *TCU*, sec. 6.

87   *ECHU*, I, IV, sec. 17; *STCE*, sec. 136.

88   John Locke, *A Letter Concerning Toleration*, ed. James H. Tully (Indianapolis, IN: Hackett, [1689] 1983), para. 1. All citations from *A Letter* are taken from this edition, hereafter cited as *LCT*.

89   *STCE*, sec. 136.

90   *STCE*, sec. 136.

91   *LCT*, para. 1.

92   *Second Treatise*, sec. 34; *ECHU*, II, XXVIII, ss. 5–6.

93   *Second Treatise*, sec. 176; *STCE*, sec. 116. Also see Peter Myers, *Our Only Star and Compass: Locke and the Struggle for Political Rationality* (Lanham, MD: Rowman and Littlefield, 1998), 37–65.

94   *ECHU*, I, III, sec. 5.

95   John Locke, *The Reasonableness of Christianity*, ed. George W. Ewing (Washington, DC: Regnery Gateway, [1695] 1965), sec. 245. All citations from *Reasonableness* are taken from this edition, hereafter cited as *RC*.

 96 *RC*, sec. 245; *STCE*, sec. 54.

 97 *ECHU*, II, XXI, sec. 70; *RC*, sec. 245.

 98 *STCE*, sec. 166.

 99 *STCE*, sec. 166.

100 *STCE*, sec. 166.

101 *STCE*, sec. 178.

102 *STCE*, ss. 193–94.

103 *STCE*, ss. 193–94.

104 *STCE*, sec. 194.

105 First Treatise, sec. 57.

106 *STCE*, sec. 185.

107 *STCE*, sec. 185.

108 *STCE*, sec. 184.

109 *STCE*, sec. 187.

110 *STCE*, sec. 186.

111 *STCE*, sec. 186.

112 *STCE*, sec. 186.

113 *Second Treatise*, ss. 1–4, 124.

114 *Second Treatise*, sec. 1.

115 *STCE*, ss. 202, 210.

116 *STCE*, ss. 204, 209.

117 *STCE*, sec. 207.

118 *STCE*, ss. 196–99.

119 *STCE*, ss. 198–200.

120 *STCE*, ss. 188–89.

121 *TCU*, sec. 32.

122 *TCU*, sec. 23.

123 *STCE*, sec. 116.

124 *STCE*, "Dedicatory Letter."

125 *TCU*, ss. 6–7; *ECHU*, I, IV, sec. 17; *RC*, sec. 243.

126 *TCU*, ss. 12, 45.

127 *STCE*, sec. 216.

128 *Second Treatise*, ch. 16; *LCT*, para. 8; Fundamental Constitutions of Carolina, Article 97.

129 *Second Treatise*, sec. 196.

130 *Second Treatise*, sec. 189.

131 Fundamental Constitutions of Carolina, Article 97.

132 *First Treatise*, ss. 56–57.

133 First Treatise, sec. 88.

134 *First Treatise*, ss. 1, 88; *ECHU* II, XXI, sec. 44.

CHAPTER 5

Vattel on Morally
Non-Discriminatory Peace

Ben Holland

Emer de Vattel (1714–67) is often considered one of the first truly "modern" writers on international law. If this is true, his comments on the subject of peace in *The Law of Nations* (1758) show that we live today in postmodern times:

> A treaty of peace can be no more than a compromise. Were the rules of strict and rigid justice to be observed in it, so that each party should precisely receive everything to which he has a just title, it would be impossible ever to make a peace.[1]

After Nuremberg and Tokyo, after the findings of international criminal tribunals on Sierra Leone and the former Yugoslavia, after the Rome Statute giving rise to the International Criminal Court—Vattel's conception of peace as morally non-discriminatory appears to have had its day. Contemporary opinion holds that wars do not conclude merely with peace, but with just peace. Peace is normative; it must be more than a compromise.[2]

In this chapter, I present Vattel's work in its intellectual and political contexts, in order to shed light on his purposes in describing peace as morally neutral. This idea of peace is certainly one of the more straightforward outlined in this book. It is less elevated than Luther's notion of peace as subsisting by the proper division of God's rule on earth into "two kingdoms," as described by Jarrett A. Carty in Chapter 1 of this volume. It is less abstract than Hegel's idea of peace as dialectically related to war, as discussed by Mark Blitz in Chapter 8. It is less metaphysical than Heidegger's concept of peace, assessed in Chapter 10 by David Edward Tabachnick, as a dynamic "settling in" in the world (made impossible by the onset of the technological era, which Heidegger views as a continuous abandonment of individual being, as people become the raw material of the age of consumption). And it is less spiritual than Benjamin's view of peace as critique and as "divine violence," as articulated by Herminio Meireles Teixeira in Chapter 11. Yet it arises from an engagement with ideals of agency that is as elevated, as abstract, as metaphysical, and as spiritual as any other in early modern theory. And if Vattel's concept of peace now strikes us at first as scandalous, there may still be something to be said for it.

I argue here that Vattel's philosophical commitment—to a law of nature requiring that individuals all seek to attain their own "perfection"—led him ultimately to maintain that justice in world affairs was a subjective rather than an objective matter. No "view from nowhere" existed by which to assess state actions.[3] Just wars could not be waged to bring about a just peace, for nobody had a right to argue about the justice of any conflict in the first place. I further show why some commentators, who do not necessarily share Vattel's underlying assumptions, nonetheless consider his understanding of peace as superior to the more normatively loaded notions that preceded it—which emanated from the "just war" tradition—and those that followed it, after the Second World War.

Vattel's Precursors: Leibniz and Wolff

The key to understanding Vattel's idea of peace as morally non-discriminatory is his notion of conscience; and in order to grasp that, it is necessary to examine the philosophical tradition in which he stood. Vattel's two principal intellectual influences are the great German polymath Gottfried Wilhelm Leibniz (1646–1716), and his less innovative (but still formidable) epigone, Christian Wolff (1679–1754).

The issue that dominated Leibniz's philosophical life was to understand why a perfect, all-knowing, all-loving, and all-powerful God would create a world of so much obvious imperfection. His answer, in essence, was that if anything were at all different, the world would be the worse for it; and this must be impossible, because God's perfection meant that he was always morally necessitated to do the best. As Leibniz puts it: "When a wicked man exists, God must have found in the region of the possible the idea of such a man forming that sequence of things, the choice of which was demanded by the greatest perfection of the universe, and in which errors and sins are not only punished but even repaired to greater advantage, so that they contribute to the greatest good."[4] It did not bother Leibniz that his theory seemed to eliminate the possibility of free action.[5] Rather, he considered that he had found a way of exculpating sinners from their misdeeds, by showing how all things contribute to the perfection of creation.

In his most famous essay, the *Monadology* (1714), Leibniz posited a world teeming with "monads"—a term he derived from the Greek word for unity. He believed that monads are the "true atoms of nature," substances resulting from aggregations of infinitely divisible material bodies.[6] Their non-complex and immaterial character means that they share certain properties with God—such as the fact that each is the sole cause of its future states. God has harmonized all monads, so that what we perceive as a clear-cut case of causality (if a bottle of milk balanced on the edge of a table is pushed, it falls to the ground) has in fact already been ordained by God (the bottle was always going to be pushed and to fall at just that moment). Both "agent" and "patient" act spontaneously to activate a "disposition," a potential future state that then becomes actual. By virtue of this harmony between monads—established by God, and involving an interconnection "of all created things to each one, and of each one to all the others"—the world that exists is therefore the best possible world. As Leibniz writes, "each simple substance has relationships which express all the others," and so each is "a perpetual living mirror of the universe."[7] As the universe must be exactly as perfect as a perfect God can make it, we see how the ever-optimistic Leibniz was able to exonerate these mirrors of the universe for whatever ills they appear to cause.

God himself is the highest monad: his perception of the relationship between the multitude of lower monads and the unity of the universe is perfect, and his perfect perception, allied to his all-goodness, provides sufficient reason for him to activate the best of all worlds. Human beings are also considered monads, although lower ones; their rationality makes them capable of understanding at least some part of "the system of the universe."[8] And if individuals to some extent mirror God, yet are caught in the imperfections of their physical faculties, the only way they can know the good is through progressively realizing the part of themselves that is divine. God has perfectly clear and distinct perceptions, which means that he does not have a point of view, as such. Individuals can therefore strive to imitate divinity by adopting a contemplative attitude, and renouncing all animal passions. Wisdom, Leibniz says, stems from such "mental concentration and renunciation of the sensible world."[9] Knowing the source of the universe's teleological order, however, is not enough; people must also develop a sensitivity or feeling for the world.[10] To find happiness in God's design, they must realize their goal, or *telos*, as rational and compassionate beings. And just as God gave the universe its own teleological order, individuals who find their own *telos*—of rationality combined with compassion—have achieved their earthly end of reunion with God.

This philosophy of Leibniz is all rather heady and forbidding material, though brought a little more down to earth by Wolff. His first step was to argue, in Timothy Hochstrasser's words, that every substance strives "merely for self-perfection, instead of its shaping out its individual characteristics in the direction of reunion with the divine."[11] Perfection is less a movement toward a higher order of perfection, like God's nature, than a form of self-perfection. As Wolff writes: "For since the human soul is receptive to the operation of grace—otherwise it could not accept grace, when confronted by it—there should be, in the essence and nature of the soul, some reason, some disposition, that enables it to receive this into itself."[12] In other words, since a person's intellect has all the resources required to apprehend God's grace, and thereby improve itself, we need look no further than the possibilities of human nature itself in order to establish what human perfection looks like.

According to Wolff, actions are good or bad only so far as they assist or hinder an individual's striving for self-perfection. Only one moral law therefore guides human conduct: "Do what makes you and your state more perfect, and refrain from what makes you and your state less perfect."[13] (This refers to personal states, not political.) And since this rule applies to "all the free actions of men there is no need for any other law of Nature." We can know this law by reason, and "a reasonable man needs no further law, for because of his reason he is a law unto himself."[14]

However, Wolff explicitly stated that individual perfection cannot be obtained through selfish behaviour. People are social beings, and therefore moral perfection must entail kindness toward others. Furthermore, it is rational to assist others, in the hope that they will return the assistance if needed. Reason dictates that individuals come together in a society so that all are in a more favourable position to achieve personal perfection; so a general duty of sociability toward others is dictated by natural law. But such duties can be suspended at the bidding of individual conscience, which Wolff defined as the ability to work out the implications of our actions for our goal of self-perfection. We all have a "perfect" duty to advance our own perfection; and if our conscience tells us that the best way to achieve this is by ignoring the requirements of sociability, then we must follow our conscience. Even when people contract obligations to one another, those obligations remain imperfect; for no duty contingent on a form of words can really be known to their conscience. If a person in good conscience desires to break a promise made to another, then so be it.

From a civil perspective, though, this is a problem: any society in which people can conscientiously extricate themselves from all commitments to others must surely be precarious. The mind has no dispositions to act other than on its motives; and if something is represented as good, that is enough reason for activity—no matter whether the representation is based on accurate or inaccurate perceptions. We are determined by the reason that most strongly moves us, Wolff argued. Errors and sins are excusable if they follow from clouded representations—sinners are closer to mad than bad—although we must still do as much as we can to ensure that our conscientious judgments are as accurate as possible.

This is why, said Wolff, individuals need the state, meaning a contract with one another to establish a security unobtainable in the condition of nature. While it might be true that nature has not precisely imposed on people the obligation of uniting together in civil society, Wolff holds that such a state, once instituted, is "a moral person."[15] (In the 18th century, "moral" meant having agency and responsibility.) The state motivates us to behave sociably by promulgating law, which threatens punishment for unsociable behaviour, and thereby motivates us to engage in some actions and refrain from others. The threat of execution, for instance, motivates someone afraid of death not to steal.[16]

Wolff's concept of "states as persons" orients his contribution, published in 1749, to modern international law: his *The Laws of Nations According to the Scientific Method*. There were two rival traditions in this field, dominated by Hugo Grotius and Thomas Hobbes. Grotius's massive tome *The Laws of War and Peace* (1625) drew on Thomist moral theology: the "law of peoples" (*ius gentium*) specified the principles that individuals had consensually reasoned to be appropriate to their ends, in given circumstances.[17] Likewise, Grotius set out to identify inductively what he called the "law of nations," by means of examining common customs of civilized nations. By contrast, Hobbes maintained—in *Leviathan* (1651) and elsewhere—that the law of nations was nothing but the law of nature, applied to sovereign states. Discovering such law was a matter of deduction, not induction.[18]

Wolff himself subscribed to a modified version of this Hobbesian perspective. He too argued that "the law of nations is originally nothing except the law of nature applied to nations."[19] Nations are persons, initially inhabiting a state of nature, in which there is no law but the law of nature. Yet he believed it important to recognize that nations are different from biological individuals, and this fact alters the character of the law of nations. States are more than merely embodiments of the persons of their sovereigns. As moral persons, states bear the natural obligations of conscience; but that refers to their nature *qua* states, not the nature of biological persons. Individuals' obligations of conscience under the law of nature are translated into a state's duties to its subjects under the law of nations. States also have some duties of sociability toward each other, though these are always subordinate to sovereigns' obligations to their subjects. Similarly, sovereigns may make promises to each other; but these are always imperfect, and refutable if conscience dictates.

Just as a civil state must mitigate the problems caused by prioritizing conscience, means must also be found to mitigate war between states. Wolff calls for the establishment of a *civitas maxima*, or maximal association of states. Such an association, he said, should be headed by a *rector*, "who, following the leadership of nature, defines by the right use of reason what nations ought to consider as law among themselves."[20] This rector must promulgate a "positive law of nations" by which states regulate their external conduct with one another (though it would not apply to their internal affairs).

Vattel: Morally Neutral War and Peace

Now that we have thoroughly examined the background to Vattel's thinking, we can turn to his own ideas. The book that eventually became *The Law of Nations* had modest beginnings, as Vattel tells us in the preface. His initial ambition was only to publish and clarify "for the greater number of readers, the knowledge of the luminous ideas" of Wolff on the law of nations.[21] Wolff's original exposition made little sense to anyone not conversant with the methods of formal geometry, and assumed that readers were acquainted both with the difficult perfectionist metaphysics of Leibniz, and with his own ideas on the subject. The more Vattel studied Wolff's opus, however, the more he "ventured to deviate from the path" Wolff had pointed out, and "adopted sentiments opposite to his."[22]

One path from which Vattel ventured to deviate led him to contend, *contra* Wolff, that the idea of the *civitas maxima* was an impossible one. Vattel's own biography is relevant to this point. He came from Neuchâtel, today a Swiss canton, but in his day a pawn in the game of dynastic politics. Neuchâtel was by long tradition a hereditary principality; but in 1707, with the death of Mary, Princess of Neuchâtel, the throne fell vacant with no direct successor. The most credible candidate was one of the many French princes, the claim of one of whom was supported by Louis XIV. However, recent French annexations of parts of the Holy Roman Empire provoked fears of French designs on Neuchâtel's political autonomy, while Louis' harassment of French Protestants had prompted large numbers of refugees into exile in Switzerland—stoking yet more resentment against France. Vattel's family was deeply involved in arranging for one of France's enemies to assume the throne. An ancient feudal right was discovered in support of William III of England, a country that was at the time fighting against France in the War of the Spanish Succession. But William relinquished the title of King to his nephew Frederick I of Prussia, who was officially recognized in November 1707. Vattel himself, though a Prussian subject, worked as a diplomat in Saxony—until Saxony was invaded by Prussia, which believed that the territory had allied itself with Prussia's rival, Austria.[23]

So Neuchâtel was at the same time a supposedly sovereign state, a part of the Holy Roman Empire, a part of the Swiss Confederacy, and a territory about to be welded into what would soon become the state of Prussia. Neuchâtel's status in the Empire was precarious, since all parts of it—though ostensibly subordinate to the Emperor—were in a seemingly constant state of internecine hostility.[24] Wolff's idea of the *civitas maxima*, in some senses an abstraction from the reality of overlapping political authority in the Holy Roman Empire, now appeared an abstraction from a moribund political system. "This idea does not satisfy me," Vattel wrote. "Nor do I think the fiction of such a republic either admissible in itself, or capable of affording sufficiently solid grounds on which to build the rules of the universal law of nations which shall necessarily claim the obedient acquiescence of sovereign states."[25] If not the *civitas maxima*, then what? Vattel set out to explore the law of nations in the context of yet another abstraction, given the messy political actualities of his day—but an abstraction he felt better justified by the evidence: a law of nations for legally equal, autonomous sovereign units.

Vattel began to build his own schema of international law by examining the law of nature. He commenced, in Wolffian fashion, by arguing that individuals are brought to act by physical and psychical motivations. There is, he wrote in an essay of 1746, "no will in the soul without motivation; therefore to bring about the moral necessity to undertake a particular action, some motivation must be linked to this action, which you cannot separate from it."[26] No inclination, desire, or affection is more basic than self-love, and the motive attaching to self-love is "our *well-being*, our *expediency*, our *advantage*."[27] Self-love "causes us to desire or seek for our happiness or the perfection of our condition," of our soul, of the well-being of our body, and of our prosperity.[28] There is nothing morally objectionable about this, Vattel believed. It would be absurd to claim that an individual was ever under an obligation to act against his self-interest.[29] For this is how God created us; and reason tells us that the first principle of the law of nature must be to seek our own perfection:

> When we have a correct understanding of *self-interest*; when we have constituted it mainly in the perfection of the soul, a perfection that already defines our happiness in itself, and which reconciles us with the good will of the Creator, what danger is there in confusing the meaning of *integrity* with *expediency*?[30]

Vattel went on to adopt Wolff's nomenclature of states as "moral persons."[31] The purpose of a writer on the law of nations was to discover the law of nature as it fitted the distinct nature of these persons. Hobbes, he believed, was mistaken to have imagined that the law of nature underwent no changes when states themselves became its subjects, and Wolff corrected that mistake. States had a perfect duty under the law of nations to strive for their own perfection.[32] As Frederick Whelan has pointed out, Vattel seems to have meant a number of things by this. Sometimes he explained that this duty meant that the state should promote the pursuit of self-perfection by its individual members, "the individual finding in a well-regulated society the most powerful succours to enable him to fulfil the task of which Nature imposes upon him in relation to himself, for becoming better, and consequently more happy."[33] At other times, he suggested a more collective understanding of civil perfection: if the perfection of a thing consists in "the perfect agreement of all its constituent parts to tend to the same end," then if all citizens "conspire to attain the end proposed in forming a civil society, the nation is perfect."[34] But more often, Vattel argued that a state, as a moral person, had a duty to its own corporate self to perfect itself. The state had its own conscience, which (for Vattel as for Wolff) was the faculty of assessing actions in respect of their contribution to the final goal of self-perfection. The state's first duty under the law of nations was to do the bidding of its conscience.

Vattel went further than Wolff, though, in insisting that the stipulations of conscience were primarily self-interested, and only secondarily about advancing the cause of sociability among nations. It "exclusively belongs to each nation to form her own judgment of what her conscience proscribes to her—of what she can or cannot do—of what it is proper or improper for her to do; and of course it rests solely with her to examine and determine whether she can perform any office for another nation without neglecting the duty which she owes to herself."[35] As he also observed, "Our obligation is always imperfect with respect to other people, while we possess the liberty of judging how we are to act; and we retain that liberty on all occasions where we ought to be free."[36] And nations ought to be free on all occasions to pursue their duties of conscience.

This has enormous implications for Vattel's concept of peace. War is not morally discriminatory, he said, and therefore neither is peace. If a sovereign decides in good conscience to undertake hostilities against another state, then who is to judge whether that course of action is right or wrong? There is no *rector* to make such a determination. War, it is true, cannot be just on both sides; but "since nations are equal and independent, and cannot claim a right of judgment over each other," it follows that "two parties at war are to be accounted equally lawful."[37] States are not able to judge the justice of the cause of one of their number who elects to wage war, for that is a choice made by the sovereign to advance the perfection of the state. In Vattel's view, such conscientious choices do not admit of objective scrutiny by outsiders. To be sure, he did try to establish many ground rules for the proper conduct of hostilities, on topics such as rights of pre-emptive warfare, reparations, booty, treatment of prisoners of war, rights of neutrals, and safe passage. Yet these rules were not binding judgments of the conduct proper to sovereigns and diplomats, according to a stipulative law of nations. They were proffered as good advice, but never superseded the dictates of sovereign conscience.

Ian Hunter writes, in a locution I shall adopt, that Vattel "elaborates a conception of morally non-discriminatory peace as the partner to his conception of [morally] non-discriminatory war."[38] The end of a just war, in that tradition, was to be a just peace. Only one side was in fact fighting a war, if war was a form of enforcement of the natural law. It fell to law enforcers, should they win, to punish the lawbreaker, and to be indemnified by the loser for the costs incurred in prosecuting the struggle. By contrast, Vattel's intellectual horizons did not admit the possibility of a just war in this sense. From the point of view of international law, equivalence of justice had to be assumed when two parties to a conflict disputed the matter of right. Therefore, the making of peace had nothing to do with doing justice either. Objective justice was in fact suspended by peacemaking—which, Vattel wrote, is no more than a sensible compromise between exhausted belligerents:

> No other expedient remains than that of coming to a compromise respecting all claims and grievances on both sides, and putting an end to all disputes, by a convention as fair and equitable as circumstances will admit of. In such convention no decision is pronounced on the original cause of the war, or on those controversies to which the various acts of hostility might give rise; nor is either of the parties condemned as unjust ... but, a simple agreement is formed, which determines what equivalent each party shall receive in extinction of all his pretensions.[39]

In this view, Vatell wrote, peace treaties are not determinations of justice or injustice; they are instruments of amnesty, "a perfect oblivion of the past."[40]

> As each of the belligerent powers maintains that he has justice on his side,—and as their pretensions are not liable to be judged by others,—whatever state things happen to be in at the time of the [peace] treaty, is to be considered as their legitimate state; and if the parties intend to make change in it, they must expressly specify it in the treaty. Consequently all things not mentioned in the treaty are to remain on the same footing on which they stand at the period when it is concluded. This is also a consequence of the promised amnesty. All damages caused during the war are likewise buried in oblivion; and no action can be brought for those of which the treaty does not stipulate the reparation: they are considered as having never happened.[41]

By now, we can anticipate Vattel's attitude should one party later decide to reopen hostilities. No matter whether "the new cause which gives birth to hostilities be just or not, neither he who makes it a handle for taking up arms, nor he who refuses satisfaction, is reputed to break the treaty of peace, provided the cause for complaint on the one hand, and the refusal of satisfaction on the other, have at least some colour of reason."[42]

Vattel on Peace: Cynical or Good Sense?

Like Leibniz and Wolff before him, Vattel considered that the first duty of all individuals under natural law was to pursue their own perfection. As moral persons, precisely this same duty fell to states. The faculty possessed by all persons to deduce the appropriate means of achieving the goal of self-perfection was the conscience. It is the nature, though, of consciences that they are inscrutable by other persons. No state is ever in a position to challenge the judgment of any other that it acted in good conscience in pursuing some foreign policy. "Every free and sovereign state has a right to determine, according to the dictates of her own conscience, what her duties require of her, and what she can or cannot do with justice," Vattel wrote.[43] Out of the window, then, went the idea of just war and its appurtenances. Justice was now a subjective notion; a state might well be condemned by others for what it chose to do, but such condemnations were also subjective and had no more moral force than whatsoever the condemned state could itself muster in justifying its actions. The corollary of the idea of just war was the idea of just peace: a just war was waged to make the world a more just place.[44] Vattel instead conceived of peace as morally non-discriminatory. The resumption of peace did not necessarily increase justice in the world. Rather, peace treaties were amnesties, meaning not pardons for wrongs done—for no wrongs were admitted—but burials in oblivion of claims against the other party.

This may grate on contemporary sensibilities; but Vattel had his own pragmatic justification of the position to which his philosophical commitments had led him. Wars are terrible events, he argued, made worse by each party's belief that justice is on their own side. They all "arrogate to themselves all the rights of war, and maintain that their enemy has none, that his hostilities are so many acts of robbery, so many infractions of the law of nations, in which all states should unite. The decision of the controversy, and the justice of the cause, is so far from being forwarded by it, that the quarrel will become more bloody, more calamitous in its effects, and also more difficult to terminate."[45] But the subjectivization of the concept of justice—the realization by both sides that the other was a legal equal who also had legitimate reasons for supposing that they too were in the right— would moderate conflict. The rigours of justice and just peace could cede to the requirements of reality. The end of war need not be just peace but a fair "compromise."

Some historians of international law have lent support to Vattel's thesis that peace as a morally neutral compromise moderates conflict. Stephen Neff argues that the "very essence" of the just-war tradition that Vattel sought to supplant was "the idea of war as a law-enforcement operation." A just war could not, therefore, "be seen as a conflict between legal or moral equals, in the manner of a duel or sporting contest. Instead, every armed conflict must be seen as a case of right and wrong, of crime and punishment."[46] The just side waged war in the name of right; the other side were mere bandits. In its treatment of the conduct of hostilities, just-war doctrine "remained resolutely lodged at the level of [one] broad general principle": necessity.[47] The just side was permitted to take whatever extreme measures were necessary in order to prevail.[48] Vattel's influential argument that the same justice for their respective causes should be attributed to all warring parties, Neff claims, helped to bring some restraint to conflicts: no longer were wars waged in the name of righteousness or objective right. A concept of peace as morally non-discriminatory is the corollary of a concept of war as morally non-discriminatory. The former moderates conflict, and there are solid grounds to regard the latter favourably in comparison to the doctrine of just peace that preceded it.

In many respects, Neff's argument restates more fully that of Carl Schmitt, a German legal scholar and political theorist whose active involvement in the Nazi Party in the early 1930s led to his internment for potential war crimes after the Second World War (although he was eventually released without charge for lack of evidence).[49] According to Schmitt, just wars were in fact inhumane: the aggressor's view of his opponent as a criminal, perhaps even an enemy of humanity, permitted the use of any and all means of violence to bring him to heel.[50] "To confiscate the word humanity, to invoke and monopolize such a term, probably has certain incalculable effects, such as denying the enemy the quality of being human and declaring him to be an outlaw of humanity; and a war can therefore be driven to the most extreme inhumanity."[51] To Schmitt's mind, nuclear weapons—which threatened absolute physical annihilation— presupposed such just-war thinking: the enemy was not a lawful opponent but one who must be exterminated.[52] By contrast, Vattel's writings helped to usher in (for a time) a golden period when the notion of just war lost its substantive meaning, and justice was reduced to a matter of "form"— such as whether there had been a proper declaration of war, for instance. As Schmitt argued, the "problem of just war had been divorced from the problem of *justa causa*, and had become determined by formal juridical categories," leading to "the rationalization and humanization of war."[53] War was now a properly legal status, rather than a series of individual coercive acts. In Vattel's writings, peace also acquired a contractual, procedural, and morally neutral character. In Schmitt's opinion, this should be a cause not for despair but for celebration.[54]

We should not, however, push this argument too far. Neff may overstate the significance of necessity in just-war thinking. As Chris Brown points out, just-war doctrine in its most elaborately articulated versions was interrogative, requiring disputants to make various kinds of judgment in deciding whether military action was just: judgments about absolute moral imperatives, but also about legal authority, about circumstances and consequences, and about their own mental and spiritual state.[55] Contemporaries of Vattel, such as Voltaire and Montesquieu, also perceived clearly that the priority allotted to the "inscrutable" consciences of state-persons could rationalize the pursuit of aggrandizing foreign policies at the expense of peace.[56] As wars came to be seen as having less to do with interpersonal morality, and more as a kind of transaction between corporate juridical equals, they were also "nationalized," as Neff put it.[57] This development would eventually bolster some of the conflagrations most inimical to peace in world history—a factor Schmitt completely overlooked in his account of the humanization of war in the early modern period.[58] (Schmitt's commendation of Vattel's contractual idea of peace, it should also be noted, is part and parcel of his broader argument attacking the Nuremberg trials for daring to criminalize a legitimate "conventional" enemy—a posture that is morally bankrupt.)[59] Still, in this post-Nuremberg epoch, we ought not to dismiss outright Vattel's concept of peace as morally non-discriminatory. The United States and its allies continue to wage a global War on Terror that they claim is a just war.[60] That war has become an "institution of international hierarchy," in which combatants are criminalized, and the inhumane tactics of the irregular fighter reciprocated, as the battlefield is globalized and deterritorialized.[61] It almost beggars belief that this War on Terror has not mobilized even more hatred of its prosecutors.[62] Scandalous as they may seem to us today, we may ponder whether Vattel's ideas of morally non-discriminatory war and peace may yet have something to recommend them.

Notes

1   Emer de Vattel, *The Law of Nations*, ed. Béla Kapossy and Richard Whatmore (Indianapolis: Liberty Fund, 2008), IV.ii.§18, 662.

2   Oliver P. Richmond, ed., "A Genealogy of Peace and Conflict Theory," *Palgrave Advances in Peacebuilding: Critical Developments and Approaches* (Basingstoke: Palgrave Macmillan, 2010).

3   The phrase is from Thomas Nagel, *The View from Nowhere* (New York: Oxford University Press, 1986).

4   Gottfried Wilhelm Leibniz, *Theodicy: Essays on the Goodness of God, the Freedom of Man, and the Origin of Evil*, ed. Austin Farrer (London: Routledge and Kegan Paul, 1952), 335.

5   Gottfried Wilhelm Leibniz, *Textes inédits*, Vol. 2, ed. Gaston Grua (New York: Garland, 1985), 482. There is a large secondary literature on Leibniz's conception of freedom. Some useful discussions can be found in these works:

> Donald Rutherford and J. A. Cover, ed., *Leibniz: Nature and Freedom* (New York: Oxford University Press, 2005).
> G. H. R. Parkinson, "Sufficient Reason and Human Freedom in the *Confessio Philosophi*," *The Young Leibniz and his Philosophy*, ed. Stuart Brown (Dordrecht: Kluwer, 1999).
> Pauline Phemister, *Leibniz and the Natural World: Activity, Passivity and Corporeal Substances in Leibniz's Philosophy* (Dordrecht: Spinger, 2005).

6   Gottfried Wilhelm Leibniz, *Philosophical Texts*, ed. R. S. Woolhouse and Richard Francks (Oxford: Oxford University Press, 1998), 268.

7   Leibniz, *Philosophical Texts*, 275.

8   Leibniz, *Philosophical Texts*, 280.

9   Gottfried Wilhelm Leibniz, *Philosophical Writings*, ed. G. H. R. Parkinson (London: J. M. Dent, 1973), 367.

10   Gottfried Wilhelm Leibniz, *New Essays on Human Understanding*, ed. Peter Remnant and Jonathan Bennett (Cambridge: Cambridge University Press, 1996), 340.

11   Timothy J. Hochstrasser, *Natural Law Theories in the Early Enlightenment* (Cambridge: Cambridge University Press, 2000), 161. Another good account of Wolff's development of Leibnizian ideas on consciousness and personal identity is Udo Thiel's *The Early Modern Subject: Self-Consciousness and Personal Identity from Descartes to Hume* (Oxford: Oxford University Press, 2011), 279–314.

12   Christian Wolff, "Discourse on the Practical Philosophy of the Chinese," *Moral Enlightenment: Leibniz and Wolff on China*, ed. Julia Ching and Willard G. Oxtoby (Nettetal: Steyler, 1992), 160.

13   Thomas P. Saine, *The Problem of Being Modern, or the German Pursuit of Enlightenment from Leibniz to the French Revolution* (Detroit: Wayne State University Press, 1997), 144.

14   Wolff is quoted in J. B. Schneewind, *The Invention of Autonomy: A History of Modern Moral Philosophy* (Cambridge: Cambridge University Press, 1998), 439.

15   Christian Wolff, *Jus Gentium Methodo Scientifica Pertractatum*, Vol. 2, ed. J. H. Drake (Oxford: Oxford University Press, 1934), 10. The phrase "moral person" was one that Wolff adopted from the Saxon natural lawyer Samuel von Pufendorf, who introduced the term into political theory. See Ben Holland, "Pufendorf's Theory of Facultative Sovereignty: On the Configuration of the Soul of the State," *History of Political Thought* 33 (2012): 427–54.

16   Schneewind, *Autonomy*, 438.

17   Annabel Brett, *Changes of State: Nature and the Limits of the City in Early Modern Natural Law* (Princeton: Princeton University Press, 2011), 23.

18   David Armitage, *Foundations of Modern International Thought* (Cambridge: Cambridge University Press, 2013), 59–89.

19   Wolff, *Jus Gentium*, 9.

20   Wolff, *Jus Gentium*, 19.

21   Vattel, *Law of Nations*, Preface, 12.

22   Vattel, *Law of Nations*, 13.

23   These details are from the best biography of Vattel: Edouard Béguelin's *Recueil de travaux* (Neuchâtel: Attinger, 1929), 35–176.

24   On this political context, see especially Frederick G. Whelan, "Vattel's Doctrine of the State," *History of Political Thought* 9 (1988): 50–90.

25   Vattel, *Law of Nations*, Preface, 14.

26   Vattel, "Essay on the Foundation of Natural Law, and on the First Principle of the Obligation Men Find Themselves Under to Observe Laws," from *Law of Nations*, 751 (hereafter referred to as *Obligation*).

27   Vattel, *Obligation*, XXI, 753.

28   Vattel, *Obligation*, XX, 753.

29   Vattel, *Obligation*, XXIV, 754.

30   Vattel, *Obligation*, XXX, 762.

31   Vattel, *Law of Nations*, Preface, 12.

32   Vattel, *Law of Nations*, Preface, 9.

33   Vattel, *Law of Nations*, I.ii.§21, 88–89.

34   Vattel, *Law of Nations*, I.ii.§14, 86.

35   Vattel, *Law of Nations*, Preliminaries, §16, 74.

36   Vattel, *Law of Nations*, Preliminaries, §17, 75.

37   Vattel, *Law of Nations*, III.iii.§39–40, 489.

38   Ian Hunter, "Vattel's Law of Nations: Diplomatic Casuistry for the Protestant Nation," *Grotiana* 31 (2010): 108–40, 137.

39   Vattel, *Law of Nations*, IV.iii.§18, 663.

40   Vattel, *Law of Nations*, IV.iii.§20, 664.

41   Vattel, *Law of Nations*, IV.iii.§21, 664.

42   Vattel, *Law of Nations*, IV.iv.§40, 674–75.

43   Vattel, *Law of Nations*, III.xii.§188, 589.

44   Randall Lessafer, "A Schoolmaster Abolishing Homework? Vattel on
       Peacemaking and Peace Treaties" (Leuven: Tilburg Law School Working Papers
       Series, 2008), http://papers.ssrn.com/sol3/papers.cfm?abstract_id=1091170.

45   Vattel, *Law of Nations*, III.xii.§188, 589–90.

46   Stephen C. Neff, *War and the Law of Nations: A General History* (Cambridge:
       Cambridge University Press, 2005), 57.

47   Neff, *War*, 64.

48   Neff, *War*, 65.

49   Gopal Balakrishnan, *The Enemy: An Intellectual Portrait of Carl Schmitt*
       (London: Verso, 2002).

50   Carl Schmitt, *The Nomos of the Earth in the International Law of the Jus
       Publicum Europaeum*, ed. G. L. Ulmen (New York: Telos Press, 2003).

51   Schmitt, *The Concept of the Political*, ed. George Schwab (Chicago: University of
       Chicago Press, 1996), 54.

52   Schmitt, "Theory of the Partisan: Intermediate Commentary on the Concept of
       the Political," *Telos* 127: 11–78 (2004): 77–78.

53   Schmitt, *Nomos of the Earth*, 141.

54   For a detailed engagement with Schmitt on Vattel, see Isaac Nakhimovsky,
       "Carl Schmitt's Vattel and the 'Law of Nations' between Enlightenment and
       Revolution," *Grotiana* 31 (2010): 141–64.

55   Chris Brown, *Practical Judgement in International Political Theory: Selected
       Essays* (Abingdon: Routledge, 2010).

56   Voltaire and Montesquieu, contemporaries of Vattel, outlined their views
       in these works: Voltaire, *Philosophical Dictionary*, ed. Theodore Besterman
       (Harmondsworth: Penguin, 1971), 232; and the Baron de Montesquieu, *The
       Spirit of the Laws*, ed. Anne M. Cohler, Basia C. Miller and Harold S. Stone
       (Cambridge: Cambridge University Press, 1989), 512.

57   Neff, *War*, 101.

58   William E. Scheuerman, "International Law as Historical Myth," *Constellations*
       11.4: 537–550 (2004): 546–47.

59   Gabriella Slomp, "The Theory of the Partisan: Carl Schmitt's Neglected Legacy,"
       History of Political Thought 26 (2005): 503–519.

60   Jean Bethke Elshtain, *Just War Against Terror: The Burden of American Power
       in a Violent World* (New York: Basic Books, 2004). On the continuities and
       discontinuities in the global War on Terror post-Bush, see these writers:

          Richard Jackson, "Culture, Identity and Hegemony: Continuity and (the
              Lack of) Change in US Counterterrorism Policy from Bush to Obama,"
              International Politics 48 (2011): 390–411.
          Trevor McCrisken, "Ten Years On: Obama's War on Terrorism in Rhetoric
              and Practice," *International Affairs* 87 (2011): 781–801.

61   Jason Ralph, "War as an Institution of International Hierarchy: Carl Schmitt's *Theory of the Partisan* and Contemporary US Practice," *Millennium: Journal of International Studies* 39 (2010): 279–298. On inhumane tactics, see Stephen F. Eisenman, *The Abu Ghraib Effect* (London: Reaktion Books, 2007).

62   Alex Danchev, *On Art and War and Terror* (Edinburgh: Edinburgh University Press, 2009), 172–96.

CHAPTER 6

In Search for Laws above Nations: Jean-Jacques Rousseau on Perpetual Peace

René Paddags

Among the key concepts usually associated with Jean-Jacques Rousseau—such as *amour-propre*, the general will, the social contract, or the sentiment of existence—the concept of peace has a much less prominent role. Still, Rousseau did not entirely ignore the subject. He wrote two essays on peace: the awkwardly titled *Abstract of Monsieur the Abbé de Saint-Pierre's Plan for Perpetual Peace*, and the later *Judgment of the Plan for Perpetual Peace*.[1] These works, which Rousseau took up at the behest of his employer, Madame Dupin, were written in order to honour the memory of the Abbé de Saint-Pierre, who had been a favourite of Mme. Dupin. While Rousseau speaks in his own name in the *Judgment*, in the *Abstract* Rousseau takes on the persona of the Abbé in order to safely convey some of his own ideas.[2] Rousseau's ideas were influential enough to inspire Immanuel Kant to write his famous essay *On Perpetual Peace: A Philosophical Sketch*—now considered a foundational text for modern international organizations, such as the United Nations and the European Union.[3] Rousseau's influence on us extends to the ideas we hold about peace; and this makes a study of his ideas on the subject a worthwhile endeavour.

In this chapter, I elaborate on Rousseau's definition of peace, and demonstrate that Rousseau believes that a limited peace through the rule of law could prevail among people—though primarily for domestic politics, rather than as a practicable solution for international relations. I conclude with a consideration of Rousseau's understanding of peace in the context of the contemporary debate on the future of the European Union.

Rousseau's Definition of Peace

It is useful to begin with a synopsis of the frequency of Rousseau's use of the term peace (*paix*) in his best-known works: *On the Social Contract* (1762), *Emile, or On Education* (1762), and *Discourse on the Origin and Basis of Inequality Among Men* (1754).[4] The term occurs fourteen times in *Social Contract*, twenty-five times in *Emile*, and eleven times in *Discourse on Inequality*. Because the works are of considerably different lengths, we can say that it appears much more frequently in *Social Contract* than in the other two works; and somewhat more frequently in *Discourse on Inequality* than in *Emile*.

In each work, Rousseau uses peace in three distinct meanings. Most often it refers to an individual's internal state, in the sense of "peace of mind." The other two uses are political. Rousseau distinguishes between two conditions: a state of domestic peace—of unity among citizens, and absence of conflict between ruler and ruled—and a state of external peace, meaning the absence of a foreign enemy. The individual state of peace is unambiguously positive, while the other two may or may not be good (one example Rousseau gives is a domestic peace when a tyrant rules over slaves).[5] The same ambiguity can be found in his references to an external state of peace.

In a fragmentary essay often titled *The State of War*,[6] Rousseau elaborates his understanding of peace by distinguishing its characteristics from a state of war. As this is a central passage for the purposes of this discussion, it is worth quoting at length:

> Although these two words of war and peace appear exactly correlative, the second contains a much more extended signification, considering that one can interrupt and disturb the peace in several ways without proceeding as far as war. Rest, union, concord, all the ideas of benevolence and mutual affection, seem included in this sweet word, peace. It brings to the soul a plenitude of feeling that makes us love our own existence and someone else's at the same time; it represents the linkage of beings that unites them in the universal system; it has its entire extent only in the mind of God

whom nothing that exists can harm, and who wants the preservation of all the beings he has created. The constitution of this universe does not allow all the sensitive beings that compose it to cooperate at the same time for their mutual happiness.[7]

In this essay, Rousseau differentiates between two types of peace whose distinctions run parallel to the categories suggested above: a fundamental and perfect state of peace; a state of disturbed peace; and, finally, a state of war.

The first type of peace is one that Rousseau describes as the "feeling that makes us love our own existence and someone else's at the same time."[8] Peace can therefore only be truly complete for a being like God, "whom nothing that exists can harm and who wants the preservation of all the beings." People cannot attain such an exalted position, and Rousseau gives a twofold reason for this human limitation. First, individuals cannot avoid seeking their own self-preservation, and this often harms others' chances of self-preservation. This argument is based on the assumption that our fundamental drive is self-preservation, and also that the natural resources that would ensure our survival are limited.[9] Furthermore, individuals can be harmed by other beings, either human or animal, and therefore our love for others can be disturbed.

The second reason, which Rousseau only implies, is that people might be limited in their capacity to extend love to all beings. His definition of experiencing peace is feeling the love of "one's own existence and someone else's at the same time." The question of peace therefore becomes one of defining the conditions and limits of love—a question that is raised many times in Rousseau's work, particularly in his discussions of self-love and *amour-propre*. In *Discourse on Inequality*, he suggests that the fundamental experience of extended love in the state of nature is based on compassion.[10] While people may feel revulsion at seeing others suffer, compassion develops when people begin to live together in families and villages, and turns into conjugal and parental love.[11] The bonds that tie people to family and village can then be extended beyond the tribe to all members of a community. Rousseau pursues the possibility of extending love of others even further, to a whole country, through patriotism or *amour de patrie*. Further extension seems unlikely, however. While the possible limitations of *amour de patrie* are intensely debated, it is certain that Rousseau believed that this love could not be extended as far as to all mankind.[12]

The necessity of extending the love of one's own existence through *amour de patrie* only arises, however, when the unity of the state of nature has been destroyed, and the state of war has replaced the state of peace. In the state of nature, as Rousseau describes it in *Discourse on Inequality*, peace is not fundamentally disturbed.[13] Only the advances of the arts and sciences give birth to the state of war.[14] Therefore Rousseau focuses on establishing peace through the proper ordering of just political society, and *amour de patrie* is one of his instruments. This leads him to shift from the sociological conditions of peace to its political-institutional conditions.

Peace Through the Rule of Law

Rousseau addresses political-institutional conditions most famously in his *Social Contract*, setting down the "true principles of political right."[15] These are meant to overcome the difficulties whose genesis is only elaborated in *Discourse on Inequality*.[16] These difficulties can be overcome through the rule of law and the general will, as *Social Contract* provides the foundation for a "legitimate and sure rule of administration."[17] The social contract constitutes the community out of individuals, and provides laws that rule over all. The standard of legitimacy becomes the guarantor of domestic peace, as all individuals agree to abide by the rules established through the legislature. Since they are part of that legislature, they obey rules they have established themselves. Yet even if a society was able to fully follow the principles set forth in *Social Contract*, it would only succeed in creating domestic peace; the external world would remain in a state of war. Among the many conditions that prevent a legitimate political society from existing, a major one is the necessary limitation of size: the smallness needed to make direct participation possible also makes a society vulnerable to attack from outside. Rousseau refers to this fragility at the end of *Social Contract*, and emphasizes the necessity of establishing international peace.[18] In his view, this must be either a consequence of establishing a republic, or a precondition for its existence.[19]

Yet what international order would most likely lead to peace? In *Abstract of Monsieur the Abbé de Saint-Pierre's Plan for Perpetual Peace* (or *Abstract*, as I will call it henceforth), Rousseau outlines the contradiction between the state of war among nations and the civil state, and the threat the former poses to the latter. In his view, only "a form of confederative government, which, uniting Peoples by bonds similar to those which unite individuals, equally subject both of them to the authority of Laws" could remedy this situation.[20] The question of external peace turns on the same difficulty as he outlines in *Social Contract*, and demands the same solution: the rule of law.[21]

Rousseau argues that the current state of European international law "is not at all established or authorized in concert, has no general principles, and constantly changes in accordance with times and places." It is also, he claims, full of contradictory rules that "can be reconciled only by the right of the stronger."[22] This situation makes Europe war-prone. In addition to the lack of leadership and effective international law, he believes, states are not properly ruled because rights and duties, and the matter of who rules, are often confused both across borders and even within countries.[23] Neither is a balance of power a properly moderating force: "Let us not think that this much-vaunted equilibrium has been established by anyone, and that anyone has done anything on purpose to preserve it."[24] Alliances also fail to effectively address these difficulties. "I doubt that since the world has existed, three or even two great Powers have ever been seen to be well united in subjugating others without falling out over the contingents or the shares," Rousseau writes in *Abstract*, adding that such falling out soon gives "new resources to the weak by means of their disagreement."[25]

At that time, in the mid-18th century, the relative stability of what we now call the Westphalian system depended on the German Empire. Any change or disruption there would throw Europe back into struggles it experienced before the Treaty of Westphalia.[26] In contrast to Locke or Montesquieu, Rousseau argues that commerce fosters war. "Since ideas about commerce and money have produced a sort of political fanaticism, they cause the apparent interests of all Princes to change so promptly that one cannot establish any stable maxim based on their true interest," he writes. "Now everything depends on some economic system, most of them extremely bizarre, which run through the heads of Ministers."[27] In his view, none of the solutions suggested are apt to create peace in Europe; still less a peace sufficient for Rousseau's hypothetical republics.

Instead, Rousseau offers an alternative path for achieving domestic peace based largely on the model he outlined in *Social Contract*: he proposes the establishment of a European federation. In establishing the rule of law, Europe would benefit from its many historical, geographical, and religious ties, which together constitute a de facto European society. In *Social Contract*, Rousseau refers to mores as the most important law: "I speak of morals, customs, and above all opinions."[28] Still, the mere existence of these ties does not automatically lead to peace; and Rousseau concludes that "the relative state of the Powers of Europe is properly speaking a state of war."[29] (This situation resembles *Social Contract* as well as his *Second Discourse*[30] : individuals established ties among themselves that made their situation so volatile that a political solution became necessary.) With European society constantly teetering on the brink of war, it seems perfectly reasonable to put into practice any solution that exists. A treaty among European sovereigns would establish the rule of law among them, as Rousseau argues in *Abstract*:

> If I have insisted on the equal distribution of force which results from the present constitution in Europe, this was to deduce from it a consequence important for the establishment of a general association; for, in order to form a solid and durable confederation, it is necessary to put all its Members into such a mutual dependence that none might be in a position to resist all the others by itself, and that particular association which could harm the great one, may encounter sufficient obstacles in it to impede their execution: without which the confederation would be vain; and each would be really independent under an apparent subjection.[31]

The terms of the federative treaty again recall the principles Rousseau sets forth in *Social Contract*. First, every constituent party is equal to all the others; second, the aim of the treaty is the preservation of all parties; and third, each party will be maintained after the contract has been concluded. Rousseau outlines five articles that he believes would establish all necessary parts of an effective government, providing for executive, legislative, and judicial branches; these would have the power to raise taxes and troops, to determine the form of domestic government, and to establish foreign policy. The treaty also provides an important mechanism to guard against its most likely danger: unity dividing into factions. The alliance is not threatened by its constituent states, since the treaty effectively thwarts the passions—ambition and fear—that might cause the emergence of factions. [32] Rousseau gives this advice in *Social Contract*, where he writes that if factions cannot be avoided altogether, they should at least be prevented from exercising any power.[33]

Such a treaty would provide material benefits to all its participants, and to sovereigns in particular. Rousseau here questions the benefits of warfare, and emphasizes its true costs: the losses of soldiers, widespread depopulation, increase in taxes, decline of national productivity, interruption of trade, etc.[34]

Conversely, the absence of war would almost certainly make all countries wealthier.[35] Rousseau also suggests, several times, that the establishment of a European federation should replace personal sovereignty with the sovereignty of laws. A common tribunal, he claims, "will decrease none of the rights of sovereignty, but on the contrary will strengthen them." In his view, sovereigns would be guaranteed security not only "against all foreign invasions, but also … against all rebellion of his Subjects."[36] Perhaps the rule of law would render individual sovereigns much weaker than before, but it would provide a stable source of authority at the federal level. In the present situation, the authority of Germany's permanent leader "must necessarily constantly tend toward usurpation," Rousseau claims; but in a European Diet, the same would not be true. "The presidency ought to alternate … without regard to the inequality of power."[37] This political concept of an alternating presidency (known as polysynody) is further elaborated on by Rousseau in two essays, *Polysynody* and *Judgment on the Polysynody*. In the first he provides an abstract of the Abbé de Saint-Pierre's work of the same title, and in the second he gives his own opinion. This pair of works obviously parallels the two on the subject of perpetual peace.

Member countries would depend for their power on the treaty, and the institutions it establishes: the European Diet, the common Tribunal, and the presidency. Any conflict that threatens peaceful relations among European states would be dealt with by the alliance. Effectively, sovereignty would pass from individual monarchs to a community of monarchs. The treaty establishing a federation differs from the otherwise similar project of *Social Contract* by the absence of any requirement for submission under a general will. The focus of the treaty is establishing a rule of law, with the goal of ensuring the absence of violence. The social contract, on the other hand, begins with the assumption of an absence of violence, and then aims for more far-reaching goals, in accordance with the general will. The treaty ensures more freedom for states; but in Rousseau's opinion, this is insufficient to guarantee the stability of the federation over time.

The Limits of International Peace

In his *Abstract*, Rousseau speaks about the practical usefulness of setting the rule of law above sovereigns. In *Judgment*, Rousseau speaks in his own voice to criticize the plan for perpetual peace. Some commentators have therefore ignored *Abstract*, and taken Rousseau's dismissal of the "Abbé's" ideas for his true opinion.[38] However, this interpretation fails to consider Rousseau's own initiative in writing his *Abstract*, as well as his sympathetic references to it in *Emile* and *Social Contract*. He also explicitly endorses the ideas of the Abbé de Saint-Pierre in parts of his *Abstract*.[39] Even in his *Judgment*, Rousseau writes that his own work is "a solid and well-thought-out book, and it is very important that it exist."[40] He obviously considers at least parts of *Abstract* as relevant to his political philosophy, even if other parts of its argument is flawed. Rousseau does not attack the usefulness of his plan for perpetual peace in *Judgment*; he merely defends it against simple-minded criticism. He describes as a moral truth "the general and particular utility of this plan," and claims that its advantages, "both for each Prince and for each people, and for all Europe are immense, clear, undeniable."[41] But though he supports the Abbé de Saint-Pierre's moral argument, he also considers the work deeply flawed in other regards. To begin with, even the idea of bringing about peace through a book is naive. "Although the plan was very wise, the means for executing it make one feel the author's simplicity," he writes.[42] That same simplicity is "in all this honorable man's plans," he claims: "He saw rather well the effect of things if they were established, [but] judged the means for establishing them like a child."[43]

The Abbé's flawed judgment, Rousseau believes, is the result of his character. "It seems that this healthy soul, attentive only to the public good, measured the efforts it gave to things solely upon the greatness of their utility, without letting itself be rebuffed by the obstacles or ever considering personal interest."[44] This benign myopia explains his inability to see that most people are not, like himself, rational beings. Instead, they are propelled to action by forces other than reason. If people were in fact like the Abbé, Rousseau believes that the European federation would indeed exist. Rousseau goes even further and suggests that in such a case, the problem of politics would not exist either—because if individuals were purely rational, peace would establish itself naturally. He describes the Abbé's work as "useless for producing [peace], and superfluous for preserving it," adding that "some impatient Reader will say it is a vain speculation."[45] In reality, mankind is constantly in a state of conflict; and the Abbé seems incapable of understanding the reason for war's existence.

Rousseau himself claims to view people in a realistic light.[46] He does not, he says, assume individuals "to be as they ought to be, good, generous, disinterested, and loving the public good out of humanity; but as they are, unjust, greedy, and preferring their self-interest to everything."[47] But these assumptions too are unrealistic, since Rousseau admits in his *Abstract* that he makes another important assumption: that people have "sufficient reason to see what is useful to them, and enough courage to bring about their own happiness. Thus, if, in spite of all of this, this Plan remains unexecuted, it is not because it is chimerical; it is because men are insane, and because it is a sort of folly to be wise in the midst of fools." In other words, his plan of perpetual peace falters because of the powerlessness of reason.[48]

The fact that people are driven by their passions—particularly the passion of *amour-propre*—rather than by wisdom, makes them blind to their real interest: peace under the rule of law. Instead, Rousseau says, they chase the false advantage of absolute independence.[49] In *Judgment*, he draws attention to the flawed assumption he had only hinted at in *Abstract*:

> It is the great punishment of the excess of *amour-propre* always to have recourse to means that deceive it [to see their advantage]; and the very ardour of the passions is almost always what diverts them from their true goal. Let us distinguish, then, in politics as in morality, real interest from apparent interest.[50]

The critique of assuming people to be reasonable was not only anticipated at the end of *Abstract*; Rousseau also highlighted it in the only passage that explicitly speaks in his own voice.

> I would not dare respond along with the Abbé de Saint-Pierre: That the genuine glory of Princes consists in procuring the public utility, and their Subjects' happiness; that all their interests are subordinate to their reputation; and that the reputation that one acquires among the wise is measured by the good one does for men; that, since perpetual Peace is the greatest undertaking that has ever been done, it is the most capable of covering its Author with immortal glory; that, since this same undertaking is also the most useful for Peoples, it is also the most honourable for Sovereigns; and finally that the surest way to distinguish oneself in the crowd of Kings is to work for the public happiness.[51]

In *Judgment*, Rousseau analyzes the interests that truly drive the actions of monarchs—a list that acts as a scathing critique of the Abbé's assumptions about their rationality. Monarchs do not seek the common good, Rousseau says, or to be useful to their people, or to increase their subjects' happiness; even their reputation is not their foremost concern, especially not their reputation for wisdom Consequently they do not look for glory or seek to distinguish themselves by working for the public benefit on such a goal as perpetual peace. Instead, he writes, monarchs are interested in only two objects: "extending their dominion abroad, and rendering it more absolute at home."[52] Under such assumptions, they would obviously never support the proposal for peace.

Least obvious from *Abstract* is Rousseau's opinion that a European federation based on the rule of law would interfere with a sovereign's privileges, such as the right to wage war.

> For one feels very well that the government of each State is no less settled by the European Diet than its boundaries are, that one cannot guarantee Princes against the revolts of subjects without guaranteeing the subjects against the Tyranny of the Princes at the same time, and that otherwise the institution could not continue to exist.[53]

While Rousseau makes a very similar argument in *Abstract*, it appears that a European federation would in fact shield monarchs from possible rebellion.[54] He assures his readers that "princes will not be any less absolute for [the federation], and their Crown will be more certain for it."[55] From *Judgment* it becomes clear that this argument is incomplete and misleading. The truth is that the European federation could not guarantee its security, and the performance of the treaty, if monarchs abused their subjects. This could cause a civil war, which could then spread to other parts of the federation and threaten its external defences of the federation—thereby losing the benefits of the peace. In order to be effective, a federation must involve a true and irrevocable transfer of sovereignty, from the national to the supranational level. Securing sovereignty, not securing monarchy, was Rousseau's goal in his description of the rotating presidency, in the sense of *Social Contract*:

> Moreover, there is a great deal of difference between depending on someone else, or only on a Body of which one is a member and of which each is the leader in his turn; for in this latter case one does nothing but secure one's freedom by the pledges one gives for it; it would be alienated in the hands of a master, but it is strengthened in those of Associates.[56]

In a European federation, members would retain their sovereignty just as individuals retain their freedom—though the civil liberty they enjoy is different from natural freedom.[57] The same would hold for a country entering into a federation.

Rousseau's tongue may be in his cheek when he asks, in *Abstract*, whether a sovereign—"limited [in] his dearest plans"—would ever "without indignation put up with the mere idea of seeing himself forced to be just, not only with Foreigners, but even with his own subjects."[58] This indicates another reason why the European federation could not come about: it is the essence of a sovereign to determine justice, and none would willingly conform to someone else's version of it. A federation, able to force its subordinate parts to submit to its notions of justice, would be the only effective sovereign.

In addition to critiquing the Abbé's misjudgment of human self-interest, and foreseeing the resistance of sovereigns, Rousseau also suggests that a federation's institutions would also not attain their goals—at least not in the long run. In *Abstract*, Rousseau had suggested that the establishment of the rule of law also establishes an executive power capable of enforcing those laws. "As soon as there is a society, a compulsory force is necessary, which orders and concerts its Members' movements, in order to give the common interests reciprocal engagements the solidity they cannot have by themselves."[59] Especially in times of military crisis, this force must be led by an effective representative of the federation. Yet Rousseau doubts that a polysynody—that is, a rotating presidency—will provide the necessary leadership for a stable government. In *Abstract* and *Polysynody*, Rousseau seems to suggest that a rotating presidency would achieve its end. But in *Judgment of the Polysynody*, he admits to not believing "that such an administration could last long without abuses."[60] In his assessment, the polysynody would be unable to adequately protect the federation against the influence of internal factions, and of alliances hostile to its intention of peace.

Finally, in his *Judgment*, Rousseau addresses the question of founding a European federation. Having dismissed the Abbé as naive for believing in the power of a book to persuade, he suggests a different manner for creating a federation. In *Judgment*, Rousseau uses about half of the essay to refute the Abbé's claim that Henry IV had almost established a European federation through peaceful means. Instead, Rousseau portrays the English king as a master politician who—if he had lived longer—might in fact have united the continent through a combination of diplomatic skill and force. In this view, the best hope for a European federation would be through the actions of such a founder-statesman. In contrast, Rousseau claims, the Abbé's peace would most likely have to be achieved by means of a devastating war. Would the goal be worth all those lives? "Let us admire such a fine plan, but console ourselves for not seeing it executed; for that cannot be done except by means that are violent and formidable to humanity."[61]

Since Rousseau rejects the Abbé's ideas on human rationality, shows the impossibility of a voluntary founding of the federation, critiques its institutions, and even concludes that the dream itself is not entirely harmless, one has to wonder why Rousseau took up his pen at all to abridge the Abbé's work, and firmly maintained that "it is important that it exist." The solution seems to lie in *Abstract*'s main argument, addressing the political problem of establishing a rule of law in the context of international relations. Even though Thomas Hobbes claimed that the rule of law is usually considered to be inoperative in that area, Rousseau shows that it can in fact be established.[62] His assertion also counters Grotius's claim that international relations are subject to natural laws. If, instead of natural laws or the rule of the stronger, the rule of law could be extended to international relations, then the actions of monarchs would become less inevitable and more questionable. Such a change would serve multiple purposes. First, it would create the hope that progress in international relations is possible. Second, it would demonstrate that societies are not inevitably founded by force, but can be based on contracts in accordance with human nature. Third, it would weaken the legitimacy of monarchs, as well as their freedom to conduct foreign policy in pursuit of selfish goals. All these would serve to advance Rousseau's advocacy of a European federation, and his goal of establishing a just domestic order through the moulding of public opinion of international relations.

Another important point about *Abstract* is that its ideas are written for ordinary educated people, especially women—in other words, people far removed from positions of authority and influence. Rousseau evidently believes that it would be foolish to address a book like *Abstract* to those currently in power, and aims for a change in the opinion of the people regarding war, peace, and the potential benefit of limiting the power of monarchs. His work is also a gentle warning to all those thinkers who, like the Abbé de Saint-Pierre, harbour unrealistic hopes for world peace. A European federation, if it could exist, would have to come into being through force and fraud—so instead of world peace, believers in reason are more likely to reap war and tyranny.

In all his essays, Rousseau claimed to encapsulate the work's central argument in the epigraph he chose for it. For *Abstract* he used a passage by the Roman poet Lucan, taken from his *Pharsalia*: "May the human race consult with itself, all weapons being laid down, and in turn may peoples all love one another."[63] Lucan's yearning call for peace, however, was not heeded by Julius Caesar, whose ambition could be thwarted or redirected but never eliminated. Perhaps we can assume that Rousseau was not only pointing to the main flaw in the Abbé's proposal, but also flagging his intention to criticize the monarchies of his days.

Rousseau's Judgment of the European Union

Because of his influence on Immanuel Kant, Rousseau is often regarded as one of the founding fathers of the European Union—a reputation he gained primarily due to his *Abstract*. Yet Rousseau's own later criticism of *Abstract* raises the question whether his reputation is truly deserved. If he could assess today's European Union, he would likely argue that it both operates on false principles, and lacks the power to rule effectively. He might also point out that the Union is unlikely ever to be a true sovereign power, because its constituent parts lack the will to ever fully relinquish their own authorities. In other words, a proper founding of a European federation, as Rousseau conceived it, has not yet occurred. But unlike many modern believers in the European Union, Rousseau would not consider its failure a tragedy but a blessing.[64]

There are several reasons for this. First, all the institutions of today's Union stop short of the real transfer of sovereignty necessary to the institutions of the federation for a true federation—which Rousseau clearly considers the only true and sufficient guarantee of the treaty's effectiveness. In the European Union, this would imply control of foreign relations; the power to raise taxes; a federal law superior to national law; and, most importantly, a monopoly on the use of force. The present European Union lacks most of these decisive powers, such as the power to raise money and use force—both of which remain exclusively in the hands of individual governments. It should also be able to prevent any secession by force. Instead, the Treaty of Lisbon permits countries to secede after negotiating a withdrawal treaty.[65]

Because of this incomplete transfer of sovereignty, and the resulting absence of the rule of law, Rousseau would claim that the European Union remains merely an alliance based on international law, rather than a true federation. It is founded not on any notion of justice, but rather on the principles of commerce, balance of power, and public right—which is to say, on wealth, fear, and interest, none of which were sufficient for the attainment of peace when Rousseau first discussed them in *Abstract*. Even worse, in Rousseau's eyes, would be the Union's current emphasis on the pursuit of wealth and luxury. This pursuit, instead of creating peace, only makes war even more likely, as the gap between the haves and the have-nots grows ever larger, exaggerating the *amour-propre* of both alike. Religion plays a part as well. Rousseau's original conception was of a federation based on a Christian society; but in the European Union this common bond is weakened by secularism, immigration, and communism.

Finally, we may ask: is Rousseau's criticism of a European federation blunted by the change in Europe from monarchies to democracies? In *Judgment*, Rousseau refers to the political benefits that monarchs derive from war. In his view, war, conquests, and "the progression of Despotism mutually reinforce each other."[66] Since modern republics do not derive the same advantages from war as monarchs, in theory they should be more open to a federation. And indeed, history shows that republics hardly ever, if at all, wage war against one another.[67]

That does not mean, though, that republics are any more willing than monarchies to transfer their sovereignty. Rousseau assumes that republics are necessarily smaller than monarchies, and hence more vulnerable to international threats—giving them an inherent interest in protecting themselves against foreign states.[68] Yet as Rousseau also makes clear, federation would deprive them of their sovereignty; and republics might hesitate to submit to an authority that might deprive them of their republican way of life. They are moved by mores, the most important law, which leads them to consider their land, their language, and their common history as the foundation of their state. Their *amour de patrie* is based on these factors.[69] These primordial origins of European peoples make it exceedingly difficult to imagine a unity based on constitutional principles, which could manifest itself in a federation. This means that a European republican state is as unlikely to relinquish its power to a supra-national entity as a monarch would be. In Rousseau's view, establishing a federation would require a founder-legislator who would deprive members of their sovereignty, give European states new laws, and then relinquish power to the people again.[70]

In the early years of the eurozone crisis of 2010, it was repeatedly asserted that the euro should not be allowed to fail because it would jeopardize the prevailing peace among European countries.[71] Yet Rousseau might argue that the Union is an imperfect instrument for securing peace, since it is not a true federation under the rule of law. Even though constituted by democracies in its current form, it is still dedicated to the pursuit of luxury rather than the pursuit of equality. Perhaps, after all, a return to the old system of nation-states, with its inherent risk of war, is preferable to the grave danger of a new economic tyranny. Despite Rousseau's best efforts, this unfortunately seems to be the best we can attain.

Notes

1   Hereafter referred to as *Abstract* and *Judgment*. I have used the following English edition of Rousseau's works: Jean-Jacques Rousseau, *The Plan for Perpetual Peace: On the Government of Poland, and Other Writings on History and Politics*, trans. Christopher Kelly and Judith R. Bush, ed. Christopher Kelly, *The Collected Writings of Rousseau*, Vol. 11, ed. Roger D. Masters and Christopher Kelly (Hanover: Dartmouth College Press, 2005), hereafter cited as *Perpetual Peace*.

2   Jean-Jacques Rousseau, *The Confessions and Correspondence, Including the Letters to Malesherbes*, trans. Christopher Kelly, ed. Christopher Kelly, Roger D. Masters, and Peter G. Stillman, *The Collected Writings of Rousseau*, Vol. 5, ed. Roger D. Masters and Christopher Kelly (Hanover: Dartmouth College Press, 1995), hereafter cited as Rousseau, *Confessions*.

3   Immanuel Kant, "Idee zu einer allgemeinen Geschichte in weltbürgerlicher Absicht"; and also "Über den Gemeinspruch: Das mag in der Theorie richtig sein, taugt aber nicht für die Praxis." Both from *Gesammelte Werke Akademie Ausgabe: Abhandlungen nach 1781* VIII (Berlin: De Gruyter, 1971), 313.

4   I have used the following editions of Rousseau's works:

  Jean-Jacques Rousseau, *Social Contract, Discourse on the Virtue most Necessary for a Hero, Political Fragments, and Geneva Manuscript*, trans. Judith R. Bush, Roger D. Masters, and Christopher Kelly, ed. Roger D. Masters and Christopher Kelly, *The Collected Writings of Rousseau*, Vol. 4, ed. Roger D. Masters and Christopher Kelly (Hanover: Dartmouth College Press, 1994).

  Jean-Jacques Rousseau, *Discourse on the Origins of Inequality (Second Discourse), Polemics, and Political Economy*, trans. Judith R. Bush, Roger D. Masters, Christopher Kelly, and Terence Marshall, ed. Roger D. Masters and Christopher Kelly, *The Collected Writings of Rousseau*, Vol. 3, ed. Roger D. Masters and Christopher Kelly (Hanover: Dartmouth College Press, 1992).

  Jean-Jacques Rousseau, *Emile, or On Education*, trans. Allan Bloom (New York: Basic Books, 1979).

  These three works are cited, respectively, as *Social Contract*, *Second Discourse*, and *Emile*.

5   Rousseau, *Perpetual Peace*, 61.

6   This fragment, which has no title its own, is commonly referred to as "The State of War." It is included in *Perpetual Peace*, 61–73.

7   Rousseau, *Social Contract*, 70–71.

8   Rousseau, *Social Contract*, 70–71.

9   Rousseau, *Second Discourse*, 14.

10   Rousseau, *Second Discourse*, 15, 37.

11   *Second Discourse*, 47. Rousseau believes that the development of the emotions was made possible by the development of primitive technology, which allowed the strongest early humans to settle in huts. Contrast this with Aristotle, who argues that households are natural because of the mutual attraction of men and women. Rousseau does not ascribe to mankind a desire to leave someone behind like oneself. Aristotle, *Politics*, trans. Carnes Lord (Chicago: University of Chicago Press, 1984), 1252a29.

12   Rousseau, *Emile*, 253. Rousseau believes that while love of the self, and its extension to spouse and children, is a natural sentiment, its extension to fellow citizens is artificial and requires further deliberation.

13   Victor Gourevitch, "Rousseau's Pure State of Nature," *Interpretation* 16.1 (1988): 36; and Rousseau, *Second Discourse*, 52–55.

14   Rousseau, *Second Discourse*, 49. Compare Arthur M. Melzer, *The Natural Goodness of Man: On the System of Rousseau's Thought* (Chicago: University of Chicago Press, 1990), Ch. 3.

15   Rousseau, *Social Contract*, IV.9.

16   See Hilail Gildin, *Rousseau's Social Contract: The Design of the Argument* (Chicago: University of Chicago Press, 1983), 2.

17   Rousseau, *Social Contract*, Intro.

18   The *Social Contract*'s epigraph, *"foederis aequas Dicamus leges"* ("in an equitable federation we will make laws," taken from Virgil's *Aeneid*) refers to the unfulfilled desire to be ruled by law instead of force.

19   Olaf Asbach, *Die Zähmung der Leviathane: Die Idee einer Rechtsordnung zwischen Staaten bei Abbé de Saint-Pierre and Jean-Jacques Rousseau* (Berlin: Akademie Verlag, 2002), IV.2.

20   Rousseau, *Perpetual Peace*, 28.

21   As Leah Bradshaw points out in Chapter 7 of this volume ("Kant, Cosmopolitan Right, and the Prospects for Global Peace"), Immanuel Kant claims to have found in cosmopolitan right a solution to this problem of setting law above force.

22   Rousseau, *Perpetual Peace*, 32. Also, as outlined by Ben Holland in Chapter 5 of this volume ("Vattel on Morally Non-Discriminatory Peace"), Emer de Vattel is equally sceptical about the strength of the law of nations to bring about peace.

23   Rousseau, *Perpetual Peace*, 32–33.

24   Rousseau, *Perpetual Peace*, 33.

25   Rousseau, *Perpetual Peace*, 34.

26   Rousseau, *Perpetual Peace*, 34–35.

27   Rousseau, *Perpetual Peace*, 35. As well, in Chapter 5 of this volume ("John Locke's Liberal Path to Peace"), Jeffrey Sikkenga refers to "peaceful extra-curriculars," and quotes Locke as advocating the study of "merchant's accounts." Sikkenga also summarizes the beneficial effects of Lockean education.

28   Rousseau, *Social Contract*, II.12.

29   Rousseau, *Perpetual Peace*, 32.

30   Rousseau, *Social Contract*, I.6, and Rousseau, *Second Discourse*, 178–79.

31   Rousseau, *Perpetual Peace*, 35–36.

32   Rousseau, *Perpetual Peace*, 40.

33   Rousseau, *Social Contract*, II.3.4, FN.

34   Rousseau's view resembles here the "neo-Machiavellian tradition" of an Andrew Fletcher of Saltoun against the comparative advantage of David Ricardo. The former favours confederations in order to secure republican independence, as well as gains from trade. See István Hont, *Jealousy of Trade: International Competition and the Nation-State in Historical Perspective* (Cambridge, MA: Harvard University Press, 2005), 261–63.

35   This argument has since been found in many different variations, most famously in Norman Angell, *The Great Illusion: A Study of the Relation of Military Power to National Advantage* (New York: G.P. Putnam's Sons, 1910). Angell argued that from his time on, war would be irrational because it would be too costly.

36   Rousseau, *The Perpetual Peace*, 44. Also see the "deprivations" the sovereigns will "suffer" by being subject to the rule of law.

37   *Perpetual Peace*, 45.

38   See Pierre Hassner, who mentions Voltaire, Madison, Kant, and Kenneth Waltz. Pierre Hassner, "Rousseau and the Theory and Practice of International Relations," *The Legacy of Rousseau*, ed. Clifford Orwin and Nathan Tarcov (Chicago: University of Chicago Press, 1997), 205.

39   Rousseau, *Social Contract*, IV.9; see also *Emile*, 466–67.

40   Rousseau, *Perpetual Peace*, 53.

41   Rousseau, *Perpetual Peace*, 53.

42   Rousseau, *Perpetual Peace*, 56.

43   Rousseau, *Perpetual Peace*, 57.

44   Rousseau, *Perpetual Peace*, 53.

45   Rousseau, *Perpetual Peace*, 53.

46   Rousseau, *Social Contract*, I. Intro; also *Perpetual Peace*, 49.

47   Rousseau, *Perpetual Peace*, 49.

48   Rousseau's critique of the Abbé de Saint-Pierre's *Perpetual Peace* is at the same time a critique of the enlightenment's faith in reason. As Leah Bradshaw remarks, Kant later tries to leave politics behind by introducing cosmopolitan right.

49   As Laurie M. Johnson points out in Chapter 3 of this volume ("Thomas Hobbes on the Path to Peace"), Rousseau agrees with Hobbes on this point, if Hobbes's concept of honour is equivalent to Rousseau's *amour-propre*.

50   Rousseau, *Perpetual Peace*, 54.

51   Rousseau, *Perpetual Peace*, 42.

52   Rousseau, *Perpetual Peace*, 54.

53   Rousseau, *Perpetual Peace*, 54.

54   Rousseau, *Perpetual Peace*, 44.

55   Rousseau, *Perpetual Peace*, 44.

56   Rousseau, *Perpetual Peace*, 54.

57   Gildin, *Rousseau's Social Contract*, 9, 30–31.

58   Rousseau, *Perpetual Peace*, 54.

59   Rousseau, *Perpetual Peace*, 33. This parallels Rousseau's argument in the *Social Contract*, II.6.2.

60   Rousseau, *Perpetual Peace*, 98.

61   Rousseau, *Perpetual Peace*, 60.

62   As per Johnson, note Rousseau's surprising agreement with Hobbes on alliances, and the role played by natural law in international relations.

63   Rousseau, *Perpetual Peace*, 27.

64   George Soros, "The Tragedy of the European Union and How to Resolve It," *New York Review of Books* (September 27, 2007). For a related analysis, see Hassner, "Rousseau and the Theory and Practice of International Relations," 215–18.

65   European Union, "Treaty of Lisbon," Consolidated Versions of the Treaty on European Union and The Treaty on the Functioning of the European Union (Luxembourg: Publications Office of the European Union, 2007), Article 50.

66   Rousseau, *Perpetual Peace*, 54.

67   Michael Doyle, "Kant, Liberal Legacies, and Foreign Affairs," *Philosophy and Public Affairs*, 12.3 (1983).

68   In Rousseau's defence, the feasibility of a large republic was proved after his lifetime. Compare Alexander Hamilton, John Jay, and James Madison, *The Federalist Papers* (New York: Random House, 2000), 10.

69   A different model is suggested by the United States, and to some extent by France, which take as their foundation the political principles of the state. See Liah Greenfeld, *Nationalism: Five Roads to Modernity* (Cambridge: Harvard University Press, 1992).

70   As Jeffrey Sikkenga makes clear, Locke would agree with Rousseau that a European federation first requires the proper education of its citizens.

71   Three exemplary reactions by the French and German governments, as well as a key reaction by the former presiding judge of the German Constitutional Court:

Paul Kirchhof, "Verfassungsnot!" FAZ, (July 12, 2012), http://www.faz.net/
    aktuell/feuilleton/debatten/europas-zukunft/paul-kirchhof-zur-krise-der
    -eu-verfassungsnot-11817188.html.
Angela Merkel, "Regierungserklärung von Angela Merkel zum
    Europäischen Rat und zum Eurogipfel," Presse und Informationsamt der
    Bundesregierung (October 26, 2011), http://www.bundeskanzlerin.de/
    ContentArchiv/DE/Archiv17/Regierungserklaerung/2011/2011-10-27
    -merkel-eu-gipfel.html.
Nicholas Sarkozy, "Discours du Président de la République à Toulon," Élysée,
    (December 1, 2011), http://www.archives.elysee.fr/president/les-actualites/
    discours/2011/discours-du-president-de-la-republique-a-toulon.12553
    .html.

CHAPTER 7

Kant, Cosmopolitan Right, and the Prospects for Global Peace

Leah Bradshaw

"Give peace a chance" is not a mantra shared by all, and certainly not by most canonical figures in the tradition of political thought. In many of the formative texts of the Western tradition, peace is given nary a mention. Arguably the best practicable state in Plato's *Republic* is the *timocracy*, the "regime that loves honour," a highly disciplined and war-inclined *polis* that resists the complacent enjoyments of peacetime, such as commerce, consumption, and domesticity.[1] In Aristotle's characterization of the best regime, he remarks that "all concerns [with] a view to war are to be regarded as noble."[2] Machiavelli famously proclaimed that a prince "must not have any other object nor any other thought, nor must he adopt anything as his art but war, its institutions, and its discipline."[3] And perhaps most notoriously, Hobbes grounded his innovative notion of political contract in the ontological premise that man is by nature a creature at war.

There is, however, an alternative tradition in Western thought that resists the call to war, and proclaims the higher calling of peace—though it generally resides in the religious sphere rather than in the unruly world of politics. Not until the Enlightenment do we find compelling accounts of the goal of peace in the works of political thinkers. In the Two Worlds doctrine of Christianity—the kingdom of God and the kingdom of man—

we find the promise of peace only in an otherworldly transcendence of the sinful and conflictual temporal order. Christians are familiar with the Bible's proclamation of faith in the world to come: "The peace of God, which passeth all understanding, shall keep your hearts and minds through Jesus Christ."[4] For centuries, because of those two kingdoms, Christian philosophers such as St. Augustine had no trouble defending peace while simultaneously defending the concept of "just war." Because the kingdom of God is universal and homogeneous, and collapses all political and state identities into the holistic embrace of the believer, there can only be peace for the faithful after death unites them with God.

A much later thinker, Hannah Arendt, captures well the tension between the "peace that passeth all understanding" and the active turbulence of our worldly activities. As Diane Enns points out in Chapter 12 of this volume, Arendt parallels the Christian promise of salvation with earlier (Greek) notions of the subordination of political activity to the higher goals of philosophical contemplation; and she identifies the highest reaches of both philosophy and faith with a kind of quietude, or stillness. "Just as war takes place for the sake of peace, thus every kind of activity, even the processes of mere thought, must culminate in the absolute quiet of contemplation," Arendt writes. "Truth, be it the ancient truth of Being or the Christian truth of the living God, can reveal itself only in complete human stillness."[5] To be at peace is to be beyond politics—either withdrawn into the stillness of philosophical contemplation, or dead and saved in the kingdom of God. As we know, Arendt sought to rescue the nobility of politics from what she regarded as the "tyranny" of the philosophical and religious traditions of the West. But my task here is different: instead, I explore how in the modern West, the stillness of peace was transformed into a political project.

What has changed is that the two kingdoms have collapsed into one: the worldly and the immanent. There are still faithful believers in the kingdom of God and the kingdom of man, and there are still a few philosophers who see themselves as set apart from the futile business of politics. But we now live in an age largely governed by the Enlightenment goals of universal rights, equality of all people in the here and now, and (in many quarters) the hope for peace on earth. I will make a sweeping claim: that the prospects for world peace cannot be contemplated without recourse to the stillness and universality of Hannah Arendt's characterization. To make a case for peace in the world is necessarily to abrogate difference, honour, and frankly, anything worth fighting for. This is captured in the humanistic Baha'i faith's declaration in *The Promise of World Peace*, directed to "the peoples of the world." As it proclaims, "the Great Peace toward which people of good will throughout the centuries have inclined their hearts ... is now at long last within the reach of nations. For the first time in history, it is possible for everyone to view the entire planet, with all its myriad diversified peoples, in one perspective. World peace is not only possible but inevitable."[6]

The Baha'is possibly demonstrate greater faith in the prospects for world peace than most political thinkers would generally exhibit; but their invocation of the single goal of pacifying the whole planet, rather than pursuing the multiple goals of myriad states, is a strong thrust of modern thought. Many contemporary political theorists now argue that state sovereignty is an outmoded idea, and that we inhabit a common world in which the erosion of state boundaries can, and should, lead us to a global universality and peace.[7] All such theorists embrace what I would call a "transpolitical" understanding of justice: one that reaches beyond the defence of state-centric identity for universal claims about the rights and entitlements of individuals. These cosmopolitan thinkers all start with assumptions about the fundamental equality and autonomy of human beings; and all wrestle with the obvious tensions between the goals of global peace, equality, and universal justice, and the opposing claims of state sovereignty, ethnic and racial identity, and religious fundamentalism.

How do we establish secular, universal claims for world peace in a world fractured by difference and conflict? If peace is a practical goal, and not just a utopian thought, is there any way to bring together the stillness of peace with the antinomy of war? To my mind, the most ambitious thinker to attempt this was Immanuel Kant, the 18th-century philosopher who waded carefully through this conflict with a realistic eye on political differences, combined with an unwavering faith in world peace. That does not necessarily mean that Kant was successful in his endeavour, as I will discuss later; but for me, he is still the most significant theorist of a realistic peace project.

In the 18th century, Kant formulated the Enlightenment notion of cosmopolitanism; and he is, I believe, the most powerful exponent of right in the modern political tradition. Universal right is the immanent, worldly equivalent of the Christian notion of the equality of all souls before God. Rights belong to everyone, regardless of kinship, nationality, race, or language. Kant was the first important thinker in the Western tradition to argue that perpetual peace is a realistic goal toward which we ought to strive; and that goal is contingent on the expansion of the principles of right. For Kant, rights are universal because they defend the fundamental autonomy of all people, and they can be known by everyone who is rational. In his view we all have a duty to uphold right, once we recognize that our own freedom has to be commensurate with the freedom of others.

Like all theorists of right, Kant emphasizes the concept of protecting people's right to make their own choices, and to be self-determining agents. This emphasis on reasonable choice is central to his understanding of what is most important about individuals, and what is required to create just political institutions. He defines right as "the sum total of those conditions within which the will of one person can be reconciled with the will of another in accordance with a universal law of freedom."[8] The protection of right relies on our recognition of the universal law that, in our actions toward others, our free will must coexist with everyone else's.

Kant had no intention, he stressed, "to teach virtue, but only to state what is *right*."[9] He emphasized the political institutions that guard external actions, since there is no right without a state to guarantee it. The natural condition, Kant affirms, is one "devoid of justice," because in any dispute over right, there is no "competent judge" to resolve the argument. Any contract between individuals must be provisional "until it has been sanctioned by a public law."[10] The only legitimate form of state, he believes, is the republican model that includes a division of powers among the legislative, executive, and judicial branches. The people who unite together in such a state have three rightful attributes that are "inseparable from the nature of a citizen." These are the lawful freedom to obey only those laws to which one has given consent; the recognition of civil equality among all citizens; and the preservation of an independence of will that accords with each person's "rights and powers as a member of the commonwealth."[11]

These attributes tie the protection of right irrevocably to the political institutions of the state: no state, no right. Kant is not a natural rights theorist, like John Locke; for him, right is the willed and institutionalized framework of citizenship. In such a framework, people have not "sacrificed a part of their inborn external freedom for a specific purpose"; rather, they have "completely abandoned their wild and lawless freedom, in order to find their entire and undiminished freedom in a state of lawful dependence"— that is, in a state of right. As Kant points out, "this dependence is created by their own legislative will."[12]

Kant further tells us that all the nations of the world "may unite for the purpose of creating universal laws to regulate the intercourse they have with one another," and this unity he terms cosmopolitanism.[13] This view creates something of a conundrum, however: while he holds that rights are universal, and can be embraced by reason, they can be upheld only by political institutions. The idea of right is universal; but its practical enforcement requires regulating by law, and backing up by force. We need particular states to enforce universal laws. When Kant anticipated that—despite the great oceans that divide the peoples of the world—trade and mobility would increase, he accurately foresaw (in the mid-18th century) the commercial realities of our modern age. Presciently, he declared that cosmopolitanism would demand an attitude of hospitality that would allow the citizens of the world to enter other countries, and expect to be welcomed by them. That was the limit Kant set to cosmopolitanism, however: its universal laws govern hospitality, but do not confer the right to settle on foreign land.

In fact, Kant identifies cosmopolitan right as something entirely separate from international right. The latter consists of the legally binding treaties among sovereign states, principally for regulating (and, Kant hopes, eventually for eliminating) war. "The idea of a world republic cannot be realized,"[14] he writes. The concept seems to him impossible for two reasons: because independent states do not wish to forfeit their sovereignty, and (more practically) because the extension of dominion over the whole world is more likely to induce tyranny than right. As Kant comments, "nature wisely separates the nations" by differences both linguistic and cultural. Kant does not appear to regard these differences as being as intrinsically important as his own principles of right, but he does regard them as useful in containing states within manageable borders. He hopes that international agreements among states will generate a peace "created and guaranteed by equilibrium of forces and a most vigorous rivalry"—a balance he regards as far preferable to the state of "universal despotism which saps all man's energies and ends in the graveyard of freedom."[15]

In his specific articles for peace among states, Kant recommends that every state in the world should have a republican civil constitution; and he prohibits the practice of strong states acquiring weaker ones by "inheritance, exchange, purchase, or gift." He also proposes to abolish standing armies, prohibit foreign national debt, and condemn any state that interferes "in the constitution and government of another."[16] In the larger view, Kant concedes that the only rational way for states to rise above the "lawless condition of pure warfare" would be for them to form an international state, "which would necessarily grow until it embraced all the peoples of the earth." But this is not the will of nations, he acknowledges, and so they must work with the articles of peace toward an "enduring and expanding federation likely to prevent war."[17]

For Kant, the idea of cosmopolitanism is not intended to be implemented in any formal manner (beyond the laws governing hospitality). He anticipates a time when all "the peoples of the earth have entered in varying degrees into a universal community, and it has developed to the point where a violation of rights in one part of the world is felt everywhere. The idea of a cosmopolitan right is therefore not fantastic and overstrained; it is a necessary complement to the unwritten code of political and international right, transforming it into a universal right of humanity."[18] With regard to perpetual peace, Kant warns that "we have a duty to act in accordance with such an end, even if there is not the slightest probability of its realization, provided that there is no means of demonstrating that it cannot be realized either."[19] This is one of Kant's notoriously cryptic statements. How can people have a duty to act in accordance with an end, when there is little probability of its realization?

Two threads in Kant's arguments support this stubborn hope. First, Kant is a deontological thinker, meaning that principles of right are neither derived from nor challenged by experience. In his essay on theory and practice, he raises the possibility that "history may well give rise to endless doubts about my hopes, and if these doubts could be proved, they might persuade me to desist from an apparently futile task." But Kant is unwavering. "So long as [these doubts] do not have the force of certainty, I cannot exchange my duty (as a *liquidum*) for a rule of expediency which says that I ought not to attempt the impracticable."[20] He insists that we have a present duty to work toward peace, albeit within the limits of present practicality, and of respect for the legitimacy of state autonomy. "It is quite irrelevant," Kant says, "whether any empirical evidence suggests that these plans [for peace] which are founded only on hope, may be unsuccessful."[21]

A second thread worth noting is his faith in progress: Kant believes that we are getting better. "In our age, as compared with all previous ages, the human race has made considerable moral progress, and short-term hindrances prove nothing to the contrary," he points out. Most of history may have been a tale of war, conflict, and division, but in Kant's reading this has been a kind of dialectical (and necessary) path toward enlightenment.

Not easily deterred from his goals, Kant even affirms that contemporary laments about decadence or decline are typical indicators of progress: they mean that people are more enlightened and self-aware. If there are setbacks in the march of civilization, we can pause and self-correct. Kant's faith in progress is so firm, that he calls it a "criminal" act for one generation to bind future generations to any kind of contractual arrangement.[22]

So the picture Kant gives us is one of universal rights, known by reason, that champion individual autonomy above all other ends. These rights are not "natural," but rather the products of an enlightened consciousness on the part of a progressive species that has become capable of erecting self-governing institutions that recognize the primacy of right. Republican institutions are the only just form of political organization because they protect the sovereignty of right. Citizenship in discrete states is preferable to a world constitution (despite the universal nature of rights), because of the practical problems of monitoring rights, and also because of the lively rivalry among states that keeps them "vigorous" in their defence of freedom. International federations of states are to be encouraged as a way of deflecting conflict and war. Cosmopolitan right is the unwritten code that complements political and international rights—one that is the most universal, yet also the most abstract. Perpetual peace is our ultimate goal, but one that has to be embraced and worked toward, in a realistic assessment of our present condition. Even if peace "were forever to remain a pious hope, we should still not be deceiving ourselves if we made it our maxim to work unceasingly towards it, for it is our duty to do so."[23]

What is most interesting to me about Kant is that he seems to be trying to stay true to the distinction between philosophy and politics that has been a brake on tyranny ever since Socrates, two thousand years ago, acknowledged the tension between his loyalty to truth and his loyalty to the Athenian polis. In his *Apology*, I see Socrates' decision to accept the death penalty inflicted on him by his fellow citizens as an acknowledgement that while he found the decision unjust, he accepted the fact that he had implicitly agreed to live and die by the laws of the polis. He told the assembly that he has always been a good citizen, and would not defy the democratic ethos that had nurtured him.[24] This acceptance did not negate Socrates' view of the higher claim of truth; it merely highlighted the paradox of being a "citizen of the world" (or citizen of "truth") as well as a citizen of Athens.

Socrates' and Kant's paths are not parallel: Socrates' muse is the timeless one of philosophical contemplation, while Kant's is the timely one of realizing his project of peace. Nevertheless, I view Kant's three tiers of right as conceived in a similar mode. Cosmopolitan right for Kant is a noble cause, and any reasonable person in the modern world can understand that a violation of right anywhere on earth is essentially a violation at home. At the same time we are all citizens of our own states, living under laws of external right that bind us in contractual obligations with our fellow citizens. These obligations protect and sustain not just formal rights, but also aspects such as property, family relations, social policies, infrastructures, and public goods. State-centred right and citizenship is the catalyst for cosmopolitan sentiment. It is important to understand this. Citizenship right keeps us grounded in the very real state contours of external right that make it possible at all for us to exercise our will and autonomy, and to comprehend our obligations toward the rights of others.

For Kant, right begins with the protection of external right within the state, extends outward to a defence of federations at the international level, and culminates in cosmopolitanism. The structure cannot be inverted. Cosmopolitanism is not the inspiration for the political protection of right. Cosmopolitanism, married to right, is not a modern day substitute for natural law. If states, committed to republican institutions that protect individual rights, do not fulfill their mandate, the entire structure of right collapses. No one is better on this than Hannah Arendt. As she famously declared: "The Rights of Man, supposedly unalienable, proved to be unenforceable—even in countries whose constitutions were based upon them—whenever people appeared who were no longer citizens of any sovereign state."[25] Of course, for Kant, rights are not "unalienable"; they are primarily political. Following Arendt's logic, Kant would no doubt agree that a loss of state does indeed mean no right. "The calamity of the rightless is not that they are deprived of life, liberty and the pursuit of happiness, or of equality before the law and freedom of opinion—formulas which were designed to solve problems within given communities—but that they no longer belong to any community whatsoever."[26] What really expels a person from humanity under the modern rights-regime is the loss of a polity.[27]

Cosmopolitan responsibilities, as Kant and Arendt would agree, do not help in the crisis of statelessness, expelled populations, or exterminated peoples. The "right to have rights," Arendt says, should theoretically be guaranteed by being human, but it is not. Arendt hopes for firmer declarations and enforcement of human rights from international organizations, and she criticizes "the present sphere of international law which still operates in terms of reciprocal agreements and treaties between sovereign states."[28]

But like Kant, she backs off from attaching any institutional prerogative to cosmopolitanism. World government, based on a common humanity that forgoes the traditional structure of state citizenship, is a possibility, writes Arendt, but one that by no means necessarily holds the promise of greater freedom. Just as likely would be an outcome of tyranny, what Kant terms a "graveyard" of freedom. At the end of Arendt's discussion of the "rights of man," and her considerations on world government, she cites Plato as having said: "Not man, but a god, must be the measure of all things."[29] This seems a cryptic close to her discussion, but I understand what she means. When the rights-protecting state collapses, all right implodes, as there is nothing outside that rights-conferring framework that could be called up to redress the calamity. As Arendt says, rightly, I think: "If a human being loses his political status, he should, according to the implications of the inborn and unalienable rights of man, come under exactly the situation for which the declarations of rights provided. Actually, the opposite is the case. It seems that a man who is nothing but a man has lost the very qualities which make it possible for other people to treat him as a fellow-man."[30]

Kant and Arendt, I believe, both have the capacity to hold onto an idea, such as world peace, or universal right, as an inspirational guide to our moral conduct, without moving from that idea to its institutionalization. For all the reasons cited above in Kant and Arendt, this instrumental application of theory to practice bodes disaster. Kant famously deplored revolutions. There should be no attempt to put ideas into practice by force, because this would mean that in the act of forcible revolution "there would be an interval of time during which the condition of right would be nullified." Gradual reform, carried out in accordance with "definite principles" (meaning the protection of right) and public enlightenment, for Kant is the path to "the supreme political good—perpetual peace."[31] Kant consistently rejects the possibility of world-government, remarking that "nature has wisely separated the nations" on linguistic and religious grounds.[32] Kant anticipated that as "culture grows and men gradually move towards greater agreement over their principles [principles of universal right]" progress would be made toward peace, but not at the behest of eradicating these differences. The peace that Kant envisages is "created and guaranteed by an equilibrium of forces and a most vigorous rivalry."[33]

In their introduction to *Perpetual Peace; Essays on Kant's Cosmopolitan Ideal*, authors James Bohman and Matthias Lutz-Bachmann assert; "Cosmopolitan law and institutions are, if anything, solutions to contemporary problems more urgent and threatening than the threat of war was for Kant. Aside from the inescapable connections between the fate of Western democracies and the fates of all other political communities resulting from such dangers as global warming and new forms of violence, it is clear that living up to democratic ideals of political and economic justice (democratic self-determination and freedom from destitution, abject suffering, hunger and environmental catastrophe) is now truly and unavoidably a cosmopolitan project."[34] In light of these historical developments, can the middle way that Kant theorized hold? That is, is it possible in the 21st century to defend a universal, cosmopolitan peace theory that sits firmly on the defence of a world of discrete sovereign republican states, each of which may defend its autonomy (even its linguistic and religious identity)?

Seyla Benhabib is a contemporary champion of cosmopolitanism, and she takes her bearings from a revision of Hannah Arendt and Kant, claiming "we have entered a phase in the evolution of global civil society, which is characterized by a transition from international to cosmopolitan norms of justice."[35] Benhabib declares that this transition marks a leap over the sovereign state, recognizing the rights of individuals in a "worldwide civil society." This is a significant departure from Arendt, whom Benhabib terms a "Kantian" who "remains committed to a civic republican vision of self-determination."[36] Benhabib's prescriptions for a new cosmopolitanism include fostering transnational juridical institutions that will constitute an "international human rights regime," and encouraging what she calls "democratic iterations" that can disaggregate citizenship from state boundaries. She sees the possibility of "new political configurations and new forms of agency, inspired by the interdependence—never frictionless, but ever promising—of the local, the national and the global."[37]

Benhabib's relationship with Kant and Arendt is an ambivalent one. Like Arendt, Benhabib looks at human rights through the catastrophe of the Nazi state and the dispossession and genocide that that state inflicted on its citizens. Benhabib identifies Arendt's "dilemma," as her realization that the legal framework of rights within the sovereign state is inadequate to protect the people within its borders (as Arendt said, the Nazis showed it was possible to expel people from humanity); at the same time, Arendt thought that natural law doctrines were "obsolete." Where does one turn to rescue individuals who are marginalized and expelled from rights protection within the state under such conditions? Benhabib thinks it is time to harness

Kant's notion of cosmopolitan right and confer on it the legal status that it deserves. It is by turning to cosmopolitan right that we can secure the foundations for what Arendt called the "right to have rights," and to ensure that we can punish "crimes against humanity." These categories, Benhabib states, "are intended to provide not only precepts of individual conduct but also principles of public morality and institutional justice. They transcend the specific positive laws of any existing legal order by formulating binding norms which no promulgated legislation ought to violate."[38]

Benhabib seems puzzled that Arendt did not herself make this "leap" to cosmopolitan justice. In the postscript to *Eichmann in Jerusalem*, Arendt's first-hand account of the trial of Adolf Eichmann, Arendt ends on what Benhabib thinks a "surprising" note. Arendt says there that it is conceivable that one day an international court might adjudicate political responsibilities of nations, but "it is inconceivable that such a court would be a criminal tribunal which pronounces on the guilt or innocence of individuals."[39] Arendt's position is "baffling" to Benhabib, because "[Arendt's] insistence on the juridical as opposed to the merely moral dimension of crimes against humanity suggests the need for a standing international body that would possess the jurisdiction to try such crimes committed by individuals."[40] Advocating for a new cosmopolitan order, Benhabib writes that "the modern sovereign draws its legitimacy not merely from its act of constitution, but equally, significantly, from the conformity of this act to universal principles of human rights that are in some sense said to precede and antedate the will of the sovereign and in accordance with which the sovereign undertakes to bind itself."[41]

Arendt's position is not baffling when we consider her (and Kant's) position that rights have no substance that "antedates" the will of the sovereign. Consistently throughout her work on rights, Arendt speaks to the Kantian problem that rights are political artifacts. To repeat some of the fundamentals of Kantian logic here, for Kant, rights are things we grant to ourselves in the building of political institutions of republican representation. Rights are primarily external, that is they are understood in relation to the rights of others as law in a sovereign state circumscribes us all. Cosmopolitan right is derivative, first from republican citizenship, and second from international right in the agreement among states. Cosmopolitan right cannot stand on its own as a bellwether. Cosmopolitan right has no foundation in nature, no foundation in religion, and no foundation in philosophy independent of political sovereignty. On Arendt's (and Kant's) ground, cosmopolitan right cannot address the calamities of statelessness, dispossession and genocide. Moreover, the transcendence of the state into the universal ether of cosmopolitan right may actually exacerbate these calamities. "The paradox involved in the loss of human rights," Arendt warns, "is that such loss coincides with the instant when a person becomes a human being in general—without a profession, without citizenship, without an opinion, without a deed by which to identify and specify himself—and different in general, representing nothing but his own absolutely unique individuality which, deprived of expression within, and action upon, a common world, loses all significance."[42]

Arendt thus provides (for me) a convincing rebuke to the cosmopolitan theorists who advocate for the dismantling of the sovereign state in favour of some trans-state world. These thoughts are echoed in this volume by Diane Enns, in her analysis of Hannah Arendt's thoughts on violence, political action, and political space. Arendt decried violence, contrasting it with what she termed the "power" of collective action in politics, and Enns draws on this distinction in her discussion of peace. Rather than speak to the end of violence, Enns advises, why don't we learn from Arendt the importance of protecting "spaces of exchange and agreement." Such spaces, of course require contours, rules, lawful boundaries and respect for speech over guns. Political spaces for exchange and agreement also tend to be those in which people have a shared vision of the common good, and that common good is frequently bound up with identities of ethnicity, nationhood and belonging. As Arendt pointed out, even stateless people do not see themselves as cosmopolitans, but rather, are likely to "insist on their nationality, the last sign of their former citizenship, as their only remaining and recognized tie with humanity."[43] And so we have the obverse of cosmopolitanism: the assertion of particular cultural, or national, or ethnic identity and the insistence that this identity be afforded political recognition. If a place in the world is of central concern to people, a space in which it is possible to act together, make decisions as a community, and advance individual rights within a context that is meaningful, then cultural/national/ethnic belonging is an anchor. Theorists of multiculturalism have taken up the cause of these identities, attempting to graft them onto a preservation of Kantian individual autonomy.

Foremost among these theorists is Will Kymlicka, who has defended a rights-based state that can accommodate cultural particularity. I do not know if Kymlicka sees himself lodged within a Kantian legacy, but certainly we find in his work the Kant-like effort to wed universal norms (rights-based) with state sovereignty. Kymlicka writes, "within recent Anglo-American political philosophy, the predominant idea of political community and citizenship has two main features. The first concerns the underlying values which typically have been defined in liberal-democratic terms … the second concerns the boundaries of citizenship which invariably have been defined in national terms."[44] Liberal commitments are universal and include the classic freedoms (speech, conscience, etc.) as well as the (very Kantian) commitment to autonomy, the "freedom of choice about how to live our lives."[45] The defence of the nation state rests rather on the commitment to self-rule: "political participation, self-government, and solidarity."[46] Kymlicka terms this marriage of liberal democratic norms, and commitment to self-rule within the nation-state a model of "liberal nationhood."

The model of liberal nationhood, according to Kymlicka, has been hugely successful in the modern world except for one glaring problem: the supposedly neutral and universalistic tenets of liberal nationhood exclude or marginalize many, including recent immigrants, historic sub-state groups (such as indigenous peoples) and neighbouring nation-states perceived as hostile and threatening. Kymlicka's formula for addressing these injustices, as is well known, is to adopt a multiculturalism that adapts to the model of liberal nationhood. States can, and ought to, move to adopt: (1) a "multicultural nationhood" more welcoming to immigrants; (2) "a more "multination" conception of the state that recognizes the existence of sub-state nations and indigenous peoples, and accords them a significant degree of national autonomy"; (3) better international security arrangements that can diminish conflict among states.[47]

Kymlicka calls his project one of "taming" liberal nationhood so that it is more accommodating of the very real differences that mark people's identities, especially those of the relatively powerless. Examples he gives of successful "tamed liberal nations" are Australia, Canada, the United States and Britain (interestingly, all primarily English-speaking). Kymlicka does not see his project as an abandonment of cosmopolitanism, but rather as a different version of cosmopolitanism—one that brings together cosmopolitan ideals (universal notions of freedom and autonomy) with retention of the primacy of state citizenship, albeit expanded to include cultural identity.[48]

I cannot help but think of Kant here again, and his comment that nature has acted wisely in populating the world with peoples of differing languages and cultures. Although Kant anticipates that trade, commerce and communications will open up the world in such a way that there is a great deal of cultural "cross-fertilization," he nonetheless sees the entrenched differences among peoples as intrinsically linked to the modern sovereign state. Kant also sees these differences as a good thing because they mitigate against the drift toward ever larger units of political control, which he regarded as inherently dangerous. However, there is nothing as far as I know in Kant that would connect cultural identity to claims of a thick conception of justice. Justice for Kant is about freedom, autonomy and external right.

This is how I see the principal debates on political theory and citizenship as they stand in Kant's legacy. The Kantian tension among the three levels of right—republican, international, cosmopolitan—on the slow, incremental but sure road to perpetual peace has proven unsustainable. I think this is the case, because the very foundations of right, as conceived by Kant, are not capable of bearing the weight of the edifice he constructs on them (but this is the subject of another paper, where I have written of the contrast between the Aristotelian conception of politics and the Kantian conception of right).[49] The Kantian project, held together by the absolutely primary commitment to republican government and the state guarantee of public right, has splintered off into the "universals" and the "particulars" that it was intended to contain. We have the cosmopolitans on the one hand, who take Kant's sentiments on the global reach of right, and turn them into frameworks for law and justifications for the erosion of state sovereignty. And we have the multiculturalists who, fearful of the sterility and rootlessness of cosmopolitan autonomy, look for ways to defend cultural belonging within a fabric of democracy and rights. The loser here is civic republicanism.

For all the reasons given by Kant and Arendt, which I believe still hold true, global transcendence of the state, movements toward a human rights regime, and international law are misconceived because they reach too far, too wide, and ultimately cannot provide the security or the harbour that citizenship can. There is a great danger in bypassing the political for the cosmopolitical. I do not think that the cosmopolitan advocates understand this danger, specifically, the danger of closing the gap between the ideal (if not utopian) and the actual. World peace requires the universal embrace of common ends, and that means that all states in the world would have to legislate as their primary mandate the security of individual rights and autonomy. We do not live in this world. The danger lies in the possibility (and one might argue, the empirical reality) that efforts to reach for a universal right regime, and its corresponding call for the suspension of national sovereignty, may exacerbate conflict.

There may be an even bigger problem with the Kantian formulation of perpetual peace that brings us back to my opening comments about the "stillness" of peace. Is it possible to imagine a world without friends and enemies, us and "others," struggles for honour, wealth, and power? Was Kant fundamentally misguided in transporting the notion of a "peace that passeth all understanding" into a project for historical realization? Was he wrong to have hope that we are getting better, more enlightened? Does the idea of perpetual peace not mean ultimately that all difference is collapsed into a universal calm? A century after Kant, we have Karl Marx's prescriptions for a universal world order in which the project for peace is mapped out as an historical inevitability. Man, according to Marx, will become a "species-being," and communism will be the "definitive resolution of the antagonism between man and nature, and between man and man. [Communism] is the true solution of the conflict between existence and essence, between objectification and self-affirmation, between freedom and necessity, between individual and species. It is the solution to the riddle of history and knows itself to be this solution."[50] Definitely resolving all antagonisms, as we well know from Marx, requires not just an apocalyptic shift in how we think, but violent revolution. If we think that universal peace is a tenable historical project, it may well be that we cannot resist the impetus to hurry it along with draconian measures. The moderate Kant, with his allegiance to law (and his abhorrence of revolution), is surpassed by the messianic.

Still another consideration on the prospects for peace is raised by David Tabachnick in his essay in this volume. Tabachnick assesses Heidegger's claim that only in the trauma of war can we experience "a deeper or richer reality that leads us to a free harmonious and peaceful pose that entails a full awareness of the conflictual character of existence." Heidegger's concern with the contemporary world is that under the sway of technology, we can no longer even distinguish between war and peace. "The division between war and peace is obliterated in that there continues on unabated by declaration of war or peace treaties, an overarching age of consumption." In this world picture, "peace and war are really part of the same inexorable process of taking up everything, man included, as standing reserve." This is a deep rebuke of the Kantian hope that we are moving inexorably toward a perpetual peace.

I am drawn to Kant because of his commitment to peace, his moderation and his respect for the integrity of politics, law and sovereignty, but I think his philosophy of history "undoes" him: the trajectory of perpetual peace into the future fosters children who lack Kant's sense of measure. I retain some faith in our capacity to think peace in the midst of conflict. Perhaps the best route is to retreat from historical narratives, either of the Kantian sort (history is unfolding progressively) or of the Heideggerian sort (technology is swamping our capabilities). We need states because we need laws and security apparatuses that can actually protect people from harm, and that can sustain communities of identity that are clearly important to the members of those communities. And we also need to work with the idea that we share a common humanity, grounded in the irreversible modern commitment to human right. Perhaps we need to understand that these two threads will never merge into one. I like Pamela Huber's characterization of Derrida in her contribution to this volume. "For Derrida, peace is not a state but an active concept, a work in progress, a perpetual promise of democracy to come." Huber invokes the images of "stillness" and "truth" with which I began this paper. She asks: "can there really be peace without a static vision of friendship or the common good?" For Derrida, she tells us, "absolute inclusion and universal peace are impossible. No political program, whatever its optimistic tone, can achieve it." That does not mean, however, that we give up. "An unconditional hospitality," Derrida said, "is practically impossible to live; one cannot, in any case, and by definition, organize it … no state can write it into its laws."[51] And yet, Derrida continues, without the idea of unconditional hospitality, we would not even have the commitment of living together, of being open toward alterity. Derrida rejects contemporary theories of cosmopolitanism, because he sees these as presupposing something like a "world state, whose concept can be theologico-political or secular."[52] Derrida mounts a surprisingly strong defence of the state. "I believe that everything must be done to extend the privilege of citizenship in the world: too many men and women are deprived of citizenship in so many ways." Hospitality and universal obligation are Derrida's "measures" for how we judge our political actions. For Derrida, it seems, we hold onto the notion of a "peace that passeth all incarnation," if not understanding, and this is likely to make us better citizens, and better human beings.

Notes

1   All references to Socrates taken from Allan Bloom, ed., *The Republic of Plato* (New York: Basic Books, 1968). After Socrates' consideration of the "man who is both good and just" (544e), the prototype of the philosopher-king, he discusses with his interlocutors the four descending orders of cities, beginning with timocracy as the best, and concluding with tyranny as the worst. The timocracy is a regime dominated by a spirited type of man, one whose distinctive characteristic is the "love of victories and of honours" (548c). The rulers in a timocracy base their claim to rule on "warlike deeds and everything connected with war." I take from this Socrates' suggestion that in politics, but not in philosophy, the discipline of war is central. The themes of the *Republic* may be challenged by those of Plato's *Laws*. In that much later dialogue, suggestions are made by a wise old man (not necessarily Socrates) that a good regime will include "an extensive new educational system for women as well as men, presided over by one magistrate who holds the highest administrative office in the regime; an unprecedented penal code based on the premise that no one ever voluntarily does wrong; and a new civil theology grounded on astral gods and elaborated through evident demonstrative reasoning." See Thomas Pangle, ed., "Interpretive Essay," *The Laws of Plato* (New York: Basic Books, 1980), 379.

The more pacific tone of the *Laws*, in my view, does not undermine the power of the war images in the *Republic*, or the implications for politics. Plato's works are dialogues, not treatises, so we may consider Allan Bloom's remark that "in the *Laws*, the Athenian Stranger engages in [a] narrower task of prescribing a code of laws for a possible but inferior regime. His interlocutors are old men who have no theoretical gifts or openness" (Preface to *Republic*, xvi–xvii).

2   Carnes Lord, ed., *Aristotle: The Politics* (Chicago and London: University of Chicago Press, 1984), 1325a5.

3   Peter Bondanella, ed., *Niccolò Machiavelli: The Prince* (Oxford: Oxford University Press, 2005), XIV: 50.

4   King James Bible, Phil. 4:6.

5   Hannah Arendt, *The Human Condition* (Chicago: University of Chicago Press, 1958), 14.

6   Declaration of the Baha'i Faith, *The Promise of World Peace: A Statement from the Universal House of Justice*, 1985.

7   Some of the most forceful cosmopolitan theorists are Arash Abazideh, Anthony Appiah, Seyla Benhabib, Jürgen Habermas, David Held, Martha Nussbaum, and Thomas Pogge. There are variations in the kinds of institutional prescriptions they advocate, but all these thinkers embrace some universalist or cosmopolitan understanding of politics. Thomas Pogge summarizes the cosmopolitan agenda as consisting of three primary loyalties: individualism, universality, and

generality. He defines individualism thus: "The ultimate units of concern are human beings or persons—rather than, say, family lines, tribes, ethnic, cultural or religious communities, nations or states. Universality is the ultimate concern that "attaches to every living human being equally—not merely to some subset, such as men, aristocrats, Aryans, whites or Muslims." The special status of generality, he claims, has global force: "Persons are ultimate units of concern for everyone—not only for their compatriots, fellow religionists, or such like." See Thomas Pogge, "Cosmopolitanism and Sovereignty," *Ethics* 103 (October 1992): 48–49.

8   H.S. Reiss, ed. "The Metaphysics of Morals," *Kant: Political Writings* (Cambridge: Cambridge University Press, 1991), 43.

9   Reiss, "Metaphysics of Morals," 134.

10   Reiss, "Metaphysics of Morals," 138–39.

11   Reiss, "Metaphysics of Morals," 139.

12   Reiss, "Metaphysics of Morals," 140.

13   Reiss, "Metaphysics of Morals," 172.

14   Reiss, "Perpetual Peace: A Philosophical Sketch," *Political Writings*, 105.

15   Reiss, "Perpetual Peace," 114.

16   Reiss, "Perpetual Peace," 93–102.

17   Reiss, "Perpetual Peace," 105. As well, the "realism" of Kant's views on international politics, and of Kant's unshakeable commitment to the nation-state as the fundamental unit of modern politics, is something emphasized throughout the work of the (recently deceased) Enlightenment theorist István Hont. He writes that efforts to develop international law in the 18th century were mainly attempts to regularize the rules of conflict in a world of might, not right. It was for this reason that Kant denounced the early modern classical exponents of natural law and international rights as "sorry comforters," thinkers who could not manage to lift their eyes from accepting the power games of nation-states as an inescapable game of politics. What Kant showed was that modern international law was ultimately an expression of the principles of "reason of state." István Hont, "The Permanent Crisis of a Divided Mankind: Contemporary Crisis of the Nation State: Historical Perspective," *Political Studies* XLII (1994): 176.

18   Reiss, "Perpetual Peace," 107–108.

19   Reiss, "Metaphysics of Morals," 174.

20   Reiss, "Theory and Practice," *Political Writings*, 89.

21   Reiss, "Theory and Practice," 89.

22   Reiss, "What Is Enlightenment?," *Political Writings*, 57.

23   Reiss, "Metaphysics of Morals," 174.

24   Socrates, *Apology*, 30a, 39b. Thomas West and Grace Starry West, trans., *Plato and Aristophanes: Four Texts on Socrates* (Ithaca, NY: Cornell University Press, 1984).

25   Hannah Arendt, *The Origins of Totalitarianism* (New York: Harcourt, Brace, Jovanovich, 1951), 293.

26   Arendt, *Origins of Totalitarianism*, 295.

27   Arendt, *Origins of Totalitarianism*, 297.

28   Arendt, *Origins of Totalitarianism*, 98.

29   Arendt, *Origins of Totalitarianism*, 299.

30   Arendt, *Origins of Totalitarianism*, 300.

31   Reiss, "Metaphysic of Morals," 175.

32   Reiss, "Perpetual Peace," 114.

33   There is in Kant this strong sense of preserving differences within unity. While defending linguistic and religious differences, and the organization of autonomous states around those differences, Kant nonetheless collapses these differences into the higher calling of universal principles. He writes: "Religious differences—an odd expression! As if we were to speak of different moralities. There may certainly be different historical confessions, although these have nothing to do with religion itself but only with changes in the means used to further religion, and are thus the province of historical research. And there be just as many different religious books (the Zend-Avesta, the Vedas, the Koran, etc.). But there can only be one religion which is valid for all men and at all times" (Kant, *Perpetual Peace*," 114).

34   James Bohman and Matthias Lutz-Bachmann, *Perpetual Peace: Essays on Kant's Cosmopolitan Ideal* (Cambridge, MA: MIT Press, 1997), 19–20.

35   Seyla Benhabib, "The Philosophical Foundations of Cosmopolitan Norms," ed. Robert Post, *Another Cosmopolitanism: The Berkeley Tanner Lectures* (Oxford: Oxford University Press, 2006), 15–16. Jürgen Habermas also shares this position. In his essay, "Kant's Idea of Perpetual Peace, with the Benefit of Two Hundred Years' Hindsight," Habermas advocates for the establishment of a cosmopolitan order that would mean that "violations of human rights are no longer condemned and fought from the moral point of view in an unmediated way, but are rather prosecuted as criminal actions within the framework of a state-organized legal order according to institutionalized legal procedures." *Kant's Cosmopolitan Ideal*, 140.

36   Benhabib, "Cosmopolitan Norms," 15.

37   Benhabib, "Cosmopolitan Norms," 74.

38   Benhabib, "Cosmopolitan Norms," 25.

39   Hannah Arendt, *Eichmann in Jerusalem* (New York: Penguin, 1973), 298.

40   Benhabib, "Cosmopolitan Norms," 15.

41   Benhabib, "Cosmopolitan Norms," 32.

42   Arendt, *Origins of Totalitarianism*, 302.

43   Arendt, *Origins of Totalitarianism*, 300.

44   Will Kymlicka, "Liberal Nationalism and Cosmopolitan Justice," *Another Cosmopolitanism*, 128–29.

45   Kymlicka, "Liberal Nationalism," 128.

46   Kymlicka, "Liberal Nationalism," 129.

47   Kymlicka, "Liberal Nationalism," 130.

48   Kymlicka, "Liberal Nationalism," 133.

49   Leah Bradshaw, "Empire and Eclipse of Politics," *Enduring Empire*, ed. David
      Tabachnick and Toivo Koivukoski (Toronto: University of Toronto Press, 2009).

50   Karl Marx, *Economic and Philosophic Manuscripts of 1844*, ed. Eugene
      Kamenka, *The Portable Karl Marx* (New York: Viking Penguin, 1983), 149–50.

51   Jacques Derrida, "Autoimmunity: Real and Symbolic Suicides," *Philosophy
      in a Time of Terror: Dialogues with Jürgen Habermas and Jacques Derrida*,
      ed. Giovanna Borradori (Chicago and London: University of Chicago Press,
      2007), 131.

52   Derrida, "Autoimmunity," 131.

CHAPTER 8

Hegel on Peace

Mark Blitz

Georg Wilhelm Friedrich Hegel (1771–1831) believed that war is inevitable and, in some ways, desirable; and he believed this because reason demanded it.[1] His ideas, indeed, led some people to hold him partially responsible for the First World War. In their view, Hegel was an apologist not just for militarism in general but for Prussian monarchists in particular. More broadly, he was thought to suffer from the disease called conservatism.

Today, however, most academics consider Hegel a philosopher of freedom.[2] They notice how his political argument begins with the individual, and see Kant's influence on him. They recognize the importance in his work of civil society, and his openness to the free market. If he is a political traditionalist, he is a very unusual one. Some who are won over to the liberal view of Hegel also notice that he believes a rational state should limit unbridled markets and private property. Perhaps Hegel is not only a friend of freedom, but Marx without the excess; not merely a liberty-lover, but a left-of-centre one. Moreover, his discussion of recognition is a useful resource for theorizing about identity politics. As well, there seems in him a more than incipient communitarianism that makes him appear superior to thinkers viewed as too liberal and individualistic, such as Locke or Kant. To many people today, Hegel seems usefully up to date—a *New York Review of Books* intellectual before his time. There is not only a conservative and a liberal Hegel, but a modishly leftist one.

Still, there are annoying obstacles to this fashionable picture, such as the politically incorrect things that Hegel said about war, perpetual peace, and international law. Perhaps, the thinking goes, we can best use Hegel's acceptable claims about other matters to reinterpret the remarks that jar—allowing us to defend a Hegel who is not only sound domestically, but also a proponent of international equalization and (the right sorts of) globalization. Or, if we balk at actually ascribing such views to Hegel himself, we can at least give him great-great-grandfatherly credit for providing the intellectual resources to help us achieve healthy thoughts. The logic of his original arguments, or of a new Hegelianism, may defend the utility of war; but today we prefer to view it as a war on global poverty, or disease. We can indeed transfer everything acceptable he says about freedom and mutual recognition between individuals to the relations among states, seen as individuals. The pleasant result is the discovery that he advances the cause of global civil society, and even promotes extra-national legal institutions such as the European Union. If only Hegel had lived longer, he would have become—just like us.

The errors and false consciousness of this view do not justify the old ideas about Hegel the German militarist—though at least those ideas attempted to understand the actual Hegel, rather than merely project today's neo-Marxist ideas onto him. What I intend to do in this chapter is to examine Hegel's views in order to understand what we might call a conservative version of the liberal Hegel, one that focuses on his concern for individual freedom. I believe it more important to keep the actual Hegel clearly in sight, than to discuss his position on this or that topic.

Hegel's understanding of war, peace, and international affairs is distinguished mainly by its sobriety. He considers states to be in a natural situation with regard to each other, yet their substance as individuals differs from the substance of natural persons singly. He does not restrict individual or political welfare to satisfaction of desire, however, nor does he consider self-preservation to be the dominant fact. His international realm is not identical to a Hobbesian state of nature, but neither is it a fully moral realm. He does not engage in moralistic hopes, though he gives considerations of international justice a reasonable place. He does not invent schemes of permanent international peace, but he does indicate how wars should be limited by the necessities of the peace that should follow. He believes that war has a place in making the state a vital whole, but he does not advocate European war detached from public welfare (despite his belief that some historical wars may have been accidentally responsible for spreading freedom).

What Hegel had in mind was wars less massive than some of our contemporary kind. We can understand, today, his view that a state's welfare could only rarely justify the carnage, or even the risk of it, inherent in modern war. But rarely does not mean never, especially if the response to a threat is defensive or pre-emptive. Hegel does not support mechanisms that put war out of bounds. Standing armies are a central concern among those who expect perpetual peace, along with issues like the arms race and force build-up; but Hegel does not worry about such things. Armies merely permit the establishment of a separate class devoted to valour. As with other political matters, he is liberal but not egalitarian, hard-headed but not materialist, and an idealist but not a fantasist.

For Hegel, no matter what the subject, his view is systematic rather than casual or episodic. International affairs have a particular place in his overall system, and in his discussion of justice or right—namely, one associated with his presentation of politics. He does not choose this location lightly or conventionally. (Plato's Laws, for example, begins with the topic of war.) Rather, Hegel chooses to first develop the existence of a state that fully embodies the practices of individual right, moral freedom, and ethical institutions. International affairs reflect this state as a whole, and each state is a version of this embodiment (even if not a fully developed or conscious one).

Let us very briefly trace Hegel's overall political argument until we arrive at international affairs. He begins with individual right, but argues that this is substantive, not formal: neither an abstract personality and its rights, nor the arbitrary interests to which it directs itself, are stable. Each half collapses when we seek to consider or act upon it alone. The true first subject of justice is a concrete individuality. Hegel then proceeds along a path on which each whole reveals itself to be a part, or is negated by its opposite, which is in turn negated, and so on. This is Hegel's dialectic, the way that reason proceeds to form and understand its subjects. This process also proves that even the combined world of individual rights and property cannot stand on its own: the natural-rights liberalism of Locke, and its roots in Hobbes, are insufficient. Nonetheless, the transformation of what is merely material stuff into property, into what is owned, is an important clue to the power of our reason to shape things beyond (but not apart from) natural material. The material world does not know or contain property. The limits of property and abstract right become visible once we notice that we are able not only to act freely, but to grasp ourselves in our freedom; and, ultimately, to act freely on the basis of this self-grasping.

Hegel traces the incipient presence of this power through the processes of making contracts, and of codifying crime and punishment. Especially in morality, which is universal, we see how we choose free action as such, not tied to separate interests. In morality, we choose our rights simply because we recognize ourselves as universal and free. Although acting morally goes beyond satisfying our interests, and may limit or focus us in those satisfactions, it does not tell us which among many morally acceptable things it is best to choose. Free, universal, rational choice cannot show its full power until we recognize our subjective interests, and ourselves, as integrally connected to an objective form that permeates or pervades them. This organizing principle of making the universal concrete, and assimilating it with self-interest, occurs in three bodies: the family, civil society, and the state. All require complex duties from us, such as citizenship, that enable us to go beyond both empty morality and selfish interest, and arrive at articulated reasoned choice. In a well-governed market economy, for example, I can meet my needs only if I belong to a rational system of money, police, division of labour, general education, and public welfare. The individual who satisfies his needs, and whose own freedom and choice are respected, exists only as part of such an economic or civil whole.

But even such a whole is insufficiently rational and universal: the next step in combining individual needs and universal reason involves belonging to a structured order in which free government and rational law prevail. Any political constitution has a lawmaking (or universal) part; an executive (or particularizing) part; and a sovereign who stands for (or activates) this composite singularity, through international actions and decisions. When I act as a dutiful and patriotic citizen, I unite my personal interest with my universal or moral good. The state, of course, cannot be itself and be completely isolated. This does not mean, however, that the next stage in uniting particular and universal is to place the state in a still larger legal framework. Rather, sovereigns direct foreign affairs with the welfare of their own states in mind. The progress of world history—from the Orientals to the Greeks, then to the Romans, and finally to the Germanic realm of freedom—illustrates the universal principles that states serve, though without full understanding.

This outline shows Hegel's understanding of the possibility and desirability of peace, and his understanding of war, as it connects to foreign affairs. This helps to explain his opposition to the ideal of perpetual peace, especially as we see it in Kant.[3] Sophisticated efforts to deny, minimize, or transform Hegel's understanding deny Hegel himself. The independent state has a central place in Hegel's understanding, and the independent state is inseparable from the rationality of war. "The true valour of civilized peoples is their readiness for sacrifice in the service of the state so that the individual merely counts as one among many," he wrote in the *Philosophy of Right*. "Not personal courage but integration with the universal is the important character here. In India, five hundred men defeated twenty thousand who were not cowards, but who simply lacked the disposition to act in close association with others."[4] And again: "The significance of valour as a disposition lies in the true, absolute, and ultimate end, the *sovereignty* of the state. The *actuality* of this ultimate end, as the product of valour, is mediated by the surrender of personal actuality."[5]

Hegel conceives of the state as an individual subject that faces outward to other states, and is directed by the sovereign who stands for, and has, this independence. The sovereign thus directs all relations with other states: treaties, ambassadorial representation, the armed forces, and making war and peace. Hegel denies that responsibility for this power can belong to the various estates that compose the constitution: rulers are not more likely to press for war than their people (as some who sought perpetual peace believed), since the people are subject to unruly passions. The complexity of foreign affairs also demands that they be conducted by the sovereign. Still, the occasional popularity of war does not always make war a sensible choice. Writing of England and its wars at the end of the 18th century, Hegel observed: "The popularity of Pitt arose from the fact that he knew how to comply with the nation's current wishes. Only after, when emotions had cooled, did people realize that the war was useless and unnecessary, and that it had been entered into without calculating the cost. Besides, the state has relations not just with *one* other state, but with several; and the complexities of these relations become so delicate that they can be handled only by the supreme authority."[6]

Although both states and private persons are individuals, in a sense, Hegel makes the difference between them clear. This means, among other things, that attempts are misguided to equate connections between states, or among states and their citizens in a global civil society, to the relationships among individuals. States differ from private persons, although they are not the final actualizing of spirit, which is inseparable from art, religion, and philosophy. "States are not private persons but completely independent totalities in themselves, so that the relations between them are not the same as purely moral relations or relations of private right," Hegel claims. Furthermore, he says:

> Attempts have been made to apply private right and morality to states, but the position of private persons is that they are subject to the authority of a court that implements what is right in itself. Now a relationship between states ought also to be inherently governed by right, but in worldly affairs, that which has being in itself ought also to possess power.... No power is present to decide what is right in itself in relation to the state and to actualize such decisions, this relation must always remain one of obligation. The relationship between states is a relationship of independent units which make mutual stipulations but at the same time stand above these stipulations.[7]

Hegel goes on to say that "the people as state is the sprit in its substantial rationality and immediate actuality, and is therefore the absolute power on earth; each state is consequently a sovereign and independent entity in relation to others. The state has a primary and absolute entitlement to be a sovereign and independent power in the eyes of others, i.e., to be recognized by them. At the same time, however, this entitlement is purely formal, and the requirement that the state should be recognized simply because it is a state is abstract. Whether the state does in fact have being in and for itself depends on its content." Recognition among states differs from the mutual recognition of individuals as, say, property holders, because the state is an absolute power, and "the sprit in its substantial rationality and immediate actuality."[8] Still another way to say this, as Hegel does, is that the legitimacy of the sovereign is a purely internal matter. Recognition by other states supplements this legitimacy: such recognition demands mutual recognition among states. From this point of view, a state cannot be indifferent to others, even though legitimacy is internal.

The relationship of independent states with one another, as wholes, is primarily contractual. This fact restricts the complexity of their connections, since they are not interdependent to the degree that individual citizens are. It is precisely a state's greater wholeness, the presence of reason in the range and relations among its parts, that differentiates it from ordinary individuals.

One standard for a state's relations is international law, defined by the principle that treaties must be observed since mutual obligations depend on them.[9] This universal right is distinct from the content of any treaty in particular. International law is not the product of any single sovereign, or enforced by any police force. States are sovereign, and no power supervenes over them. In this sense, states exist in a state of nature with each other. Their rights are not made actual in a universal will, as individuals' rights are, but rather through their own will. Their only obligation is to observe treaties, and they sometimes fail to do so. For states to resolve disputes without war, perhaps achieved by a federation of the sort Kant describes (or what people once believed the League of Nations or United Nations to be) will always be contingent on their choice. As a result, conflicts that do not yield to agreement can be settled only by war.

It may never be determined exactly which of a state's many relationships may suffer an injury that the state perceives as a slight to its honour, or as a breach of treaty. No moral standard can determine what offences justify war. Indeed, a state long at peace may even seek out "an occasion for action abroad."[10] Another might see an injury that others do not see. In any event, states are subject to conjectures and contingencies while considering other states' intentions; and all relate to one another as individual wills, each concerned in general with its own welfare. This is its supreme law. In a state, what is otherwise the opposition between "right as abstract and the particular content which fills it" is superseded or unified. States recognize each other as concrete wholes.[11]

So what must guide a state, as Hegel says, is its own specific interest and condition, and its distinctive external circumstances. In its relationships with other states, and in its principles for justifying both treaties and wars, its goal is not a philanthropic idea but its welfare—whether merely offended, or actually threatened—"in its specific particularity."[12] The relation between politics and morality is not such that politics can (or should) simply comply with an abstract demand for peace, or place itself under a higher legal authority. The reason, again, is that a state's welfare is justified differently from an individual's. The state, unlike the person, exists immediately as an ethical individual, whose right is embodied in its concrete existence. This is its principle of action, not "any of those many universal thoughts which are held to be moral commandments."[13] The other view, indeed, is a superficial one. As Publius writes in *Federalist #8*, "Safety from external danger is the most powerful director of national conduct. Even the ardent love of liberty will, after a time, give way to its dictates."

How precisely do states recognize each other; and how does this recognition relate to war and peace? Recognition comes from states' contingencies, choices, and their use of force in war. In this sense, any war is determined as a condition that must end, so that separate states may continue to exist. The conduct of war, Hegel points out, "entails the determination in international law that it should preserve the possibility of peace."[14] Among his examples of the limits to war are these: "Ambassadors should be respected, and war should on no account be waged either on internal institutions, and the peace of private and family life, or on private individuals."[15] Hegel's view of these rightful and substantial limits show, as it were, war's orientation to peace. Hostilities must be humane and, even in the army, must take "second place to the duty which each respects in the other."[16] Beyond this, customs determine the actions of states. Customs are, he writes, "the universal spirit of behaviour which is preserved in all circumstances."[17] The European nations form a family with respect to these. Nonetheless, the relations between states are unstable.[18] Similarity in principles of law, custom, and culture does not properly demand a transnational European government.

After discussing international law, Hegel turns to the activity of states in world history—a topic that leads into his discussions of art, religion, and philosophy. The destiny of "the concrete Idea as absolute universality" is partially achieved, he thinks, in "the right of heroes to establish states."[19] The same determination entitles nations to treat as barbarians other nations that are less substantially advanced, just as agriculturalists may treat pastoralists in the same way (and both may look down on hunting societies).[20] In these circumstances, wars are significant for world history as "struggles for recognition with reference to a specific content."[21] Hegel's views on how institutions are shaped and progress rationally, and how individuals live freely and self-consciously within such institutions, argue against avoiding war altogether or favouring peace altogether. But his opinions also argue against the propriety of ignoring war's rightful limits, or engaging in it foolishly.

The utility of Hegel's understanding of foreign affairs lies in the power of his reason and the good sense of his views. The general ways in which foreign affairs should serve a state's welfare—its interests such as security and economy—are not ignored. The importance for freedom of the state and its associated institutions (such as family and civil society) is clarified: neither what is larger or smaller than the state is fully reasonable or sufficient. The standpoints of morality and rights are given their due, and the state is not dignified simply in its self-interest. But the state does not properly bow down to hazy generalities and hopes, untethered by interest or reason. What is contingent in politics is not wished away. Hegel understands that politics are moving in the direction of freedom, and that states may be concerned with the internal affairs of others, without giving rules for interventions or validating political crusades.

Hegel sees war as a necessity—but, I would argue, a necessity limited or eschewed when foolish; and not engaged in when agreements could make it unnecessary. He may perhaps too confidently elevate the reasonable elements in politics, art, and religion, but not in a manner that unleashes the harm or destruction of an attempt to realize utopian dreams for permanent peace.

Notes

1   In this chapter, I draw my remarks on Hegel from his *Elements of the Philosophy of Right*, first published in 1821 as *Grundlinien der Philosophie des Rechts*. In this paper, I have generally followed this translation: Georg Wilhelm Friedrich Hegel, *Elements of the Philosophy of Right*, trans. H.B. Nisbet, ed. Allen Wood (Cambridge: Cambridge, University Press, 1991), and I refer to its specific sections and additions (for example, 331, 331A). For the original German, I have used the Suhrkamp edition: Eva Moldenhauer and Karl Markus Michel ed., Frankfurt: Suhrkamp, 1979. Hereafter I will refer to this as *Philosophy of Right*.

2   For good studies of Hegel generally, his political thought, and *The Philosophy of Right*, see the works of the following writers (among many others):

> Shlomo Avinieri, *Hegel's Theory of the Modern State* (Cambridge: Cambridge University Press, 1972).
> Andrew Buchwalter, ed., *Hegel and Global Justice* (Heidelberg: Springer, 2012).
> Andrew Fiala, "The Vanity of Temporal Things: Hegel and the Ethics of War," *Studies in the History of Ethics* (Feb. 2006).
> Paul Franco, *Hegel's Philosophy of Freedom* (New Haven: Yale University Press, 2002).
> Stanley Rosen, *G.W.F. Hegel* (New Haven: Yale University Press, 1974).
> Mark Shelton, "The Morality of Peace: Kant and Hegel on the Grounds for Ethical Ideas," *Review of Metaphysics* 54.2 (Dec. 2000): 379–408.
> Constance I. Smith, "Hegel on War," *Journal of the History of Ideas* 26.2 (Apr.–June 1965): 282–85.
> Steven B. Smith, *Hegel's Critique of Liberalism* (Chicago: University of Chicago Press, 1989).
> Charles Taylor, *Hegel* (Cambridge: Cambridge University Press, 1975).
> Merold Westphal, *Hegel, Freedom and Modernity* (Albany: State University of New York, 1992).

3   For a discussion of some contemporary views of issues that are relevant to Kant's discussion of peace, see Leah Bradshaw, "Kant, Cosmopolitan Right, and the Prospects for Global Justice," in Chapter 7 of this volume.

4   Hegel, *Philosophy of Right*, #327A.

5   Hegel, *Philosophy of Right*, #328.

6   Hegel, *Philosophy of Right*, #329A.

7   Hegel, *Philosophy of Right*, #330A.

8   Hegel, *Philosophy of Right*, #331.

9   For a discussion of an influential understanding of international law that was current during Hegel's time, see Ben Holland's discussion "Vattel on Morally Non-Discriminatory Peace," in Chapter 5 of this volume.

10   Hegel, *Philosophy of Right*, #334.

11   Hegel, *Philosophy of Right*, #336.

12   Hegel, *Philosophy of Right*, #337.

13   Hegel, *Philosophy of Right*, #337.

14   Hegel, *Philosophy of Right*, #338.

15   Hegel, *Philosophy of Right*, #338.

16   Hegel, *Philosophy of Right*, #338A.

17   Hegel, *Philosophy of Right*, #339.

18   Hegel, *Philosophy of Right*, #339A.

19   Hegel, *Philosophy of Right*, #352, 350.

20   Hegel, *Philosophy of Right*, #351.

21   Hegel, *Philosophy of Right*, #351.

PART III

LATE-MODERN CRITIQUES OF
THE SECURITY OF STATES AS
APPROXIMATION OF PEACE

CHAPTER 9

Seeking Peace in Nature: A Reading of Thoreau on Ecology and Economy

Toivo Koivukoski

There is a connection between how people may come to live peacefully with one another, and how human beings find their relations with nature. It is reasonable even to suppose that humanity's relationship with nature, at a system level, preconditions the potentials for peace among and between people; that is, peace in the social sphere is mapped out from the possibilities inscribed into the human-nature connection.[1] I suggest that there is in this sense something natural about peace, both as a subjective aspiration and as a set of objective conditions. These are describable in much the same way that the natural world is: that is, based on observation of the actual conditions under which people live—be they peaceful or otherwise, driven by domination, or enjoyed at ease with the world and in the company of others.[2]

One finds a notable source of such first-hand observations, of a life aimed at being at peace, in the writings of Henry David Thoreau. His record of day-to-day life in the woods near Concord, Massachusetts, reveal his composite perceptions of the symphonic movement of life through the seasons. His best-known work *Walden, or Life in the Woods*, is supported by a number of his other social commentaries, such as "On the Duty of Civil Disobedience," "Captain John Brown," "Walking," and his *Journal*, filled with social critique, naturalist observation, and a poetics of nature. All of these inform Thoreau's personal ethics, including his view of peace.

This poetic experiment of a person seeking to live life sincerely and critically in contact with the world translates directly into Thoreau's social, political, and ethical writings. For Thoreau, the duty to disobey is grounded in humanity's relation with nature, in the form of a pact with personal conscience that is ultimately testable in a person's accounting for their life. As *Walden* begins, Thoreau's basic aim was to spend a year in the woods at Walden Pond, living life simply, in a manner worth writing about critically and sincerely. For him, the experiment would lead to peaceful resistance that set the commands of his conscience at odds with what society expected of him. This kind of ethical engagement, through acts of peaceful disobedience, has been shown to bring about greater social justice: examples include Ghandi's independence movement in India, and the civil-rights movement in America. These represent progress sustained by the direct involvement of individuals who feel duty-bound to act ethically for a more just society.

An Altered Version of Thoreau's Title

Thoreau's most politically influential work is likely his essay on the duty of disobedience—originally titled "Resistance to Civil Government," and later rendered as the less radical "On the Duty of Civil Disobedience."[3] I see the change as a telling one. In the original title, the qualifier was attached not to the form of resistance but to the government—which, though outwardly civil, might still be resisted, since its authority was contingent on individual consent, and individuals always retained their right of conscientious non-cooperation. The point of the essay is not to qualify certain kinds of disobedience as being allowable, because they share some virtue of civility that supposedly overarches both lapses in good governance and breaches of consent—as, for example, when Thoreau and his jailer carried on cordial discussions through the bars of his cell when he was briefly jailed for not paying his poll tax.[4] Rather, his essay is an incitement to non-cooperation, and the imagining of moral codes more real and more personally demanding than the mere appearance of civility.

Mahatma Gandhi describes Thoreau's essay on resistance as containing "the essence of his political philosophy, not only as India's struggle related to the British, but as to his own views of the relation of citizens to government."[5]

Interestingly, in Gandhi's critical engagement with Thoreau, he alters the attributed phrase "civil disobedience" to "civil resistance," arguing that the former "failed to convey the full meaning of the struggle" by assuming hierarchical relations of command and obedience as the framework for action.[6] In a similar spirit of conscientious resistance, Martin Luther King reflects that his reading of Thoreau convinced him that "non-cooperation with evil is as much of a moral obligation as is cooperation with good."[7] Complicity in the domination of man by man is in this sense an excuse of inaction, with the duty to act being borne out whether the person does something or not.

It is reported that during a visit to the jailed Thoreau, Ralph Waldo Emerson asked him what he was doing behind bars; to which the prisoner of conscience responded by asking Emerson what he was doing outside. Slavoj Žižek observes that "This is the properly radical answer to the liberal's sympathetic concern for the excluded: 'How come that they are out there, excluded from public space?'—'How come that you are in here, included in it?'"[8] What did Thoreau not want to be included in at that time? What perspective and sense of rightness was liberated by his resistance? In this sense, it appears that the disavowal of the possibility of fundamental change has a perennial quality to it:

> All men recognize the right of revolution; that is, the right to refuse allegiance to and to resist the government, when its tyranny or its inefficiency are great and unendurable. But almost all say that such is not the case now. But such was the case, they think, in the Revolution of '75. If one were to tell me that this was a bad government because it taxed certain foreign commodities brought to its ports, it is most probable that I should not make an ado about it, for I can do without them: all machines have their friction; and possibly this does enough good to counterbalance the evil. At any rate, it is a great evil to make a stir about it. But when the friction comes to have its machine, and oppression and robbery are organized, I say, let us not have such a machine any longer.[9]

The situation that occasioned this rejection, with domestic freedoms underwritten by military occupations, still unfortunately characterizes regimes where violence is relocated to the hinterlands of empire, while day-to-day life in the metropole is made to seem nominally peaceful.[10] Identifying these systemic forms of violence is a first order of practice for peace-building: laying bare these connections, so that they can be addressed in individuals' lives.

A Source of the Idea of Peace

The idea of peace functions for us moderns in much the same way that an idea of "the Good," or "*to Agathos*," did in the classical Greek pagan tradition: it provided a source of shared longing in a world that was seemingly often characterized by fragmented perspectives and divergent interests. In the very notion of peace, however partially grasped, there is an intimation of a shared bond of unity with others, of harmonious belonging and spontaneous beneficence. The challenge for us, as moderns, is to speak and act in a way that approaches such a common good, in the context of a political consensus that it is freedom that makes life meaningful; for clearly we do not enjoy our freedoms in a vacuum, as if inheriting liberty *ex nihilo*, or as if being thrown into the abyss of indeterminate freedom in every act we initiate.[11] Even during Thoreau's sojourn of independent life in the woods, someone had to make his axe for him. Hence the importance of social concepts of economy, of neighbours, and of the relations between town and country—all chapters in a book ostensibly about one person living in nature.

How do we reconcile this conscientious striving for freedom with the peaceful co-presence of others? Drawing on a combination of Thoreau's writings on nature and society, I suggest that the experience of nature offers a powerful common bond, an inkling of what peace feels like, that transcends the inner/outer divisions of individual and environment, of us and them—situating us in a world that is shared not only with other people, but in a sense also with the world itself. Our collective human action into nature both reflects on our treatment of other people, and conditions the range of free choices available in the future.[12] If by "world" one understands a whole that encompasses human artifacts alongside the spontaneously regenerating regime of natural things, then to be at peace with the world means reconciliation both with one's fellow human beings (including what we have made of ourselves historically), and with the basis of our own potential for regeneration as a species, that is nature.

That this would be an act of reconciliation, unfulfilled by casual gestures of quietude, is implied in the existence of the world as a whole, containing both these self-generating and artificial dimensions. These components of reality, the natural and the human-made, are becoming increasingly difficult to differentiate, as the technological and the natural co-penetrate into a systemic order that amplifies the effects of human making on a global scale. Even the natural world now has human acts embedded in its very being. Marshall McLuhan made the prescient observation, in 1970, that it only became possible to think ecologically on a global scale—that is, to adopt a perspective on the world as an ecosystem—at the precise moment when satellite technologies enveloped the earth.[13] Thinking thus—from what is literally a meteorological perspective, as if seeing the world from above the earthly sky—we find ourselves in a nature that is now clearly affected by human doings: the weather, for example, from brutally hot days to violent storms, has become something we have a hand in. And at the micro-perspective, the very self-generating capacity of the natural world is now open to re-engineering through genetic modification. This makes Thoreau's faith in a seed seem perhaps quaint and anachronistic, compelling precisely for its evocation of an interval between hope and history. He writes: "Though I do not believe that a plant will spring up where no seed has been, I have great faith in a seed. Convince me that you have a seed there, and I am prepared to expect wonders."[14]

What Thoreau contends, in this worldly faith, is that the possibility of life is predicated on what was here to begin with. In this quote from Thoreau's last unfinished manuscript, *Faith in a Seed* (representative of his late botanical writings, which resolved into a charmingly boring focus on simply describing what is in nature, in which he found a basis of trust), he makes a case against an argument that he traces back to Pliny—who thought that living beings could come into being out of spontaneous generation, like frogs supposedly born out of the mud, or (thinking forward) like machines that would make themselves.[15]

Against this faith in a seed—a trust in the self-generating presence of nature—there stood, for Thoreau, the new order of technology, introduced to his pastoral woodland in the form of railway lines laid down over the already path-marked forests. One can imagine the shock people must have felt when first seeing a steam locomotive charging through new country, the first machine borne into an erstwhile wilderness, and in its very being and operation changing the ecology in an essential way. In lieu of the seasons of nature's births, the careful counts of the philosopher-botanist—noting the appearance, as Thoreau did: "By the 10th of May at least, the winged seeds or samara of elms"[16]—there is the work of historical humanity, driving forward with unprecedented speed, in a new form of linearity that would turn the cycles of nature into raw resources. And following this shift—this change in comportment towards what exists, and what we may use it for—goes both a change in self-perceptions, and a corresponding social shift: people as well start to be viewed in the conceptual framework of resources. As humanity would do unto nature, humanity would also do unto itself: treating people as raw materials, as it does with water and trees, and with all things living and inanimate. As Thoreau wrote:

> The mass of men serve the State thus, not as men mainly, but as machines, with their bodies. They are the standing army, and the militia, jailers, constables, *posse comitatus*, &c. In most cases there is no free exercise whatever of the judgment or of the moral sense; but they put themselves on a level with wood and earth and stones; and wooden men can perhaps be manufactured that will serve the purpose as well.[17]

This has become a characteristic effect of technological development: the tools engineered to serve human freedom effectively reshape conceptions of what is worth doing with our freedom—producing a kind of violent compulsiveness, rather than putting humanity at peaceful ease with the natural world. Observing that symbol of an emergent industrial economy, the railway, Thoreau comments that:

> We do not ride on the railroad; it rides on us. Did you ever think what those sleepers are that underlie the railroad? Each one is a man.... The rails are laid on them, and they are covered with sand, and the cars run smoothly over them. They are sound sleepers, I assure you. And every few years a new lot is laid down and run over; so that, if some have the pleasure of riding on a rail, others have the misfortune to be ridden upon.[18]

Thoreau sees the introduction of the railway as representative of the new kind of society then in formation, one that would register human and non-human nature both as resources to be efficiently organized, making mere stuff of each at the expense of their inherent qualities: the distinctiveness of the individual person, or the manifold richness of natural phenomena. It is in these claims to particularity—the individual's call to conscience, and the pristine specificity of all living beings—that Thoreau finds an ethical ground for critique of the seemingly neutralized forms of systemic violence. In particular, he objected to those political formations that connected, by wheels and gears, his taxes paid (or not paid) in Concord, Massachusetts, to the institution of slavery, and to the Mexican war of invasion and occupation.

As for what can be done against those kinds of circumstances, what matters for Thoreau the botanist-philosopher is simply to notice what stands out, both in nature and in a person. This allows us both to gain a sense of critical perspective on patterns of domination, and to act ethically in the face of them. That sensitivity to distinctiveness takes on what is, in many ways, a Kantian imperative—to treat each person as if they were an end in themselves, never a means—while recasting that hypothetical "as if" into the specific context of a real person. True, at that point one is already at some distance from the intent of transcendental idealism: one describes the value of a person, or of a plant, according to its specific qualities—that is, people are distinguished by their habits, as plants are by their morphology. As seasons describe the lives of flora and fauna, days to be accounted for make up a person's life. For Thoreau, the question then is just what these days and seasons mean. What sense of purpose is encoded in the unfoldings of things, both human-made and natural?

What saves Thoreau's American form of transcendentalism from reducing beings to their objective qualities is the poetic value he sees in those particularities. His view is something like pre-modern Aristotelian science, in that it involves seeing purpose in nature—though not in the sense of a cosmological order that perceives the purposes of all things as interwoven in a graduated hierarchy of means and ends, with the ends of one becoming the means of another. If the purpose of a being does manifest itself through the act of observation, then, for Thoreau, this manifestation is ultimately a poetic event. Something is seen so that one can ask what it means, and observe how a being truly is—both in its own distinctiveness, and in its relations to what is around it. A being is never reducible to a simple quality, as if in answer to the question "What is this for?"

The seed of a white birch tree may be suited to floating on streams, or blowing over a crust of snow, or landing in the ruts of disused cart tracks, putting down roots, and filling the furrows with even rows of saplings. But for Thoreau, it is not enough to simply say that the birch seed is intended for the propagation of the species. In Thoreau's poetic ethics, the patterns laid out in the growth of seeds contain lessons of an ethical order. When he so carefully describes the natural world around him, especially in his early writings and in *Walden*, he searches for some lesson for humanity in the shape of what exists around him. So, in the case of the dispersion of birch trees, Thoreau sees their capacity for regeneration throwing into relief the comparative precariousness of the human order. "I noticed the other day a little white birch tree, a foot high, which had sprung up in the gutter on the main street in front of my house.... It suggested how surely and soon the forest would prevail here again if the village were deserted."[19] And in a more prosperous spirit:

> How rich and lavish must be the system which can afford to let so many moons burn all the day as well as the night, though no man stands in need of their light! There is none of that kind of economy in Nature that husbands its stock, but she supplies inexhaustible means to the most frugal methods. The poor may learn of her frugality, and the rich generosity.[20]

Even in his tendency to mythologize nature, Thoreau retains that critical discernment that observes the sense of nature's spontaneous beneficence as being both true poetically, and as a perspective conditioned by experience. Subjectivity is thus informed by one's specific relations to nature. We see ourselves in the frame of this essential relation, though we may imagine that there is something essentially independent to who we are:

> Each generation thinks to inhabit only a west end of the world, and have intercourse with a refined and civilized Nature, not conceiving of her broad equality and republicanism. They think her aristocratic and exclusive because their own estates are narrow. But the sun indifferently selects his rhymes, and with a liberal taste weaves into his verse the planet and the stubble.... Let us know and conform only to the fashions of eternity.[21]

The concept that nature could be suggestive of a new political order belies the usual assumption that nature and society are somehow antithetical: a realm of given necessity versus a realm of human freedom. Human freedom is rather born from an experience of nature that is so demanding on the self and the senses that it requires a critical imagination to reconcile perspective and reality. Nature is the source of a wonder that is the beginning of both myth and philosophy, brought together at times in flashes of poetic expression. As Thoreau writes in his *Journal*:

When Nature ceases to be supernatural to a man, what will he do then? Of what worth is human life if its actions are no longer to have this sublime and unexplored scenery? Who will build a cottage and dwell in it with enthusiasm, if not in the Elysian fields?[22]

Whatever the specifics of one of these poetic reflections on an ethic in nature, it is the ability to be attuned to "what is" that would moderate the unthinking appropriation of nature as resources, and the enslavement of humanity to progress for the sake of progress. Just asking, "What is this thing in itself?" would provide a vantage point more substantial and situated than the technological view of the world as mere horizon. This situation could then be used to critique that new historical order.

For such a perspective, traced out at the margins of nature and civilization in one man's years of walks in pastoral fields and forests, we have the *Journals*.[23] Thoreau was only ever able to publish a small part of his output: his volume of unpublished writing is simply enormous, including a comprehensive record of his life. No matter how notable the political effects of "On the Duty of Civil Disobedience," and how commended *Walden* became as literature, the journals are perhaps the richest source of his thoughts. In many ways, this process is precisely the essence of his works: Thoreau's writing was an exercise in accounting for himself and his days, through the act of writing expressed as a call of conscience.[24]

Reading Thoreau, one gets the sense of the author suffering from pangs of conscience—of a clash between ideas of stern puritanical zeal and the still-emergent mass culture—a culture that consists of rather loose subjective frameworks of corporate individuality, with identities reconfigured as job-holders, and daily patterns of living dictated by technology. Thoreau felt no evident remorse for slacking and sauntering, but he did feel a call to conscience in deriding mass society as oppressive to the free spirit and an ethical life. His critique of mass society at his time was that "the mass of men lead lives of quiet desperation,"[25] resigned to following cart tracks and habitually unaccountable to ethical judgment. How one lives thus becomes both sign and symbol of an ethical order: patterns of behaviour are both the direct consequences of that order, and at the same time function as the symbolic renderings of an ethic—with certain archetypes then offered up by society as status symbols for advancement. What Thoreau's ethical imperative demands from society (in much the same spirit as Emerson's and Nietzsche's exhortations to greatness in thought and conduct)[26] is that each person, and not some de-personified abstraction of a person, so consider their days as to give an account of themselves. Hence Thoreau's focus on living simply, emphasizing simplicity in order to gain the capacity to give a full account of what was said and done in any given day.[27]

Thoreau's volumes of reflections on life in the natural world cue us to the sense of wonder he felt, irreducible to the effects of objectification. He writes:

> The mystery of the life of plants is kindred with that of our lives, and the physiologist must not presume to explain their growth according to mechanical laws, or as he might explain some machinery of his own making. We must not expect to probe with our fingers the sanctuary of any life, whether animal or vegetable. If we do, we shall discover nothing but surface still. The ultimate expression or fruit of any created thing is a fine effluence which only the most ingenious worshipper perceives at a reverent distance from its surface even.[28]

In much the same spirit of inspired observation, or what Thoreau calls his "subjective philosophy," he situates the observer as participant in the phenomenon. This creates an openness to what the thing itself may mean:

> Some incidences in my life have seemed far more allegorical than actual; they were so significant that they plainly served no other use. That is, I have been more impressed by their allegorical significance and fitness; they have been like myths or passages in a myth, rather than mere incidents or history which have to wait to become significant. Quite in harmony with my subjective philosophy.... The boundaries of the actual are no more fixed and rigid than the elasticity of our imaginations. The fact that a rare and beautiful flower which we never saw, perhaps never heard [of], for which therefore there was no place in our thoughts, may at length be found in our immediate neighbourhood, is very suggestive.[29]

For Thoreau, to look on nature is to register this suggestive sense that it must somehow mean something; that even a glancing experience of nature—like seeing a species of flower for the first time—must have a kind of intentionality to it; that there is in reality a presence to which our perceptions are held in thrall. For no matter through what prisms of cultural representations we obtain our various perspectives on nature, or what slew of constructed environments fragment our human sensorium, there is no overlooking the fact that nature can be so tasty to the senses. The unadorned fact that nature happens to be edible—that an apple is as desirable to us as excrement is delicious to a dung beetle—shocks the senses with the recognition that the world so happens to be accommodating to life. This propensity to see meaning in nature, finding in it a source of poetic inspiration, is connected with the proclivity to feel at peace in nature. Both modes are inherently good for human beings. So Thoreau enthuses, in one of his flights of secular evangelism:

> For all Nature is doing her best each moment to make us well. She exists for no other end. Do not resist her.... Why, "nature" is but another name for health, and the seasons are but different states of health. Some men think that they are not well in spring, or summer, or autumn, or winter; it is only because they are not *well in* them.[30]

That capacity to look for and to see meaning in nature is born from the essential relationship with it that sustains humanity. The state of being "in" nature reflects on the constitution of a person (who one is), with that Other (nature) inflected into subjectivity via the lives that people actually live—which, beyond all function and routine, take on an ethical value if those lives are seen to have meaning.[31] In his poetics of nature, the ethical standard would be whether a person's life is lived in a free relation with the natural world, with nature giving them sustenance; or, conversely, whether it is lived rather frantically, with nature appropriated as a mere resource for compulsive humanity.

In our own time, we see the global technological condition as being characteristically unfree in its relations to otherness; barbed wire fences quarantine a dispossessed humanity into zones of world-alienation that border on bubbles of virtual abundance. The scarcity of resources may or may not be the actual causes of wars and conflicts:[32] causality is not a singular phenomenon, but rather the result of a skein of relationships—as if one were to ask, "What causes this tree to be?" And while violence may be ascribed to the structural distribution of resources themselves, with inequalities viewed as signs of underlying modes of domination—still, at the level of experience, all forms of violence coalesce into a feeling of ontological dispossession. Victims may have a feeling of being un-worlded, as if the world were not for oneself. At its extremes, the biological consequences of such dispossession may be hunger, thirst, imprisonment, torture, and even death.

At the polar opposite of such violent experiences of world-alienation is the experience of a leisurely, unencumbered walk through bountiful fields and forests—sustained by an Other that is as constant in its presence as it is precarious in its withdrawal. This is a wonder that helps to sustain our humanity.

On Economy and Ecology

Thoreau was perhaps the quintessential slacker, registering the feeling of peace in days spent sauntering, noting the passage of the seasons in the changes of nature and in the habits of the country folk.[33] Just as Socrates defended his "unproductive" days of philosophizing, arguing that his gadfly services to the community deserved free meals at the Prytaneum,[34] Thoreau gave himself the title of "inspector of snow-storms and rain-storms,"—a post well suited to his demonstrated capacity for leisurely walks in nature.[35] In this kind of leisure economy, much time was spent in berry-picking and fishing, with the work of the day elegantly tuned to the free appropriation of nature's plentitudes.[36] This consideration of economical living would be, for Thoreau, the most visceral approximation of what peace would mean to how a person lived their life: either dictated to by material compulsion, or enjoyed at ease with the world and other people. And because economics pertains to relations between people, as well as to the choices they make for themselves, this commonly accepted bargain—of compulsive consumption with intervals of hard-gained leisure—essentially translates into the choice between a violent economy or a peaceful one. Thoreau would describe the difference between the two as a choice between a slave-dependent imperial society, or one characterized by pastoral autonomy.

The chapter in *Walden* on "Economy" can be considered as a blueprint of the habits for frugal living, with a do-it-yourself ethic guiding every day's activities. Thoreau devotes considerable energy to the economic considerations of means, precisely so that economic imperatives can be met, and free days enjoyed in peace, without the compulsions of material necessity. It can be quite difficult to set work aside: Thoreau built his own cabin from salvaged materials, and tended his bean field daily. But the difference is a clear one between availing oneself of the fruits of economical living, versus giving oneself over to economics as if it were an end in itself.[37] The former course is how Thoreau sees personal freedom: as a life lived as much as possible without compulsion, enjoyed in that spirit of peaceful ease. Thus, at this basic level of distinction between necessity and freedom, it is natural that we would find peace when the insistence of work stops and the fields of leisure open up, inviting one to perhaps nothing more productive than an afternoon's walk.

Thoreau recoils at the idea of indentured servitude to an economy where labour is traded for commodities (often in an uneconomical and unfair exchange for the workers), and in which natural riches are viewed merely as resources, or simply destroyed in order to make way for an economy of material accumulation. As he observes:

> My neighbours would not hesitate to shoot the last pair of hen-hawks in the town to save a few of their chickens! But such economy is narrow and groveling. It is unnecessary to sacrifice the greater value to the less. I would rather never taste chickens' meat nor hens' eggs than never to see a hawk sailing through the upper air again. This sight is worth incomparably more than a chicken soup or a boiled egg.[38]

In Thoreau's view there are different kinds of economies, some "narrow and groveling," others concerned with what we would call "higher laws." The two have quite different modes of valuation. One measure, which today is often passed off as the whole of economics, consists just of what one would pay for a boiled egg. The other measure registers the sort of value that cannot be reciprocated with a compensatory exchange—like the impossible question of what a person would pay for there to be hawks in the sky. This impasse of values in many ways defines the shift from the classical economics of Adam Smith, Karl Marx, and David Ricardo (who asked what was the ultimate source of value in an exchange item), to the neo-liberal emphasis on marginal valuations. This neutralizing approach to value has been carried on in capitalist economic regimes from Alfred Marshall to the present day: that is, how much someone is willing to pay for one more unit of a commodity, without any ontological questions as to what its value really is, what its origins are, what it is made of, etc. In a way, this neo-liberal turn—the foundational assumption of contemporary capitalist economics—does away with the issue of things that cannot be given a discrete value, replacing that consideration with a kind of betting game on disaster. What would one be willing to wager on the continued existence of an animal species, or of clean air to breathe?[39]

Those kinds of impasses between exchangeable values and intrinsic values is registered even in a capitalist economy grounded on the levelling of values to monetary worth. Milton Friedman, an archetype of the capitalist mindset, aims to make sense of such unsettling examples as environmental pollution by observing that those systemic issues are difficult to resolve because of the so-called "third-party effects" or "externalities" linked to supposedly individual market choices. The challenge here (as in any theoretical instance) is to define precisely what is "external" to decisions made, and what lies entirely in the private domain of the decider—be it a household or a corporation, an individual or a labour union.[40] Economic choices, after all, connect the participants in an economy—in part by establishing what factors matter in valuation, and which can be set aside from cost-benefit evaluations, and not considered in the ledgers.

The choice to work in the first place, for example, and what kind of work is considered worth remuneration, was framed by the prevailing economic system; and that personal choice, in turn, affects the potential future choices available to others (as in the historical effects of organized labour, for example). From the perspective of a young Irish woman, as Thoreau recounts in his *Journal*, a day spent cleaning and cooking from four in the morning until nine at night, for little pay, seemed like not much of a choice to make.[41] Similarly, Thoreau's advice to an impoverished bog-cutter and his family, to live cheaply and independently by wanting less, comes across as fanciful. The reality of the family's situation was that they had to toil all day just to supply themselves with the tools of their toil.[42]

In the context of a wage economy, the matter of how to recognize a person's intrinsic value must somehow bracket their economic exchange value, in order to reflect how the person values their own freedom. Here Thoreau's poetic habit of looking for meaning in nature, and in the lives of individuals, offers a compelling rejoinder to that instrumental logic that sees in both merely material for manipulation. There is a telling difference between imposing value onto the passive stuff of human and non-human nature, and the openness of Thoreau's almost mythological commitment to a world imbued with meanings.

In the technological world view, all of nature—including human nature—is in essence nothing but so much matter in motion, subject to certain forces. This supposed neutrality of existence opens up the potential for historical humanity to master both its own nature—through such tools as social engineering, propaganda, crowd control, etc.—and to appropriate nature itself, as inputs into a technological system of production and consumption. The apparently limitless potential for dominating nature is made possible by removing any sense of intrinsic meaning from the things themselves. Once they are considered as having no purposes of their own, either manifest or implicit in their being, then humanity is free to do whatever it wishes to nature—limited only by the mandate of efficiency, with technological limits replacing ethical or natural ones.

Thoreau's poetic ethic—or, as he calls it, his "subjective philosophy"—is in some ways a result of the same insistence on human freedom that undergirds all modernity: that is, the purposes of natural things are not given *sub specie aeternitatas*, within the framework of ahistorical ends or designs, nor are the ends of individuals assigned by nature through some archetypal portioning of duties and purposes. For Thoreau, there is no ultimate set purpose for either man or for nature; one can imagine him drawing out a host of interpretations from a newly discovered species of flower. But that suggestive general sense that the new flower *has* meaning is significant for moderating the violence inherent in the appropriation of human and non-human nature as mere resources.

Here again, Thoreau's insistence on the value of individual conscience—that it matters very much what individuals do—has quite different consequences than the Kantian ethic of proposing a similar valuation of individuals as ends in themselves. While Kant makes a strict (and in many ways, now familiar) separation between the human realm of freedom, and the material realm of necessity that he sees in nature—conditioned by laws and reflex responses—for Thoreau freedom and the capacity for conscience are found in crossing over that boundary between the social and the natural orders. The natural world provides occasion for allegory, myth, and reverie, as well as a critical distancing from the technological world view (which can be overwhelming) that the natural world is merely instrumental to human freedom. This intermingling of the natural and the human-made stem from the intimation that nature has meaning, and that human freedom can have a place in that field of meanings. From this pair of possibilities arises a question: what is worth doing with our freedom? How can we best give an account of our days and ourselves?

Because the search for meaning translates into both an appreciation of the natural world, and an inspiration to live poetically, Thoreau trespasses on another rigid separation in Kant's transcendental idealism: the boundary between our critical capacity—that is, the freedom of the rational imagination to see things as they might be otherwise—and our duties to perform our public functions and fulfill the social contract. However much that Kantian kind of idealism may protest against war, or imagine an international community of rational agents enjoying perpetual peace—in the end, because of Kant's separation of freedom and necessity, if the pacifist is ordered to go to war, then it is his public duty to fight. There is something retrograde about this notion of critical conscience, as a faculty suited to expression only in the form of petitions to the throne.[43] What makes Thoreau's transcendentalism distinct, in the modern tradition, is his emphasis on observing the given quality of nature and its changes, and seeing some meaning for individuals in the world they observe. For how is it possible for nature to have the inspiring effect on us that it does, if there is not some attunement in us to its purposes, some point of connection between it and us? That the romance of nature is even possible as an intimation suggests that the potential for enchantment is embedded in the simple act of sensation—observing the world, and noticing that it is beautiful.

Phenomenologically, how is this possible? From whence this common bond to the beautiful in nature? There is a sense in which to "get" the natural world, or to be at peaceful ease with one's environment, means seeing it as meaningful. Seeing the animate and inanimate elements of nature as mere functions and processes cannot account for this. Much the same is true of the elements that sustain human life. Thoreau's shopping list for construction materials for his cabin, described with his characteristic detail, is meaningful only to the extent that economy, or the meeting of necessity under conditions of relative scarcity, contributes to autonomy and the feeling of peaceful ease it engenders. And this autonomy is predicated on the capacity to give an account of oneself, rather than to be accounted for.

Peace for Thoreau has its basis at this level of individuals and the lives they lead, whether autonomously chosen or dominated by material necessity. This is a kind of noble "slacker ideal" of a life devoted to freedom, seeing in our days both the simple, sweet pleasure of being, and the transcendental fulfillment of having a life worth accounting for.[44] The fact that this would, at times, require a practical form of resistance indicates the gaps in civility in our society, and the modes of domination practised by the economic system and its political correlates.

Such entrenched modes of domination represent forms of systemic violence, and this substructure not only echoes explicit manifestations of violence—as, for example, wars of invasion and occupation—but also sustains the concept of violence as a supposedly fixed potential in the fabric of nature itself. This is not simply a structural matter, although structural imbalances such as economic inequality, racism, and sexism obviously do sustain the potentials of explicit violence. At the deepest level, this systemic violence manifests itself in the habitual patterns of social relations: Who gathers with whom? Who speaks, and who is spoken to? Who can move freely, and whose mobility is constrained? Taken together, these ordinary patterns of behaviour describe the actual peacefulness of a society, inversely indexed by the modes of domination that structure people's lives. As Slavoj Žižek observes, "Innermost beliefs are all 'out there,' embodied in practices which reach up to the immediate materiality of my body."[45] Ethical beliefs are realized in people's actual daily practices, and these frames of belief and practice describe the real limits and possibilities in any society. Thus, considering the potentials for resistance, Žižek argues that:

> Every legal order, or every order of explicit normativeness, has to rely on a complex network of informal rules which tells us how to relate to explicit norms: how we are to apply them; to what extent we are to take them literally; and how and when we are allowed, even solicited, to disregard them.[46]

What Žižek is calling our attention to here are the codes of civilization that are already broken: the contradictions of principle and practice—such as slavery in a liberal society—that turn resistance into a positive duty, demanding an act that would make an otherwise casual disregard for ethical coherence into an explicit denunciation of injustice. It is obvious that even an apparently peaceful order can have violence embedded in its modes and orders, as if the flower of a secure society had human blood composted into its very being. What is needed is to turn that society over, subvert its ethical codes, define as injustice what is termed justice, and put peaceful disobedience in the place of violent pacification. Thus Thoreau has it that:

> The greater part of what my neighbors call good I believe in my soul to be bad, and if I repent of anything, it is very likely to be my own good behavior. What demon possessed me that I behaved so well? You may say the wisest thing you can, old man—you who have lived seventy years, not without honor of a kind—I hear an irresistible voice which invites me away from all that. One generation abandons the enterprises of another like stranded vessels.[47]

And from thence, to save the stranded, where to? How to even tell violence apart from peace, and justice from injustice? Thoreau's answer would have us reorient our imaginations away from the twisted collective fantasy that makes machines out of men,[48] and toward a vision of nature set not as law, but as that which presents itself at the margins of our understanding—a nature "well adapted to our weakness," that traces out the limits of an otherwise compulsive economy.[49] This is nature viewed not as raw materials, as means and resources, but as end in itself: potent with meaning and the capacity to change, and suggesting some more noble purposes for humanity.

This is what Thoreau, the natural philosopher, intimates when he writes: "When one man has reduced the fact of the imagination to be a fact to his understanding, I foresee that all men will at length establish their lives on that basis."[50] This would be the basis of a peace derived from nature. Imagination and critical understanding are joined in an autonomy made real by the will to account for oneself, worked out through the peaceful resistance to injustice, and enjoyed in the actual lives that people lead.

Notes

1   The connection between environmental change, resource scarcity, and conflict is well documented in the work of Thomas Homer-Dixon, who demonstrates a deep connection between the health of societies measured in terms of human security, and the shared substance of nature. Indeed, the very consideration of environmental factors as externalities belies a certain abstraction from the worldly conditions that sustain human life. See Thomas Homer-Dixon, "On the Threshold: Environmental Changes as Causes of Acute Conflict," *International Security* 16.2 (Fall 1991): 76–116. The article is also available online at http://www.homerdixon.com/projects/evidence/evid1.htm.

Bridging security studies and political philosophy, Homer-Dixon's research taps into a foundation of classical political thought: the premise that political community has its origins in the biological and economic necessities that bind us to nature and to one another, with people organizing together in order to meet their bodily needs—and, in the process, liberating the human potential for free association. Thus Plato describes the origins of war in terms of land grabs and the "unlimited acquisition of money, overstepping the boundary of the necessary." (Allan Bloom, ed. *The Republic of Plato* [New York: Basic Books, 1991], 373d.) Plato's ideal city must begin by overcoming material scarcity, and enjoying its benefits in equal partnership, "keeping an eye out against poverty or war" (*Republic*, 372b). Likewise, Aristotle promotes a peace policy that discourages wars of acquisition and empire-building. For him, the aim of security is the attainment of a condition of leisure, freed from the precariousness of biological and economic necessity. (Aristotle, *Politics*, trans. Ernest Barker (Oxford: Oxford University Press, 1958), 1333a–1334a.) In this sense, peace in and between political communities is contingent on the measure of prosperity that nature allows.

2   See, for example, the phenomenological approach of the Global Peace Index (GPI), which indexes a multivariate set of conditions—ranging from primary school education to participation in the arms trade—in order to rank countries' relative peacefulness. (View the index online at http://www.visionofhumanity .org/gpi-data.) This conception of peace as multi-dimensional, as any working social concept must be, is emphasized in discussion with GPI director Camilla Schippa, who says it is important that peace means different things to different people. The genuine subjectivity of peaceful agency requires public forums to articulate those differences, as well as to make objective determinations about real-world conditions. See Nipissing University Peace Research Initiative, *Agents of Peace Project* (North Bay, 2011), http://vimeo.com/42779363.

3   Henry David Thoreau, "On Resistance to Civil Government," in *Aesthetic Papers*, ed. Elizabeth P. Peabody (Boston, 1849), http://en.wikisource.org/wiki/ Aesthetic_Papers. The phrase "civil disobedience" was posthumously attached as the essay's title in an 1866 collection of Thoreau's works, *A Yankee in Canada, with Anti-Slavery and Reform Papers*, and was retained in later editions. The change has the effect of smoothing over the concept, making a liberal platitude out of what is an essentially radical idea. I refer to the essay by the conventional title in *Henry David Thoreau: Walden and Other Writings*, ed. Brooks Atkinson (New York: Modern Library, 2000).

4   Thoreau, "Civil Disobedience," in *Walden and Other Writings*, 682–83.

5   See George Hendrick, "The Influence of Thoreau's 'Civil Disobedience' on Gandhi's Satyagraha," *New England Quarterly* 29.4 (Dec. 1956).

6   Letter from Gandhi to P. Kodanda Rao, 10 September 1935, in *The Collected Works of Mahatma Gandhi*, online edition, http://www.gandhiserve.org, 67, 400.

7   See Brent Powell, "Henry David Thoreau, Martin Luther King Jr., and the American Tradition of Protest," *OAH Magazine of History* 9.2 (Winter 1995), 26–29.

8   Slavoj Žižek, *Living in the End Times* (London: Verso, 2011), 124.

9   Henry David Thoreau, "Resistance to Civil Government," http://en.wikisource .org/wiki/Aesthetic_Papers/Resistance_to_Civil_Government.

10 On the division between imperial hinterland and metropole, see Harold Innis, *Empire and Communications* (Lanham: Roman and Littlefield, 2007).

11 For such a version of freedom, and the free act as strictly indeterminate, see Slavoj Žižek, *The Abyss of Freedom* (Ann Arbor: University of Michigan Press, 1997). Following F.W.J. Von Schelling's conception of freedom as a recovery of the unconditioned status of origins, Žižek presents freedom as a kind of worldly miracle, though one made manifest through violent means. However timely and current this argument may be, in terms of understanding fundamentalist and fascist social movements (both secular and religious), I think that here

Hegel's original argument criticizing Schelling still holds: that this notion of freedom as unconditioned origin represents a "night in which all cows are black," lacking the barest discriminatory functions, for example to distinguish violence from peace, or compulsion from freedom.

12   Barry Cooper, *Action into Nature: An Essay on the Meaning of Technology* (Notre Dame: University of Notre Dame Press, 1991).

13   Marshall McLuhan, television interview with Dick Cavett, December 6, 1970, http://soundcloud.com/toivokoivukoski/marshall-mcluhan-on-ecology. The thinking here is very much like Heidegger's world view of the unique possibilities opened up by technology. See Martin Heidegger, "The Age of the World Picture," *The Question Concerning Technology and Other Essays*, trans. William Lovitt (New York: Harper, 1982). See also the essay commentary by Don Ihde, "What Globalization Do We Want?," *Globalization, Technology and Philosophy*, ed. Toivo Koivukoski and David Edward Tabachnick (Albany: SUNY, 2004).

14   Henry D. Thoreau, *Faith in a Seed: The Dispersion of Seeds and Other Late Natural History Writings*, ed. Bradley P. Dean (Washington: Island Press, 1993).

15   The examples Pliny uses are trees that supposedly bear no seeds, like the tamarack, the poplar, and the elm, which he comments "are regarded as sinister and are considered inauspicious" (*Faith in a Seed*, 23). Thoreau notes that "sinister" (in the original Latin, *infelices*) is perhaps better translated as "unhappy"—an idea that reflects on the unhappy status of modern seeds, now genetically engineered to produce seedless crops—meaning that we effectively bring forth fatal seeds that contain their own demise, building a kind of kill-switch into nature. The spontaneous beneficence of nature is thus programmed out of it by the formation of a new regime that requires human intervention for its continued survival.

   If there is an element of anthropomorphism in Pliny's attribution of emotion to plants, it represents an understanding inaccessible to us as moderns: the attribution of human values to nature now occurs not in our reflections on their qualities, but rather in the programming of those qualities into their very patterns of growth and regeneration.

16   Thoreau, *Faith in a Seed*, 53.

17   Thoreau, "Resistance to Civil Government," 670.

18   Henry David Thoreau, *Walden* (Signet: New York, 1960), 67.

19   Thoreau, *Faith in a Seed*, 45.

20   Journal entry for April 3, 1842. Henry David Thoreau, *The Journal of Henry D. Thoreau* (hereafter *Journal*), ed. Bradford Torrey and Francis H. Allen (New York: Dover, [1842] 1962), 108.

21   Thoreau, *Journal*, Sept. 1, 1841, 88.

22   Thoreau, *Journal*, Nov. 2, 1843, 74. *Selected Journals of Henry David Thoreau*, ed. Carl Bode (Scarborough: Signet, 1967).

23 Thoreau had a remarkably poor career in publishing; the family business of pencil manufacturing was more profitable, though boring to him. He records in his *Journals* that he is the proud, if self-deprecating, owner of a library of "nearly nine hundred volumes, over seven hundred of which I wrote myself." Thoreau, *Journal*, Oct. 28, 1853, 643.

24 The ethical centrality of conscience, and of the related concept of resoluteness, is echoed in Heidegger, for whom "conscience manifests itself as the call of care." Martin Heidegger, *Being and Time*, trans. John Macquarrie and Edward Robinson (San Francisco: Harper, 1962), II.2.277. On the practical side of conscience, in terms of action, Heidegger notes that this term "must be taken so broadly that 'activity [*Activität*] will also embrace the passivity of resistance." *Being and Time*, II.2.300.

25 Thoreau, *Walden*, 10.

26 See Herman Hummel, "Emerson and Nietzsche," *The New England Quarterly* 19.1 (Mar. 1946). Nietzsche begins his *Gay Science* with a quote from Emerson:

> I live in my own place,
> have never copied nobody even half,
> and at any master who lacks the grace
> to laugh at himself—I laugh.

Friedrich Nietzsche, *The Gay Science*, trans. Walter Kaufmann (New York: Vintage, 1974).

27 Thoreau, *Walden*, 66.

28 Thoreau, *Journal*, XII, 23, Mar. 7, 1859, 1438.

29 Thoreau, *Journal*, V, 203–4, May 31, 1853, 579.

30 Thoreau, *Journal*, V, 395, August 23, 1853, 627.

31 Thoreau recounts: "I left the woods for as good a reason as I went there. Perhaps it seemed to me that I had several more lives to live, and could not spare any more time for that one. It is remarkable how easily and insensibly we fall into a particular route, and make a beaten track for ourselves." *Walden*, 214.

32 Thomas Homer-Dixon, "Environmental Scarcities and Violent Conflict: Evidence from Cases," *International Security* 19.I (Summer 1994), 5–40.

33 In his essay "Walking," Thoreau suggests two possible French etymologies of the verb "saunter": either from "*sans terre*"—that is, without land—or from "*à la Saint Terre*," on a pilgrimage to the Holy Land. The latter, with its dual sense of uplifted motives and humble circumstances, must have been very agreeable to the way the author spent his days. In *Walden and Other Writings*, 627; also online at http://thoreau.eserver.org/walking1.html.

34 Thoreau, *Apology*, 36d.

35 Thoreau, *Walden*, 17.

36 "Yesterday, toward night, gave Sophia and mother a sail as far as the Battle-Ground. One-eyed John Goodwin, the fisherman, was loading into a hand-

cart and conveying home the piles of driftwood which of late he had collected with his boat. It was a beautiful evening, and a clear amber sunset lit up all the eastern shores; and that man's employment, so simple and direct,—though he is regarded by most as a vicious character,—whose whole motive was so easy to fathom,—thus to obtain his winter's wood,—charmed me unspeakably. So much do we love actions that are simple. They are all poetic. We, too, would fain to be so employed." Thoreau, *Journal*, V, 444, Oct. 22, 1853, 639.

37   For contemporary examples, consider the do-it-yourself, ethical eating, and environmentalist movements. In this video, two modern homesteaders, Yan Roberts and Sherry Milford, describe a nature-based ethic that in many ways mirrors the "close to the bone" economy of Thoreau's original environmentalism (*Walden*, 66). Nipissing University Peace Research Initiative, *Agents of Peace Project* (Nipissing Village, 2012), http://www.youtube.com/ watch?v=c4McLIT6zy8&feature=BFa&list=UULfYrK9caWyOpf7GG5MdKOQ.

38   Thoreau, *Journal*, June 13, 1853. The punctuation of the quote has been corrected.

39   For more on the neo-classical shift in economics, and its evisceration of the notion of intrinsic values (so crucial to liberal political and ethical discourses), I put forward a more extensive argument. See Toivo Koivukoski, "The Hopeful Science," *After the Last Man: Excurses to the Limits of the Technological System* (Lanham: Lexington Books, 2008).

40   Milton and Rose Friedman, *Free to Choose* (New York: Avon, 1979), 203–8.

41   Thoreau, *Journal*, June 9, 1853.

42   Thoreau, *Walden*, 170.

43   Immanuel Kant, "What Is Enlightenment?," *Foundations of the Metaphysics of Morals*, trans. Lewis White Beck (London: Macmillan, 1990), 84.

44   Aristotle, *Politics*, 1278a40.

45   Slavoj Žižek, *Violence: Six Sideways Reflections* (London: Profile Books, 2009), 166.

46   Žižek, *Violence*, 158.

47   Thoreau, *Walden*, 194.

48   Thoreau, *Walden*, 191.

49   Thoreau, *Walden*, 191.

50   Thoreau, *Walden*, 194. The passage is echoed in "Resistance to Civil Government," where Thoreau writes:

> I know this well, that if one thousand, if one hundred, if ten men whom I could name,—if ten honest men only,—aye, if one honest man, in this State of Massachusetts, ceasing to hold slaves, were actually to withdraw from this copartnership, and be locked up in the county jail therefor, it would be the abolition of slavery in America. For it matters not how small the beginning may seem to be: what is once well done is done for ever.

CHAPTER 10

Heidegger's Polemical Peace: Outer Violence for Inner Harmony

David Edward Tabachnick

The German philosopher Martin Heidegger is not known as a philosopher of peace. His commitment to National Socialism marks him as notorious for endorsing the horrors of the Second World War. Yet there is still a strange and disturbing link between the Heidegger who wrote about "the inner truth and greatness" of the Nazis, and the Heidegger who decided that "Care" is "the Being of Dasein."[1] He believed that the leadership of Adolph Hitler, the National Socialist movement, and the war somehow represented—at least for some people—an opportunity to return to a more authentic, spiritually rich, and (in the end) peaceful existence. In the exceptionally trying times of mid-20th-century Europe, Heidegger seemed to think that the massive perpetration of external violence would in some way recapture a nearly lost "inner harmony."

But can the Heidegger of war and the Heidegger of peace really be reconciled? In part, answering this question will uncover a Heideggerian conception of peace that rejects the enlightened, Kantian, progressive model, and embraces what will be explained as a polemical definition. In one sense, this effort to link Heidegger's philosophy and politics has become a surprisingly mainstream approach.[2] Previously it might have seemed as though there were two different Heideggers: the apolitical "radical individualist" scholar who advocated personal freedom from an oppressive, "inauthentic" society; and the foremost philosopher of the Nazi party, whose political views infused all his thinking.[3] It now seems clear that his political commitments were an outgrowth of his philosophy; and by studying that philosophy, we can better understand the horrifying nature of his politics.

Like many of the thinkers discussed in this volume, Heidegger spends little time explicating a specific definition of peace. Very few passages in his work even reference the term. One of them is his 1951 lecture "Building Dwelling Thinking" ("*Bauen Wohnen Denken*"). There he attempts to uncover an overlooked connection between building and dwelling to articulate a possible avenue to thinking that stands outside of the dominant metaphysical, technological, and scientific view. Instead of describing building as a product of objectifying and controlling or as a means for humans to escape the harshness of the natural world, Heidegger suggests that building should serve as a setting for a kind of dwelling that enables a more intimate and genuine relationship between human beings and nature.

He asks, "But in what does the essence of dwelling consist?" He then claims that "Building is really dwelling," in part because "the Old High German word for building, *buan*, means to dwell." He then further connects *buan* to the Gothic word *wunian*, which means "to be at peace, to be brought to peace, to remain in peace" because both can also mean "to remain, to stay in place."[4] So, in the technological conception of building, we are homeless but, by returning to a more authentic kind of building, we can return home and finally be at peace.

The key point is not that a dormant peace somehow awaits us at home, but that our experience of peace only comes from leaving, a homecoming and a settling in. Heidegger's definition of *wunian* presents three different poses of peace: "to be at," "to be brought to," and "to remain in." The first pose is one of stillness and quietness—perhaps an undisturbed, original and naive sense of peace. The second pose clearly suggests a journey away from and a return to peace; something that has been disturbed or disrupted but then, through some kind of action, has been brought back to a place of peace after a difficult displacement. The third pose suggests a resolution or perseverance "to remain at peace" in the face of efforts to once again disturb or disrupt it through some violence or conflict that tests or challenges the ability to endure in a peaceful place.

These movements—involving peace, displacement, returning, and remaining with a renewed sense of peace—are suggested in Heidegger's further effort to define peace (*Frieden* in German) as meaning "the free";

derived from the Old High German word *fry*, meaning "preserved from harm and danger, safeguarded."[5] In the same essay, Heidegger connects this dwelling and remaining in peace to our essential relationship with nature, and our responsibility to it. He explains that our proper place as mortals, on earth, under the sky and before the divinities, is among a "fourfold" that we must safeguard and preserve. However, we only can arrive at this place and take up this responsibility to safeguard once we recognize our mortality in "death *as* death."[6] Because in our original naive pose of peace we have not experienced the disruption and violence that allows us to recognize our finitude, we cannot yet properly play our proper role in caring for the fourfold. Critically, we are only able recognize our responsibility once we have experienced the difficult journey away from, and back to, peace.

This description of the relationship between peace and dwelling can be linked to Heidegger's earlier writing on anxiety.[7] In *Being and Time*, he describes anxiety as the uncanny experience of being thrown from our normal understanding—a feeling that "everyday familiarity collapses."[8] Because Heidegger thinks that most people live inauthentic lives among the "they," the public or the somnambulistic mob, anxiety is a moment when we can, at least momentarily, grasp something authentic. Still, he defines it as Dasein's "fleeing *in the face of* itself,"[9] since our first reaction to anxiety is usually to push it away and return to everydayness.

He continues a few passages later decrying that, "When in falling we flee *into* the 'at-home' of publicness, we flee *in the face of* the 'not-at-home'.... This uncanniness pursues Dasein constantly, and is a threat to its everyday lostness in the 'they.'"[10] With a sense of great struggle, uncanny anxiety is presented as a threat to our everydayness just as the falling back into everydayness is presented as a threat to the mood of anxiety that can serve as a "disclosive state of mind" that allows us to begin the journey to an authentic life.[11]

Heidegger clearly sees most people losing this struggle for authenticity, and falling back into everydayness. The few who attain authenticity, from the exceptional experience of anxiety and beyond the narrowness of the "they-world," are led to "care," which is "the Being of Dasein."[12] As Heidegger explains, care is profoundly linked to people experiencing a sense of place or belonging on the earth, which is the source of our Being: "'Being-in-the world' has the stamp of 'care,' which accords with Being."[13] Care, as Heidegger describes in *Being and Time*, is quite similar to the peace of the fourfold, outlined in "Building, Dwelling, Thinking." In both, Dasein is described as being in harmony or balance with the earth. Yet again, this harmony only comes through an anxious displacement. We need some kind of violent shock, knocking us out of our inauthentic stupor or "tranquillized self-assurance,"[14] to give us the opportunity to "dwell" authentically.

However, for most people, this violent shock induces fear. Unlike anxiety, fear is experienced as a paralyzing or overwhelming terror that does not move one from inauthenticity to authenticity but rather stupefies them in displacement with no sense of uncanniness. In turn, Heidegger decides that 'real' anxiety is a rare and individualized experience, "In anxiety there lies the possibility of a disclosure which is quite distinctive; for anxiety individualizes. This individualization brings Dasein back from its falling, and makes manifest to it that authenticity and inauthenticity are possibilities of its Being."[15] So, where one person may experience paralyzing fear in the face of violence or war, which we would take as a rather typical response, it might spark anxiety in another type of person, awakening them to new possibilities.[16]

We might now be able to more clearly connect "outer violence" with "inner harmony." Only through some disruption from the everyday can we be awakened to the possibility of a deeper or richer reality that leads us to a free, harmonious and peaceful pose that entails a full awareness of the conflictual character of existence. Only by experiencing war can we appreciate peace; an appreciation gained for the few who survived the journey. Overall, Heidegger is describing what could be called a polemical definition of peace in the sense of the ancient Greek word for war: *Polemos*. This odd pairing of war and peace is not all that surprising when the role of war, strife, confrontation and struggle is understood in the larger context of Heidegger's work. He understands existence itself as a struggle in that all beings have an essence that comes into being and goes out of being, unconcealed and concealed, disclosed and then hidden, presenced and then absenced, lives and dies, participating in the larger movement, movedness, or "emerging power" of nature or *physis*.[17] In a sense, then, all things must struggle to emerge from the manifold of Being, to distinguish themselves as discrete beings and maintain their essence in the face of overpowering nature.[18]

The central role of struggle is considered more directly in his work on the "Polemos Fragment" or Fragment 53 from Heraclitus. In a 1966–67 seminar on Heraclitus, the fragment is presented via the standard Diels translation, "War [*Polemos*] is the father and king of all things. He established some as gods and the other as humans; some he made slaves and the others free."[19] From this, Heidegger decides that *Polemos* as "father and ruler" is then responsible for the movement of all things.[20] But, as Gregory Fried points out, he provides a far more provocative, alternative translation in his lectures on Hölderlin over three decades earlier, "Struggle [*Polemos*] is indeed the sire to all beings, but for all beings also ruler, and some he makes manifest as gods, the others as humans, some he sets forth as servants, the others as masters."[21] Heidegger goes on to explain that:

> Struggle is the power of the generation of beings, but not in such a way that struggle, after things have come to be through it, then draws itself back from them. Rather, struggle also preserves and governs beings precisely in their essential condition. Struggle is indeed progenitor, but also ruler. And where struggle as the power of preservation and standing true [*Bewährung*] ceases, there begins standstill, compromise, mediocrity—and harmlessness, atrophy, and decline. But such struggle … is not arbitrary quarreling and discord and mere disturbance, but rather the strife of the great opposition between the essential powers of Being, so that in such struggle the gods as gods, and humans as humans first come to appearance against each other, and thereby to an inner harmony. In themselves, there are no gods or humans, nor are there masters and servants in themselves who then, because they are what they are, come into strife or harmony. Rather the reverse: struggle first creates the possibility of decision about life and death. Through proving true to a test [*Bewährung*], a being in one way or another first becomes in each case what it is and how it is. And this "is"—Being—essentially unfolds only as standing true to a test [*Bewährung*].[22]

Strangely, just as struggle "preserves and governs," peace is preserved and safeguarded. We might conclude then that *Polemos* safeguards peace or war keeps the peace. As Dianne Enns explains in Chapter 12 of this volume ("Hannah Arendt on Peace as a Means to Politics"), Hannah Arendt, one of Heidegger's best-known students, rejects this strange notion that violence and war brings about balance, harmony, and peace, noting that "the most likely outcome of violence is more violence"; but she still recognizes the problem of simply associating peace with utopic predictions. For Arendt, peace is necessarily political. Heidegger, distinctly, argues that without struggle we see the beginning of a "decline" and the end of the "inner harmony" which allowed a being to be "what it is and how it is." So, his polemical peace is a sustained balance between opposing powers. Without this struggling opposition, the essence of the thing at peace descends into nothingness, its unique character waning and withdrawing from existence. Just like Dasein is lost in the meaningless chatter of the "they," or in its disconnection from the fourfold, the authentic self can only emerge from an anxiety inducing event or circumstance that restores a sense of opposition that brings back a lost inner harmony or peace.

So far, Heidegger has explained this experience as exceptional and individualized. Elsewhere, though, he seems to suggest that a much broader experience of violence and anxiety could free an entire people (*Volk*) from the grip of inauthenticity.[23] Just as the individual experience of anxiety is rare, so too is this anxiety of the *Volk*; an exceptional experience, or what he later calls "spiritual mission" for only the German people. This movement from individual to people relates to the link between his earlier philosophy of individual freedom, mentioned above, and his later calls for the political liberation of the German *Volk* through an embrace of National Socialism.

Heidegger was not alone in this kind of thinking. Vigorous assertions about the German people were quite common in German philosophy and culture in the early 20th century: they were experiencing a precipitous decline, and required some sort of release or emancipation from the pressures of modern life. The leading thinkers and commentators of that era frequently described Western civilization as drained of spirit, oppressed by narrow thinking and materialism, and on the verge of collapse. Perhaps more than any other work, Oswald Spengler's tremendously popular two-volume *The Decline of the West* articulates the idea that the disorder, lack of direction, and weakness of leadership that plagued Germany was the historical fruition of the degradation of civilization in the Western world. In the introduction, he presents his earliest rationale for writing the book, which was begun in 1911 but first published in 1918:

> At that time [in 1911] the World War appeared to me both as imminent and also as the inevitable outward manifestation of the historical crisis.... Consider the decline of art and the failing authority of science; the grave problems arising out of the victory of the megalopolis over the country-side, such as childlessness and land-depopulation; the place in society of a fluctuating Fourth Estate; the crisis of materialism, in Socialism, in parliamentary government, the position of the individual *vis-à-vis* the State; the problem of private property with its pendant problem of marriage.[24]

For Spengler, the coming war was thought to be the necessary consequence of the cultural, intellectual, social, economic, political and familial decline of Western World. He also argues that discussions about "'The Age of Reason,' Humanity, the greatest happiness of the greatest number, enlightenment, economic progress, national freedom, the conquest of nature, or world-peace"[25] and their associated philosophy and politics had led nowhere and only a world war could resolve this "historical crisis."[26] Michael Zimmerman explains Spengler's keen sense of the German state of mind:

> Germans were searching desperately for something that would exalt their narrow lives, that would free them from social isolation, that would restore meaning in their lives, and that would unite them in a primal bond that must have been available to Germans in a simpler, more genuine era. That longed-for event, so they concluded, was the outbreak of the Great War in 1914.[27]

Yet as the later success of *The Decline of the West* attests, the violence and destruction of the Great War resolved nothing for the Germans. It only exacerbated social tensions and inspired further drastic plans to fight against the paralyzing effects of modern society. The desperate circumstances of Germany during this period led to ever more radical calls to respond to what was viewed as the abject failure of the Western Enlightenment to deliver on the promised free and peaceful rational society.[28]

In this time and place, Heidegger comes to the fore. But unlike Spengler and his ilk, he does not blame the crisis on civilization, social decline, or degraded culture. In his 1929–1930 Freiburg Lectures (later published as *The Fundamental Concepts of Metaphysics*), he argues that such "convoluted idle talk about culture" was itself a product of a more fundamental problem:

> We said that this philosophy of culture most sets out what is contemporary about our situation, but does not take hold of *us*.... Our flight and disorientation [*Verkehrung*], the illusion and our lostness become more actute.... Why do we find no meaning for ourselves any more, i.e. no essential possibilty of being? Is it because an *indifference* yawns at us out of all things, an indifference whose ground we do not know? Yet why can we speak in such a way when world trade, technology, and the economy seize hold of man and keep him moving? And nevertheless *we* seek a *role for ourselves*. What is happening here?, we ask anew. Must we first make ourselves interesting to ourselves again? Why *must* we do this? Perhaps

because we ourselves have become *bored* with ourselves? Is man himself now supposed to have become bored with himself? Why so? *Do things ultimately stand in such a way with us that a profound boredom draws back and forth like a silent fog in the abysses of Dasein?*[29]

This description of the experience of disorientation and being lost, the sense of insignificance, indifference, and "profound boredom," is not offered as a critique of the decline of the West, or as a conservative commentary on the deprivations of modern society. Instead, Heidegger aims to spur his readers to further and deeper thinking. Unlike Spengler, he does not call for some sort of cultural revival of a glorious past Germany, or attempt to inspire a new sense of purpose for the German Dasein. For him, the crisis offers an opportunity to clear away the fog that covers the German Dasein; to attune and awaken the *Volk* to their estrangement from the authentic, and to help them somehow begin the journey back home.[30]

When Heidegger asks "How do we escape this boredom?,"[31] he is not referring to our attempts to preoccupy ourselves, pass the time with trivial distractions, or try to ignore boredom. He means that instead, we should listen to what the mood of boredom is trying to tell us, and pay attention to its true significance. The real problem with contemporary society is not (as the ranting philosophers of culture contend) that it is flat, static, and dull; but that it is actually designed to divert us from grasping the real meaning of our "contemporary situation." So we should not run away from boredom, but "bear it" and "wait for its effect"—allowing everyday boredom to grow into *profound* boredom. As Heidegger advises, instead of adopting "emergency measures for the protection of culture in a kind of spurious instant response" or "some general collective enthusiasm," as is the counsel of Spengler, "we must principally concern ourselves with preparing man the very basis and dimension upon which and within which something like a mystery of his Dasein could once again be encountered."[32]

Here, in these opaque passages that include a description of Heidegger's hours long wait in a train station, is an ominous call for a new kind of politics that rejects the modern project for safety, security and world peace. Because modernity attempts to abolish the mystery and the terror, strife and confrontation, that are critical to the "inner harmony" of Being, we now need something or someone drastically different and powerful to awaken us:[33] "We must first call for someone capable of instilling terror into our Dasein again. For how do things stand with our Dasein when an event like the Great War can to all extents and purposes pass us by without leaving a trace?"[34]

Amazingly, the terror and turmoil of the First World War was not enough and, consequently, "our Dasein" or the German *Volk*, requires someone capable of instilling even greater terror. With this alarming passage firmly in mind, we can better understand the meaning of his "Rectoral Address" of May 27, 1933 presented under the title "The Self-Assertion of the German-University." He speaks of being "led by the inexorability of that spiritual mission which impresses onto the fate of the German Volk the stamp of their history." He explains the idea of self-governance as the task of being "what we ourselves ought to be," and links this concept to "the historical spiritual mission of the German Volk that knows itself in its state."[35] But this spiritual mission or fate is under "extreme distress," in constant danger, and thus in need of an "active perseverance" or constant struggle to keep this all important task ongoing.[36] Some of the stresses and dangers Heidegger lists include the "Christian-theological interpretation of the world," and the "mathematical-technical thinking of the modern age."

He also mentions the role of "international organizations" in obscuring the possibility for Germany to "recapture" greatness. This reproach of international organizations is a knowing reference to German animosity to the role of the League of Nations. In fact, later that same year—echoing his call for self-assertion in the Rector's address—Heidegger appeals to the German people to vote for a November 12 plebiscite that would see Germany withdraw from the League:

> It is not ambition, not desire for glory, not blind obstinacy, and not hunger for power that demands from the Führer that Germany withdraw from the League of Nations. It is only the clear will to unconditional self-responsibility in enduring and mastering the fate of our people.[37]

With this call for withdrawal, we see an obvious connection between Heidegger's philosophy and the politics of the day. The plebiscite—held at the same time as the first parliamentary elections under National Socialism—ushered in both the country's rejection of involvement in the international community, and the Nazis' further consolidation of domestic power. Heidegger and Germany were not only turning away from the League of Nations but also its conception of peace based in the prevailing Enlightenment philosophies of the past century.

Heidegger's views on how the deprivations of global politics imprison the German people can be compared to Kant's earlier ideas about the way states can be emancipated from conflict through international cooperation (outlined in Chapter 7 of this volume by Leah Bradshaw). In the seventh thesis of his *Idea for a Universal History from a Cosmopolitan Point of View*, written in 1784, Kant states:

> Through war, through the taxing and never-ending accumulation of armament, through the want which any state, even in peacetime, must suffer internally, Nature forces them to make at first inadequate and tentative attempts; finally, after devastations, revolutions, and even complete exhaustion, she brings them to that which reason could have told them at the beginning and with far less sad experience, to wit, to step from the lawless condition of savages into a league of nations. In a league of nations, even the smallest state could expect security and justice, not from its own power and by its own decrees, but only from this great league of nations (*Foedus Amphictyonum*), from a united power acting according to decisions reached under the laws of their united will.

Here, Kant articulates what became the prevailing view after the First World War: individual states cannot take "self-responsibility" for their fates because—as history has shown, and reason tells us—this leads only to endless war. The alternative way to peace can only come from the subordination of state power to the "united will" of a "league of nations." But Heidegger's depiction of the League as an obstacle to the recapturing of the still existent but hidden greatness of the German *Volk*, indicates that this kind of peace, and the way of life that goes along with it, is illusory and superficial. This distinction is also clear in his "Declaration of Support for Adolph Hitler and the National Social State," on November 11, 1933:

> The choice that the German people must now make is, *simply as an event in itself*, quite independently of the outcome, the strongest expression of the new German reality embodied in the National Socialist State. Our will to national [*völkisch*] self-responsibility desires that each people find and preserve the greatness and truth of its destiny [*Bestimmung*]. This will is the highest guarantee of peace among nations, for it binds itself to the basic law of manly respect and unconditional honor. The Führer has awakened this will in the entire people and has welded it into *one* single resolve. No one can remain away from the polls on the day when this will is manifested. Heil Hitler![38]

In Heidegger's view, peace—rather than being found in the united will of all states—is expressed in the singular will of the German people, "embodied in the National Socialist State." This, he claims, is the violent struggle necessary to recapture the home of the *Volk*, where they can remain in peace and harmony. In lock-step with fellow Nazi philosopher Carl Schmitt, and his unbending support for the undemocratic, authoritarian character of the regime, Heidegger maintains that without struggle, violence, and war, there can never be peace for Germany.[39] Yet by the start of the Second World War, he seems resigned to the failure of this spiritual mission, and the prospect of peace. In a passage from "Overcoming Metaphysics," written just as the war begins, he considers contemporary society characterized by an abandonment of Being:

> The "world wars" and their character of "totality" are already a consequence of the abandonment of Being. They press toward a guarantee of stability of a constant form of using things up. Man, who no longer conceals his character of being the most important raw material, is also drawn into this process. Man is the most "most important raw material" because he remains the subject of all consumption. He does this in such a way that he lets his will be unconditionally equated with this process, and thus at the same time become the "object" of the abandonment of Being. The world wars are the antecedent form of the removal of the difference between war and peace. This removal is necessary since the "world" has become an un-world as a consequence of the abandonment of beings by Being's truth.[40]

For Heidegger, the massive technological effort epitomized by two world wars (which a generation before Ernst Jünger had called Total Mobilization)[41] obliterates the distinction between war and peace: in either state, there continues an age of mass consumption, unabated by declarations of war or peace treaties. Understandably, "the abandonment of Being" also means "the removal of the difference between war and peace": existence can no longer move from peaceful dwelling to violent disruption, because now everything is held static and captive, obstructed, "enframed" by the demands of technology. Now, human beings are nothing more than "raw material" or what Heidegger calls in "The Question Concerning Technology," published in 1954, "standing-reserve": stuff waiting to be processed through the massive technological infrastructure that develops hand-in-hand with the vast war machines of 1914 and 1939.

For him, in that day and age, peace and war, then, are really part of the same inexorable process of taking up everything, man included, as standing-reserve. As he writes in the same section of "Overcoming Metaphysics": "Changed into their deformation of essence, 'war' and 'peace' are taken up into erring, and disappear into the mere course of the escalating manufacture of what can be manufactured, because they have become unrecognizable with regard to any distinction" and "The question of when there will be peace cannot be answered not because the duration of war is unfathomable, but rather because the question already asks about something which no longer exists, since war is no longer anything which could terminate in peace."[42] For Heidegger, the triumph of the technological world means that struggle, balance, and inner harmony are no longer possible; and so the possibility of peace also disappears.

While unconventional, his conclusion that war becomes ever more technological, all-encompassing, and endless matches the reality of the "long war" or "Cold War" that followed the Second World War. The arms race, and the related concept of Mutually Assured Destruction, align with Heidegger's notion that war and peace are fused through the acceleration of technology to a global scale. In the 21st century, the so-called war on terror also represents a confusion of war and peace: it is empowered by ever more ubiquitous technology, including spy satellites that can monitor the homes of potential enemies, and drones able to kill anyone, anywhere, at any time. In the modern world, it may be that Heidegger was right: war is both everywhere, all the time, and also nowhere and never.

Notes

1   Martin Heidegger, *An Introduction to Metaphysics*, trans. Ralph Manheim (New Haven: Yale University Press, 1959), 199; and also Martin Heidegger, *Being and Time*, trans. John Macquarrie and Edward Robinson (Oxford: Blackwell, 2000), 241.

2   For some examples of efforts to link Heidegger's philosophy and politics, see these works:

> Miguel Beistegui, *Heidegger and the Political* (London: Routledge, 1998).
> Hubert Dreyfus, "Heidegger on the Connection between Nihilism, Art, Technology and Politics," *The Cambridge Companion to Heidegger*, ed. Charles Guignon (Cambridge: Cambridge University Press, 1993), 289–316.
> Luc Ferry and Alain Renaut, *Heidegger and Modernity*, trans. Franklin Philip (Chicago: University of Chicago Press, 1990).

Gregory Fried, *Heidegger's Polemos: From Being to Politics* (New Haven: Yale University, 2000).

Tom Rockmore, *The Heidegger Case: On Philosophy and Politics*, ed. Tom Rockmore and Joseph Margolis (Philadelphia: Temple, 1992).

Richard Wolin, "French Heidegger Wars," *The Heidegger Controversy*, ed. Richard Wolin (Cambridge: MIT Press, 1993), 272–300.

Richard Wolin, *The Politics of Being* (New York: Columbia University Press, 1990).

Michael Zimmerman, *Heidegger's Confrontation with Modernity: Technology, Politics, Art* (Bloomington: Indiana University Press, 1990).

3   Frederick A. Olafson, "The Unity of Heidegger's Thought," *The Cambridge Companion to Heidegger*, ed. Charles Guignon (Cambridge: Cambridge University Press, 1993), 97–121.

4   Martin Heidegger, "Building, Dwelling, Thinking," *Martin Heidegger: Basic Writings*, ed. David Farrell Krell (San Francisco: Harper Collins, 1993), 348–50.

5   Heidegger, "Building, Dwelling, Thinking," 351.

6   Heidegger, "Building, Dwelling, Thinking," 352.

7   Heidegger, *Being and Time*, 227.

8   Heidegger, *Being and Time*, 233.

9   Heidegger, *Being and Time*, 229.

10   Heidegger, *Being and Time*, 234.

11   Heidegger, *Being and Time*, 230.

12   Heidegger, *Being and Time*, 241.

13   Heidegger, *Being and Time*, 241.

14   Heidegger, *Being and Time*, 233.

15   Heidegger, *Being and Time*, 241.

16   *Being and Time*, 230–33. Heidegger continues, "Being-anxious discloses, primordially and directly, the world as world…. That which anxiety is anxious about is Being-in-the world itself." Again, anxiety is the state-of-mind by which Dasein can be authentic. Also, "Anxiety brings Dasein face to face with it Being-free for (*propensi in*) the authenticity of its Being, and for this authenticity as a possibility which it always is."

17   For Heidegger's analysis of nature as movedness, see Martin Heidegger, "On the Essence and Concept of φύσις in Aristotle's *Physics* B, I," *Pathmarks*, ed. William McNeil (Cambridge: University Press, 1998).

18   In his article, W.R. Newell explains that for Heidegger:

> Being must be understood in terms of the origin, the generative process from which things emerge, not as a realm of eternal ends or substance in which human nature seeks its perfection and has a permanent place. Instead, according to Heidegger, man experiences Being or life as an "overpowering" force. It is a *Polemos* (the ancient Greek word for war) in which man is engaged as a kind of chief warrior, struggling to make his

> home in the matrix of history. Like all other things, man is generated out of this overpowering force. But he alone is capable of turning back against it to achieve his "being-free."

W.R. Newell, "Heidegger on Freedom and Community: Some Political Implications of His Early Thought," *American Political Science Review*, 78.3 (Sept. 1984): 776.

19   As quoted in Martin Heidegger and Eugen Fink, *Heraclitus Seminar*, trans. Charles H. Seivert (Evanston, IL: Northwestern University Press, 1993), 23. See also *Die Fragmente der Vorsokratiker* (Berlin, 1903; 6th ed. rev. by Walther Kranz [Berlin: Weidmann, 1952]).

20   Heidegger and Fink, *Heraclitus Seminar*, 24. Heidegger also considers the Polemos Fragment in *An Introduction to Metaphysics*: 61–62. See also Hans Sluga's essay "'Conflict Is the Father of All Things': Heidegger's Polemical Conception of Politics," *A Companion to Heidegger's Introduction to Metaphysics*, ed. Richard Polt and Gregory Fried (New Haven: Yale University Press, 2001), 205–25.

21   Gregory Fried, *Heidegger's Polemos: From Being to Politics* (New Haven: Yale University Press, 2000), 29. Translated from the German by Gregory Fried.

22   As quoted in *Heidegger's Polemos,* 30.

23   As W.R. Newell notes in reference to *An Introduction to Metaphysics*: "In one of Heidegger's rare concrete descriptions of 'primordial' political activity, we learn that the resolve to recover the greatness of a people's origins cannot exclude violence" (Newell, 780).

24   Oswald Spengler, *The Decline of the West*, trans. Charles Francis Atkinson (London: George Allen & Unwin, 1918), Vol. 1, 46–48.

25   Spengler, *Decline of the West*, 20.

26   This is the same notion described by Friedrich Nietzsche a generation earlier. In his Preface to *Beyond Good and Evil*, Nietzsche explains that Western thinking (i.e., the legacy of Plato) and religion (i.e., Christianity) "has created in Europe a magnificent tension of the spirit the like of which has never yet existed on earth: with so tense a bow we can now shoot for the most distant goals … we still feel it, the whole need of the spirit and the whole tension of its bow. And perhaps also the arrow, the task, and—who knows?—the goal" (2–3). Ominously, Nietzsche later explains that the relief of this tension, exhibited in the "internal upheavals" of Europe, would come "by means of a new caste that would rule Europe, a long, terrible will of its own that be able to cast its goals millennia hence—so the long-drawn-out comedy of its many splinter states as well as its dynastic and democratic splinter will would come to an end. The time for petty politics is over: the very next century will bring the fight for the dominion of the earth—the compulsion to large-scale politics." Friedrich Nietzsche, *Beyond Good and Evil*, trans. Walter Kaufman (New York: Vintage Books, 1989), 131.

In his assessment of the period, Michael Zimmerman decides that "Germans were searching desperately for something that would exalt their narrow lives, that would free them from social isolation, that would restore meaning in their lives, and that would unite them in a primal bond that must have been available to Germans in a simpler, more genuine era. That longed-for event, so they concluded, was the outbreak of the Great War in 1914." Michael Zimmerman, *Heidegger's Confrontation with Modernity: Technology, Politics and Art* (Bloomington: University of Indiana Press, 1990), 13.

27 Zimmerman, *Technology, Politics and Art*, 13.

28 As Ernst Breisach puts it, "The proponents of progress, including Condorcet, had failed to grasp the real outcome of the modern quest for absolute knowledge and its correlate, absolute control. Instead of the ideal union of reason and freedom, a life with a narrow-gauged routine would mark the static or quasi-static postmodernity." Ernst Breisach, *On the Future of History: The Postmodernist Challenge and Its Aftermath* (Chicago: University of Chicago Press, 2003), 21.

29 Martin Heidegger, *The Fundamental Concepts of Metaphysics*, trans. William McNeill and Nicholas Walker (Bloomington: Indiana University Press, 1995), 77.

30 For a further discussion, see David Tabachnick, "Modern Boredom, the Human Element and Creative Politics," *The Primacy of Persons in Politics: Empiricism and Political Philosophy*, ed. Thomas Heilke and John von Heyking (Washington: Catholic University of America Press, 2013).

31 Heidegger, *Concepts of Metaphysics*, 78.

32 Heidegger, *Concepts of Metaphysics*, 172.

33 Heidegger, *Concepts of Metaphysics*, 163–64.

34 Heidegger, *Concepts of Metaphysics*, 172.

35 Martin Heidegger, "The Self-Assertion of the German University," *The Heidegger Controversy*, ed. Richard Wolin (Cambridge: MIT Press, 1993), 29–30.

36 Heidegger, "Self-Assertion," 32.

37 Heidegger, "German Men and Women!," *The Heidegger Controversy*, 47–48.

38 Heidegger, "Declaration of Support for Adolph Hitler and the Nationalist Socialist State," *The Heidegger Controversy*, 52.

39 See, for example, Carl Schmitt, *Political Theology* (Cambridge: MIT Press, 1985); and also Carl Schmitt, *The Concept of the Political* (Chicago: University of Chicago Press, 2008). As well, Michael Zimmerman notes Heidegger's rejection of Kantian international relations as part of a broader movement: "German discussion about the cultural despair was heightened by defeat in World War I, which further eroded the leading status of the liberal-progressive view of history propounded by the influential neo-Kantians." From

Zimmerman's essay "The Ontological Decline of the West," *Companion to Heidegger*, 192.

40   Wolin, *The Heidegger Controversy*, 84.

41   Wolin, *The Heidegger Controversy*, 128.

42   Wolin, *The Heidegger Controversy*, 84–85.

CHAPTER 11

The State of Exception, Divine Violence, and Peace: Walter Benjamin's Lesson

Hermínio Meireles Teixeira

When engaging with the diverse works of Walter Benjamin one can, at best, only piece together a possible vision of what one would properly call a philosophy of peace. The same must be said for how such a vision would appear in practice. But once accomplished, this piecing together of a vision of peace is disturbingly clear and remarkably prescient. For Benjamin, peace, as non-violent political conflict and agreement, exists only in collective actions that break or evade the legal monopoly of violence so integral to the sovereign authority of the Western nation-state system. This monopoly, he explained, is defined and fully active in the Western state's constitutional right to declare, and use, a state of emergency, or "exception," as the primal source of law and order.[1] In such a state, the authorities legally suspend the provisions of the law (rights, due process) so as to unleash the full force and violence of the law.

Importantly, as the authorities must proclaim, such a legal suspension is done so as to restore or preserve the ends of power and authority in the law. But, as Benjamin shows us, this violent restoring and preserving of the legal ends of power and authority contains the insoluble paradox of all justifications of the foundations of legal violence: the contingency of violence itself is exposed as the most, and perhaps only, secure means of founding and justifying law. Peace, therefore, in Benjamin's sense, is the historical struggle to sever this nexus between violence and law in political experience. A confrontation with Max Weber's paradigmatic justification of the legal-rational foundations of the modern state is therefore unavoidable, as we shall see below. Yet how does this peace actually translate into practice? It is here that Benjamin's vision of peace turns out to be a most prescient one.

In his work, the historical practice of peace transpires, paradoxically, as what he calls "divine violence"[2]—a unique form of violence that breaks the legal monopoly by seeking neither to make and restore law, nor to preserve it, but simply to depose it. Benjamin calls it divine because he locates this violence in the historical material of Scripture itself, especially in the allegories of Jewish and Christian messianic traditions.[3] In them he discovers a type of violence that opposes the mythical justifications of violence at the heart of royal, theocratic, and imperial rule.[4] Crucially, Benjamin sees in these allegorical appeals to the divine a violence that does not repeat the cycles of sovereign rule, but simply destroys them. Its end is neither restoration nor preservation of legal violence, but an active purifying commitment to its destruction as a source of political organization.

Divine—that is, mythical—violence often cannot avoid responding with the same physical violence as the cycles of legal retribution. But the true potency of its means, as we will see below, is a radically different form of destructiveness that the cycles of legal violence can never appropriate. Rather than assaulting or smashing the state, divine violence is a simple withdrawal of essential support: one that starts to occupy the daily functioning of state institutions themselves. Rather than engaging the forceful demands or compromising reforms of a state-declared crisis, it appears as the dissolution of the very possibilities of participation and cooperation; and rather than defer to the urgent need for results and resolutions there may be in true (but politically manipulated) states of emergency, divine violence occupies the heart of the latter with a devastating indifference. Have we not seen the recent "Occupy" movements, from Arab Spring to Wall Street to student protests, betraying the essence of this violence? All these were different in their conditions, but linked by common means. If one seriously considers this possibility, then the voices who find relief in the ending of these events[5]—those who gain a sense of vindication in the failed results of their poorly organized plans and commitments, and who rejoice over the return of a sovereign order that relegates these occupying events to the detritus of history—may have missed the most important dimension of what Benjamin meant by "divine" violence. Like the divine of Scripture, it is never reducible to the durations of its actions, or the results of its visitations on history. Instead it is a spectral image, a fractured burning memory, illuminated only in the failures of historical struggles for peace.

But how can these fragments of historical failures, with their short durations and unaccomplished results, evoke a divinely violent end to the cyclical hold of legal violence? We will elaborate the difficulties of Benjamin's response to this question later, but for now a brief answer is worthwhile. The failures of historical struggle do not always signify a slide into oblivion, but instead, with time and event(s), can retain images that resonate as preparatory efforts to enact an impossible idea (at the time of its expression) that now, in its failure, lies waiting to be repeated in the difference of its time to come. In this sense, the greatest threat facing the victorious political authorities today is not the return of the vulnerability of law and order, but the recent history of Occupy movements—strewn mainly with the melancholia of failure, and unresolved political efforts to depose legal violence. The potent work of divine violence, therefore, is actually in the spectres of debris, the aftermaths of destruction (both historical and natural),[6] and especially in the residual ruins of historical struggles. Benjamin ends his masterwork *The Origins of German Tragic Drama* with exactly this point, highlighting our disturbed but irresistible attraction to the ruins of great buildings: in them, he declares, "the idea of the plan speaks more impressively than in lesser buildings, however well preserved they are."[7]

Let us now move on to identifying the two difficulties in Benjamin's vision of peace and its practical enactment in divine violence—though a caution is necessary: these are not merely problems of interpretation, or theoretical lacunae in Benjamin's work on peace and divine violence. They are rather the irresistible and creative difficulties immanent to any pieced-together work. The two difficulties are this: Why, for Benjamin, must peace be conceived in the shattered remnants of history, in tumults such as a state of emergency that has become the rule? And how does the peace of divine violence actually manifest itself? For though it resides in events such as the Occupy movements, it is never reducible to their durations, or to the programs of new social movements wrought by self-conscious occupiers.

Peace in the State of Exception

The first difficulty we encounter in trying to link Walter Benjamin's work to peace is that he has no philosophy or theory of peace. This does not mean, however, that he did not provide critical insights into the concept, as we will see below. As Hannah Arendt rightly notes in her introduction to *Illuminations*, what this means is that he worked in the fields of history, theology, and literature without actually being a historian, theologian, or writer; and that he "thought poetically, but was neither a poet nor philosopher."[8] Arendt's point is that Benjamin's work in these scholarly fields was oriented by a different historical method of inquiry, one that could only be described as that of "the critic"—the term Benjamin himself used to identify his work.[9] Yet he penned such a unique conception of critique through his works that only the impact of historical event and distance could bring to light what he called the life of a work: "more the moving truth than the resting truth." This is how Benjamin described his critical work in the opening pages of his essay "Goethe's Elective Affinities."[10]

Carefully distinguishing critique's concern for this moving truth from commentary's concern for mere subject matter, Benjamin explains that the true critic understands how both the durations and vicissitudes of historical time are integral to the essential truth of a work. "If, therefore, the works that prove enduring are precisely those whose truth is most deeply sunken in their material content, then, in the course of this duration, the concrete realities rise up before the eyes of the beholder [the critic] all the more distinctly the more they die out in the world," he writes.[11] A critical inquiry into the concept and practice of peace, therefore, defines its enduring image only in the fragmented unfolding of its history. As Benjamin explains in the opening section of *Origins of German Tragic Drama* (duly titled, "Epistemo-Critical Prologue"), no historical phenomena ever enter the realm of ideas whole and unadulterated, which in philosophy and politics means a submission to the conceptual demands of representation. It is critique, in Benjamin's sense, that avoids the "destructive sophistry" of unified philosophies, theories, or systems (the "false unities"), by making its purpose "the salvation of phenomena in ideas."[12] In this sense, the lack of a philosophy or theory of peace in fact privileges the study of peace, for Benjamin understands, as we shall argue below, that peace is the critical life itself.

We are now prepared to redress our first difficulty—how to piece together Benjamin's fragmentary vision of peace, and the means by which it has emerged, and can emerge, in historical time. However, a warning is in order. To say that peace is the critical life, and vice versa, implicates any ideas of peace in its living history: that critical peace as critique is essentially implicated in temporal destructions with its own unique form of violence, which Benjamin calls divine violence. This paradoxical affirmation of the intimacy of peace and destruction is contained in our second difficulty, and will occupy the latter part of this essay.

Benjamin's image of peace emerges by juxtaposing three key writings that address three topics that appear at first sight disparately related to each other, though much more to peace: violence in "Critique of Violence" of 1921 (1978); theatrical tragedy (*Trauerspiel*) in *Origins of German Tragic Drama* of 1928 (1998); and historical materialism in "Theses on the Philosophy of History" of 1940 (1968). In the first, Benjamin examines how the history of the institution of sovereign law has always required a monopoly of violence at its foundation, and as a result conceives of justice and peace only in relation to this historical founding of sovereign law. With a special disdain for pacifists, he warns them that a priori commitments to peace in the Western tradition of state sovereignty have mainly emerged in the historical settlements of a relationship of war.

Why, Benjamin asks, do conquerors and oppressors, with the submission of the conquered in full grasp, still require from them a legally sanctioned peace treaty?[13] This peace, he warns, is the historical correlative of sovereign war. "Indeed the word 'peace,' in the sense in which it is the correlative of war … denotes this a priori sanctioning, regardless of all other legal conditions, of every victory."[14] In this sense, commitments to peace often denote the historically constituted supports for commitments to the settled dominance of war relations. For Benjamin, therefore, a first defining moment in the vision of peace resides in a critical severance of the essential nexus between the violence of sovereign law and the norms of life—a severance, that is, of sovereign law's hold on life in the warlike conditions of what Benjamin calls "the state of exception, or emergency."[15]

Writing on the topic of violence at almost exactly the same time (1919–1921 in Germany), Benjamin's peace has to emerge as a direct confrontation with Weber's paradigmatic justification (done not without disenchantment) of violence as an essential necessity in the legitimacy of the modern nation-state. Recall Weber's classical formulation in *Politics as a Vocation*: "We must say that the state is the form of human community that (successfully) lays claim to the *monopoly of legitimate physical*[16] *violence* [italics are

Weber's] within a particular territory."[17] One cannot exaggerate the varied and continuing dominance of this justification of the foundations of legal violence. In the present day, at almost a century's distance from Weber's assertion, and equally from the left and right, one now finds its uncritical presence stretching from the simple civics taught in introductory political texts, to the philosophical depth of Heidegger's fundamental ontology.[18] With what means, therefore, does Benjamin confront this paradigm?

In *Origins of German Tragic Drama*, Benjamin relates how the tumults of the Reformation and Counter-Reformation wars generated crises about how sovereign authority and power affect individuals and populations. But he does not turn for elucidation to the classics of political philosophy, or the masterpieces of Baroque drama; nor to the natural-rights theorists, or the works of Shakespeare or Calderon, for example. These recognized authorities spanned the periods from the 16th to at least the 18th centuries. Instead, he turns to obscure, vulgar, and failed Baroque dramas, by German authors such as Griphius, Lohenstein, Orpitz, and Hallmann, all written in a twenty-year period in the middle of the 17th century. Benjamin believes that this helps him to better understand the crises at the heart of early modern sovereignty.

Readers would be mistaken to read this scholarly choice as merely another sympathetic attempt to give dignity and recognition to the history of the downtrodden classes—a misinterpretation that underestimates the importance of these early Baroque dramas.[19] For Benjamin, these failed, fractured images of historical struggles to define the actual conditions of sovereign power and authority, are important precisely because they are failures; ideas relegated to the detritus of history. These are the shattered images of mournful, deteriorating sovereigns losing control of their sovereign rule to tumults and intrigues, precisely at that moment when they try to restore and maintain it with decisions on exceptions and declared emergencies. As Benjamin reveals, if one takes these voices of a declining art form seriously, on their own terms, one may examine what they struggled to articulate—but could do so only in the mournful figures of imploding sovereigns. This was the fear that sovereign rule had no other basis than the tumults of historical, earthly, "creaturely" time.[20]

The dramatists' expression of this fear was, it must be said, a Counter-Reformation reaction: a sad clinging to the restoration of Catholic princely and papal rule in the face of Protestant princes, who were solidifying their rule with decisions on exceptional threats and emergencies. But in the mad, mournful figure of the sovereign, these dramas shape and confront the intractable problem of the sovereign's rootedness in historical time: in the melancholia of the *Trauerspiel* are the unique words that express this in their own time. To formulate the problem carefully: sovereigns who found their earthly rule in decisions on emergencies implicated themselves and their realms in the tumults and struggles of earthly time, in which emergencies cannot be limited to the decision, because they become the rule of sovereignty itself. In fact, it should be said that these early Baroque dramas mourn what they see as the core of early modern sovereignty itself: an "indecisiveness" with respect to both its own rule, and to the lives of its people, wrought by exceptions and emergencies that are now the rule. The melancholia of the *Trauerspiel* is the normative disintegration of sovereign rule—indecisiveness expressed in *acedia*: listlessness, sloth, dullness of heart.[21] No doubt these represent a catastrophic scenario for the Counter-Reformation, Benjamin notes.[22] Yet what he also finds in these dramatic images, buried in the state histories of sovereign evolution, is a real catastrophe of a "fruitful and preparatory kind."[23]

We can now identify a second moment in Benjamin's vision of peace, one that brings us closer to how this peace may be attained in earthly life. If peace emerges only in the severance of the historically constituted nexus between sovereign violence and normative life, then the exception that becomes the rule is the very historical expression of that severance. This is exactly what Benjamin announces in 1940, in one of the last works of his life: "Theses on the Philosophy of History." He writes these theses knowing full well that a decision on the "exceptional case" of his own life had already been made by the Nazi sovereign. This gives a special poignancy to his words in Thesis VIII: "The tradition of the oppressed teaches us that the 'state of emergency' in which we live is not the exception, but the rule ... we [must] clearly realize that it is our task to bring about a real state of emergency."

As we read in the *Origins of German Tragic Drama*, the conception of history to which we must attain is itself situated in the early modern struggles of Christian theology over the question of sovereign authority. In their very fragmentation, the phenomena of the *Trauerspiel*—such as sovereign madness, melancholia, and martyrdom—retain an unrefined occupancy, often in mere images, or flashing memories, within the theological ideas and symbols to which they are intimately connected, such as sovereign authority or God's providence in history. A key fact for Benjamin here is that the *Trauerspiel* expresses the images of a sovereign power entirely abandoned by God to the ruptures of earthly time—to nothing but history (at least as the Reformation and Counter-Reformation sides saw it). The images and memories of historical rupture, therefore, become a historical condition of the possibility of an idea such as sovereign right, in their very negative relation.

More importantly, and paradoxically, the fractured image of a past can also lend itself to the future subversions of the very idea that has housed it through history—again, image as a historical decline of a "preparatory kind." This insight contains Benjamin's critical renewal of the theory of historical materialism, which he explains in Thesis VI: "Historical materialism wishes to retain that image of the past which unexpectedly appears to man singled out by history at a moment of danger. The danger affects both the content of tradition and its receivers."[24] A few sentences later, Benjamin articulates the greatest threat to the apprehension of those moments of danger: "In every era, the attempt must be made anew to wrest tradition away from a conformism that is about to overpower it."[25] Needless to say, for Benjamin this reading of the history of sovereign law and violence, as the terrain on which struggles for justice and peace are resolved, is just such a conformism.

Yet when Benjamin shatters conformity, he does not only seek to save justice and peace from the ideas of sovereign decision; he also focuses on redeeming the concept of violence—saving the images of its history from the appropriations of sovereign law. This is why he emphasizes the destructiveness that afflicts these melancholic sovereigns as they meet their demise. It is a type of violence that escapes sovereign right precisely in those moments of decision when the latter seeks to restore and maintain its rule through the capture and monopoly of violence. Borrowing the images of an eschatological violence from the Counter-Reformation concerns of these Baroque dramatists, Benjamin finds a rather non-eschatological moment in their concern for a singular form of violence, essentially defined by divine abandonment. This is not merely the withdrawal of the Divine in history, or withdrawal as history, but the experience of historical withdrawal itself—of what Benjamin calls "an irresistible decay."[26]

This is exactly what a genuine state of emergency means: a violence that breaks the nexus by withdrawing from the subjective and systemic means of violence in sovereign decisions. Such a violence is divine precisely in the sense that—as a means of withdrawal from sovereign decision, and a withdrawal therefore from the means of such decisions—it comes neither to restore nor maintain the law, but simply to depose it.[27] So crucial is this type of violence to Benjamin that he goes back further than the Christian eschatology of the Baroque period, to the Talmudic interpretations of the original Jewish commandment, "Thou shalt not kill." In Benjamin's view, what relates the commandment to the act of transgression signified by killing it is not judgments, vengeance, punishments, or negotiated interpretations of the application of the law. Rather, it is the withdrawal of the commandment itself, its abandonment of the life of the evil-doer at the moment of decision and deed. As Benjamin writes, "the injunction becomes inapplicable, incommensurable, once the deed is accomplished."[28] Herein also resides the meaning of divine violence: it is not some return to an uncorrupted state, or a leap to the good days to come, but actively purifying violence.[29] It is a freeing of the means of life, of life as means, from the subjugations of origins and the over-determining violence of imposed ends.

We are now in a position to address a key element of our second difficulty: the dangerous intimacy of this pure, divine violence with the very form of violence it comes to depose: what Benjamin called the "mythical violence" of state sovereignty.[30] He does not evade this intimacy or its dangers. The withdrawal of state sovereignty can be even more annihilating and destructive than any intentional acts of sovereign violence.[31] To clarify, the difficulty here is not so much the affirmation of types of violence or destruction in both the mythical and divine traditions of violence. As we have seen so far, Benjamin expounds carefully on their differences. More profoundly, it is a question of whether the two may be differentiated. Has not the mythical violence of the state traditionally made use of this divine violence in the reinforcement of its sovereign rule? Does not mythic violence use withdrawal and abandonment as well, in the capture and destruction of life? It took no less a figure than Jacques Derrida to address this difficulty.[32]

Peace Enacted in Divine Violence

In 1990, Derrida conducted a presentation on the violence of law twice in the span of a few months. He did this as a sort of homage to Benjamin's severance of the force of sovereign law from the norms of life, and especially from the norms of justice. For the second event, Derrida wrote a new addition, to his earlier work, titled "Force of Law: The Mystical Foundations of Authority." In this postscript, he questions the very capacity to decide between Benjamin's divine violence, and the worst of contemporary mythic violence—Hitler's Final Solution. The quotation is worth repeating:

I do not know whether from this nameless thing called the final solution one can draw something which still deserves the name of a lesson. If there were a lesson to be drawn, a unique lesson among the always singular lessons of murder, from even a single murder, from all the collective exterminations of history, the lesson that we can draw today—and if we can do so we must—is that we must think, know, represent for ourselves, formalize, judge the possible complicity between all these discourses [Benjamin's divine violence] and the worst (here the final solution). In my view, this defines a task and responsibility the theme of which (yes, theme) I have not been able to read in either Benjaminian "destruction" or Heideggerian "Destruktion."[33]

Derrida's concern is certainly not unwarranted. There is complicity between the destruction facilitated by Benjamin's concept of divine violence,[34] and Heidegger's affirmation of the "Destruktion" of Western metaphysics.[35] The difficult question is whether this affirmation of destruction leads both Benjamin and Heidegger to an implicit complicity with the totalizing destruction of the Final Solution. As we contended above, the violence of a sovereign decision on the exceptional case of life is exactly what Benjamin's concept of divine violence exists to prevent. In a sense we saw how such a decision must contain, not just in the sense of an internal property but of a hold on life, the very existential conditions that rule and override it: exceptions and states of emergency.

These, in the bounded confines of sovereign decision, always contain the potentiality of a ruling urgency that overwhelms the very decision itself, that empties it into the "indecisiveness" of an exceptional state; in its withdrawal from sovereign decision, this brings about the real state of emergency we mentioned above. But is this incompatible with Heidegger's "Destruktion" from *Being and Time*? That destruction, as we will see shortly, unfolded from 1933 onwards as a support for the "inner truth and greatness" of the Nazi movement, hurtling itself into the implosions of the Final Solution. Such proximity is unavoidable; its meaning is another matter. Here is Heidegger on ontological destruction:

It has nothing to do with a vicious relativizing of all ontological standpoints. But this destruction is just as far from having the negative of shaking off the ontological tradition. We must, on the contrary, stake out the positive possibilities of that tradition, and that means keeping it within its limits;

and these in turn are given factically in the way the question is formulated at the time, and in the way the possible field for investigation is bounded off. On the negative side, this destruction does not relate itself toward the past; its criticism is aimed at today and at the prevalent way of treating the history of ontology, whether it is headed towards doxagraphy, toward intellectual history, or towards a history of problems. But to bury the past in nullity (*Nichtigkeit*) is not the purpose of this destruction; its aim is positive; its negative function remains unexpressed and indirect.[36]

Destruction is here positive with respect to tradition, allowing the concealed positive possibilities of tradition to emerge. Its negative function, like the withdrawal and abandonment of divine violence, "remains unexpressed and indirect," in Heidegger's phrase. But is it not at this point of proximity that the glaring difference erupts—a small but irreducible gap between the two destructions? For Heidegger, the positive aim of unexpressed destruction is conditioned by a staking out of possibilities, a keeping of tradition within its limits, and a "bounding off" of fields to be investigated.[37] These latter presupposes decisiveness. Moreover, any reader of Heidegger knows that it is not some self-conscious subject of history that chooses to stake out, keep limits and bound off. Rather, destruction in the history of Being calls human being, Dasein, to these decisive moments of the possibility of historical ontology itself.

Nothing could be further from Benjamin's sense of the "indecisiveness" of destruction in the very staked-out spaces of sovereign decision. It is precisely in the intimacy of this destructive moment that the *Trauerspiel* of Benjamin's sovereign loses not only the meaning of both the transcendent and earthly life, but the experience of eschatology itself—of an end, an eschaton, that would redeem the tumults of historical Being. As Benjamin explains: "The religious man of the Baroque era clings so tightly to the world because of the feeling that he is being driven along to a cataract with it. The Baroque knows no eschatology, and for that reason knows no mechanism by which all earthly things are gathered in together and exalted before being consigned to their end."[38]

It is here that crucial differences must be articulated: Benjamin's complicity with the philosophies of the Final Solution is the obverse of Derrida's (and Heidegger's) sense of complicity. Complicity is defined as giving approval or support, whether tacitly or explicitly. But when complicity is experienced (in those fragmentary moments of life, as

Benjamin might say), approval and support can quickly be transfigured into an intimate access to what is most precarious, disturbing, and vulnerable in the approved and supported.[39]

To explain this, let us try an analogy. Imagine that a community is trying to integrate strangers—perhaps immigrants or refugees—and needs to teach them its norms and traditions. In order to integrate them, the community must presuppose two things: that the strangers will comply with these norms in their own ways, and that—by making the choice to enter the community—they have freely chosen to comply. Then imagine that such an immigrant—perhaps a woman, still a stranger in the community, still struggling to be part of it, and to understand its norms—might one day accidentally wander into a less visible part of the society, and there witness an act of extreme violence; one that flies completely in the face of the traditions the community venerates. Worse, she realizes that this violence is not simply fortuitous; it is ritualistic, systemic even. She realizes that those who commit the violence are in fact joined by those who condemn it, including the community's leaders. The latter may express disapproval, even moral indignation, but they clearly do not, will not, and cannot envision their community without this violence, which is also a venerated tradition. It is an unfortunate fact of life, they say. The stranger must then confront the unbearable fact that this ritualistic, systemic violence, this destruction of normative life itself, its anomic essence, is in fact an essential part of what sustains the community's norms.

This allegory is in fact laid out with harrowing precision, in only eight pages, by an artist of short stories. Writer Shirley Jackson brought these images to life in her 1949 story "The Lottery," published in *The New Yorker*.[40] Jackson's sparse prose tells us as much about what she does not write about, as what she does. The story, set in contemporary small-town America, deals with a ritualized lottery performed every year to honour the harvest. Names are drawn on slips of paper; and at the end of the story a member of the community, selected by the pure contingency of the draw, is stoned to death by the rest of the townspeople.

What lies unsaid at the end, deafening in its silence, is the fact that at this particular lottery, one of the participants is a relative stranger, an included outsider (rare in this idyllic, isolated rural community) who joins in the lottery without fully knowing the rules—unwittingly risking his own life. When he witnesses the horrific and arbitrary violence that results, he realizes that this is how the community preserves the integrity of its norms.

Unlike the residents of the community, such as Bill and Tessie Hutchison, the stranger is still so removed from these long-standing norms that he sees the ritualized violence for what Benjamin would call it: an arbitrary, contingent use of systemic violence. As well, the stranger's presence in their midst forces the townspeople to confront an image of how this arbitrary violence shows an impossible complicity with the community's venerated norms. They can no longer evade the fact that what shapes and supports their integrity—that is, systemic violence—is the very condition of their demise.

The stranger's witnessing of the lottery parallels the only form of complicity Benjamin could have offered the Nazis and their Final Solution. In the story Bill Hutchison, a respected pillar of the community, draws one of the last papers; and with great relief, he announces that his is blank. Without missing a beat, and with an uncanny ability to suspend his normative commitments to his wife, Bill proclaims, "It's Tessie!" Then he moves to join the murderous crowd. This, we contend, is Heidegger's own experience of complicity.[41]

But our allegory is not complete. We need to understand the different ways in which these two contrasting figures, Heidegger and Benjamin, responded to the same events: the rise of a communally supported murderous fascism in the period of 1930–1940. These events can help explain the need for the allegory, though not in the sense that the different actions of these contemporary scholars can be explained by their differing philosophical and political thought. It is rather the other way around. We need to understand how the events and actions of their lives, the temporal unfolding of the truths of their works, and even the contemporary events of our own time, in fact help to explain their scholarly works and commitments.

On July 25, 1940, Benjamin crossed the French–Spanish border into the Catalan town of Portbou, along with a few other Jewish refugees. But they had no exit visas from the Vichy government, so the Catalan authorities detained them, with the aim of handing them over to the Gestapo. Rather than being held in a detention centre or police cell, however, Benjamin was separated from the other refugees, allowed to keep all his possessions, and put up in a hotel.[42] Possibly this was because the Catalan guards—renowned for both their republican and communist sympathies, and their anti-Franco sentiments—were implicitly offering a Benjamin the chance to escape from the Gestapo.

But if that was the case, Benjamin did not take the opportunity: the next morning, July 26, he was found dead in his hotel room from a self-

induced overdose of morphine pills. He knew he would be murdered by
the Gestapo if they ever caught him. He had known this since 1933, when
the Nazi government enacted its exceptional, emergency powers of Article
48 of the rights-based Weimar Constitution, and set in motion new laws
proclaiming the necessity of protecting the German race and culture.[43] We
will never know if Benjamin entertained the idea of escape; sorrowful and
tantalizing rumours of the possibility still persist to this day. What we do
know is that, even if he was aware of the hopeful possibility of saving his
life, he chose to ignore it in favour of thwarting the decision of the Nazi
state. Benjamin's ending of his own life prevented the carrying out of a
sovereign decision by the Nazis—a decision that was to treat him (as it did
other Jews and minorities) as a legal exception to the norms underlying the
basic rights and civil protections of the Weimar Constitution.

In a very real sense, Benjamin's last act took exception to the Nazis'
sovereign claim to decide on the exception. We need not be reminded that
this claim to legally determine exceptions is no historical aberration, limited
to the Weimar Republic under Nazi rule. Today, in the post-9/11 era, it is
the normal state of affairs for all Western liberal-democratic governments.
This is not the simplistic and greatly abused warning of forgetful returns
to fascist politics in contemporary liberal democracies. Instead, it simply
points out that though fascism has died out, the need for states to decide on
the exception, the emergency, the security threat, etc., may be more normal
now than ever.

So in the one mortal act of his death, Benjamin evokes images of the
two critical concepts that break any nation-state's legal claim to found or
preserve itself through a monopoly of coercion and violence. These concepts
are the nations whose "states of emergency" are no longer the exception
but the rule;[44] and the divine violence that neither restores nor preserves
the legal right of sovereign violence, but deposes it. Before we complete
our elaboration of these two concepts, let us first complete the contrast by
describing the events and actions in Heidegger's political life around the
same period.

In the spring of 1936, about four years before Benjamin's untimely death,
Heidegger visited a former student, Karl Löwith, in Rome. Like Benjamin,
Löwith was a Jew who had assimilated to German culture, but was now on
the run from the Third Reich. Knowing that his mentor was in Rome to
preside over a conference on Ancient Greek studies, he asked Heidegger for
a meeting. When the two men met, Löwith (who was fearful for his safety,

and impoverished by the current condition of German politics) noticed that Heidegger still wore his Nazi insignia on his lapel.[45] He knew it had been two years since Heidegger had unceremoniously resigned from his position as Rector of Freiburg University, and as the Nazis' first philosopher, in 1934. So Löwith asked: Did Heidegger still support National Socialism? Here is Lowith's account of the answer:

> He was convinced, now as before, that National Socialism was the right course for Germany; one only had to "hold out" long enough. The only aspect that troubled him was the ceaseless organization at the expense of "vital forces." He failed to notice the destructive radicalism of the whole movement, and the petty bourgeois character of all its "power-through-joy" institutions, because he himself was a radical petty bourgeois.[46]

Let us pause over this image, for it contains Benjamin's critical reflections on the workings of an emergency state that claims to make and preserve law by deciding on the exception. What is profoundly disturbing is not merely the fact that Heidegger supported a regime that set out to destroy the lives of people close to him. It is his ability to explain to Löwith his good reasons for holding on until the "truth and inner greatness" of the movement finished the job. What horrified Löwith was no doubt the way Heidegger could suspend the basic norms of friendship, community, and even civilized humanity, and cordially explain his decision to honour his political commitments. (This might remind us of how Bill Hutchison treats Tessie in the last scenes of *The Lottery*.) The Heidegger that Löwith talked to in 1936 (and wrote about again in 1977)[47] was still very much the figure for whom the unexpressed, quietist destruction, revealed by authentic Dasein in *Being and Time*, had to find its expression in a decisive event—a mobilization of the collective existence of a people, such as the National Socialist Movement. As Habermas[48] explained in 1984,[49] before 1934–1935 there was nothing in the internal development of Heidegger's work that pointed to the need for destruction of the history of Being. It is only with the external events of 1933, 1934, and 1935, with time and distance from his 1927 masterwork *Being and Time*, that Heidegger works the unfolding truth of this work as such a mobilization.[50]

The original state of exception theory is largely the brainchild of the Nazi philosopher and constitutional jurist Carl Schmitt, author of such works as "On Dictatorship" (1921), *Political Theology* (1922), *The Crisis of*

Parliamentary Democracy (1923), and *The Concept of the Political* (1932). By 1928 Benjamin had developed an amicable relationship with Schmitt, based on his interest in Schmitt's exception theory—a topic Benjamin had already explored in his own 1921 essay "The Critique of Violence."[51] The relationship so scandalized his friends that no evidence of their correspondence was included in the first posthumous compilation of Benjamin's collected works.[52] It was not until 1998 that Giorgio Agamben showed that Benjamin's complicity with Schmitt's theory was, in fact, an attempt to expose its radical collapse.[53]

When Schmitt defined the true foundation of authority (especially in *Political Theology*), his claim was not only theological, legal, and philosophical, but also historical: "Sovereign is he who decides on the exceptional case."[54] Aware of the legal authority of this formulation, Benjamin was already working on material for his dissertation on the *Trauerspiel*, the mournful, dissolute speeches of sovereign Kings in the early Baroque dramas of German theatre. He saw in this historically specific art form a stark contrast between the theatrical sovereigns and Schmitt's formulation. The artistic images are so disruptive of sovereign authority precisely because, in Benjamin's view, those images were unavoidably juxtaposed with any historical formulation seeking to ground the legitimacy of sovereign decision. With this in mind, Benjamin believed that Schmitt's now-classic definition in *Political Theology* was in fact built on the very theological concept it cannot depend on: the exception as a messianic moment when a sovereign is unable to decide. Benjamin had clearly understood the deeper theological implications of Schmitt's thesis. In *Political Theology*, Schmitt speaks of deciding "on the exceptional case":

> All significant concepts of the modern state are secularized theological concepts ... for example, the omnipotent God became the omnipotent lawgiver.... The exception in jurisprudence is analogous to the miracle in theology. Only by being aware of this analogy can we appreciate the manner in which the philosophical ideas of the state developed in the last centuries.[55]

In response to Schmitt's secular attempt to appropriate such theological concepts as miracles and sovereign decision, Benjamin employs his unique form of revolutionary Marxism. Emptying the science of historical materialism of any conformist claims to the doctrine of progress, he demonstrates that fragmented images of miracles and messianic time— resiliently present in their secular, state variations even as outmoded religiosity—in fact signify the exceptions, the exceptional, that is life itself, that are never the decisions of a political sovereign. How else to imagine a miracle if not as the uniqueness of an irreducible event, a "monad," a reality that in its occurrence refers to nothing but itself, whose decisiveness exists only in its own expression, always withdrawn from the appropriations of a political sovereign? And how can one ignore in such an image of the miraculous event, the flashing presence of its messianic time? This was conceived by Benjamin as the time of a singular event that puts a halt to all other happenings. Benjamin tells us as much in his Thesis XVII: "A historical materialist approaches a historical subject only where he encounters it as a monad. In this structure he recognizes the sign of a Messianic cessation of happening, or, put differently, a revolutionary chance in the fight for the oppressed past."[56]

In 1928, he sent a complete manuscript copy of *The Origins of German Tragic Drama* to Schmitt, with a note attached that read, "With Gratitude and Admiration."[57] But as Agamben shows, what Benjamin wanted was to critically engage Schmitt with the central thesis of his dissertation; namely, that the tragic demises of the Baroque sovereigns in the *Trauerspielen* were in fact true states of exception, precisely in sense that the sovereign could not decide on the exception.[58] For Benjamin, the destruction and transformation of a sovereign's rule ensues when a community—increasingly accustomed to an emergency state where the exception has become the rule—is no longer moved in the normative sense by the sovereign claim that it alone has the right to decide on the exception. Importantly, here the destruction of the sovereign's authority is not defined by the violent responses of the community against the legal monopoly on, and deployment of, violence by a republic or a king. Instead, the destruction is brought on by a communal, anomic indifference to sovereign decisions that are founded on the legal appropriation of coercion, force, and violence.

The conditions of this mournful inability to decide on the exception is, for Benjamin, a form of violence that is most effective only when it does not strike out against a sovereign authority with the same kind of violent means reserved for the state. It is therefore a violence that destroys by facilitating the deterioration of a sovereign government, mired in the exceptional moment of sovereign indecision—a violence that, as in the prophetic lessons of Biblical literature, comes neither to make or restore law, nor to preserve it, but simply to depose it. This is what Benjamin means by "divine violence." He explains it in "Critique of Violence"; fascinatingly, he cites the example of the "educative power" of schools and universities (and especially in student activism), as a prime illustration of the peace of non-violent violence:

> This divine power is attested not only by religious tradition but is also found in present-day life in at least one sanctioned manifestation. The educative power, which in its perfected form stands outside the law, is one of its manifestations. These are defined, therefore, not by miracles directly performed by God, but by the expiating moment in them that strikes without bloodshed and, finally, by the absence of all law-making. To this extent it is justifiable to call this violence, too, annihilating; but it is so only relatively, with regard to goods, right, life, and suchlike, never absolutely with regard to the soul of the living.[59]

It should be no surprise that today, in this era of Occupy movements and student protests (such as the Quebec students whose intransigence forced an election and brought down a government), some of the most prominent scholars and activists are returning to Benjamin's concept of divine violence. Some recent interventions are even more affirmative of Benjamin's understanding of violence, since Derrida's caution regarding the possible complicity of divine violence with the Final Solution in 1990. Slavoj Žižek, for example, cites models of divine violence in the civil disobedience of Ghandi and Martin Luther King;[60] Judith Butler coins the expression "a violent non-violence," commonly found in states of normative loss such as mourning and grief;[61] and Simon Critchley invokes divine violence as a way for anarchic resistance to evade mimicking the "archic violence" of sovereign violence.[62] We may be witnessing the emergence of this interruptive divine violence as a structural feature of a new politics. The problem now is how to envision it.

Epilogue: The Original Wall Street Occupier

"Bartleby, the Scrivener: A Story of Wall Street," a short story by Herman Melville, is told from the point of view of the narrator—a successful lawyer who hires Bartleby as a legal copyist for his Wall Street firm.[63] One day, when told to copy some text, Bartleby responds that he "would prefer not to." This "preference not to," expressed with calm, unaggressive indifference, soon extends from copying to the normative basics of eating, speaking and even shelter—Bartleby simply lives in the office, silently staring out of the window at a brick wall, upsetting the day-to-day activities not only of his employer but also of his increasingly hostile co-workers. The narrator does not fire him, thinking that Bartleby's unfathomable strangeness seemed so foreign to the habits of his office that maybe his own firm's practices were in the wrong, that "all the justice and all the reason is on the other side."[64] Most importantly, this seasoned lawyer senses that Bartleby's strangeness is all too familiar to the legal offices and decisions of Wall Street. Through his strangeness, Bartleby seems increasingly to belong in this place.

So the lawyer moves his office to the "safer" area of city hall, at the urban centre of Wall Street. But when a new law firm moves into the old premises, where Bartleby still remains, it threatens legal action if the former scrivener does not leave immediately. The narrator even offers his own home to Bartleby, hoping this will resolve the impasse on Wall Street. To which Bartleby responds, "No, at present I would prefer no change at all."[65] The force of the law must step in and remove Bartleby, first to the police station, then to jail. The narrator visits Bartleby there, taken to him by a prison cook concerned that he does not eat. Finding him reclined under a tree in the prison yard, the lawyer realizes that his former scrivener is dead. The unknowing cook asks, "Eh! He's asleep, ain't he?"[66] Sensing the strange condition he shares with Bartleby, the lawyer murmurs, "With kings and counsellors."[67]

We will leave the last word to Giorgio Agamben, who was one of the first to draw a parallel between Benjamin's divine violence and the pure contingency of Bartleby's life.[68] The potentiality of Bartleby's condition is not an adversarial response, or a planned resistance. It is the ancient Aristotelian secret of the doctrine of potentiality, the "potential not to do." It is certainly not the heroic deed of the ancients, but a fragment of the ancient sceptics' defining experience, *epokhe*, a suspension of imposed norms of life.[69] It is Bartleby's life as the "point of indifference between potentiality and in-potentiality," of life freed from the politico-theological decision over life and death.[70]

Notes

1 In the original text, Benjamin puts the expression "state of emergency" in quote marks, signifying that the phrase is not his own, but that of a history of state practices. Walter Benjamin, *Illuminations*, trans. Harry Zohn (New York: Zone Books, 1968), 257.

2 Walter Benjamin, *Reflections: Essays, Aphorisms, Autobiographical Writings*, trans. Edmund Jephcott (New York: Harcourt Brace Jovanovich, 1978), 297.

3 Benjamin, *Illuminations*, 254.

4   Benjamin, *Reflections*, 296–97.

5   As of the time this study was written, in April 2013, the Occupy Wall Street event in New York had ended without significant consequence; the Arab Spring was increasingly contained by the Mersi regime in Egypt; and the Quebec student protests in Canada had gone dormant with the electoral defeat of the provincial government.

6   In Chapter 9 of this volume ("Seeking Peace in Nature: A Reading of Thoreau on Ecology and Economy"), Toivo Koivukoski relates peace to Henry David Thoreau's affirmation of the "non-cooperative" resistance of nature. Koivukoski does not emphasize the destructiveness of nature as a source of peace, as Benjamin does with divine violence.

7   Walter Benjamin, *The Origins of German Tragic Drama*, trans. John Osborne (London: Verso Books, 1998), 235.

8   Benjamin, *Illuminations*, 3–4. Hannah Arendt may be closer to Benjamin's notion of peace, as an essential means that refuses the ends of sovereign violence, than to any other part of his work. In Chapter 12 of this volume ("Hannah Arendt on Peace as a Means to Politics"), Dianne Enns points out Arendt's explanation of peace as the essential means of politics in her political philosophy.

9   Benjamin, *Illuminations*, 4.

10   Benjamin, *Illuminations*, 4.

11   Walter Benjamin, *Selected Writings, Volume Two, Part Two, 1931–1934*, trans. Rodney Livingstone, ed. Michael W. Jennings, Howard Eiland, and Gary Smith (Cambridge: Harvard University Press, 1999), 297.

12   Benjamin, *German Tragic Drama*, 33.

13   This is a question that should go to the heart of the sovereignty of the settled "new societies" of all of the Americas, as Louis Hartz called them. (Hartz, *The Liberal Tradition in America: An Interpretation of American Political Thought since the Revolution* [New York: Harcourt Brace, 1955]). Why, for example, more than a generation after the Conquest and Royal Proclamation Act of 1763, would the government of Canada still be pursuing a peace treaty with the indigenous peoples under its rule, such as the Jay Treaty of 1794?

14   Benjamin, *Reflections*, 283.

15   Benjamin, *Illuminations*, 257; 2009, 66; see also Walter Benjamin, *The Origins of German Tragic Drama* (London: Verso Books, 1998); and Giorgio Agamben, *Homo Sacer: Sovereign Power and Bare Life*, trans. Daniel Heller-Roazen (Redwood City, CA: Stanford University Press, 1998), 112–15.

16   Max Weber, "Politics as Vocation," *The Vocation Lectures*, trans. Rodney Livingstone; ed., intro. David Owen and Tracy B. Strong (Cambridge: Hackett Publishing, 2004), 33. It is important to note how the reference to physical violence here cannot be reduced to the mere legal right to coerce, punish, and

destroy bodies—a reduction too often found in the textbook definitions of the social sciences. There is another reason why, after the italicized emphasis, Weber links physical violence with the essential feature of control over the populations of a legally defined territory. Far more than just the visceral retributions of the law, physical violence is intended here to signify the spectre of a sovereign decision on the uses of life and death in the governance of a population. Weber tells us as much a couple of lines after the classical definition: "For what is specific to the present is that all other organizations or individuals can assert the right to use physical violence only insofar as the *state* [Weber's italics] permits them to do so."

17 Weber, *Vocation Lectures*, 33.

18 For how the understanding of peace in Heidegger's fundamental ontology requires a polemical encounter (from *Polemos*, ancient Greek for the embodiment of war) with ontological upsurge, strife, and violence, see David Edward Tabachnick's study ("Heidegger's Polemical Peace: Outer Violence for Inner Harmony") in Chapter 10 of this volume.

19 Benjamin, *German Tragic Drama*, 51–53.

20 Benjamin, *German Tragic Drama*, 152–55.

21 Benjamin, *German Tragic Drama*, 70–72; 155–56. Benjamin goes to great pains to distinguish these *Trauerspielen* from the tragic pathos of the classical tradition: these sovereigns are not heroes, measured by the fate of their gods or God, nor do they deliver popular catharsis through the images of their sufferings. They are rather martyrs, mourning their impossible abandonment by God to the finite struggles of earthly, historical time. And as martyrs, importantly, they are even more exposed to destruction with impunity than those lives subjected to sovereign decision. For the sovereign is always held accountable for the decision, especially in times of indecision (Benjamin, *German Tragic Drama*, 57–60, 155–58).

22 Benjamin, *German Tragic Drama*, 65.

23 Benjamin, *German Tragic Drama*, 56.

24 Benjamin, *Illuminations*, 255.

25 Benjamin, *Illuminations*, 255.

26 Benjamin, *German Tragic Drama*, 178.

27 Benjamin, *Illuminations*, 294–95, 297.

28 Benjamin, *Illuminations*, 298.

29 Giorgio Agamben, *Means Without Ends*, trans. Vincenzo Binetti and Cesare Casarino (Minneapolis: University of Minnesota Press, 2000), 115–17; and Giorgio Agamben, *The State of Exception*, trans. K. Attell (Chicago: University of Chicago Press, 2005), 61–62.

30 Benjamin, *Illuminations*, 297.

31 Benjamin, *Illuminations*, 297.

32   For Derrida, the deeper issue is clearly the inherent instability at the heart
      of the crucial distinctions between divine and mythical state violence. Peace
      exists only in the unstable acts of doing and saying peace, and not in a priori
      definitions; for it exists in the acts of definition itself. For a fine elaboration
      of the point in this volume, see Pamela Huber's account of Derrida's ideas in
      Chapter 13 of this volume ("Defining Peace: Jacques Derrida's 'Impossible
      Friendship' and 'Democracy to Come'").

33   Jacques Derrida, "Postscript to the Force of Law," trans. Mary Quintance
      (French original with English attached), *Cardozo Law Review* 11 (1990): 1045.

34   Benjamin, *Reflections*, 294

35   Martin Heidegger, *Being and Time*, trans. J. Macquarrie and E. Robinson (New
      York Harper, 1962), 44.

36   Heidegger, *Being and Time*, 44.

37   Tabachnick elaborates this point in Chapter 10 by stressing that, in Heidegger's
      ontology, peace has to be explained as that which must be protected.

38   Benjamin, *German Tragic Drama*, 66.

39   For example, in his infamous approval of the Nazi movement in 1959, with
      the publication of *Introduction to Metaphysics*, Heidegger chastises people
      who went "fishing in the troubled waters of 'values' and 'totalities'" for failing
      to see, and comply with, the movement's "inner truth and greatness." By
      contrast, Benjamin would see this exposed, precarious vulnerability of the
      "encounter between global technology and modern man," together with these
      compromisers "fishing for values," precisely as the complicity of this encounter
      with the sovereign violence of Nazism. Martin Heidegger, *Introduction to
      Metaphysics*, trans. R. Mannheim (New Haven: Yale University Press, 1959),
      199.

40   Shirley Jackson, *The Lottery and Other Stories* (New York: Farrar and Straus,
      1949), 8.

41   Bill even joins the effort to mobilize the crowd into an adjacent field where
      Tessie is to be encircled and viciously stoned to death. Jackson, *Lottery*, 8.

42   Christopher Rollason, "Border Crossing, Resting Place: Portbou and Walter
      Benjamin," *Lingua Franca* 5.8 (2002): 4–9. This is well documented in the
      documentary film by Dhurjah Bhattacharyya, "One-Way Street: Fragments for
      Walter Benjamin," 2011, online at www.vimeo.com.

43   Agamben, *Means Without Ends*, 14–16.

44   Benjamin, *Illuminations*, 257

45   Richard Wolin, ed., *The Heidegger Controversy* (Cambridge: MIT Press, 1993),
      141.

46   Wolin, *Heidegger Controversy*, 142.

47   Richard Wisser, ed., *Martin Heidegger in Conversation*, trans. Srinivasa Murthy
      (New Delhi: Arnold-Heinemann, 1977), 24–25. The collection contains
      eleven tributes to Heidegger on the occasion of his eightieth birthday, and in

the context of a renaissance of his ideas (especially in France). Karl Löwith's piece, "Heidegger's Existentialism: Some Implications," stands out for its subtle critique of the renewal of this external, collectivist interpretation of destruction in *Being and Time* in the 1960s and 1970s. Though staying true to the demands of a tribute, Löwith nevertheless ends by trying to define Heidegger against the mobilization of their images into a history of Being itself. He terms the man and his masterwork quiet, solitary, singular, and individualist. In 1977, he is therefore still cautioning Heidegger's followers, his new students, who associate the thinking of Being with destruction in the collective histories of Being.

48　For Habermas' own philosophy of peace, see David Borman's study ("Habermas on Peace and Democratic Legitimacy") in Chapter 14 of this volume.

49　Wolin, *Heidegger Controversy*, 189.

50　These external interventions into the meaning of destruction in *Being and Time* emerge as follows: in 1933 Heidegger accepts his appointment as the Nazis' first philosopher, and seeks to mobilize Germany's universities—in favour of the inner truth and greatness not of Dasein, but of the Being of the collective movement itself. In 1934, as Heidegger reveals to Karl Löwith in 1936 (Wolin, 1993, 142), he leaves the position and the party; not because the mobilization is wrong but because its "vital forces" had been compromised by "ceaseless organization" (142). And in 1935, he confirms his view of the vital forces of the movement, and its inner truth and greatness, in his lecture "An Introduction to Metaphysics." This is reaffirmed a quarter-century later, in 1959, with the publication of the latter as a text (Heidegger, *Introduction to Metaphysics*, 199).

51　In an early essay "The Critique of Violence" (1921), Benjamin uses the expression, "the state's emergency measures" (*Reflections*, 282). He uses the term "exception" only in one of his last works, "Theses on the Philosophy of History" (*Illuminations*, 257), when he questions the state's ability to limit emergency measures to exceptional cases that suit its sovereign power and authority.

52　From the first collection of Benjamin's works, assembled by Benjamin and four others: Theodor Adorno, Gretel Adorno, Walter Benjamin, Friedrich Podzus, *Schriften* (Frankfurt: Suhrkamp, 1955). See also Agamben, *Means Without Ends*, 53.

53　Agamben, *Means Without Ends*, 57–59.

54　Carl Schmitt, *Political Theology: Four Chapters on the Concept of Sovereignty*, trans. George Schwab (Cambridge, MA: MIT Press, 1986), 5. Borrowing from Tracy B. Strong's insightful Introduction ("The Sovereign and the Exception: Carl Schmitt, Politics, Theology and Leadership"), and from Schwab's careful English translation, we must point out a key ambiguity intended by Schmitt in the German uses of the latter two terms, "exception" and "case." An exception pertains to law whose provisions and existential norms are suspended in favour of the pure force of law; it need not identify a case—individuals, groups, religious forms of life—when declaring this sovereign, exceptional decision. But this contingent relation between exception and case is covered over by an imposed necessity: if the exception is the legal "force" of law deployed in the suspension of the provisions of law, all in the name of restoring or preserving the law, then a threatening life, lives, or cases must at some point be captured by this force of law, if the restoration or preservation of the law is to be defined in the exception (Schmitt, *Political Theology*, xii).

55   Schmitt, *Political Theology*, 38.

56   Benjamin, *Illuminations*, 263.

57   Agamben, *Means Without Ends*, 52–53.

58   Agamben, *Means Without Ends*, 57; Benjamin, *German Tragic Drama*, 69–72.

59   Benjamin, *Reflections*, 297–98.

60   Slavoj Žižek, *Violence: Six Sideways Reflections* (London: Profile Books, 2009). See also Slavoj Žižek, "Language, Violence and Non-Violence," *International Journal of Žižek Studies* 2.3 (2008).

61   See Judith Butler, *Frames of War: When Is Life Grievable?* (London and New York: Verso Books, 2009); and her "Critique, Coercion, and Sacred Life in Benjamin's 'Critique of Violence,'" *Political Theologies in a Post-Secular World* (New York: Fordham University Press, 2006).

62   Simon Critchley, "Žižek Has Been Telling Lies about Me," Harvard Kennedy School of Government, October 21, 2009, http://www.hks.harvard.edu. See also Critchley's book *Infinitely Demanding: Ethics of Commitment, Politics of Resistance* (London and New York: Verso Books, 2007).

63   Herman Melville, "Bartleby, the Scrivener: A Story of Wall-Street" (1853), Great Books Online, 1993, http://www.bartleby.com/129, para. 22.

64   Melville, "Bartleby," para. 40.

65   Melville, "Bartleby," para. 212.

66   Melville, "Bartleby," para. 248.

67   Melville, "Bartleby," para. 249.

68   Giorgio Agamben, *Potentialities: Collected Essays in Philosophy*, trans. & ed. Daniel Heller-Roazen (Redwood City, CA: Stanford University Press, 1999), 245.

69   Agamben, *Potentialities*, 256.

70   Agamben, *Potentialities*, 270.

CHAPTER 12

Hannah Arendt on Peace as a Means to Politics

Diane Enns

At first glance, Hannah Arendt's political philosophy appears to offer few insights into the meaning of peace. It is no wonder that almost no one has examined her work in this light.[1] We find neither a sustained discussion of peace in her writings, nor an absolute stand against violence. What we find instead is a complex analysis of violence and non-violence that foregrounds historical contingencies, and highlights the pragmatic conditions necessary for politics to thrive. In the 1940s Arendt made an impassioned plea for a Jewish army to take up weapons against Hitler, advocating self-defence for a people in danger of becoming "a victim of world history."[2] In the 1960s, with palpable impatience, she criticized the glorification of violence in the decolonization and civil rights struggles of her time; yet she also pointed out that violence sometimes does achieve its political and economic goals. Throughout, she never failed to stress that the most likely outcome of violence is more violence, leading, inevitably, to the destruction of politics.[3]

My argument here is that this apparent ambivalence is precisely the reason we should turn to Arendt for an understanding of peace—a concept dogged by utopian traditions on one side, and by the charge of passive surrender on the other. In the first case, the reverent attention given to such figures as Gandhi or Martin Luther King Jr.—stripped of their own complex historical contexts and personal contradictions—has tended to ghettoize peace scholarship. And in the second case, peace is aligned with the state's repression of political dissent in the name of security, and equated with defeat by those engaged in violent emancipatory struggle. The need to "politicize" peace is thus twofold: to steer clear of utopian horizons and religious dreams of transcendence that remain permanently out of reach, and to dislodge peace from its association with passive acceptance of the status quo. Most importantly, unless we bring peace into the realm of the political, violence will retain its uncontested reign there—either as the state's default method for containing conflict, or as the first line of defence for dissenting non-state actors. The danger, according to Arendt, is that we might "confuse politics with what would put an end to politics, and present that very catastrophe as if it were inherent in the nature of things and thus inevitable." When this happens, "politics may vanish entirely from the world."[4]

If we are in danger of confusing violent measures with politics, we are also in danger of confusing peace with the absence of politics. My discussion here avoids the "stillness" of peace evoked by David Tabachnick and Leah Bradshaw in Chapters 10 and 7 of this volume; since both the "inner harmony" that appealed to Heidegger, and the stillness that Bradshaw believes can be recovered from the midst of antagonistic politics, stand in relief to an Arendtian politics. The risk of "safeguarding" or preserving peace is that we either ignore politics, or eliminate it altogether. As Bradshaw puts it, "To be at peace is to be beyond politics, either withdrawn into the stillness of contemplation in the solipsism of philosophy, or dead and saved in the kingdom of God"[5] (p. 130). Neither am I concerned with the "legal pacification" that David Borman describes in his discussion of Habermas in Chapter 14 of this volume. Although Arendt certainly respects the rule of law, she is also aware that the very "normatively legitimated rules" that transform political relations for Habermas, may also sabotage politics. Peaceful relations cannot be a matter of obeying the law.

Politicizing peace is no easy task, however, given that current global politics are caught in cycles of violence: on the one hand resistance in the name of justice for victims, and on the other hand military incursions, pre-emptive strikes, occupations, or drone warfare in the name of state security. Insurgency and counter-insurgency forces are locked in a deadly embrace, each fortified by claims to self-defence. Arendt's view of politics responds to both of these tendencies. First, her persistent focus on human freedom and agency undermines the justification of violence in the name of victimhood; and second, her own justification of violence in self-defence renders problematic current state-sanctioned violence in the name of security. In the process of elaborating these ideas, Arendt provides an understanding of peaceful relations *as a means to politics*, one that dissociates politics from violence and peace from passivity.

A Good Peace

Arendt was never one to shy away from tackling challenging political issues. She leaped into the fray of the most contentious debates on historical events, including the nature of totalitarianism and fascism, anti-Semitism, racism, revolution, political protest, and American and Middle East politics. Given the philosopher's tendency to look for a coherent set of ideas in a work, reading Arendt on politics and peace poses something of a challenge, which explains why philosophers so often ignore her work. Her critique of violence is not based on moral absolutes but on pragmatic political concerns specific to particular situations. In order to understand Arendt's ideas, therefore, we must attend to the historical events out of which they arise. Political concepts are messy, and unlike universal moral principles, they must bend with the winds of contingency. Arendt's lack of an absolute stand against violence might make peace scholars uncomfortable; but her phenomenological approach to politics—caring more about the experience of human relations in the public sphere than about structures of governance—might make political theorists equally uneasy. In her emphasis on the "splendour" of human interaction in the *polis*, we find alternative approaches to dealing with conflict that render her work essential to discussions of peace—albeit a qualified notion of peace.[6]

The association between peace and politics is most explicit in Arendt's few references to peace, found in her commentary on the formation of the state of Israel. Arendt was very much in favour of establishing a Jewish state in Palestine, and was committed to a version of Zionism—"I am not against Israel on principle, I am against certain important Israeli policies," she wrote—but quickly became critical of the extremes to which Zionist leaders went in their quest for a safe territory for survivors of Hitler's Final Solution.[7] She made the insightful but contentious claim, reiterated now in current analyses, that a generation of European Jews was "trying to wipe out the humiliation of Hitler's slaughterhouses with the newly won dignity of battle and the triumph of victory."[8] They did this in the attempt to isolate themselves from the world, according to Arendt, to inhabit a promised land forever safe from anti-Semitism.[9]

This would constitute a state of peace as the absence of conflict, but it is also the destruction of a world, Arendt tells us. In her view, Zionists like Theodor Herzl dreamed of an organic national body that would isolate Jews from relations with other nations, and hence from hatred and persecution. But even if Palestine had been "a country without a people," she notes, the country Herzl envisioned did not and could not exist: "There was no place on earth where a people could live like the organic national body he had in mind"—there was no escape from the world.[10]

Arendt thought a different kind of peace was essential for the region. She spells this out in a 1950 essay, "Peace or Armistice in the Near East?" which is both remarkable and discouraging for its foresight. Her point is that peace is not an armistice or truce; a "good peace" can result only from negotiation, mutual compromise, and eventual agreement between Jews and Arabs. The distinction is significant; mere armistice would force the new Israeli state to organize the Jewish people for permanent potential mobilization. Such a move, Arendt warned, could lead to the permanent threat of armed intervention and possibly end in a military dictatorship. If this were to happen, the result would be cultural and political sterility, and endless "chauvinistic violence."[11] Tragically, Arendt's predictions have turned out to be fairly accurate. Israel's lust for security is driven by the perception of itself as an island of democracy in a sea of hostile Arab neighbours, perpetually facing threats to its existence.

In Arendt's formulation, then, peace is neither armistice nor isolation from the world of human relations. The conditions for a good peace that results from negotiation and compromise are "good relationships" fostered by common political bodies or institutions among Jews and Arabs. These bodies were all too rare, she complains; in the years before the birth of the Israeli state, with the exception of the Haifa municipality, not a single common political body or institution was created among the Jews and Arabs in Palestine.[12] The only sources of Arab-Jewish friendship were to be found in the active workers' cooperatives in the labour movement. For Arendt, these were the most promising demonstrations of the desire to build a new type of society in which there would be no exploitation.

With little modification, we could substitute "politics" for "peace" in these writings. The conditions for politics, as we will see, are the good relations that result from negotiation, compromise, and taking into account a plurality of perspectives. Keeping in mind that we are talking about politics as the public realm of human relationships, action and speech, politics becomes sterile when replaced by "chauvinistic violence." The decades since Arendt made these observations have certainly borne out this point: the Israeli occupation of the Palestinians, and military incursions against a nearly defenceless population, continue to be justified on the basis of self-defence against terrorism. In the process, political imagination and inventiveness have all but died. Arendt's brief essays—reflections made in the midst of events whose outcome could not be known or predicted—open up a range of questions for us regarding the nature of politics and peace, and their unique relationship.

Politics: "Sheer Human Togetherness"

Arendt's consideration of politics pivots around three inextricably related conditions of human existence: plurality, natality, and freedom. In order to grasp these conditions, we must suspend our common perception of politics as the mechanics of governance and structural relationships, and think instead in phenomenological terms, highlighting the experience of what Arendt calls "sheer human togetherness."[13] Politics should not be reduced to the question of who rules whom—it is not merely a competition for domination.[14] Quite simply, politics is what arises between human beings; it is established as relationships.[15] Not relationships of kinship in the private realm—these are domains of refuge and retreat for Arendt—but those of a public or common space in which a plurality of individuals appear, speak and act freely, together creating something absolutely new. Arendt describes this plurality in the opening pages of *The Human Condition*: "Plurality is the condition of human action because we are all the same, that is, human, in such a way that nobody is ever the same as anyone else who ever lived, lives, or will live."[16] The sameness here is not the elimination or assimilation of difference, but the recognition of a shared human singularity. We are singular and plural at once.

Without human plurality there would be no politics, for politics is contingent on a public space, a "world," that both gathers human beings into it and separates them from one another. "Wherever people come together," Arendt writes, "the world thrusts itself between them, and it is in this in-between space that all human affairs are conducted."[17] This world is not necessarily always a harmonious one. Indeed, the very plurality of this "in-between" space entails risk; it ensures that both agreement and disagreement are indispensable for politics, the potential for both peaceful relations and violent conflict being present in equal measure. Arendt's dual emphasis on difference and commonality puts her in tension both with those who seek to repress conflict in the name of social harmony, and with those who argue that the whole content of politics is agonism, or disagreement.[18] She insists, however, that the political realm is more than "a battlefield of partial, conflicting interests." For Arendt, the content of political life is "the joy and the gratification that arise out of being in company with our peers, out of acting together and appearing in public, out of inserting ourselves into the world by word and deed, thus acquiring and sustaining our personal identity and beginning something entirely new."[19]

This understanding of politics is exemplified by Arendt's unusual (and not very popular) formulation of a different concept of the state, a "council system" in which power is "horizontally directed." It provides an alternative to state sovereignty, global governance, and the ubiquitous war that forms their backdrop. From the 18th century onwards, revolutions have provided examples of such councils—from small neighbourhood associations to more complex workers' or professional organizations—groups that spontaneously erupted wherever people lived or worked together. These were the "common political bodies" she hoped would arise among the Jews and Arabs living together in the new state of Israel.

At the heart of these organizations, Arendt tells us, is the need for participation. "The councils say: We want to participate, we want to debate, we want to make our voices heard in public, and we want to have a possibility to determine the political course of our country."[20] Politics, for Arendt, demands that we take into account multiple perspectives, bringing all those who choose to participate in public life into dialogue regarding the events and issues that bind them. The significance of this emphasis on horizontal and participatory relations should not be underestimated, given its potential to challenge the us-versus-them attitude particularly pronounced in post-9/11 state politics. Violence is an easy choice when the enemy is outside the range of discourse; killing becomes acceptable when others are rendered un-human, their speech reduced to noise.

In the space of politics, the freedom to begin—again and again—is characterized by Arendt as natality; for action always gives birth to novelty, to what is unpredictable or unexpected. She elaborates:

> It is in the nature of beginning that something new is started which cannot
> be expected from whatever may have happened before. This character of
> startling unexpectedness is inherent in all beginnings.... The fact that

man is capable of action means that the unexpected can be expected from him, that he is able to perform what is infinitely improbable. And this again is possible only because each man is unique, so that with each birth something uniquely new comes into the world.[21]

We find this freedom disconcerting, Arendt observes, unable to accept the very burden of "irreversibility and unpredictability" that empowers our actions. Instead, we choose to believe in the inevitability of historical events, and so deny our responsibility for events that our indifference or complicity did nothing to prevent. We hold freedom in contempt, feeling entangled in the web of human affairs to such an extent that we appear "much more the victim and the sufferer than the author and doer" of what we have done.[22] But if "startling unexpectedness" is the outcome of human freedom, our actions are never inevitable; violence is no more inevitable than kindness. It is action that most expresses natality, since action is what instigates the unexpected. To act requires an appearance in public; this act does not mean an individual act carried out in isolation from others. It is meaningful only to the extent that it occurs in a context of plurality.

To grasp what Arendt means by this freedom to initiate the unexpected, we need only note the exceptions to what might seem the norm in human behaviour. Exceptions are found among those who resisted Nazi policies in Denmark, for example—an extraordinary refusal that inspired dissent even among the Nazi officials stationed there—or among German soldiers like Anton Schmitt, who was executed for participating in the Jewish underground while a sergeant in Poland.[23] These exceptions were highlighted in brief moments of the trial against Nazi war criminal Adolf Eichmann, covered by Arendt for *The New Yorker* in 1961. Their significance can hardly be overstated, as she notes in her description of the courtroom scene after the story of Schmitt was recounted:

> And in those two minutes, which were like a sudden burst of light in the midst of impenetrable, unfathomable darkness, a single thought stood out clearly, irrefutably, beyond question—how utterly different everything would be today in this courtroom, in Israel, in Germany, in all of Europe, and perhaps in all countries of the world, if only more such stories could have been told.[24]

The lesson of such exceptions, Arendt argues, is that while most people will comply under conditions of terror, some will not: "Humanly speaking, no more is required, and no more can reasonably be asked, for this planet to remain a place fit for human habitation."[25]

Plurality, natality, and freedom are thus the conditions we must protect in order to preserve a space for politics in which all are invited to participate. These conditions are perpetually under threat from forces and authorities with a vested interest in a mute and obedient population—conditions, therefore, in need of cultivation and protection. Expressions of public discontent, dissent, disagreement, and moral outrage are as necessary as the negotiation and deliberation required for agreement: these are not destructive of politics, but a vital part of human relationships. It is only when all discussion of this discontent is silenced through the use of violent measures that the conditions needed for politics are destroyed. And the longer these conditions are disabled, the more difficult it is to rehabilitate them.

The essential question for politics is thus not what we would normally think—"Who has power over whom?"—but rather, "What can we do to preserve the capacity for politics?" How can we act in such a way that we protect our freedom to enact something of "startling unexpectedness," and so resist the belief that events are inevitable? What actions will continue to foster sheer human togetherness, the power of solidarity that arises from acting in concert? We can first respond in the negative: violence destroys the capacity for politics. In times of crisis, we may be tempted to react to provocation or victimization with violence, swift and satisfying, but this will rob us of the capacity for alternative responses, and often the will to invent them.

The Destruction of Politics

Violence destroys the worlds created between individuals, according to Arendt; it is thus decidedly anti-political. Words and action are meaningless when violence is used against an enemy as a means to an end, she writes, when human togetherness is lost, and people are only for or against others.[26] Isolated from a public space of exchange and interaction, individuals become powerless, unable to speak or act. The ultimate example of such isolation is totalitarianism, for "terror can rule absolutely only over men who are isolated against each other."[27] The task of the tyrant, therefore, is to ruin all relationships between individuals. Arendt's dissociation of violence from power, and her emphasis on the power of non-violence—indeed, as she observes, "to speak of nonviolent power is actually redundant"—has significant implications for an understanding of how we might reverse this process of isolation.[28] The recognition of the immense power of non-violent practices must be at the root of any discussion of peace, if only to counter the frequent dismissals of peace as a state of passivity.

Contrary to our common perception that violence and power go hand in hand, for Arendt these are opposites—"where the one rules absolutely, the other is absent."[29] Power is held in the hands of the many against one—it requires numbers, and appears when individuals act in concert. But violence is only instrumental, wielded by one against the many. A tyrant is not powerful on his own, and will quickly fail without the support of his subjects. An authoritarian regime will typically employ violence when the power of its supporters weakens, but without loyal henchmen, no tryant can wield power.[30] The violence he unleashes when he fears the loss of his control might destroy power but he will never acquire power through violence. Thus, "Everything depends on the power behind the violence," Arendt writes, "where commands are no longer obeyed, the means of violence are of no use."[31] Without obedience, even the most well-equipped military would be utterly powerless.

Her emphasis on the link between disobedience and power—essentially between dissent and politics—places Arendt in the good company of history's best advocates of non-violent civil disobedience. Václav Havel, for example, who describes the "power of the powerless" as the force of "living within the truth" rather than the outcome of any direct struggle for power,[32] would no doubt agree with Arendt's remark that "it is precisely in [the] admission of one's own impotence that a last remnant of strength and even power can still be preserved even under desperate conditions."[33] The "direct action" of the American civil rights movement, influenced by Martin Luther King Jr.'s call for "non-violent gadflies" to create the tension necessary for social revolution, is similarly compatible with Arendt's view of power. If Rosa Parks had not been joined by the majority of blacks in Montgomery, Alabama, in a boycott of the public bus system in 1955, it is unlikely that her refusal to give up her seat for a white passenger would have led to desegregation.[34] The power to transform society arises when individuals act together, supporting or withdrawing their support.

This explains why revolutions, like social movements, might succeed against all odds; and why a people armed only with righteous rage against injustice might overcome a brutal regime. Gene Sharp provides numerous historical examples in his studies of nonviolence, but recent years have again brought to the world's attention the power of collective action, particularly across the Arab world, where mass public dissent succeeded in dismantling several authoritarian regimes.[35] Needless to say, we have plenty of evidence that these successes do not spell the end of political turmoil, but they might inaugurate—or at least provide a glimpse of—a political culture that values the plurality, dissent, deliberation, and agency that Arendt admired in the revolutionary councils. It is this political culture that will assist in both the recovery from violence, and the prevention of further violence.

As we know from the severe repression of dissent in Syria, Bahrain, or Yemen, however, the power of the powerless doesn't always win against the violence of the violent—a phenomenon of which Arendt is well aware. In fact, she argues that the outcome is hardly in doubt when there is a "head-on clash between violence and power."[36] She speculates that even Gandhi's powerful non-violent resistance would not have ended in decolonization had he been standing up to Stalin's Russia or Hitler's Germany, rather than a British colonial rule that was characterized by restraint. The outcome would have been "massacre and submission."[37] Violence might bring victory, Arendt concludes from this, but the price is extremely high, paid by both the conquered and the conqueror.[38]

We are currently witnessing an example of this outcome in Syria, where the non-violent revolution that began in 2011 has developed into a horrendous civil war (if asymmetrical in terms of military power and responsibility), with atrocities committed by both sides. The international community, stymied by various state interests and power plays, takes sides, deliberates over whether and how to intervene, and waits. With some 160,000 dead at the time of writing, the Syrian conflict has become the longest and bloodiest of the Arab uprisings.[39] We can't be certain that if the uprising had continued to be non-violent, President Bashar al-Assad would have responded with less brutality and collective action would have led to his downfall. But surely we can claim that the price paid for the opposition taking up weapons has been the incalculable loss of the capacity for politics. Arendt states that since we can never reliably predict the ends of human action, "the means used to achieve political goals are more often than not of greater relevance to the future world than the intended goals."[40] Syria is one such case where the means have overwhelmed the end, the gravest concern is now what this horrific violence engenders for any kind of future. Just as a culture of disobedience among the Danish public transformed the attitudes of the Nazi officials in their midst, a culture of violence will transform the public institutions and communities charged with preserving a space for speech and collective action. A politics defined by natality will turn into a politics of mortality; death will become a way of life.[41]

This fact alone can explain why cycles of violence are difficult to stop; once begun, the erosion of a political space means that fewer and fewer alternatives to violence are imagined or considered. Violence appears necessary and inevitable in the absence of politics; once voices are silenced, and human interaction abruptly cut off, it is easy to perceive violence as synonymous with action. We witnessed this situation in the desperate call to the international community, from Syrians and many others around the world, for military intervention to stop Assad; the underlying assumption was that anything short of killing was a shameful display of impotence. This is not to suggest that diplomacy or negotiation will *always* work to put an end to authoritarian rule; but that violence will not *always* work either. Whether one works or not, depends not only on a host of factors concerning the kinds of political institutions and means for communication in place—in short on the power of public support—but on how we define "works." In other words, to what end are we employing our strategies?

All too often we forget the effects and legacies of the means, sacrificing countless lives for an unknowable future in the persistent belief that the effects of killing in the name of a just cause will somehow cease to matter in this imagined future—that the suffering will prove to have been worth it. But any new society is built on the actions of the old, Arendt reminds us. The psychological legacy of violence—in the form of ongoing hostility, intergenerational memory, and fantasies of vengeance—and the devastation violence wrecks on economies, infrastructures, and institutions—will form a cracked, unstable foundation for the future. Without politics there can be no peaceful relations. Indeed, the one provides the means for the other. There is still, however, the matter of the exception—when the preservation of life itself must come before the preservation of politics.

Critique of Violence

Despite her dissociation of violence from power, and therefore violence from politics, Arendt does not take an absolute moral stand against violence. She does not share the spiritual or religious emphasis—with its veneration of martyrdom—of Gandhi, for example, who believed that non-violence necessitated an ascetic way of life; or of King, who called for Christian self-purification as essential for non-violent action. Arendt is uncompromising on the point that violence is illegitimate, that we pay too high a price for it in terms of the destruction of politics and untold human misery. But this still leaves open the question of its justifiability after the fact. Moral outrage, and the violence it may spawn, are not necessarily irrational, and in fact quite typical responses to injustice, Arendt points out, and to cure us of such emotion would essentially dehumanize us. While rage does not necessarily lead to violence, "to resort to violence when confronted with outrageous events or conditions is enormously tempting because of its inherent immediacy and swiftness."[42] But, she adds—and this might strike us as surprising—such swift action might be the "only appropriate remedy" following acts of injustice, and the only way to balance the scales of justice.[43]

This qualification is worth a closer look. We find Arendt's most incisive critique of violence in her reflections on her own "century of wars and revolutions," as she puts it in her introduction to *On Violence*. She expresses frustration with the "glorification" of emancipatory violence that she finds in Frantz Fanon's anti-colonial manifesto, *The Wretched of the Earth*, reinforced with exaggerated rhetorical flair by Jean-Paul Sartre in his preface to the work. Fanon, who famously claimed that decolonization is always a violent phenomenon, is taken to task by Arendt for his "irresponsible grandiose statements" that glorify the rage and violence of those who dream of taking the oppressor's place and appropriating his wealth.[44] By this "mad fury," Arendt argues, the wretched of the earth are not recreating themselves, as Sartre insists, but turning dreams into nightmares for everyone.[45]

The colonized subject is inevitably consumed by the fantasy of the absolute destruction of his enemy, Fanon explains—a destruction necessitated by the Manichean division of the world instigated by the colonizer. This is an irreconcilable world in which negotiation has no place; a world reduced to two sides—one is either for or against—no longer characterized by plurality and the free exchange of speech. To respond to this situation with violence is to keep the dualism intact, a dynamic that should have worried Fanon. The solidarity factor, in revolutionary movements and militaries alike, creates a kind of "intoxicating spell" that binds actors together into "the great organism of violence which has surged upward."[46] Death is a potent equalizer, Arendt concludes.[47]

All too often the outcome of this "great organism of violence" is an even more brutal response by the colonizers, who fear the loss of power over those they subjugate. Fanon's writings inspired the more militant wing of the American civil rights movement—increasingly active after the assassination of King—which was criticized by Arendt for undermining the successes of non-violent action. She speaks approvingly of the boycotts, sit-ins, and demonstrations, but complains that the black riots could provoke a much more violent white backlash.[48] While violence in interracial struggle is logical, she says, a rational consequence of racism—much like Fanon's conclusion about decolonization—and may be the only way to ensure a hearing, it could bring about a "full-fledged racist ideology for which 'law and order' would indeed become a mere façade." No doubt Arendt was thinking of Nazi ideology in this instance.[49]

Given Arendt's position on the use of violence (or at least its glorification) in emancipatory struggles such as decolonization and anti-racism, we might be taken aback by the vehemence with which she calls for Jews to take up weapons against Hitler. Her contributions in the 1940s to the German-Jewish publication *Aufbau* are brimming with anguish and fury over Hitler's Final Solution, the indifference of the world, and the lack of widespread political will among the Jewish people.[50] She justifies a Jewish army to fight the forces of Nazism on the basis of self-defence: "A people that no longer defends itself against its enemies is not a people but a living corpse. A people whom others will not allow to defend itself against its enemies is condemned to a fate that is perhaps humanly quite lofty but politically completely unworthy: a victim of world history."[51]

Indeed, Arendt claims that the certainty of Hitler's determination to exterminate the Jews is matched by the certainty that his downfall will come about *only* if those under threat confirm their existence "by defending themselves with their own hand."[52] She echoes Fanon's palpable rage when she asserts: "We do not want promises that our sufferings will be 'avenged,' we want to fight; we do not want mercy, but justice."[53] This is the Arendt who had no moral qualms about sending convicted Nazi war criminal Adolf Eichmann to his death. "He who does not practice justice has no right to mercy," she explains, for "mercy without justice is one of the devil's most powerful accomplices—it calms outrage and sanctions the structures that the devil has created."[54]

In her criticism of Fanon and of the militant civil-rights activists, Arendt does not appear to recognize the same desire for justice *before* mercy among those who fight for an end to racism. We should note, however, that she does not explicitly refute Fanon's claim that decolonization is necessarily violent; her critique is focused on his rhetoric, which romanticizes and justifies the violence of the oppressed. Arendt's own demand for Jewish self-defence is not a glorification of the violence of resistance, but a pragmatic recognition of the needs of survival. She shows compassion for victims of political violence, but intolerance for a world view determined by victimhood. Violence cannot be justified solely on the basis of suffering. It is certainly this attitude that contributed to the fierce public controversy aroused by her discussion of the Jewish councils in *Eichmann in Jerusalem*, and to the criticism of her impatience with some aspects of the African American struggle.[55]

Arendt's insistence that only armed Jews could defeat Hitler, and her criticism of what she calls the "cowardly" hearts of the oppressed, must be read in the context of her emphasis on the agency of the individual, whether victim or perpetrator. Jews must not be sacrificial lambs led obediently to the slaughter. She does not mince words on this point, complaining bluntly of a "slave mentality" among Jews. "It is not true that we have been the persecuted innocents of history, always and everywhere," Arendt protests; this attitude, far more than persecution, would remove Jews from history completely. Rather, she argues, Jews must "do battle" with all those in their own ranks who claim that they have always been the victims and targets of history.[56] The anger that this perspective provoked among Jews shocked Arendt, who believed herself entitled—as a Jew herself—to be self-critical, insisting that "self-criticism is not self-hatred."[57] But Arendt's concern remains, above all, with exercising political will and power through collective action, and refusing an identity of victimhood. No wonder she complains of the attitude she witnessed first-hand, in her own brief detention in a camp: "We Jews sat there, quite peaceful and unpolitical, in French internment camps and consoled ourselves with how much worse Dachau was."[58]

Arendt stresses often enough the devastating effects of violence on politics, arguing that violence is at cross-purposes with political life. But ultimately, faced with the grim reality of the Holocaust, she is unable to say that violence is never justifiable. In one of the most intriguing passages of *On Violence*, we read: "Violence can be justifiable, but it never will be legitimate. Its justification loses in plausibility the farther its intended end recedes into the future. No one questions the use of violence in self-defence, because the danger is not only clear but also present, and the end justifying the means is immediate."[59] The distinction she makes between legitimate and justifiable helps us to manage the contradiction between the belief that harming or taking another human life is wrong—unlawful, illegitimate—

and yet, after the fact, it may appear paradoxically just or reasonable, provided that there was no means of escape or possibility of resistance.

This may seem a contradiction—that the violent resistance of the Jews is justifiable, but not the violent resistance of the colonized, or of Black Americans. But there is no contradiction if we follow Arendt in her attentiveness to the singularity of historical circumstances. Self-defence is justifiable when the danger confronted is immediate, when the protection of one's own life demands swift action—indeed, when the threat to one's life is greater than the threat of the destruction of politics. It presupposes that the individual or group facing this threat is utterly defenceless, bereft of the capacity for politics. Arendt might have suggested that slaves need to be armed; but blacks in the civil-rights era did have options (albeit extremely limited ones), and were not entirely without support from the white population.

Genocide thus provides our best justification for self-defence in Arendt's terms, since in the case of genocide a people finds itself completely defenceless, and often without any outside support. Once again, the capacity for politics is at the heart of the matter. If—like the Jews during the years of the Final Solution—a people has no recourse to a public space where they can come together, no capacity for speech or action, no institutions or council-like collectives by which to generate solidarity and action, then they must defend themselves, with weapons if need be. This is when violence is justifiable: protecting life itself is a prerequisite for protecting politics.

Peace as a Means to Politics

We do not need to establish an absolute principle of non-violence if we agree that self-defence is a right. The challenge is rather to consider, in each individual case, at what point self-defence ceases to be self-defence and becomes something else: pre-emptive attack, revenge, terrorism, premeditated murder, counter-insurgency, or a "disposition matrix."[60] The temporal aspect matters—we can't justify violence as self-defence if its proposed ends are far in the future. The Israeli occupation of the Palestinian people or its military operations in Gaza; the Syrian opposition's acts of torture; the American use of drones in Pakistan—these are not justifiable acts of self-defence, but illegitimate acts of violence. Arendt could not have predicted the use to which her self-defence arguments would be put today—supporting a global extension of the Zionist views she criticized, in which the Jewish people appeared as "surrounded and forced together by a world of enemies."[61] But her equally severe criticisms of violence carried out in the name of liberation, and state violence carried out in the name of repression—both of which claim that their aim is peace—can help us to condemn both violence and a false notion of peace in this era of security politics.

But rather than repeat the well-worn question—when is violence justifiable?—we might instead ask: what can we do at this very moment to protect spaces of exchange and agreement? How do we keep them open and guard their fragility from those who would destroy them, especially in the face of tyranny, when fear of the just rage of the masses legitimates brutality? These are not simple questions, and demand careful analysis, discussion, and engagement with events as they unfold. Here, again, Arendt can help us. Her formulation of politics as the realm of human appearance and action—governed by speech, pluralism, and conflict, but also by negotiation and consensus—will shift our understanding of peace from a passive state to an active means. The operative word is "peaceful" rather than peace, to qualify relation, action, and conflict: not peace but *peaceful relations* as a means to politics. Important for this shift is an antithetical relationship between power and violence that banishes the latter from the territory of politics; power lies in collective action and solidarity, not in weaponry. Hannah Arendt's critique of the use of violence in politics is pragmatic rather than moral; contingent rather than normative; attentive to historical detail, and to our human freedom to enact something utterly new. The possibilities are endless.

Notes

1   One of the few exceptions is Dan Jakopovich, "Hannah Arendt and Nonviolence," *Peace Studies Journal* 2.1 (2009): 1–15.

2   Hannah Arendt, *The Jewish Writings*, ed. Jerome Kohn and Ron H. Feldman (New York: Schocken Books, 2007), 134ff.

3   For the purpose of this discussion, I define violence rather more narrowly than is currently popular: as serious physical harm resulting in injury or death, intentionally carried out by one human being against another.

4   Hannah Arendt, "Introduction into Politics," *The Promise of Politics*, ed. Jerome Kohn (New York: Schocken Books, 2005), 96.

5   Leah Bradshaw, "Kant, Cosmopolitan Right, and the Prospects for Global Peace," this volume, p. 129.

6   The reference to "splendour" comes at the close of *On Revolution*: "It was the *polis*, the space of men's free deeds and living words, which could endow life with splendour." Hannah Arendt, *On Revolution* (New York: Penguin Books, 1963), 281.

7   Arendt was quoted in Elisabeth Young-Bruehl, *Hannah Arendt: For Love of the World*, 2nd ed. (New Haven: Yale University Press, 2004), 361.

8   Hannah Arendt, *The Jew as Pariah: Jewish Identity and Politics in the Modern Age*, ed. Ron H. Feldman (New York: Grove Press, 1978), 196. For more on this subject, see Diane Enns, *The Violence of Victimhood* (University Park, PA: Penn State Press, 2012), Chapter 2; Idith Zertal, *Israel's Holocaust and the Politics of Nationhood*, trans. Chaya Galai (New York: Cambridge University Press, 2005); and Yael Zerubavel, *Recovered Roots: Collective Memory and the Making of Israeli National Tradition* (Chicago: University of Chicago Press, 1995).

9   Arendt, *The Jewish Writings*, 385.

10 Arendt, *The Jewish Writings*, 383–85.

11 Arendt, *The Jewish Writings*, 425.

12 Arendt, *The Jewish Writings*, 434.

13 Hannah Arendt, *The Human Condition* (Chicago: University of Chicago Press, 1958), 180.

14 Hannah Arendt, *On Violence* (New York: Harcourt Brace, 1970), 43–44.

15 Arendt, "Introduction into Politics," 95.

16 Arendt, *The Human Condition*, 8.

17 Arendt, "Introduction into Politics," 106.

18 Two authors with especially insightful views are Jacques Rancière, *Disagreement: Politics and Philosophy*, trans. Julie Rose (Minneapolis: University of Minnesota Press, 1999); and Chantal Mouffe, *On the Political* (New York: Routledge, 2005).

19 Hannah Arendt, "Truth and Politics," *Between Past and Future* (New York: Penguin Books, 1993), 263.

20 Hannah Arendt, "Thoughts on Politics and Revolution," interview with Adelbert Reif, *Crises of the Republic* (New York: Harcourt Brace, 1972), 232. See also Arendt's *On Revolution*, Chapter 6, 215–81.

21 Arendt, *The Human Condition*, 177–78.

22 Arendt, *The Human Condition*, 233–34.

23 Hannah Arendt, *Eichmann in Jerusalem: A Report on the Banality of Evil* (New York: Viking Press, 1963), 172, 231.

24 Arendt, *Eichmann in Jerusalem*, 231.

25 Arendt, *Eichmann in Jerusalem*, 233. The matter of individual conscience—which for Arendt is expressed as the need to be able to live with oneself and one's deeds—is beyond the scope of my discussion here, but of course the "exceptions" can be individuals refusing to comply, or entire populations.

26 Arendt, *The Human Condition*, 180.

27   Hannah Arendt, *The Origins of Totalitarianism* (New York: Harcourt Brace, 1973), 474.

28   Arendt, *On Violence*, 56.

29   Arendt, *On Violence*, 56.

30   Arendt, *On Violence*, 42–44.

31   Arendt, *On Violence*, 49.

32   Václav Havel, "The Power of the Powerless," *Open Letters: Selected Writings 1965–1990* (New York: Vintage Books, 1985), 149.

33   Hannah Arendt, "Personal Responsibility Under Dictatorship," *Responsibility and Judgment*, ed. Jerome Kohn (New York: Schocken Books, 2003), 45.

34   In fact, there were several cases of women refusing to give up their bus seats to white passengers before Rosa Parks; but they did not receive much public attention, or spark mass resistance.

35   Gene Sharp, *Waging Nonviolent Struggle: 20th Century Practice and 21st Century Potential* (Manchester, NH: Porter Sargent, 2005).

36   Arendt, *On Violence*, 53.

37   Arendt, *On Violence*, 53.

38   Arendt, *On Violence*, 53–54.

39   Anne Barnard, "Syria Death Toll Reported to Rise by 10,000 in Less than 2 Months," *New York Times*, May 19, 2014. http://www.nytimes.com/2014/05/20/world/middleeast/syria.html?_r=0.

40   Arendt, *On Violence*, 4.

41   This expression is borrowed from David Grossman, *Death as a Way of Life: From Oslo to the Geneva Agreement*, trans. Haim Watzman (New York: Picador, 2004).

42   Arendt, *On Violence*, 63.

43   Arendt, *On Violence*, 64.

44   Arendt, *On Violence*, 20–21.

45   Arendt, *On Violence*, 21.

46   Frantz Fanon, quoted in Arendt, *On Violence*, 67.

47   Arendt, *On Violence*, 67.

48   Arendt, *On Violence*, 77.

49   Arendt, *On Violence*, 77.

50   *Aufbau* was a journal for German-speaking Jews around the world, founded in 1934, and published in New York by the Leo Baeck Institute until April 2004. Its original purpose was to provide a monthly newsletter for the German-Jewish club that included information and helpful facts for Jewish refugees. *Aufbau* became one of the leading anti-Nazi publications of the German press in exile. http://www.lbi.org/collections/library/highlights-of-lbi-library-collection/aufbau-york-ny-periodical.

51   Arendt, *The Jewish Writings*, 262.

52   Arendt, *The Jewish Writings*, 263.

53   Arendt, *The Jewish Writings*, 263.

54   Arendt, *The Jewish Writings*, 263.

55   For a discussion of these reactions, see Young-Bruehl, 328–78, 412–22.

56   Arendt, *The Jewish Writings*, 143.

57   Arendt, *The Jewish Writings*, 152.

58   Arendt, *Eichmann in Jerusalem*, 167.

59   Arendt, *On Violence*, 151.

60   The term "disposition matrix" is the Obama administration's name for the continuously evolving database for current intelligence on terrorist targets, and on the various strategies and contingencies for dealing with them.

61   Arendt, *The Jewish Writings*, 385.

CHAPTER 13

Defining Peace: Jacques Derrida's "Impossible Friendship" and "Democracy to Come"

Pamela Huber

Like most of the authorities examined in this volume, Jacques Derrida offers no specific theory or definition of peace. What sets him apart from others is that for him, this lack is not a problem: in fact, it is the *raison d'être* of his work. In Derrida's concept of deconstruction, as we shall see, peace is presented as neither a reality nor a potential. Rather, it is something that may tangibly exist only when we work to make it a reality. As soon as we stop acting, it disappears. For Derrida, peace is in the doing.

This active view of peace is very different from the other views expressed here, for a reason that may seem rather peculiar. It is not a matter of mere definition; Derrida would neither agree nor disagree with others' definitions of peace. What makes his view unique is that it absolutely requires you, the reader, to exist. Without you there is nothing—only dead words on a page. For Derrida, what matters is not that you understand what he means, on this or any other subject. What matters is that you fully engage with his ideas, challenge his authority, and question every view of peace—even his own. Only by doing this, Derrida suggests, can we ever hope to grasp the true meaning of anything.

Derrida's ideas about peace will be demonstrated here via his concept of "impossible friendship." Briefly, Derrida deems friendship to be impossible because the peaceable relations it implies between persons can only ever exist in the active doing. As we will see later, it is always possible for goodwill to turn to strife and conflict. This concept both upholds and questions all issues of common good, and is linked to his related concept of "democracy to come." This idea embraces the Enlightenment promise of freedom and equality for all—but only insofar as it remains a promise, to be perpetually acted upon. To define democracy, and impose it on others, is essentially undemocratic. Finally, this chapter will examine the practical applications of Derrida's thought: his defence of a more "European approach" to a decision to go to war, whether in Iraq or elsewhere. Informed both by the Enlightenment spirit of radical critique, and the 20th-century experience of colonialism and the holocaust, Derrida aims to show that war and peace are both informed by the same logic of "us versus them." He exposes the complexity of the "other" on whom we impose our peace, by way of war; and calls us to act accordingly.

Defining by Not Defining:
Peace and Deconstruction

To understand how Derrida approaches a concept like peace, we must first understand deconstruction—Deconstruction is the radical "truth" of otherness as far as all truths, goods and ethical standards are concerned.[1] On the surface, this means that deconstruction is a method or tool used to dissect the "errors" or limitedness in all received truths, goods, and ethical standards. For Derrida, however deconstruction is much more than a method. Indeed, to restrict it as such is to risk defending another error— in effect suggesting that deconstruction can help one to finally grasp the truth. Thus, deconstruction is both a method and yet not a method. It is tool we use that is yet beyond our methodical control. This paradoxical "truth" of deconstruction reflects a broader reality that we cannot grasp. In that vein, Derrida is careful to point out that the name "deconstruction" is nothing more than his own word for a process that always happens when we express our particular truths.[2] Specifically, the "other"—the argument that questions all particular truths—always emerges alongside their expression. This means that deconstructive "othering" is not within anyone's control. This is the undoing truth of deconstruction, which Derrida also names "la différance." The only truth of deconstruction is this: in the beginning, there is not one-ness but difference, both the truth and its other.[3]

Derrida "proves" this claim by closely examining how truth is expressed in the usually accepted fount of truth: the philosophical canon. He finds no clear expression of truth. On the contrary, there are only innumerable texts—and not just primary texts like those of Plato and Aristotle, but interpretations of them; and then interpretations of the interpretations.[4] Going still further, Derrida asks us not to view expressions of truth from the usual authorial standpoint—as if we can fully know the author's intentions, and unite the lines of each text into a singular, consistent truth or definition of things. Rather, we are encouraged to view them from the perspective of the reader, the inexact interpreter, the questioner, even the perplexed.[5] Put bluntly, for Derrida there is no such thing as a pure author.

His justification for this again reflects the othering truth of deconstruction, which applies not only to all the innumerable texts in existence but also within each singular text as well. This is not to be viewed negatively, as a destruction of the author. Rather it affirms the fact that in each of us there is both an author—the individual who announces the singular truth to be presented—and a reader, who interprets (and thereby undoes) that truth as soon as it emerges.[6] This deconstructive justification of truth is laid out in Derrida's seminal work *Of Grammatology*, in which he uncovers the concept of authorial bias and the complementary need for the reader perspective. He does so by delving into the "textuality" of truth itself—that is, its written expression in the philosophical canon. This enables him to expose the foundation of the authorial bias: the tendency in philosophy to link truth and speech.[7]

Derrida begins with the obvious: the uncanny fact that truth seems to be linked to speech in a written text. Everything cannot be as it should if the traditional philosophical expression of truth, writing, is itself denounced by these same writers. The suspicion then surfaces that something is not fully right in these expressions of truth—that there might even be something forced about them.[8] We might then try to discover the reason for this speech bias. What makes its allure so powerful that philosophers are moved, in writing, to defend it as the only valid path to truth? To paraphrase Derrida's answer, the linkage of speech to truth is ultimately based on a kind of utopian dream.

Even though both speech and writing are merely signifiers or representations of truth, speech is nevertheless privileged. Defined by Plato and Aristotle as that which can more purely express the truth, speech is deemed closer to the natural, the true, the good.[9] In contrast to the abstraction of writing, speech is argued to have an intimate relationship with what is represented—even to be at one with it.[10] Because of this, the utopian dream—one that still tempts us to this day—is that perhaps people need not just philosophize about the truth, but actually come to know it.[11] So powerful is this dream, so blinding is its allure of truth, that the purity of speech is defended—in the abstraction of writing.[12] This explains the authorial bias in writing, which is a reflection of this truth-making authority of speech.

Derrida counters this vision and reaffirms the truth of otherness in *Of Grammatology*. In this work, he proposes to save philosophy from the temptation to make exclusive views of the truth universal by privileging writing over speech. He further aims to give a more equal voice to the reader, in particular that undoing "other" who is usually silenced by the more resounding voice of authorial truth. Although his many critics accuse Derrida of rejecting speech, authorship, or even the philosophical canon from whence they are derived, that is not his point here.[13] Rather, his goal is to privilege both the abstraction of writing and the interpretation of the reader. By doing this, Derrida hopes to establish truth on more firmly philosophical grounds. In particular, he believes, truth should not be based on utopian dreams of certain knowledge, but on a philosophical approach of love and pursuit of an ever-elusive knowledge.

To put this in another way, all individuals are inherently limited, particularistic, exclusive beings. Because of this, all expressions of truth, including speech and authorship, are necessarily abstractions. When we forget this and succumb to the admittedly powerful notion that there is such a thing as a direct human link to the truth, we necessarily do violence to the truth. A kind of power game of a multitude of competing truths is instituted, each asserting its truth to be the only correct one, and each excluding all others.[14]

Elucidating this deconstructive truth on more positive grounds, Derrida devotes all his writings, in one way or another, to readings of the philosophical canon. Each discussion Derrida undertakes of a given text brings out the reader-other of authorial truth.[15] And knowing that such a task can never be completed—for though the author of each text is only one, its readers are infinite—Derrida invites his readers to do the same with all the texts they read, including his own.[16]

We can conclude from this overview of deconstruction that Derrida's approach to all concepts, including peace, is to define by undefining, and to undo definitions even as they are defined. To see what this undefinitive approach means for peace, we turn now to Derrida's idea of impossible friendship—one that eschews all fixed concepts of community. Instead he argues that friendship, and the peaceable relations it implies between persons, can only ever exist in the doing.

Un-Definition of Peace 1: "Impossible Friendship"

Friendship seems a reasonable place to start discussing the subject of peace: in the bond of friendship, any disagreements there may be do not tend to lead to war, but are couched under the canopy of goodwill. The classic defender of friendship is Aristotle, who suggests that politics is a kind of friendship.[17] Speaking of a pleasure in living together, Aristotle suggests that friendship engenders a common good beyond abstract precepts and logical arguments.[18] Friendship in a society establishes a common bond among its citizenry, a more personal sense of love between the people. In this way, friendship makes the common good seem more real because this kind of love appears to overcome any fear of civil strife.[19]

And yet, as he defines the common good in terms of a bond based on human love, Aristotle is confronted with a problem. As he himself suggests in both the *Nicomachean Ethics* and the *Eudemian Ethics*, love tends to obscure the good with the seeming good. Quite simply, he asserts, it is possible for us to love a bad man. In effect, friendship—in affixing the good to love—can as easily undermine the common good as support it, and send everything topsy-turvy. [20] This confusion means that strife and warfare are always possibilities in the human bond of love.

Aristotle seeks to resolve this problem in two ways, both intended to rein in the potential boundlessness of love and affix it firmly to the singular good. First, he develops a hierarchical structure of friendship, placing good friendship at the top, claiming it to be the best kind and the only completely true version.[21] This approach confines boundless love to the category of lesser, more incidental friendships. Second, he suggests that good friendship is superior to all other kinds of friendship because it is based on the internal argument that only the good man—the "unit" of good friendship—is truly lovable.[22] In contrast to the bad man (who, in beastly fashion, is torn this way and that by his various passions) the good man, guided by his love of the good, is more in control of who he is. Because he is ruled by the good, he offers a stable and fully human personality in that there is some constant thing in him (the good) to love.[23]

But it seems unusual to consider boundless love a problem that needs resolving. Indeed, can the good of love really be defended in such an objective, "thingly" manner, and still be called love? Even Aristotle seems to vacillate here, reiterating time and again the need for friendship to instill in people a sheer pleasure in living together.[24] In either case, the possibility always remains that the love bond may over-run, or even undermine, the common good. This suggests that the power of love and goodwill amongst the citizenry to overcome conflict, as Aristotle had asserted in his introduction to friendship, is only ever tentative. At all times, peace may give way to war.

Derrida would agree. In his reading of Aristotelian friendship in his *Politics of Friendship*, he makes every effort to embrace this boundless love and thereby render Aristotle's "good friendship" argument impossible. In doing so, he suggests the process by which friendship and goodwill may bleed into civil strife and warfare. As we delve deeper into Derrida's deconstruction of Aristotelian friendship, we will uncover the source of his concept of impossible friendship—including what might be characterized as an open possibility for peace. Of particular interest in this regard is Aristotle's need to undergird his view of friendship or common good with the test of time: there is no stable friendship without confidence, but confidence needs time to establish. In the *Eudemian Ethics*, Aristotle quotes Theognis: "You cannot know the mind of man or woman till you have tried them as you might cattle." Even for Aristotle, it seems that the singular, universal good can only come to be when it is tested, questioned, and ever subject to free choice.[25] But rather than embracing this boundless common good, Aristotle takes pains to hide it, using the same argument: he cites the need to control the number of people who can truly become one's friend. People cannot have many tried-and-true friends: "it is hard to test many men, for one would have to live with each," he observes. (Nor, he adds, "should one choose a friend like a garment.")[26] Aristotle's goal remains to defend the fixed, singular good.

In outlining this, Derrida reveals what impossible friendship means in terms of the common good in particular, and of peace generally. Derrida argues backwards: the reason that Aristotle can see boundlessness only in negative, controlling terms, rather than in more hopeful, ethical ones, is because he—following the general tradition of political philosophy—

desires to put his exclusive stamp of truth on the good. Remove this desire for control, and the outlook on boundless friendship becomes infinitely more promising, with all its impossibility, open-endedness, and radical inclusiveness. We might call this Derrida's vision of peace: let friendship be what it is, in all of its boundless love.[27]

But can one propose such a perpetually open and inclusive vision of peace? Can there really be peace without a stable vision of friendship or the common good? Derrida uses deconstruction to turn this question around: a boundless vision of the good is only unthinkable from the perspective of the controlling singular tradition of the good. From a more radically open and inclusive point of view, the matter is altogether different, altogether more positive.[28] By using Aristotle's own contradiction against him, as it were, Derrida proposes a radical reframing of the philosophical tradition itself, and with it beliefs such as peace, friendship, and the common good. If we refrain from imprisoning those possibilities in singular and exclusive visions of truth, they will be guided by a new vision—one that is informed by its perpetual undoing; or rather (which is the same thing) by its perpetual openness to the other.[29] In truly universal and inclusive fashion, philosophers will be called on to be friends of the truth.[30] The truth, in all of its contradictoriness and complexity, will simply be allowed to be.

In other words, Derrida proposes a questioning stance toward all foundational concepts. He seeks to reorient the philosophical tradition from grasping or having the truth, to being a friend of truth:

> But the friends of the truth are not, by definition in the truth; they are not installed there as in the padlocked security of a dogma and the stable reliability of an opinion.... The friends of the truth are without the truth, even if friends cannot function without truth. The truth—that of the thinkers to come—it is impossible to be it, to be there, to have it; one must only be its friend.[31]

Here we have Derrida's positive ethical affirmation of impossible friendship. With this shift, Derrida in effect embraces friendship not as a singular universal truth, to be possessed by the few, but as an actual relationship—in all of its complexity, multiplicity, boundless love, and absolute otherness. Simply put, friendship is in the doing.[32]

In terms of discovering what Derrida means by friendship and ultimately peace, we have made a tentative start. Thanks to the friend of truth, the controlling tendencies of tradition are replaced by a gesture of openness and hope. As Derrida endeavours to show, the questioning or undoing of all fixed goods in the name of the other can in fact have the flavour of a universal ethical standard. However, this can only be a tentative standard; only achievable if all of us are prepared to do this work of otherness. In the end, peace lies in our fragile, finite, freely choosing hands. Peace is in the doing. Derrida ends his work *Politics of Friendship* not with a conceptual definition of friendship, but with a plea for others—people he does not know—to continue the work of otherness. "Oh my democratic friends ..."[33]

Un-Definition of Peace 2: Democracy to Come

Since we are prompted to democratic relationships, and to the system of democracy in particular, this gives us another vantage point from which to view Derrida's open-ended idea of what it means to affirm a common good, and what it looks like to be peaceable. On the one hand, it looks like nothing at all. On the other hand, it is a lot of work. Derrida reveals as much in his 1993 book *Specters of Marx*.[34] Democracy, Derrida believes, does not exist in any pure form. On the contrary, its "being" derives only from the fact that it is questioned by its Marxist other—in common parlance communism; so it would seem that democracy is made possible by its so-called enemy. Derrida's vision of democracy is a fluid and moveable one. He holds that it exists only in the doing, rather than as something definitive or graspable. It is "democracy to come," in which all the deconstructive and open-ended tropes of impossible friendship reappear in a new guise.

Approaching *Specters of Marx* for the first time, one is immediately struck by something unusual. Derrida opens this work with a quotation from *Hamlet*: "The time is out of joint."[35] His invocation of this quotation continues throughout the book, which points to its significance in his thought.[36] With this bending of the concept of time, Derrida reveals a key facet of his politics: a sense of open-endedness with no stable "now" or present context.[37] He suggests that his project will be to shake up the world of the early 1990s— a world in which the Berlin Wall has fallen, and in which a triumphalist political vision of liberal democracy has emerged. But Derrida argues that this optimistic perspective misses the point: politics goes beyond any singular or "present" vision. More precisely, the only vision that does politics justice is one in which there is no one perspective at all—since by definition, politics is utterly open to all perspectives, across distance and time.

It is helpful to contrast Derrida's view with that of one of the most famous triumphalist thinkers in the early 1990s, Francis Fukuyama. In his *The End of History and the Last Man*, Fukuyama makes a bold claim:

> Liberal democracy may constitute the endpoint of mankind's ideological evolution and the final form of human government, and as such constitutes the end of history.... This [is] not to say that today's stable democracies ... [are] not without injustice or serious social problems. But these problems [are] ones of incomplete implementation of the twin principles of liberty and equality on which modern democracy is founded, rather than of flaws in the principles themselves.[38]

Fukuyama clearly believes that liberal democracy is the best form of human government, the ideal for which all polities must aim. And if at present most actual democracies do not yet embody this ideal, the concept of "incomplete implementation" suggests that it is only a matter of time before they will do so. At bottom, ideal and actual politics are essentially collapsible, separated only by a progressive notion of time. This is Fukuyama's expression of political faith.

Derrida's critique of Fukuyama's liberal-democratic triumphalism focuses precisely on this element of time:

> Fukuyama oscillates confusedly between two irreconcilable discourses. Even though he believes in its effective realization ... Fukuyama does not hesitate all the same to oppose the *ideality* of this liberal democratic *ideal* to all the evidence that bears massive witness to the fact that neither the United States nor the European Community has attained the perfection of ... liberal democracy, nor have they even come close.[39]

In other words, Derrida argues, in order to prove that the perfect liberal democracy will be realized in a matter of time, Fukuyama ignores the very real gap that exists between ideal and actual democracies. Or more precisely, the actual gets buried under a universal logic of progress, and of end-of-history "ideality"; this allows Fukuyama to argue that the democratic ideal will in fact be realized, despite the messiness of actual politics. Derrida suggests that this is absurd, even potentially unjust. For the sake of realizing the democratic ideal, how can one completely overlook the actual attempts and failures of polities to realize democracy? Is not such blind optimism tantamount to cutting off any hope for real democracy in the world? No, Derrida hints, this one-sided optimism will not do. If we truly care about the democratic ideal, we must be more realistic. Hence Derrida's alternative vision, democracy to come.

By emphasizing the "to come," Derrida shunts aside all notions of political triumphs or endpoints and instead defends the idea of politics as a process. There will never be a complete manifestation of liberty and equality in the world, he believes. Rather, politics is a perpetual process of attempts and failures to achieve ideals. This is what democracy means; this perpetual activity is, in fact, its ideal. Derrida asserts, "if one could *count* on what is coming, hope would be but the calculation of a program."[40] In effect, the democratic ideal must always recognize its actual political failure, making its realization quite open-ended.[41] And for Derrida, the success of the ideal seems to be precisely in the attempt. Despite our failures—perhaps even spurred on by them—we continue to pursue the ever-possible democratic ideal. Such is the boundless optimism of open-endedness.

At the same time, there is a darker imperative to try to achieve greater liberty and equality. As Derrida writes, "Never have violence, inequality, exclusion, famine, and thus economic oppression, affected as many individuals in the history of the earth and of humanity."[42] This profound injustice exists in spite of all the so-called democratic societies in the world. As a result, Derrida is adamant that we must actualize the democratic ideal by way of perpetually critiquing it. Democracy is actualized insofar as it is imbued with the spirit of its other, Marxism, which challenges it.[43]

In fact, Derrida suggests that all conceptions of the democratic ideal—including Fukuyama's—are signed by Marx's eschatology.[44] Democracy, like Marxism, is defined by its promise of a better tomorrow. More precisely, the hope that encompasses both political ideals is that someday everyone will be included in a truly democratic community. Such a complete and happy life is true justice defined, including perhaps even the idea that enemies can be friends.[45] In the end, in the face of the apparent exclusionary reality of politics, Democracy and Marxism share the same ideal of absolute inclusion.

On the other hand, Derrida suggests that democratic ideals like that of Fukuyama actually require Marxism in order to exist. His concept is of a "specular circle":

> One chases after in order to chase away, one pursues, sets off in pursuit
> of someone to make him flee, but one makes him flee, distances him,
> expulses him so as to go after him again and remain in pursuit. One

chases someone away, kicks him out the door, excludes him, or drives him away. But it is in order to chase after him, seduce him, reach him, and thus keep him close at hand. One sends him far away, puts distance between them, so as to spend one's life, and for as *long a time* as possible, coming close to him again.[46]

In other words, Fukuyama's promise of democratic victory necessarily requires a Marxist defeat. More than that, the apparently defeated enemy must be repeatedly called back in order to keep alive this victory of democracy. To put it in terms of actual politics, the Cold War may be over; but democratic polities must still reference it, still continue to call up their old, dead enemies—the so-called spectres of Marx—and thwart them anew.

To underline the significance of this apparent blurring of friends and enemies, it would be useful to touch briefly on Carl Schmitt's *Concept of the Political*, and Derrida's deconstruction of it. In this short work, Schmitt draws a sharp distinction between friends and enemies. Specifically, the essence of the political is characterized as a "most intense and extreme antagonism," in which the state, "as an organized political entity decides for itself the friend-enemy distinction."[47] For Schmitt, politics is a realm in which enemies are publicly decided on in a concretely antagonistic way: by arbitrary exclusion and war.

Derrida's deconstructive reading focuses precisely on undoing this fundamental assumption of Schmitt's about the ability of states to decide between friends and enemies:

> Schmitt wants to be able to count on this opposition, and reckon with it. Even if no pure access to the essence or *eidos* is to be had, even if, in all conceptual purity, it is not known what war, politics, friendship, enmity, hate or love, hostility or peace are, one can and must know—first of all practically, politically, polemically—*who* is the friend and *who* is the enemy.[48]

Derrida suggests in *Politics of Friendship* that it is impossible to decide between friends and enemies because, in the final analysis, it is impossible to know who one's friends and enemies are. Going still further, he tells us that although for Schmitt a state's decision about its enemies is purely arbitrary, "not linked to communal appurtenance, [nor] caused by it"— still, in Derrida's view the decision nevertheless "reaffirms [communal] appurtenance."[49] In *Concept of the Political*, regardless of whether or not

Schmitt intends it, there is an *a priori* assumption that the friend exists on its own, despite the friend-enemy distinction.

The true basis of Schmitt's politics, Derrida suggests, is much more than simply deciding who one's friends and enemies are. On the contrary, Schmitt's vision relies on the pre-existence of an elite fraternity of individuals (almost certainly men) who have precisely that favoured combination of aggression and decisiveness that allows them to create and defend their kind of political community. It is yet another universal vision of exclusion, and a particularly violent one at that.

Derrida clarifies his own vision by exposing Schmitt's overconfident decisionism, and by undoing the purity of the friend–enemy distinction. In rendering Schmitt's aggressive, masculine, militant community impossible, he announces a freer, more truly open, basis for political community—one that includes everyone, friends and enemies alike. We have come full circle to Derrida's democracy to come.[50] This is the apparent truth behind democracy's promise of inclusion: it needs an enemy to exist, and it needs Marxism to define itself. Further, as Derrida's critique of Schmitt suggested, it is impossible to distinguish between friends and enemies; and so democracy effectively blurs these boundaries such that all are included. At the same time, we also learn that democracy is indebted to Marxism for the method of radical critique, which acts to promote true justice and inclusion. Enemy becomes friend, via the shared emancipatory promise.

Derrida frames the matter thus: living as we do, in (supposedly) an age of democracy, we are actually "heirs of the absolute singularity of a project—or of a promise—which has a philosophical and scientific form. The form of this promise or of this project remains absolutely unique."[51] Like Marxism, the democratic ideal is imbued with the Enlightenment critique of tradition, which embodies a futuristic hope for universal emancipation. More precisely, democracy has inherited from Marxism its principles of liberty and equality, and its desire to pursue them. As Derrida claims, the Marxist spirit of emancipation and critique is necessary to keep alive the democratic project. Without this perpetual critique of tradition, and the constant push for greater freedom, the democratic ideal of absolute inclusion would surely be a sham.[52] We would be left only with the delusionary optimism of Fukuyama.

By showing us that the Marxist and democratic ideals are essentially the same in spirit, Derrida means to open our eyes to what he calls "the radical and necessary *heterogeneity* of an inheritance."[53] Every polity—whether democratic or non-democratic—is essentially indebted to every other, for both its origin and its continuing existence. This is politics: utterly other, wholly non-deterministic. Only if we come to terms with this political fact of otherness (or, as Derrida more objectively puts it, if we simply let it do its work) will the Enlightenment spirit of freedom and equality for all live on.[54]

Put another way, Derrida suggests, if we are aware of and in tune with the truth of political heterogeneity, we will necessarily want to act in conjunction with political otherness and/or difference. We will naturally feel compelled to be hospitable to everyone, and so embody the Enlightenment ideal in our everyday actions. Why? Because the truth of politics is that no one is self-sufficient. Our existence always depends on others. Hence our responsibility—almost an existential obligation—to treat them well; to include them, enemies or not.

Of course, acting in this responsible and enlightened way, including being willing to befriend enemies, is by no means easy. Indeed, Derrida suggests, it is often fraught with despair.[55] Whether or not we recognize the concept of political otherness, we will always inevitably fail in our attempts at absolute inclusion. Revolutions for freedom and equality will always end with a fixed state from which many will be excluded. Enemies will continue to be created, and unjust traditions will persist. After all, as Derrida points out in his discussion of Stalinism, even the emancipatory spirit of Marxism could not escape this fate.[56] (This was also, as we saw above, the problem with Fukuyama's triumphal vision.) In a more contemporary vein, this failure to truly live up to the political responsibilities of otherness was certainly reflected in the policies of Osama bin Laden, Saddam Hussein, and (to a lesser extent, perhaps) George W. Bush, and now Barack Obama.

Still, failure and despair do not remove the burden of responsibility that Derrida's political otherness places on us. This is a critical point. In fact, failure only heightens our responsibility, finally bringing to light the true political import of open-endedness in the structure of Derridean politics. While for Fukuyama an optimistic political policy connotes commitment and success, for Derrida it also connotes closure, exclusion, and profound injustice for many. To quote Derrida, by ignoring the political reality of failure to live up to ideals, Fukuyama's ideal of democracy is like "law without justice." Surely if we truly care about justice and peace, we cannot be silent in a world of perpetual injustice and warfare. Given the truth of political otherness, it is manifestly our duty to act in the name of inclusion, no matter how fleeting.

So the spirit of the Enlightenment critique remains alongside the perpetuation of unjust traditions, promising that emancipation for all will one day be at hand. This highlights the significance of democracy to come, which Derrida defines as "a future modality of the *living present*."[57] For Derrida, democracy exists precisely in our failure to finally realize it; it is only alive insofar as it remains a promise that we always try to realize. Only by ceaselessly striving for absolute inclusion will we ever create a vital space for universal peace in the world.[58]

Peace in the Doing, and Contemporary Politics

We have learned that for Derrida, there is no such thing as universal peace: his ideas of impossible friendship and democracy to come tell us that peace exists only in the doing. Once we stop acting, all hope for friendship, democracy, and peace is lost. What, if anything, does this mean in terms of current political affairs? Two articles, composed shortly before Derrida's death in 2004, indicate that, in fact, his deconstructive politics can effectively speak to contemporary political issues. He asserts that if we are to have any hope for global peace in a post-9/11 world, we must take a more "European" approach to world affairs and foreign policy. In an article titled "What Binds Europeans Together" (written with Jürgen Habermas), we see Derrida's rejection of the Anglo-American approach to 9/11.[59] And in "I am at war with myself," an interview with *Le Monde* published only two months before his death, Derrida clarifies his defence of a more European approach in the context of his deconstructive politics.[60]

In "What Binds Europeans Together," composed on the eve of the Iraqi war, Derrida (speaking via Habermas) rejects what he believes this war represents: yet another assertion of "the blunt hegemonic politics of its [Europe's] ally."[61] In its response to the tragedy of 9/11, as in its response to the Soviet Union during the Cold War, the Anglo-American approach is essentially one of "if you're not with us, you're with the enemy." In terms of peace, this attitude means: peace for us is war with the other.

More specifically, Habermas and Derrida suggest, the "illegal ... unilateral, pre-emptive, and deceptively justified invasion" of Iraq signified an Anglo-American willingness to instill peace and democracy by imposing them on others via war.[62] This approach to reality is the very embodiment of everything that Derridean politics questions. So what is the alternative? What is this "European approach"?

"What Binds Europeans Together" offers the beginnings of a response. What Habermas and Derrida propose is not so much a simple rejection of the Anglo-American hegemonic approach, as a European counterbalance—embodied by the European Union (EU) ideal of politics. In theory (though not fully realized in practice), the EU model represents a geopolitics that eschews state sovereignty in favour of a pan-state political entity. This entity is much more complex than Germany or France, for example, because it is informed by the historical experience of a violent European past in which state sovereignty was extreme. For Habermas and Derrida, Europeanism means two things: confronting the terror of where extreme nationalism can lead (such as the terrors of the Holocaust, the untold destruction of two world wars, and colonialism); and learning from this experience that simple us-versus-them formulations—which impose peace by way of war—must always be regarded with suspicion.[63]

Put more positively, a robust EU offers the hope of a more global polity, in which all are included. Universal peace is not based on imposing the values of a single state by way of force or warfare, as individual European countries have done in the past, and as America has done in the Iraq war (and in others, notably the Vietnam war). Instead, peace is "put to work" via the constant negotiations that must take place between nation-states in the European Union, if the political project is to stay alive.[64] The massive peaceful demonstrations around the world, and especially in Europe, against the Iraq war proves that this kind of work-heavy peace can, and indeed does, exist.[65]

Yet while Derrida's understanding of Europe is sympathetic to this view, he sees it as in fact more complex still. In his final interview, *I am at war with myself*, he offers a somewhat different vision of Europe—less overtly geographical or institutional—from that set out in the Habermas article. Rather than focusing on the European community as it currently exists, Derrida instead proposes the idea of a "Europe to come" that opposes both the politics of American global dominance, and of Arab-Muslim theocratism.[66] This vision is essentially of the Europe that brought Enlightenment self-critique to the world—the logical conclusion of which is a deconstruction that, ironically, is also an act of defiance against Eurocentrism itself.[67]

Thus when Derrida calls for "a post-globalization Europe," he does not mean a place, or even a specific institution;, but rather an idea of universal peace to be acted upon.[68] In particular, it is a call to responsibility for all individuals and nations—including European countries, American hegemons, and Arab-Muslim theocrats—to question all fixed ways of conceiving and doing things. In this way, "the concept and the convention of sovereignty and international law" will necessarily transform themselves with every act of questioning.[69] From the time it was first instituted in Europe by the Enlightenment, this habit of self-questioning has increasingly spread throughout the world.

But how possible is this view of universal peace? Is it not self-contradictory, espousing a view that in effect exists by questioning every view? Perhaps this is true; yet Derrida suggests that we live this contradiction each day. The key is not only to accept this self-questioning, as the Enlightenment taught us to do, but to celebrate it. What this means is summed up by Derrida as follows:

> I am at war with myself. I will not find peace except in eternal rest. I say things that contradict each other, in real tension with each other, and these compose me. It is sometimes a terrifying and painful war, but at the same time I know that it is life, it allows me to live. Survival and intensity of life; life more than life.[70]

Like the ancient Greeks, Derrida posits a direct link between the political and the personal, between who I am and what the community is.[71] Unlike the Greeks, however, Derrida pursues this link between the political and the personal to its ultimate limit: at stake in self-questioning is not only political justice, but life itself.[72] When we impose our view on others, we kill not only them (both literally and figuratively), but ourselves as well, figuratively speaking. In imposing one view of peace, we necessarily and forcibly mute the multiplicity of other views, both around us and within us, We risk becoming automatons, rather than living, breathing, and feeling human beings.

At the same time, this risk gives us reason for hope. We *are* living, breathing and feeling human beings, so the possibility of questioning our singular views, and welcoming others with differing views, is always a possibility for us. This has happened ever since the Enlightenment, Derrida believes, in which time it became acceptable to question deeply held political conventions. This questioning often becomes manifest in the wider political arena, in events such as the mass demonstrations against the Iraq war. We might even assume (though these occurred after his death) that Derrida would approve of the Occupy movement that targeted those responsible for the global economic crisis, and of the ongoing protests in the Middle East that try to call their leaders to account.

In conclusion, Derrida suggests, the goal of peace may mean being at war with ourselves. Our actions must always combat all nationalisms, political positions, and singular identities. Only in undertaking such a war can we hope to be at peace with others, and in turn assert the vitality of what it means to be human.

Notes

1   Following from Heidegger's *Destruktion*. I am indebted to the following for this insight: Vincent Descombes, *Modern French Philosophy*, trans. L. Scott-Fox and J. M. Harding (Cambridge: Cambridge University Press, 1980), 77–83, 137–52. Also, Derrida implies as much in Jacques Derrida, "Violence and Metaphysics," *Writing and Difference*, trans. Alan Bass (Chicago: University of Chicago Press, 1978), 148–49.

2   "Deconstruction is not a method or a tool that you apply from the outside to something, deconstruction is something which happens, which happens inside." Jacques Derrida, "Villanova Conversations," *Villanova University*, October 3, 1994, http://www.egs.edu/faculty/jacques-derrida/articles/villanova-conversations.

3   Jacques Derrida, *Of Grammatology*, trans. Gayatri Chakravorty Spivak (Baltimore: Johns Hopkins University Press, 1976), 23, 93.

4   *Of Grammatology*, 3–26. Derrida also suggests this by pointing out the "logocentric" bias of traditional philosophy—as though being, truth, or good can be fully captured by our signs or speech. By contrast, he shows that with respect to this truth, all we have is the writing or the text, which by definition (even as the tradition defines it) is inexact.

5   For Derrida, this turn to the reader perspective is necessary because of the speech versus logocentric bias—one that has been imposed so completely that the only way to shake it up is a "patient meditation and painstaking investigation on and around what is still provisionally called writing." In short: reading the canon of western philosophy. *Of Grammatology*, 4, 19.

6   Difference, madness, duality, and schizophrenia are all perennial themes in Derrida. As he writes, "where does one then find oneself, *qua* a self?" For more on this readerly otherness in each of us, see Jacques Derrida, *Politics of Friendship*, trans. George Collins (London: Verso, 1997), 71.

7   See Note 4. Derrida refers to this linking of truth and speech as the "logocentric bias" in traditional philosophy.

8   *Of Grammatology*, 10–18. Derrida critiques the idea that there is such a thing as a direct access to reality or truth. For him, there are only speech and writing, which are but expressions or "signifiers of truth." To suggest otherwise, and

privilege speech's access to truth, implies a truth that is untrue or "forced." For Derrida, truth is necessarily beyond such significations.

9   According to Derrida, following Heidegger, this is the basis of reason in Western philosophy.

10   See Notes 4 and 5. Once again, this is based on the "logocentric bias" manifest in the canon of traditional philosophy that links truth and speech.

11   We may see from this that Plato foreshadows Hegel. See *Of Grammatology*, 3.

12   *Of Grammatology*, 6–26. Derrida also writes: "We are disturbed by that which, in the concept of the sign—which has never existed or functioned outside the history of (the) philosophy (of presence)—remains systematically and genealogically determined by that history." *Of Grammatology*, 14.

13   For example, Stanley Rosen thinks that Derrida rejects Platonic philosophy. See Rosen, *Hermeneutics as Politics* (Oxford: Oxford University Press, 1987), Chapter 2. By contrast, Derrida himself explains his approach (in Villanova Conversations) as follows:

> This has been from the beginning a terrible problem for me; not only for me—the caricature, the lack of respect for reading, and so on and so forth … because as soon as you approach a text—not only mine, but many of the texts of people close to me—you see that of course the respect for these great texts, not only the Greek ones but especially the Greek ones, is the condition of our work.… So I think we have to read them again and again; and I feel however old I am, I feel that I am on the threshold of reading Plato and Aristotle. I love them and I feel that I have to start again and again and again; it is something, it is a task which is in front of me, before me.

14   Derrida speaks of this in terms of logocentrism, which he calls "nothing but [a] most original and powerful ethnocentrism … imposing itself upon the world controlling in one and the same *order: the concept of writing* [privileging *logos*], *the history of* (the only) *metaphysics* [linking the truth to *logos* and] *the concept of science* as *logic.*" *Of Grammatology*, 3.

15   In fact, this is also true in *Of Grammatology*, which devotes a sizable chunk of its discussion (165–268) to the deconstruction of Rousseau's *Essay on the Origin of Languages*.

16   Derrida, "Villanova Conversations."

17   Aristotle, *Nicomachean Ethics*, trans. David Ross (Oxford: Oxford University Press, 1991), 1155a3–20 (192–93). The *polis* and political justice are said to have a "friendly quality."

18   *Nicomachean Ethics*, 1171b20–1172a15 (246–47). The essence of friendship is in living together and the good is augmented by their companionship.

19   *Nicomachean Ethics*, 1155a–b16 (192–93). See also Aristotle, "Eudemian Ethics," trans. J. Solomon, *The Works of Aristotle Translated into English*, Vol. 9, ed. W.D. Ross (London: Oxford University Press, 1966), 1234b10–1235b20. Aristotle says he will try to justify his opinions on friendship, in an attempt

to "put an end to difficulties and contradictions" on the topic. With respect to his "sifting" method in general, see Aristotle, *The Politics*, trans. T. A. Sinclair (Harmondsworth: Penguin, 1975), 1260b27–1261a1 (55).

20 Aristotle, *Nicomachean Ethics*, 1155b20–1156a1 (p. 194), and *Eudemian Ethics*, 1236b25–1237a35.

21 Aristotle, *Nicomachean Ethics*, 1156a6–1157b11 (195–199), and *Eudemian Ethics*, 1239a1–1239b20.

22 Aristotle, *Nicomachean Ethics*, 1165b35–1166b27 (227–30), and *Eudemian Ethics*, 1240a5–b35. The internal argument is far less systematic in the latter work. This might suggest two things: either *Eudemian Ethics* is less systematic because it is an earlier work; or else the internal argument cannot be made systematic. For more on both these insights, see Julia Annas, *Platonic Ethics Old and New* (Ithaca, NY: Cornell University Press, 1999). Annas suggests that we moderns may be missing Plato's nuanced view of the good because we have coloured it with our own progressive interpretations. If Annas is correct, Aristotle's view does not "progress" from one work to another; this suggests that the latter interpretation of his view is correct.

23 Aristotle, *Nicomachean Ethics*, 1167b15–1168a30 (232–34). Aristotle speaks of men loving more what they have won by labour; it is the "handiwork" of their love. In this way, the good man becomes a kind of product of the act of loving.

24 Aristotle, *Nicomachean Ethics*, 1171b20–1172a15 (246–47). The essence of friendship is in living together, and the good is augmented by their companionship. Aristotle appears to vacillate between the good and the pleasurable, suggests Martha Nussbaum in *The Fragility of Goodness: Luck and Ethics in Greek Tragedy and Philosophy* (Cambridge: Cambridge University Press, 1986), Chapter 12. For a less tense view of the relationship between good and pleasure, see Lorraine Smith Pangle, *Aristotle and the Philosophy of Friendship* (Cambridge: Cambridge University Press, 2003). She resolves the tension by suggesting that Aristotle's truly good friendship is akin to the pedagogical relation of an older teacher or philosopher, and a student.

25 This suggests that Derrida is simply bringing out what is already there in Aristotle. But Aristotle has a desire for control, whereas Derrida tries to see beyond the need for control. This ideally brings out the full ethical implications of friendship, Aristotelian and otherwise.

26 Aristotle, *Eudemian Ethics*, 1237b34–a3. Aristotle says that true friendship "is not found between many … for a friend is not to be had without trial nor in a single day, but there is need of time." *Nicomachean Ethics*, 1156b20–1157a1 (197). Aristotle further says:

> But it is natural that such [good] friendships should be infrequent; for such men are rare. Further, such friendship requires time and familiarity; as the proverb says, men cannot know each other till they have "eaten salt together"; nor can they admit each other to friendship or be friends till each

has been found lovable and been trusted by each. Those who quickly show the marks of friendship to each other wish to be friends, but are not friends unless they both are lovable and know the fact; for a wish for friendship may arise quickly, but friendship does not.

27   With the concept of boundless love, it could be argued that Derrida is proposing a kind of friendship that is free of any form of reciprocity, obligation, or duty. An example might be the "friendships" that now occur on Facebook: attachments are broadly inclusive, often with people one has never actually met, and with whom one feels little (if any) bond; it is as easy to "friend" people as to "unfriend" them. On the other hand, as his deconstruction of Aristotle's view of friendship suggests, it is important to keep in mind that Derrida makes his claim for boundless love and inclusive friendship against the backdrop of a desire for controlling who one's friends are; and of taking that controlling impulse as the defining concept of friendship, goodwill and peaceable relations. Derrida proposes boundless love and inclusionary goodwill in the knowledge that we will always fail to finally achieve it. This means that inclusive friendship and boundless love, like the idea of democracy to come, is based on the promise of friendship. The intent here is not to suggest that we can be friends with everyone. Rather, it is to make plain that no one person can finally define what goodwill is. At the same time, it also means that universal goodwill is only actualized by constantly working at it; Aristotle himself is all too aware of this, believing as he does that friendship requires the test of time. (I am indebted to an anonymous reviewer for the insight linking boundless love and Facebook.)

28   Derrida, *Politics of Friendship*, 29, 81. Derrida wrote: "The possibilization of the impossible possible must remain at one and the same time as undecidable— and therefore as decisive—as the future itself" (29). He also claimed: "We no longer even know whether these watchmen are guiding us towards another destination, nor even if a destination remains promised or determined. We wish only to think that we are on the track of an impossible axiomatic which remains to be thought" (81).

29   It is important to note that for Derrida, this vision is only seemingly new. Perpetual undoing or openness to the other is, for him, the only reality we truly have. This is the truth of deconstruction that we saw earlier in the essay. As he says in an interview, "Deconstruction is not a method or a tool that you apply from the outside to something, deconstruction is something which happens, which happens inside." Derrida, "Villanova Conversations."

30   I believe I am the first to explicitly link Derrida's concept of deconstruction to a gesture of friendship. I believe there is proof in Derrida's own writings, such as in *Of Grammatology*: "Only infinite Being can reduce the difference in presence. In that sense, the name of God, at least as it is pronounced within classical rationalism, is the name of indifference itself" (71). By contrast, since

we are finite, we must be aware of this difference; and so our response to being and reality must be one of difference, of accepting the otherness as absolute, of being open, even hospitable, to the other in our midst. As well, the friendship centrality in Derrida's thought is made ever more obvious, I believe, by his "friend of truth" conception in *Politics of Friendship*.

31   Derrida, *Politics of Friendship*, 43. Emphasis by Derrida.

32   Derrida, *Politics of Friendship*, 24. Derrida sees in Aristotle both exclusion, and at the same time the possibility of another experience of the possible.

33   Derrida, *Politics of Friendship*, 306.

34   Jacques Derrida, *Specters of Marx*, trans. Peggy Kamuf (London: Routledge, 1994). The reference is, of course, to Marx's famous opening line of the *Communist Manifesto*: "A spectre is haunting Europe—the spectre of communism." (Routledge follows the American spelling of "specter"; this work follows Canadian spelling, spectre.)

35   Derrida, *Specters of Marx*, 1.

36   The phrase "the time is out of joint" also has connotations of justice, as implied by Heidegger in his wordplay. He translated the Greek word *dike*, meaning justice, into the old German word *Fug*, meaning joint. This implies an idea of justice as joining. (By contrast, being not-joined, or being out of joint, was *Unfug*, or injustice.) This reading of "joint" has other echoes in the text of *Hamlet*: Gertrude is described by Claudius as the "jointress" (female heir) of Denmark's imperial state, making her the joint around which the kingship (of Claudius or of Hamlet) will revolve. As we see in the text, Derrida flips these concepts around, privileging a condition of being "out of joint" as the true justice. I am indebted to an anonymous reviewer for this insight.

37   Derrida, *Specters of Marx*, 3. He describes this as "a disjointed or disadjusted now, 'out of joint,' a disajointed now that always risks maintaining nothing together in the assured conjunction of some context whose border would still be determinable." In most of his writings, he asserts this disadjusted "nowness" via his critique of the philosophical idea of presence, or being. But in *Specters of Marx* we come to appreciate (perhaps for the first time in Derrida's writing) the political consequences of such questioning: there is no such thing as any "fixed" view of democracy or politics. What politics truly is, in other words, is not encompassed by one determinable border, but subject to numerous, often competing definitions.

38   Francis Fukuyama, *The End of History and the Last Man* (New York: Macmillan, 1992), xi. To be fair, Fukuyama qualifies these remarks by suggesting that he intends to address these claims via a more in-depth analysis of Marxist and Hegelian "end of history" philosophies. In this paper I never deal with this deeper justification, except in negative terms via Derrida's critique. On the other hand, however profound Fukuyama's future analysis may become, he

never renounces the fact that liberal democracy is the end of history, and that its effective realization is but a matter of time. This is the crux of the matter as far as my use of Fukuyama (and Derrida's) is concerned.

39   Derrida, *Specters of Marx*, 63. Emphasis by Derrida.

40   Derrida, *Specters of Marx*, 169. Emphasis by Derrida.

41   Derrida, *Specters of Marx*, 64. For Derrida, the very concept of democracy can only arise in "a *diastema* (failure, inadequation, disjunction, disadjustment, being 'out of joint.')"

42   Derrida, *Specters of Marx*, 85.

43   Derrida, *Specters of Marx*, 87. Derrida refers specifically to the link between democracy and the spirit of Marxist critique. In more general terms, it is obvious that the spirit of Marxism in contemporary politics is a persistent theme of *Specters of Marx* as a whole.

44   Derrida, *Specters of Marx*, 59. Derrida suggests that democracy is indebted to Marxism; that is, it derives the promise of emancipation from it. However, he is also careful to note that at this point, he is simply linking the ideas of Marxism and democracy—not necessarily their tangible manifestations in the world as ideologies.

45   Derrida, *Specters of Marx*, 85–87. Here Derrida speaks of his desire for a New International, which he defines as a call "to the friendship of an alliance without institution among those who, even if they no longer believe or never believed in the socialist-Marxist International, in the dictatorship of the proletariat, in the messiano-eschatological role of the universal union of the proletarians of all lands, continue to be inspired by at least one of the spirits of Marx or of Marxism (they now know that there is more than one), and in order to ally themselves in a new, concrete, and real way." That new way Derrida suggests, will be non-political or non-exclusionary. The New International includes everyone, even those traditionally conceived of as enemies. Derrida expands on this merging of friends and enemies in *Politics of Friendship* (chapters 4–6), where Derrida deconstructs Carl Schmitt's supposed political opposition of friend and enemy.

46   Derrida, *Specters of Marx*,140. Emphasis by Derrida. His context for this quotation is to use it as a critique of Marx. Thus, in the end, even Marx is closed, much like Fukuyama. The argument I make with respect to this quote is basically that Derrida believes that political theory and practice is largely influenced by this paradoxical hunt whereby the apparently defeated enemy must be repeatedly called back and re-defeated in order to keep alive the ideal of politics being defended. The problem is, most of its practitioners forget the essence of the paradox, namely that not only is politics based on the exclusion of the enemy, but that enemies must actually be summoned forth in order for politics to be possible in the first place. In effect, politics at its core requires

the enemy to exist. Seen in a positive light, this again hints that politics is essentially defined by the collapse of friend and enemy.

47 Carl Schmitt, *The Concept of the Political*, trans. George Schwab (Chicago: University of Chicago Press, 1996), 29–30.

48 Derrida, *Politics of Friendship*, 116. Emphasis by Derrida.

49 Derrida, *Politics of Friendship*, 127.

50 Derrida, *Politics of Friendship*, 302–6. Derrida also speaks of democracy to come.

51 Derrida, *Specters of Marx*, 91. This reference encompasses both quotations.

52 Derrida, *Specters of Marx*, 88. Derrida frames this sham aspect in terms of the concept of self-critique, which is one of the essential Marxist contributions to the Enlightenment. Basically, the constant or never-ending push for freedom and/or inclusion is based on the play of critique of others, and critique of self. This is why radical critique, or deconstruction, is Derrida's political method.

53 Derrida, *Specters of Marx*, 16. Emphasis by Derrida.

54 Derrida, *Specters of Marx*, 92. "[W]e wanted to announce … [an] uneffaceable and insoluble debt toward one of the spirits inscribed in historical memory under the proper names of Marx and Marxism. Even where it is not acknowledged, even where it remains unconscious or disavowed, this debt remains at work, in particular in political philosophy which structures implicitly all philosophy or all thought on the subject of philosophy." Derrida tempers this lack of acknowledgement by arguing for a state of debt: that is, the nation-state with its exclusionary principles will be replaced by an inclusionary state in which people actualize their indebtedness to all others. Needless to say, this state of debt has overtones of recognition; surely we must recognize our indebtedness to others before we can actualize a state of debt. It is perhaps Derrida's biggest weakness that he is somewhat unclear on this point—an odd shortcoming, considering that he seems to be writing this book to show us the new political way.

55 Derrida, *Specters of Marx*, 168–69. Derrida formalizes this despair by suggesting that messianism and despair should go hand in hand. In effect, politics is a promise which, by definition, is pursued but never realized.

56 Derrida, *Specters of Marx*, Chapter 5. The weakness of Marxism, which can lend itself to the horrors of Stalinism, is the subject of this final chapter of *Specters of Marx*.

57 Derrida, *Specters of Marx*, 65. Emphasis by Derrida.

58 Derrida, *Specters of Marx*, 89. "To break with the 'party form' or with some form of the State or the International does not mean to give up every form of practical or effective organization. It is exactly the contrary that matters to us here." For Derrida, to break with one idea of democratic politics is not to reject this politics. On the contrary, for him, this break with the 'party form' is itself a

defence of a truly democratic politics; as absolute inclusion that becomes real only in the doing.

59   The full title is "February 15, or What Binds Europeans Together: A Plea for a Common Foreign Policy, Beginning in the Core of Europe," by Jürgen Habermas and Jacques Derrida, trans. Max Pensky, *Constellations* 10.3 (2003): 291–97. As the abstract makes clear, the article was written by Habermas and only co-signed by Derrida, who at the time was too ill to write himself. Nevertheless, he "shares its definitive premises and perspectives."

60   Jacques Derrida, "I am at war with myself," *Le Monde*, August 19, 2004 (no page number). The European Graduate School, Graduate and Post Graduate Studies, online at http://www.egs.edu/faculty/jacques-derrida/articles/i-am-at-war-with -myself.

61   Habermas and Derrida, "What Binds Europeans Together," 295.

62   Habermas and Derrida, "What Binds Europeans Together," 295.

63   Habermas and Derrida, "What Binds Europeans Together," 296–97. Habermas sums up the point this way: "With the growing distance of imperial domination and the history of colonialism, the European powers also got the chance to *assume a reflexive distance from themselves*" (emphasis by Derrida). He magnifies this idea of reflexive distance in his article "I am at war with myself."

64   Habermas and Derrida, "What Binds Europeans Together," 293. For the EU, Habermas and Derrida claim, "it is not just the divisions that count, but also the soft power of negotiating agendas, relations, and economic advantages. In this world, the reduction of politics to the stupid and costly alternative of war or peace simply doesn't pay. At the international level … Europe has to throw its weight on the scale to counterbalance the hegemonic unilateralism of the United States."

65   Habermas and Derrida, "What Binds Europeans Together," 291. As Habermas and Derrida write, "We should also remember February 15, 2003, as mass demonstrations in London and Rome, Madrid and Barcelona, Berlin and Paris to this sneak attack [on Iraq]. The simultaneity of these overwhelming demonstrations—the largest since the end of the Second World War—may well, in hindsight, go down in history as a sign of the birth of a European public sphere."

66   In "I am at war with myself," Derrida writes: "Europe finds itself under the obligation to undertake a new responsibility. I am not talking about the European community as it currently exists, or as the currently neo-liberal majority imagines it, and literally menaced by so many internal conflicts; but of a Europe to come, and that is still in the process of seeking itself [in] geographic Europe and elsewhere."

67   Derrida, "I am at war with myself": "Deconstruction in general is a project that many have taken, rightly so, as an act of defiance toward all Eurocentrism."

68   Derrida, "I am at war with myself":

> This movement is coming. Even if the outlines are still forming, I think
> that nothing will stop it. When I say Europe, this is it: a post-globalization
> Europe, transforming the concept and the conventions of sovereignty
> and international law. And availed of a real military force, independent of
> NATO or the UN, a military power, neither offensive nor defensive, which
> would firmly enforce the resolutions of a reconstituted UN (for example,
> and with utmost urgency, in Israel, but also elsewhere). It is also the site
> from which we can reflect best on certain aspects of secularity, for example,
> or social justice, which are European legacies as well.

69   Derrida, "I am at war with myself."

70   Derrida, "I am at war with myself."

71   Plato, *Republic*, trans. Allan Bloom (New York: Basic Books, 1991), 369a. Plato
writes: "So then, perhaps there would be more justice in the bigger and it would
be easier to observe closely. If you want, first we'll investigate what justice is like
in the cities. Then we'll also go on to consider it in individuals, considering the
likeness of the bigger in the idea of the littler."

72   Derrida's view is in many ways a reversal of the Greeks'. In essence, his view
of life is one of vitality; to affirm life as it is, in the manner of Nietzsche. See
Friedrich Nietzsche, *The Gay Science*, trans. Walter Kaufmann (New York:
Vintage, 1974), Aphorism 276: "Some day I wish to be only a Yes-sayer."

CHAPTER 14

Habermas on Peace and Democratic Legitimacy

David A. Borman

Despite the centrality of the concept of peace to the tradition of political theory, Jürgen Habermas has rather little to say on the topic directly. Accordingly, some detective work is required to bring into focus what peace seems to mean to him, and what sort of transformation it might demand of our political life. Much of this work involves separating out the issue of peace from Habermas's quite voluminous discussions of cosmopolitanism, international law, and globalization—issues that are clearly related to the nature and demands of peace, but are not identical with it. Unlike a good detective story, however, in philosophy such work tends to uncover more mysteries than it solves. Certainly that will be the case here.

In pursuing this question, we face an additional difficulty that arises from an ambivalence in Habermas's own position, especially in his more recent writing. This ambivalence has already been so widely observed that I might describe it as characteristic: there is a modest Habermas and an ambitious Habermas. The latter is a proponent of radical democratization, a defender of a strong but differentiated concept of rationality, and (as we shall see) a demanding positive conception of peace. The former is a more accommodating political theorist—who makes his peace with the inner workings of capitalism as an economic system, who hopes only for a periodically reinvigorated public sphere as a check against the effects of money and power on political life, and who is resigned to the influence of *realpolitik* on at least some elements of international relations, arguably including the pursuit of peace.

On the one hand, we might be tempted to accept this ambivalence as a reflection of the real tension between what is and what ought to be, between descriptive and normative accounts of political reality. Following Cristina Lafont, we might see it as a symptom of Habermas's attempt to develop a "realistic utopia" for the post–Cold War world, which necessarily involves some trade-offs between realistic and normative considerations.[1] On the other hand, Habermas belongs to a tradition of social theorizing—known as critical social theory—which has made programmatic the demand to reconcile and mediate between norm and reality, between is and ought. This tradition tries to explain how a normatively unjust reality can be apparently legitimated and stabilized, and to point to or anticipate how that reality might be changed in the direction of justice. Thus, to the extent that these tensions remain unreconciled in Habermas's work, his theory will be found wanting according to at least some of its own criteria.[2] In short, we ought not to accept the tension.

However, while the underlying methodological issue here may be interesting, it is adjacent to our real concern. Our question is: Is Habermas's invocation of the concept of peace more realistic, or more utopian? To which Habermas does the concept of peace belong: the modest one or the ambitious one? Perhaps a better question might be: which Habermas has the more convincing view? In this chapter, I will first bring together his rather sparse direct discussions of the nature of peace, followed by a consideration (in four subsections) of the historical developments which Habermas (following Kant) regards as meeting the project of peace halfway. The latter will include some brief mention of his controversial political commentary, in response to events such as the NATO campaign in Kosovo and the first Iraq war. I will also discuss in more detail his apparently ambivalent stance on the protection of social and economic rights in a reformed global order. Stepping back from concrete political issues, I will then discuss how the issue of peace connects with Habermas's theoretical position on the relationship between democracy and the legitimacy of law—a discussion suggested by Habermas's own presentation of peace as a process of "legal pacification." Finally, I will conclude with some comments on what a non-ambivalent Habermasian position on peace might demand in our current global situation.

Habermas and the Concept of Peace

The 200th anniversary of the original publication of Kant's famous essay on perpetual peace (1795) offered Habermas the occasion to develop his own thoughts on the nature of peace.[3] One thing that emerges without ambiguity from these reflections is that, for Habermas as for Kant, peace is a legal concept, and the program of peace is therefore a program of "pacification through law."[4] This is why it will be necessary to look more closely at Habermas's theory of law, below. But for the moment, we can focus on the idea that there is some intrinsic connection between law—the "legalization" or "constitutionalization" of political relations—and peace. Habermas contrasts Kant's view on the nature of this connection with that of Hobbes. For Hobbes, the legitimacy of the legal structure imposed by the sovereign is tied exclusively to the capacity of that government to secure peace—understood negatively as preventing the collapse into the state of nature, as a war of all against all. This peace represents a modus vivendi among individuals who continue to adopt a strategic view of their relations with one another and with their government. By contrast, Kant conceives of a "law-governed relation" as one in which all persons are able (whether or not they actually adopt this normative attitude) simultaneously to see themselves as authors of the laws to which they are also subject.[5] Thus, only through democratic procedure—the institution of "a fair process of opinion- and will-formation among all those potentially affected"—can the program of legal pacification be realized.[6] To the extent that Habermas follows Kant in this, we can assert a preliminary conclusion regarding Habermas's conception of peace: that peace, for Habermas, is not merely the cessation of violence, not a merely negative concept. Rather, it is a positive concept that describes the transformation of political relations according to normatively legitimated rules and/or procedures, which we can respect because they are right. But for now I shall postpone further discussion of the nature of legal legitimacy, in order to examine in more detail the idea of peace itself, and the prospects for it, as well as its relation to Habermas's cosmopolitanism.

Despite sharing with Kant a view of peace as a legal transformation of political relations, Habermas complains that Kant's conception of peace was too much tailored to the (negative) idea of eliminating the kind of limited wars that had been part of the balance of power in Europe since the Peace of Westphalia. This peace, predicated on the "right" to go to war—a right that Kant repudiated—was constrained by the rules regarding the conduct of war. (Kant did not anticipate the development, in the 20th century, of unlimited war.) Habermas writes that "Kant was satisfied with a purely negative conception of peace. This is unsatisfactory not only because all limits on the conduct of war have now been surpassed, but also because of the new global circumstances that link the emergence of wars to specifically societal causes."[7] These developments, Habermas concludes, make it necessary for us to rethink what we mean by peace.[8] In this connection, Habermas cites with apparent approval the following proposal from Dieter and Eva Senghaas:

> The complexity of the causes of war requires a conception that understands peace as a *process* accomplished by nonviolent means. However, its aim is not merely to prevent violence per se but also to satisfy the real necessary conditions for a common life without tensions among groups and peoples. Such a strategy of nonviolent intervention works in favour of processes of democratization that take into account the fact that global interconnections have now made all states dependent on their environment and sensitive to the "soft" power of indirect influence, up to the point of explicitly threatened economic sanctions.[9]

So we can add to our developing picture of Habermas's conception of peace, the following: peace is not only the state or goal of political life, as organized by democratically legitimate law; it is also a process through which global socio-economic conditions (which seem to be what Habermas means by the "specifically societal causes" of war) are transformed to make this common, peaceful, political life possible.

This is an extraordinarily ambitious vision. Is Habermas, after all, more utopian than realist in his approach to peace? In this too, he begins with Kant's proposal for the constitutionalization of international law—a proposal that, despite its ambitiousness, Habermas insists reflects "an idealism free from illusions."[10] Although Kant initially advocated the creation of a world republic as the vehicle for subjecting international relations to legitimate republican law, his considered position—in light of the pragmatic concern that such a republic might turn into the worst sort of despotism—calls for the creation of a voluntary federation or league of (at least dominantly) free states. But this proposal faces a peculiar problem. What will motivate states that remain committed to "power politics," or the politics of sovereignty, to voluntarily "submit conflicts among themselves to an international court of arbitration, while [nevertheless] reserving the right to withdraw at any time"?[11] Kant solves this problem by appealing to a philosophy of history that suggests an eventual convergence of the self-interest of such states with the cosmopolitan project, a convergence he defines as an "agreement between politics and morality" brought about by a hidden "intention of nature."[12]

While Habermas jettisons the metaphysical underpinnings of this hopeful idea, his own account of the trends that meet the cosmopolitan project halfway reflects a dialectical critique (that is, both acceptance and rejection) of the actual evidence cited by Kant in support of this hidden intention of nature. The evidence includes three considerations: the intrinsically peaceful nature of republics, the power of global trade to create communal ties, and the development and functioning of the political public sphere.[13] To these Habermas adds another: the developments in international law since Kant's time. On the one hand, Habermas sees in the violent history of the 19th and 20th centuries a profound refutation of Kant's optimism on all three counts; on the other hand, he nevertheless believes that today we confront a constellation of historical changes that, despite all their ambiguities, do in fact represent the realization of some of the conditions necessary for the success of the cosmopolitan project.[14] I will follow Habermas in discussing these changes, under the headings listed above.

The Peaceful Nature of Republics

Kant, who died in 1804, was not able to appreciate the mobilizing and aggressive potential of nationalism in modern republics—a potential so brutally manifested in the wars and conflicts of the 19th and 20th centuries. Yet Habermas claims that "the idea that a democratic state domestically encourages a pacifistic stance toward the outside world is not completely false."[15] To wit, there is some historical and statistical evidence of a correlation between democratic government and, if not how often a nation wages war, at least the type and duration of its wars. This evidence is the basis of what is now known as the "democratic peace thesis." It is worth proceeding cautiously at this point, however, since—even putting aside a considerable dispute over the validity of the evidence itself—more than one causal mechanism would account for the apparent facts; and, in consequence, more than one conclusion might be drawn from the evidence. First, it is not the case—as Kant had hoped—that democratic nations are more peaceful *simpliciter*. On the contrary, democratic nations have not only fought numerous wars, they also appear to be somewhat more likely to initiate them than non-democratic countries. The important caveat, according to contemporary defenders of the democratic peace thesis, is that democratic nations do not initiate wars against other democratic nations, so that at least they are peaceful in their relations with one another.[16]

But since this "law" is statistical in nature, it allows some exceptions; and the significance of these may be substantial, given the small sample size. Even so, it seems a dangerous invitation to fallacious reasoning: defenders of the "democratic peace thesis" often explain away such exceptions rather than conceding them—for instance, by claiming of some apparent counterexample either that the nation in question is not really a democracy, or that the conflict is not really a war (thus rendering the thesis tautological). In any case, Habermas initially follows Kant in claiming that it is the moral orientations of democratic citizenry, coupled with the need to legitimate foreign policy domestically, that accounts for the change in the way democracies approach war. The idea is that, while citizens can be mobilized around their normative repudiation of authoritarianism, they will not accept their own government invading another country simply for a *raison d'état*.[17] As a result, a democracy can usually only legitimate military action against an authoritarian opponent. For this reason, it might seem, a world of democracies would be a world at peace.

As an empirical or historical claim, this seems to me less than convincing. But even if we grant it, Habermas's invocation of this thesis clearly reflects a reversion to the minimal, negative conception of peace. Even if it is true that democratic nations are statistically less likely to wage war against one another, that in no way entails the positive claim that such nations tend to work non-violently toward securing, domestically and internationally, the conditions that make possible "a common life without tensions." If the democratic peace thesis is to be interpreted in this positive, strong sense, evidence supporting it would be scarce indeed.

The Power of Global Trade

In citing the pacifying effects of trade relationships, Kant failed to anticipate how capitalist development would lead to class division and conflict— which would in turn threaten domestic peace and, perhaps worse, be sublimated into the sort of aggressive nationalism that serves to externalize such social conflicts. More straightforwardly, he also failed to recognize the connection between capitalist expansion and imperialist war. On the other hand, demonstrating some surprising optimism of his own, Habermas asserts that domestic class conflict was successfully pacified by means of the welfare state; though only after the horrors of the Second World War had more or less exhausted nationalist energies.[18] And only at that point did the "economization of international relations" occur, at least among and between OECD countries, which "Kant had rightly hoped would have a pacifying effect."[19] Of course, the other side of this process of expanding world markets and economic integration—globalization, for short—is the loss of economic sovereignty on the part of individual states.[20] Still, Habermas's argument seems to be that increased economic interdependence between countries eventually removes war from their foreign policy strategies.

Again, there seems room for scepticism with regard to the empirical-historical claim that globalization has in fact had this pacifying effect; but at the very least it is clear that this "effect" is also consistent only with the negative definition of peace, which Habermas has declared outmoded. He makes no effort—to his credit—to suggest that globalization is working to create the conditions that make a peaceful, democratic life possible. On the contrary, he concedes that perhaps the most visible effect of globalization, even in wealthy nations, is the way it has eroded the capacity for politico-economic self-determination. Thus, read in the light of the strong, positive conception of peace, the assertion that globalization has a pacifying effect cuts openly against the grain of Habermas's thought.

The Development of the Public Sphere

In keeping with his historical situation, Kant conceived of the public sphere as an outgrowth of the literary public—a realm whose membership was limited to the educated but which was internally, as Habermas put it, "transparent ... and open to arguments."[21] As with the earlier evidence already discussed, however, Habermas regards Kant's reading of history as insufficiently dialectical. In terms of the public sphere, there is both bad news and good news. The bad news, which only became evident in the later part of the 20th century, is that the public sphere has been substantially "refeudalized." By this, Habermas means that it is increasingly dominated by special interests that control vast amounts of the media; and it is "semantically degenerated, and taken over by images and virtual reality." Indeed, as Habermas observes, Kant could not have imagined "that the milieu of an Enlightenment of 'speech and discussion' could be so utterly transformed into forms of indoctrination without language and linguistic deception."[22] The good news is that what, for Kant, was sheer speculation— that is, the prospect of a genuinely global public sphere—has actually begun to take shape in the current era. It manifests itself through the medium of electronic communications, particularly the Internet; through the growth of international cooperation and conferences on global issues like climate change, poverty, and population; and through the formation of successful NGOs that operate globally.[23] Habermas concedes that much of this activity is episodic and issue-specific, and that the creation of a truly enduring global public sphere still remains a task for the future. However, of the three developments cited by Habermas (peaceful relations among democracies, the pacifying power of global trade, and the rise of the global public sphere), this is perhaps the most interesting: it alone seems to have any potential ties to his own ambitious conception of peace. The formation of a global public, and the changes to local identities connected with this, seem to be a genuinely important part of the task of creating the conditions for a peaceful common life, and for transforming the societal causes of war.

Developments in International Law

Kant himself had little to reflect on in terms of developments in international law; indeed, part of his motivation for formulating his account of perpetual peace was his disgust at the sort of political gamesmanship reflected in the treaties of his day. Habermas, on the other hand, believes he can point to a number of developments as steps toward a genuinely cosmopolitan legal order, beginning in the 20th century. For instance, before the formation of the United Nations, the Kellogg-Briand Pact of 1928 outlawed wars of aggression—a legal innovation that was further enshrined in the verdicts of the Nuremburg and Tokyo war-crimes tribunals. These tribunals also created the precedent for the prosecution of crimes against humanity, which was then taken up once again in the creation of the United Nations itself, and subsequently in the Universal Declaration of Human Rights. The UN's commitment to universal membership, in particular, as Habermas says, "satisfies a necessary precondition for the international community's claim to transform international conflicts into domestic conflicts."[24] That is, in order to treat violations of human rights as criminal actions within a legal order, all nations must be included as "citizens" under the force of the law. Connected with this—and apart from the reactive institution of special tribunals in response to human-rights outrages, such as in the cases of Rwanda, Sierra Leone, and the former Yugoslavia—the creation of an International Criminal Court also counts as a step toward a cosmopolitan order: citizens can now sue for protection against the criminal actions of their own sovereign governments. For Habermas, these developments are all significant, despite his justified complaints regarding the political weakness of both the World Court (which adjudicates between states) and of the International Criminal Court.

More controversially, Habermas expresses approval of UN Resolution 688 of April 1991, with which the Security Council authorized the first Iraq war. It allowed US and allied forces not only to expel the Iraqi army from Kuwait, but to intervene in Iraqi sovereignty to establish no-fly zones, and a protected area for a threatened minority in Iraqi Kurdistan.[25] Similarly, Habermas endorsed the NATO intervention in Kosovo. While he expressed regret that it had failed to win Security Council backing, he nevertheless saw it as a move beyond classical international law—according to which the intervention constituted illegitimate meddling in the domestic affairs of a sovereign state—and toward a cosmopolitan legal structure that would treat such interventions, in response to human-rights violations, as police actions in a global political order.[26] For Habermas, the arrest of former Chilean dictator Augusto Pinochet in 1998 also signalled an increasing capacity on the part of the international community to "penetrate the sovereignty of states" in pursuit of assuring "personal liability of functionaries for crimes committed by them as part of their political and military service"; Habermas anticipates that the prospect of arrest may eventually have a deterrent effect.[27] Today, we could also point to the arrests of Slobodan Milošević and Ratko Mladić, and to the conviction of former Liberian president Charles Taylor, as further developments along these lines.

Despite his support for the UN, and for its mandate as the forum for a global politics that stops short of a world republic, Habermas is still quick to concede the many faults of the organization as it presently exists. Yet if we ask what he regards as the requirements of a more effective and legitimate international organization, again we encounter the familiar ambiguities. Some of these may reflect the "transitional" status of the UN itself: its Charter commits the body to simultaneously guaranteeing and limiting the sovereignty of its member states.[28] Other ambiguities, as Lafont has argued, seem to reflect an unresolved tension between Habermas's normative commitments and his practical proposals.

Habermas's litany of complaints about the UN in its current form is mostly familiar fare.[29] Of special significance, however, is his claim that there is an urgent need for effective regional regimes (for which he believes the EU provides a model) that could serve as a "substructure" for the UN.[30] Under this proposed division of labour, the UN would restrict itself solely to its two fundamental, clearly circumscribed tasks of "maintaining peace and enforcing human rights globally"; meanwhile, the regional organizations would take charge of "political coordination in the areas of the economy, the environment, transportation, health, etc.," through systems of negotiation.[31] A move toward this two-level international system, Habermas asserts, would be "the genuinely utopian moment of a 'cosmopolitan condition.'"[32] His view is that international relations would continue to exist in a modified form at the intermediate level—that is, between the negotiating systems of continental regimes such as the EU. Habermas further claims that:

> [m]odification would already be required by the fact that, under an effective UN peace and security regime, even global players would be forbidden to resort to war as a legitimate means of resolving conflicts.... The multi-level system outlined would fulfill the peace and human rights goals of the UN Charter at the supranational level and address problems of global politics through compromises among domesticated major powers at the transnational level.[33]

The justification for this split—through which the UN would be relieved of a vast number of responsibilities that currently occupy its more than sixty organizations and sub-committees—is more than a merely pragmatic one. Rather, it is because many of the sorts of political questions that must be dealt with at the regional level—especially those that concern economic life—are not simply technical questions of regulation and management; they involve normative issues of (re)distributive justice. Habermas writes, "An international negotiating system that could place limits on the 'race to the bottom'—the cost-cutting deregulatory race that reduces the capacity for social-political action and damages social standards—would need to enact and enforce redistributive regulations."[34] For this sort of intervention to be legitimate, it requires substantive, positive solidarity and shared identities on the part of citizens. But according to Habermas, such solidarity and common identity at the global level is not only lacking today; it is inconceivable.[35]

On the other hand, there is already an emergent "negative consensus" in global society regarding the moral outrage produced by massive human-rights violations and threats to international peace; and this is sufficient to legitimate those circumscribed tasks to which Habermas thinks the UN ought to be confined.[36] Habermas's scepticism about the prospects for a positive consensus on distributive justice at the global level seems to be based on the fact of cultural pluralism—that is, the lack of shared norms and identities needed to ground substantive solidarity. As Lafont observes, this tempers his optimism about the formation of a global public sphere, and its implications for the development of cosmopolitan law.[37]

To repeat, Habermas would charge a reformed UN with two tasks: securing peace, and protecting human rights. Our interest here is in the former, but there is an ambiguity in Habermas's position on peace that mirrors his view of the latter. As Lafont notes, beyond the superficial but widespread agreement on the idea that global justice requires the protection of human rights, there is considerable disagreement over just what those rights involve. Astonishingly, almost no contemporary political theorist claims an account of justice as ambitious as the catalogue of rights to which members states of the UN have committed themselves, at least on paper.[38] Through their formal endorsement of the Charter and its associated Conventions, these signatories have accepted a wide-reaching list of social and economic rights alongside the more familiar political entitlements and protections. The question, for Lafont, is what Habermas has in mind when he insists that the protection of human rights is one of the UN's two essential functions.

> Sometimes, an ultraminimalist reading is offered, according to which, protecting human rights should be understood as 'the clearly circumscribed' function of preventing 'massive human rights violations' such as genocide by mobilizing the military forces of member states against criminal states if necessary. At other times, an ultra ambitious reading is offered, according to which implementing human rights is identified with achieving 'the human rights goals of the UN Charter.'[39]

On the one hand, Habermas's de-politicized view clearly prevents the world organization from engaging in any meaningful protection of socio-economic rights, since this would require redistributive measures. On the other hand, the character of transnational negotiating regimes makes them utterly unsuited to this task as well. Nor would they be under any apparent legal obligation to respect socio-economic rights in their negotiations, if their participation in the UN did not demand it[40] (and if the UN did not oversee their compliance with the full range of human rights, including these).[41]

Habermas certainly hopes that citizens of the democratic countries that constitute regional negotiation systems will press their governments to adopt responsible positions on issues such as global poverty and disease, the environment, and so on. He claims, without much elaboration, the acceptance of restrictions on state sovereignty—albeit "clearly circum-scribed" restrictions—will result in a "constructive transformation in the self-understanding of state actors," one that "would not leave the mode of negotiating power based on compromises hitherto dominant in international relations unaffected."[42] But why should we accept this vague and optimistic assumption? Is it not far more likely, as Lafont suggests, that democratic citizens will demand such responsible outcomes if they see them as a question of human rights, rather than as one of fair negotiations? And, inversely, if the protection of human rights is not at stake in the outcome of negotiations, would citizens be doing anything illegitimate if they continued to press their governments to pursue agreements that maximize domestic advantage?[43]

Finally, it is simply unclear how Habermas envisages the causal sequence that leads from countries' membership in a chastened UN, and in regional negotiation regimes, to the end result of a more responsible position on economic inequality in a world of limited resources. Ironically, he seems to find himself in the same position for which he criticized Kant, who could not explain how sovereign states might acquire the motivation to voluntarily relinquish elements of their own sovereignty. Habermas obviously hopes that this motivation will come from the citizens themselves; but how, and why?

This criticism of Habermas's ambivalent position on the protection of human rights, outlined by Lafont, parallels my own concerns about his conception of peace—the protection of which completes the duties of a legitimate world organization, in his view. That is, the "peace" the UN protects by prohibiting war and punishing crimes against humanity is not the same as the positive conception—the process that would create the conditions that make possible a peaceful common life under legitimate democratic law. On the contrary, the UN version of peace can only be that negative kind that Habermas himself repudiated, only to invoke it repeatedly in his assessment of the prospects for peace.

There is, in other words, a troubling lack of fit between Habermas's normative position on the nature and demands of peace, and his own practical political demands, including his sense of the realistic prospects for peace. This lack of fit ultimately leaves unclear just what he thinks peace would entail. As Lafont argues, it is similarly unclear, under Habermas's proposal, whether anyone is responsible for protecting those rights that are surely basic to securing the conditions for a common life without tensions, and for obviating or transforming the societal causes of war. We might object that the dual tasks of protecting human rights and preserving peace cannot be so neatly "circumscribed," as the modest Habermas would have us believe.

Lastly, consider the following argument: according to Habermas, if the UN is to serve as the forum for an effective coordination of global domestic politics, it must work to ameliorate the social and economic imbalances among its member states. But Habermas acknowledges that this is only possible if the world community can reach a consensus on three issues. One is "the non-simultaneity of the societies simultaneously related by peaceful coexistence"—a tendentious way of describing developmental differences. Another issue is the nature of human rights, "the interpretation of which remains disputed between the Europeans and the Asians and Africans"; the issue here seems to be not social and economic rights discussed above, but the status of the individual vis-à-vis community. The third issue is the need for "a shared understanding concerning the meaning of the goal of peace."[44] Obviously, the third requirement is of special interest here: if Habermas has ruled out the possibility of a shared understanding of distributive justice at precisely this level, what hope can he maintain for a shared understanding of peace—if by "peace" we mean the ambitious conception he himself has articulated?

It is useful to recall that the four trends we have been discussing here are introduced by Habermas as evidence that the project of legal pacification is not purely utopian—that there are indeed transformations afoot that offer realistic grounds for asserting that global society can, and might, move in the direction of genuine peace. As he has said, these trends meet the project of peace halfway; they do not represent its complete realization. Perhaps it is misleading, then, to characterize Habermas's position on peace as ambivalent on the grounds that he repeatedly refers to a merely negative conception. If we were to point this out to him, he might say: "Yes, these trends reflect progress toward peace only understood negatively, which I concede to be an inadequate understanding given the societal causes of war. Nevertheless, even these small steps represent movement toward a fuller, more positively conceived peace—a goal that appears less outrageously utopian when seen in this light."[45]

However, at least two considerations speak against this reply. First, it is difficult to make sense of the implied suggestion of a continuum of development. At one end would be a conception of peace as the cessation of organized political violence—a peace that leaves unresolved many of the basic causes of war, but which somehow is supposed to encourage movement toward the opposite end of the continuum, where we find a fundamental transformation of human relations under democratically legitimate law. Rather than stages of a single historical process, these ideas look very much like competing conceptions of the goal of the process.

Indeed, Habermas's use of the positive-negative distinction to differentiate his own view of peace from that of Hobbes and Kant suggests a difference in kind. Even if he merely insisted that peace, understood negatively, is a prerequisite to (though not in itself a cause of) deeper changes in international relations, this still leaves him (as I have already noted) without an explanation for the motive that would propel developments over the chasm that separates these divergent states of affairs. This brings me to the second consideration: there is in fact no indication that Habermas anticipates, or even regards as possible, the kind of developments in international law that would be necessary to institutionalize a legitimate global legal order—an institution that would respond to and dissolve the underlying societal causes of human conflict. This is particularly clear in light of his account of the nature of legal legitimacy, to which I now turn.

Peace and Democratic Legitimacy

Habermas's conception of peace is, like Kant's, a legal concept: both authors see in the rule of law, provided that law is legitimate, a transformation of human relations. That legitimacy in turn reflects not simply coherence with a catalogue of natural rights, nor adherence to de facto institutionalized procedures. Instead, Habermas insists on an internal connection between democracy and the rule of law—or, as he puts it in another work, on the "co-originality" or "equiprimordiality" of private and public autonomy.[46] Put simply, the view is this: we are only really free in our private lives to the extent that we have some say in the laws to which we are subject. At the same time, having a say in these laws—that is, activating our public autonomy through meaningful and equal democratic participation—requires that we have the sort of personal integrity and communal health which it is the job of law to protect, through ensuring that we enjoy meaningfully equal private liberty (including civil liberties such as access to education, health care, protection from discrimination, etc.). In the absence of such protection, any formal rights of participation are little more than a bad joke.

Thus, according to Habermas, law is legitimate only under three conditions: that I am able to understand myself as the author of the laws to which I am subject; that I am able to meaningfully participate as a free and equal individual in the public community (governed by the implicit norms of communicative interaction) regarding the justification for laws that affect me and my community; and that the political system is responsive to the outcomes of such public deliberations. Although Habermas offers us this account of legal legitimacy in the context of discussing the domestic constitutional state, we should recall that he (like Kant) maintains that there exists "a conceptual connection between the role of law in promoting peace, and the role of a legal condition that citizens can accept as legitimate in promoting freedom."[47] That legal condition is predicated on the criteria just mentioned.

This account of the legitimacy conditions for the program of legal pacification at the global level faces an immediate obstacle: the fact that transnational organizations like the UN, the WTO, and the EU suffer from a "democratic deficit" that apparently undermines their legitimacy.[48] This, again, is not merely a contingent historical problem, as Habermas tells us: "Halfway democratic procedures of legitimation have until now been institutionalized only at the level of the nation-state; they demand a form of civic solidarity that cannot be extended at will beyond the borders of the nation-state."[49] Because of this, he sees the liberal constitution as the appropriate model for the constitutionalization of legal relations at the global and continental levels. In such a constitution, political power is mutually restricted through division, and is channelled by treaties into policies that conform with human rights—rather than being rationalized through a grounding in popular sovereignty, as the major republican political revolutions of the 17th and 18th centuries attempted to do.

At the same time, Habermas concedes that this model "does not satisfy republican standards of democratic legitimation"[50]—which is to say, it does not satisfy his own conception of legal legitimacy. On the face of it, this concession would seem to give the lie to Habermas's purported commitment to a Kantian project of legal pacification, and to reveal an inconsistency in Habermas's conception of peace itself. His solution is to insist that supranational constitutions—if, indeed, we can think of the UN Charter and its equivalents as analogous to a constitution[51]—"if they are to be anything more than a hegemonic legal facade, must remain tied at least indirectly to processes of legitimation in constitutional states."[52] But Habermas is exceedingly vague about exactly what these ties would be, and exactly how they would function as conduits for legitimation.

While he notes that the basic international rights, legal principles, and criminal codes are themselves the product of "learning processes" in democratic nation-states,[53] the transfer of the product of a democratic process to other institutions in no way makes the recipient institutions democratically legitimate—particularly from the perspective of proceduralist conception of legal legitimacy like Habermas's. (By the same odd reasoning, an authoritarian regime could conceivably describe itself as "indirectly democratically legitimate" by appropriating specific laws or legal mechanisms from some actually democratic state.) And though Habermas asserts (somewhat unconvincingly, I think) that organizations like the WTO "increasingly take into account the protection of human rights, in addition to the usual legal principles," this too fails, by his own account, to constitute any form of democratic legitimation—as long as those affected have no role in articulating how those rights are to be understood. It is noteworthy that, in the case of the WTO, the human rights at issue would largely be those same social and economic rights whose status remains so unclear in Habermas's cosmopolitan vision.

In the end, Habermas's picture of a peaceful legitimate cosmopolitan world order seems to look like this: *if* member states are themselves democratically legitimate; and *if* domestic electorates "broaden their perspectives on what counts as the 'national interest' into a viewpoint of 'global governance,'" so that citizens demand that their governments adopt and act on the self-understanding of members of a global community;[54] and *if* the negotiation structures of continental regimes ensure a fair balance of powers[55]—then we could anticipate that transnational organizations might begin to move toward a more just world order, in a way that would count as progress toward securing the conditions for peace. And *if* the world organization limited itself to those basic circumscribed functions of securing (negative) peace, and protecting (a limited catalogue of) human rights, and *if* a global public sphere emerged that, although lacking in formal access to political power, could at least focus attention and discussion on the most egregious violations of rights—*then* we could anticipate that the world community might begin to move toward a fairer and less-selective defence of (certain) basic rights.

The first set of conditions outlined above is strongly counterfactual. Moreover, it fails to offer a genuine reconciliation with the ambitious Habermas's own republican conception of legal legitimacy, and so leaves unresolved an apparent contradiction in his conception of peace as a project of (democratically legitimate) legal pacification. And there remains the mystery—ironic, in light of Habermas's criticism of Kant—regarding the causal force that, operating first at the level of democratic electorates, is to create the pressure for the transformation of strategic attitudes on the part of powerful global players. At present (especially since the economic crisis that began in 2008), there is scarcely a hint of such pressure. As for the second set of conditions, they reflect the modest Habermas alone: their plausibility and even their desirability do not seem over-weighty when measured against the injustices for which they provide no remedy. It is here that we see evidence that the negative conception of peace is not, for Habermas, simply a station on the way to something more demanding and transformative.

Taking our cue from Habermas's explicit comments on the nature of peace, we must find the proposals of the modest Habermas wanting. If we want a convincing definition of peace—even a partial or incomplete one—we must look to the ambitious Habermas. It is worth thinking about how this version of Habermas might apply his definition of peace to our contemporary world. He might demand, for instance, that the citizens of countries subjected to the financial regulations of the World Bank or the IMF—predominantly poor countries, but increasingly the crisis-stricken countries of Europe as well—have a genuine say in those regulations. The ambitious Habermas might well describe as warlike actions the imposition on the developing world of structural adjustment policies, many "free trade" agreements, uncompensated environmental "externalities," and "austerity-for-others" economic politics. He might at the very least call these impositions illegitimate, and obstacles to peace.

Of course, this still leaves unanswered all the difficult questions of positive institutional design. For example, Habermas repeatedly mentions economic sanctions as the ultimate enforcement mechanism for global domestic politics. But given the terrible cost they inflict on innocent civilians—for instance, the horrendous effect of the sanctions regime on the infant mortality rate in Iraq during the 1990s—the ambitious Habermas might turn out to be a lot less sanguine regarding the "peacefulness" of such measures. What else to use as a mechanism of enforcement in a global politics that eschews war? The ambitious Habermas would insist that whatever answers we come up with for these difficult questions, they must help us to create conditions in which citizens of the world can tell one another what it would mean for them to be respected equally, to have all of their rights respected (including their social and economic rights), and to live under the protection of laws and negotiation procedures that they in turn can respect because they are acknowledged as right. These conditions must activate the autonomy of all citizens, who must come to see themselves as co-workers in the project of ensuring lasting peace for themselves and for others. Perhaps one of the most fundamental challenges for a such a position concerns the level at which this activation should occur: Habermas himself focuses on institutional innovations at the macro, or global, level, though he admits that many rights will continue to be chiefly activated through national citizenship. He has engaged rather too little, I think, with the possibility of micro-level politics and democratization—of the sort discussed in Diane Enns' treatment of Hannah Arendt, in Chapter 12 of this volume.

In any case, one thing that is arguably distinctive about an ambitious Habermas's view of peace is its intimate connection (through the proceduralist account of legal legitimacy) with the idea of justice itself. A Hobbesian—and perhaps a modest Habermasian—might countenance the possibility of a peaceful world that is nevertheless structurally unjust in some respects; for the ambitious Habermas, this is an impossibility. Indeed, for the ambitious Habermas, this sort of political realism in a world of continuing structural injustice and violence could only amount to apologetics. Typically, the apology comes from the side of the beneficiaries of these injustices: they are willing to take the good with the bad in making their peace with the victimization of other people. That Habermas's essential view of the nature of peace excludes such realism, I take as a considerable point in its favour.

Notes

1   Cristina Lafont, "Alternative Visions of a New Global Order: What Should Cosmopolitans Hope For?," *Ethics and Global Politics* 1.1–2 (2008): 41–60, 42.

2   This is not the place to enter into an extended discussion of the methodological program of critical theory. Interested readers might begin by consulting these two works: Jürgen Habermas, *Lifeworld and System: A Critique of Functionalist Reason, The Theory of Communicative Action*, Vol. 2, trans. Thomas McCarthy

(Boston: Beacon Press, 1987), especially the chapter on the tasks of critical theory; and also Max Horkheimer, "Traditional and Critical Theory," *Critical Theory: Selected Essays*, trans. Matthew J. O'Connell et al. (New York: Continuum, 1999).

As well, in her paper on Kant in Chapter 7 of this volume, ("Kant, Cosmopolitan Right, and the Prospects for Global Justice"), Leah Bradshaw argues that cosmopolitans like Habermas are insensitive to the danger of attempting to close the gap between the ideal and the actual. This seems true to me, but only because the critical theorist would return the accusation by complaining of the apologetic (and thus dangerous) character of any attempt to defend the persistence of the disjunction of "is" and "ought"—just as Marx famously complained of religion, for instance.

3   I intend to sidestep entirely the question of whether Habermas's reading of Kant is perspicuous: insofar as my aim is to clarify Habermas's view of peace, what concerns me is only how Habermas understands Kant's project.

4   Jürgen Habermas, "Kant's Idea of Perpetual Peace, with the Benefit of Two Hundred Years' Hindsight," *Perpetual Peace: Essays on Kant's Cosmopolitan Ideal*, ed. James Bohman and Matthias Lutz-Bachmann (Cambridge, MA: MIT Press, 1997), 113. This essay also appears in Habermas, *The Inclusion of the Other: Studies in Political Theory*, ed. Ciaran Cronin and Pablo de Grieff (Cambridge, MA: MIT Press, 1998).

5   Jürgen Habermas, "Does the Constitutionalization of International Law Still Have a Chance?," *The Divided West*, trans. & ed. Ciaran Cronin (Malden, MA: Polity Press, 2006), 121.

6   Habermas, "Constitutionalization," 122.

7   Habermas, "Kant's Idea," 131. For a defence of the realism of Kant's modest position, see Leah Bradshaw in Chapter 7 of this volume.

8   Habermas, "Kant's Idea," 127.

9   *Leviathan: Berliner Zeitschrift für Sozialwissenschaft* 20 (1992): 230–47.

10   Habermas, "An Interview on War and Peace," *The Divided West*, 106.

11   Habermas, "Constitutionalization," 125.

12   Habermas, "Kant's Idea," 119.

13   Habermas, "Kant's Idea," 119.

14   In what follows, I rely on Habermas's more detailed discussion in "Kant's Idea of Perpetual Peace"; however, the reader may also find useful the more condensed discussion of the same points in Habermas, "Constitutionalization," 145ff.

15   Habermas, "Kant's Idea," 120.

16   Habermas, "Kant's Idea," 120.

17   Habermas, "Kant's Idea," 120–21. This argument is not very satisfying, given the active support provided to various authoritarian regimes by democratic ones. Citizens, like their governments, are often so far from being clearly

motivated by "the universalism of value orientations of a population accustomed to free institutions," that they have historically distinguished between authoritarianisms they like, and those they do not like—because of the language they speak, the religion they practise or fail to practise, the economic practices they allow or fail to allow, etc.

18   Habermas, "Kant's Idea," 121–22.

19   Habermas, "Kant's Idea," 123. István Hont has argued that much of the contemporary discussion of the political significance of global trade recapitulates the debate carried on by Hume, Smith, and others in the 17th and 18th centuries—including the question of whether such trade would foster peace through interdependence, or encourage war through competition. See István Hont, *The Jealousy of Trade: International Competition and the Nation-State in Historical Perspective* (Cambridge, MA: Harvard University Press, 2005).

20   While Bradshaw (in Chapter 7 of this volume) accuses cosmopolitans like Habermas and Benhabib of advocating the "suspension of national sovereignty," it is worth noting that for both thinkers, a big part of the argument is that political organization needs to catch up with the facts of globalization. This process has already led to the outstripping of national sovereignty in a variety of domains: the idea that a single state could effectively protect its citizens in economic life, or with respect to environmental and food security, is today an anachronism.

21   Habermas, "Kant's Idea," 124. See also Jürgen Habermas, *The Structural Transformation of the Public Sphere: An Inquiry into a Category of Bourgeois Society*, trans. Thomas Burger (Cambridge, MA: MIT Press, 1991).

22   Habermas, "Kant's Idea," 124.

23   Habermas, "Kant's Idea," 124–25.

24   Habermas, "Constitutionalization," 165.

25   Habermas, "Kant's Idea," 130.

26   See, especially, Jürgen Habermas, "Bestiality and Humanity: A War on the Border between Legality and Morality," trans. Stephen Meyer and William E. Scheuerman, *Constellations* 6.3 (1999): 263–72, 264. For a critique of Habermas's position on the NATO intervention in Kosovo, see William L. McBride, "Habermas and the Marxian Tradition," *Perspectives on Habermas*, ed. Lewis Edwin Hahn (Chicago and LaSalle: Open Court, 2000).

Of course, from a "realist" perspective—or, as a question of legal theory, from the "positivist" perspective—what Habermas sees as the hopeful constitutionalization of international relations may be regarded as a dangerous "moralization" of international conflict. As Benjamin Holland persuasively argues in Chapter 5 of this volume ("Vattel on Morally Non-Discriminatory Peace"), Carl Schmitt's recently reinvigorated position on this issue is substantively presaged by Emer de Vattel in the 18th century. While repudiating Schmitt's fascist apologetics, Holland cautiously suggests that Vattel's position could bear a renaissance of its own: Vattel offers a useful warning against the sort of moralizing discourse we see used for the so-called War on Terror, which dehumanizes the enemies of America and licenses the circumvention of the Geneva Conventions when dealing with "enemy combatants." This complaint is well taken but, from a Habermasian perspective, it represents an overhasty conclusion. As Seyla Benhabib writes, citing Kant:

> There is a distinction between the 'political moralist,' who misuses moral principles to justify political decisions, and a 'moral politician,' who tries to remain true to moral principles in shaping political events. The discourse of human rights has often been exploited and misused by 'political moralists'; its proper place is to guide the moral politician, be they citizens or leaders. All that we can offer as philosophers is a clarification of what we can regard as legitimate and just in the domain of human rights themselves. (Benhabib, "Another Universalism: On the Unity and Diversity of Human Rights," *Proceedings and Addresses of the American Philosophical Association* 81.2 [2007]: 7–32, 23)

27 Habermas, "Bestiality and Humanity," 263. For a good discussion of the significance of this warrant as a precedent, see David Sugarman, "The Arrest of Augusto Pinochet: Ten Years On," *Open Democracy*, 29 October 2008, http://www.opendemocracy.net/article/the-arrest-of-augusto-pinochet-ten-years-on.

28 Habermas, "Kant's Idea," 127, 130. Habermas observes, for instance, that while Article 2.4 of the UN Charter prohibits offensive wars, and empowers the Security Council to act, even militarily, to enforce this prohibition, Article 2.7 "expressly forbids the intervention in the internal affairs of a state."

29 See Habermas, "Constitutionalization," 165; Habermas, "Kant's Idea," 128–35; and Habermas, "Bestiality and Humanity," 268. In the latter, Habermas concedes that the prospects for achieving the reforms he advocates seem exceedingly dim. In a later paper, Habermas goes beyond his earlier calls for an elected chamber of the UN General Assembly, and for majoritarian voting procedures for a reformed Security Council: he ambitiously recommends that the reformed General Assembly have veto powers over the reformed Security Council, as well as the right to appeal the decisions of the later to the International Criminal Court. See Jürgen Habermas, "The Constitutionalization of International Law and the Legitimation Problems of a Constitution for World Society," *Constellations* 15.4 (2008): 444–55, 451.

30 Habermas, "Kant's Idea," 127.

31 Habermas, "War and Peace," 108; see also "Constitutionalization," 136.

32 Habermas, "War and Peace," 109.

33 Habermas, "Constitutionalization," 136.

34   Jürgen Habermas, "The Postnational Constellation and the Future of
      Democracy," *The Postnational Constellation: Political Essay*, trans. and ed. Max
      Pensky (Cambridge, MA: MIT Press, 2001), 105.

35   Habermas, "The Postnational Constellation," 105, 107–8.

36   Habermas, "War and Peace," 109–10; see also "Constitutionalization," 143. In
      the latter, Habermas writes that as long as the UN limits itself to performing
      its fundamental tasks of securing peace and protecting human rights, it can
      do without the "implicit consensus on thick political value-orientations that is
      necessary for the familiar kind of civic solidarity among fellow-nationals."

37   See Lafont, "Alternative Visions," 49.

38   Lafont, "Alternative Visions," 45. Seyla Benhabib has made the same
      observation while considering the timidity of political theory when it
      comes to defending a right to democratic self-determination (see "Another
      Universalism," 10–11).

39   Lafont, "Alternative Visions," 45. For an example of the "ultra ambitious"
      reading, see Habermas, "Constitutionalization."

40   Lafont's objection is not just that the protection of socio-economic rights slips
      through the cracks of Habermas's proposed division of political labour, but that
      his justification for the division itself is faulty. For her reasons, see "Alternative
      Visions," 48–50.

41   Lafont, "Alternative Visions," 45–46, 58–59. This picture of the division of
      labour in global society, as well as the problems arising from it, are complicated
      by a more recent intervention by Habermas on this topic. While he continues
      to maintain that the primary tasks of the UN should be restricted to protecting
      human rights and securing peace, he also argues (in "Constitutionalization")
      that his proposed "cosmopolitan citizens" who would be elected to an expanded
      General Assembly would indeed exercise oversight over the outcomes of
      negotiation systems at the transnational level. As he writes: "The balancing
      of interests would take place in the transnational negotiation system *under
      the proviso of compliance with the parameters of justice subject to continual
      adjustment in the General Assembly*" ("Constitutionalization," 452; original
      italics). While those cosmopolitan citizens would also be national citizens, their
      decision-making processes would have to be responsive to both roles. These
      decisions would apparently include redistributive issues that arise, in particular,
      from the obligations "that the citizens of privileged nations have toward the
      citizens of disadvantaged nations" ("Constitutionalization," 450).
          I do not see how it is possible to square such a statement with the rest
      of Habermas's writing on this topic, since this proposal implies a reversal
      of his often-repeated scepticism regarding the scope for agreement
      around substantive issues of justice at the global level (as opposed to the
      "negative duties of a universalistic morality," to which he also appeals in

"Constitutionalization," 451). Yet no indication is given that this contradiction of his earlier views reflects a change of mind. Perhaps the resolution of the seeming contradiction is to be found in the fact that Habermas, in this paper, is no longer articulating a "realistic utopia"; on the contrary, he expressly concedes that the necessary institutions, infrastructure, actors, and attitudes are all presently lacking (451–52).

42   Habermas, "Constitutionalization," 135.

43   Lafont, "Alternative Visions," 54.

44   Habermas, "Kant's Idea," 132.

45   My thanks to Jeff Flynn for suggesting this counter-argument.

46   This is really the central thesis of Habermas's *Between Facts and Norms: Contributions to a Discourse Theory of Law and Democracy*, trans. William Rehg (Cambridge, MA: MIT Press, 1996). For a succinct defence of this thesis, see Habermas, "Paradigms of Law," *Habermas on Law and Democracy: Critical Exchanges*, ed. Michel Rosenfeld and Andrew Arato (Berkeley: University of California Press, 1998).

47   Habermas, "Constitutionalization," 121.

48   Habermas, "Constitutionalization," 138.

49   Habermas, "Constitutionalization," 139.

50   Habermas, "Constitutionalization," 139.

51   Habermas has revised his position on this question: whereas he had described the UN Charter explicitly as the constitution for the world organization (see Habermas, "Kant's Idea," 127), he is now content to assert that the Charter is at least like a constitution in a certain set of features (see "Constitutionalization," 160).

52   Habermas, "Constitutionalization," 140.

53   Habermas, "Constitutionalization," 141.

54   Habermas, "The Postnational Constellation," 111; see also "Constitutionalization," 142.

55   Habermas, "Constitutionalization," 142.

ABOUT THE CONTRIBUTORS

Paul Bagley is Associate Professor of Philosophy at Loyola University Maryland. He holds a baccalaureate degree from Loyola University, New Orleans, a master's degree from the Catholic University of America, and the degree of Doctor of Philosophy from Trinity College, Dublin. His publications include writings on the teachings of Spinoza, Descartes, and Plato, as well as essays concerning the Enlightenment, political philosophy, and the practice of esotericism. He is co-founder and former president of the North American Spinoza Society, Visiting Lecturer at the Katholieke Universiteit Leuven, and an Earhart Foundation Fellow. He is the author of *Philosophy, Theology and Politics: A Reading of Benedict Spinoza's Tractatus theologico-politicus.*

Mark Blitz (A.B. and Ph.D. from Harvard University) is Fletcher Jones Professor of Political Philosophy and Director of the Henry Salvatori Center at Claremont McKenna College. He served during the Reagan Administration as Associate Director of the United States Information Agency and as a senior professional staff member of the Senate Committee on Foreign Relations. He has been Vice President of the Hudson Institute and has taught political theory at Harvard University and at the University of Pennsylvania. He is the author of *Conserving Liberty; Plato's Political Philosophy; Duty Bound: Responsibility and American Public Life; Heidegger's "Being and Time" and the Possibility of Political Philosophy*, and is co-editor (with William Kristol) of *Educating the Prince.*

David A. Borman is Assistant Professor of Philosophy and Political Science at Nipissing University. His areas of research specialization are social and political theory, especially critical social theory, the philosophy of the social sciences, moral philosophy, and metaethics. He is the author of *The Idolatry of the Actual: Habermas, Socialization, and the Possibility of Autonomy* and has published papers in such journals as *Dialogue, Philosophy and Social Criticism*, and *Continental Philosophy Review*. He is currently working on an account of the nature and development of social and moral norms called "actual agreement contractualism."

Leah Bradshaw is Professor of Political Science at Brock University. She has a long-standing interest in comparative accounts of ancient and modern Western political thought and acknowledges an enduring debt to the ideas of Hannah Arendt. She has contributed to a number of collections edited by Toivo Koivukoski and David Tabachnick on themes of tyranny, empire, and oligarchy. Her most recent publications are "How Thinking Saves Us," in Lee Trepanier and John von Heyking, eds., *Teaching Political Philosophy in an Age of Ideology*, and "Thinking with Technology," in Thomas W. Heilke and John von Heyking, eds., *Hunting and Weaving: Essays in Empirical Political Science.*

Jarrett A. Carty is an Associate Professor at the Liberal Arts College at Concordia University, Montreal. He teaches the history of philosophy, political theory, the history of Western Civilization, and the history of science. Jarrett's specialty is early modern political thought, concentrating on the Reformation, the Renaissance, and the late middle ages. His publications include *Divine Kingdom, Holy Order: the Political Writings of Martin Luther* (2012). Jarrett also has active interests in the ancient Greek and 18th-century European enlightenments and American political thought. He lives in Ottawa with his family.

Diane Enns is Associate Professor of Philosophy at McMaster University, in Hamilton, Canada. She is the author of *The Violence of Victimhood* (2012) and *Speaking of Freedom: Philosophy, Politics and the Struggle for Liberation* (2007), and has published articles on identity, violence, political conflict, peace-building, moral agency, and responsibility. She is currently working on two projects: a book of essays that explores matters of love, writing, and philosophy, and a study of community and violence.

John Gittings was on the staff of *The Guardian* (London) newspaper for many years, as East Asia editor and foreign leader-writer. He was active in the early years of the Campaign for Nuclear Disarmament, and with the International Confederation for Disarmament and Peace. He is the author of *The Glorious Art of Peace: From the Iliad to Iraq* (2012) and a member of the editorial team for the *Oxford Encyclopedia of Peace* (2010).

Ben Holland is a Lecturer in International Relations at The University of Nottingham, UK, where he is also a Fellow of the Centre for the Study of Social and Global Justice and the Centre for the Study of Political Ideologies. His research is concerned with the history of early-modern political thought and international relations theory. He has published work in *History of Political Thought, History of European Ideas, International Studies Quarterly* and the *Journal of International Political Theory*. He is currently preparing a monograph on the history of the idea of the state as a person.

Pamela Huber obtained her Doctorate in Political Science from Carleton University in 2006. Her research interests focus on political ethics as it is described—and criticized— in Aristotle, Nietzsche, Heidegger, and Derrida, among others. She is currently investigating how an ethic of friendship can foster broad social inclusion such that all, even the most vulnerable, would be included as active members of the community. Dr. Huber has occasionally lectured part-time at Carleton University and the University of Ottawa in modern and post-modern political theory. She presently works as an analyst in the Government of Canada on the Homelessness Strategy.

Laurie M. Johnson is Professor of Political Science at Kansas State University and Director of K-State's Primary Texts Certificate program. She is the author of *Thucydides, Hobbes and the Interpretation of Realism* (1991) and numerous scholarly articles and chapters on Thucydides, Hobbes, and international relations theory. She is the author of *Political Thought: A Guide to the Classics* (2001), *Hobbes' Leviathan: A Reader's Guide* (2007), *Thomas Hobbes: Turning Point for Honor* (2009), and *Locke and Rousseau: Two Enlightenment Views of Honor* (2013). She is currently writing *Honor in America? Tocqueville and American Enlightenment,* and co-editing *Perspectives on Modern Honor.* She is co-editor with Dan Demetriou of the book series *Honor and Obligation in Liberal Societies: Problems and Prospects.*

Toivo Koivukoski is Associate Professor of Political Science at Nipissing University and Director of the Nipissing University Peace Research Initiative. He is author of *The New Barbarism and the Modern West: Recognizing an Ethic of Difference* (2014), *After the Last Man: Excurses to the Limits of the Technological System* (2008), and co-editor with David Tabachnick of a series of books on classical regimes theory, including *On Oligarchy* (2011), *Enduring Empire* (2009), and *Confronting Tyranny: Ancient Lessons for Global Politics* (2005), along with *Globalization, Technology and Philosophy* (2004). His current research and teaching are focused on the topics of love and justice through a comparative study of Plato's *Symposium* and *Republic.*

René Paddags is Assistant Professor of Political Science at Ashland University, where he teaches courses in international relations, comparative politics and regional studies. Dr. Paddags received his Ph.D. in political science from the University of Maryland, College Park, for his dissertation on Jean-Jacques Rousseau. He also received an M.A. from Johns Hopkins University, School of Advanced International Relations, in international relations and an M.A. in political science from the University of Erlangen-Nuremberg, Germany.

Jeffrey Sikkenga is Professor of Political Science at Ashland University in Ashland, Ohio, adjunct fellow of the John M. Ashbrook Center for Public Affairs, and senior fellow in the Program on Constitutionalism and Democracy at the University of Virginia. He received his Ph.D. in political science from the University of Toronto. He has published articles and reviews on political thought and the US Constitution in journals such as *American Journal of Political Science, Political Theory, History of Political Thought, Journal of Politics,* and *Political Science Quarterly.* He has contributed to a number of edited volumes, including *On Oligarchy* and *Heritage Guide to the Constitution,* and has co-edited *History of American Political Thought* (2003), edited *Transforming American Welfare* (1999), and co-written *The Free Person and the Free Economy* (2002). He is currently working on a book-length interpretation of John Locke's *A Letter Concerning Toleration.*

David Edward Tabachnick is Professor of Political Science at Nipissing University. His research focuses on linking ancient political thought to contemporary politics and ethics. He is the author of *The Great Reversal: How We Let Technology Take Control of the Planet,* and is the co-editor of *The Ancient Lessons for Global Politics* book series.

Hermínio Meireles Teixeira was born in O Porto, Portugal, and raised in Montreal, Canada. He completed his graduate studies and Ph.D. degree at Carleton University in Ottawa and is currently Assistant Professor of Political Science at Nipissing University in North Bay, Canada. Professor Teixeira's research work and writings are concentrated in the critical history of the Western tradition of political theology and its continuing encounters with indigenous forms of political thought and practice.

INDEX

Books in the Laurier Studies
in Political Philosophy Series

The End(s) of Community: History, Sovereignty, and the Question of Law, Joshua Ben David Nichols / 2013 / ISBN 978-1-55458-836-7

The Question of Peace in Modern Political Thought, Toivo Koivukoski and David Edward Tabachnick, editors / 2015 / ISBN 978-1-777112-121-7